CHASING GOLDMAN SACHS

— CHASING —
GOLDMAN
SACHS

HOW THE MASTERS OF THE UNIVERSE MELTED WALL STREET DOWN . . . AND WHY THEY'LL TAKE US TO THE BRINK AGAIN

SUZANNE MCGEE

CROWN
BUSINESS
NEW YORK

CROWN BUSINESS is a trademark and CROWN and the Rising Sun colophon are registered trademarks of Random House, Inc.

Library of Congress Cataloging-in-Publication Data

McGee, Suzanne.
   Chasing Goldman Sachs/Suzanne McGee.—1st ed.
       p. cm.
   1. Goldman, Sachs & Co.   2. Investment banking—United States—History—21st century.   3. Financial crises—United States—History—21st century.   4. Finance—United States—History—21st century.   I. Title.

   HG4930.5.M38 2010
   332.660973—dc22   2009053440

ISBN 978-0-307-46011-0

Printed in the United States of America

Design by Philip Mazzone

10   9   8   7   6   5   4   3   2   1

First Edition

In memory of my grandfather
James R. Burchell

CONTENTS

FOREWORD

On the same morning that I delivered the final page proofs of this book to my editor's offices in midtown Manhattan, fact-checked, proofread, and ready for the printer, the Securities and Exchange Commission charged Goldman Sachs & Co. and one of its executives with fraud.

The announcement came as a bombshell. It had been nearly two years since the SEC began investigating the "Abacus" mortgage-backed securities transactions at the heart of the fraud allegations. In its letter to shareholders contained in its 2009 annual report, Goldman Sachs's CEO, Lloyd Blankfein, described 2009 as "a year of resiliency" for the bank. It was also an extraordinarily profitable one for Wall Street's most famous and most envied institution: Goldman pocketed $45.17 billion in revenues and $13.4 billion of profit in 2009 and, even as the SEC was preparing to file its lawsuit, it was closing the books on a very profitable first quarter of 2010, during which it generated twice the profits that it had a year earlier, or $3.46 billion. Once again, the rest of Wall Street was left trying to figure out how to keep their shareholders happy in light of the astonishing return on equity that Goldman Sachs had delivered to its own investors—22.5 percent in 2009.

But what had Goldman Sachs done to earn that return on equity and those profits? Within hours, that was what everyone was buzzing about. Certainly, the dealings spelled out in the SEC lawsuit seemed to have little to do with the idea that Wall Street exists to connect those individuals, entrepreneurs, businesses, and governments in need of capital with investors hoping to find a way to put their capital to work in search of a return. Rather, the Abacus deal structured on behalf of hedge fund manager John Paulson was little more than a big bet on the future direction of the U.S. housing market and the credit quality of some of the country's most financially distressed home buyers. Paulson believed that the mortgage-backed securities market was about to blow up, and wanted his bankers at Goldman Sachs to find a way to let him bet on that scenario. To earn a hefty fee, all Goldman had to do was find someone willing to take the other side of that bet. And that's where the SEC claims that the blue-chip investment bank stepped over the line.

In the lawsuit, the regulatory agency claims that in order to attract buyers to the transaction, Goldman conspired to keep them from learning that Paulson not only wanted to "short" the new collateralized debt obligation (CDO) it was creating on his behalf, but took an active role in structuring it, hand-picking some of the securities on which the CDO would be based. It will take months, and possibly a year or more, before it can be established whether the SEC can prove that Goldman violated its obligation to disclose all this information to IKB, the German bank that bought a big chunk of the deal, taking the opposite side of the bet from Paulson. But what is already clear is that Wall Street is a world in which, for all the professed commitment to serving clients in need of financial services, some of those customers are more equal than others. Ultimately, Wall Street is no longer run in the interests of its clients, but in the interests of Wall Street entities themselves. The value of the Street may lie in its role as a financial utility or intermediary, but as the financial results of Goldman Sachs and most of its rivals clearly demonstrate, that's not what generates the lavish profits. And profits are what Wall Street's own investors demand.

For more than a decade, Goldman played the game better than anyone else on Wall Street. It earned returns on equity that were the envy of all its peers; its bankers were considered the crème de la crème and increasingly earned bonus packages reflecting that status. Top bankers at Merrill Lynch & Co., for instance, knew to steer clear of their temperamental CEO Stan O'Neal on the days that Goldman released its earnings. "Why can't *we* earn numbers like that?" he demanded of one subordinate on one occasion in mid-2005. O'Neal's underlings set out to try to do just that—and ended up wiping out a decade's worth of profits by taking gargantuan risks in subprime mortgage CDOs. Even in the wake of the crisis, as it became clear that Goldman had generated some of those fees by creating risk for the financial system—by, for instance, helping Greece structure its debt in such a way that the magnitude of its budget deficit was hidden from the other member nations of the European Union—the envy remained.

Goldman's bankers knew that in being "long," subprime real estate in the spring of 2007 was likely to be a risky bet for anyone who agreed to take the other side of the trade that Paulson wanted to do. In an e-mail to a friend, Fabrice Tourre, the banker who structured the deal (and who is named alongside his firm in the SEC action) wrote, "the whole building is about to collapse any time now . . . Only potential survivor, the fabulous Fab . . . standing in the middle of all these complex, highly leveraged, exotic trades he created without necessarily understanding all of the implication of those monstrousitieis!!! [*sic*]" In another e-mail, the head of Goldman's structured products correlation trading desk warned Tourre that "the cdo biz is dead" and that "we don't have a lot of time left." Nonetheless, Goldman Sachs, the SEC alleges, did whatever they could to persuade IKB to do the deal. As Lloyd Blankfein has explained repeatedly, clients like IKB are really no more than "counterparties," sophisticated investors willing to take risks and able to do their own due diligence. But even if Goldman is correct in arguing that it didn't actively mislead IKB—which later required a bailout from the German government to avoid collapsing under the weight of billions of dollars of losses on Abacus-like subprime bets—didn't it have some kind of moral obligation to warn either the client or the system?

The answer is no. On Wall Street today, clients need to be able to look out for themselves. The perception among the American public is that the game is rigged; that Wall Street is dealing cards from the bottom of the deck to its friends while saving the low-value cards for their other clients. The SEC lawsuit simply reinforces that perception, and damages any remaining confidence Main Street has that Wall Street's "financial grid" operates in their interest or serves as a de facto financial utility, through which capital flows from those that have it to those that need it. Today's Wall Street is far from being a utility, and restoring public confidence that it can still act in the interests of all those that rely on it is the challenge that confronts all of us, from the regulators and legislators in Washington to the bankers on Wall Street. As of this writing, a host of regulatory reform proposals are making the rounds, all of them hotly debated and all of them focusing squarely on the structure of Wall Street. It remains to be seen, however, whether any of these will succeed in getting Goldman Sachs and its rivals to reconsider their raison d'être and redefine their responsibilities to both their clients and to the financial system itself. They can't keep chasing Goldman Sachs if what Goldman Sachs is doing to earn its hefty profits is damaging the integrity of the financial system, as the SEC lawsuit implicitly claims.

DRAMATIS PERSONAE

Patrick Adelsbach: principal of event-driven strategies at Aksia LLC, a hedge fund research and advisory firm

Scott Amero: fixed-income fund manager at BlackRock, one of the largest asset management firms in the world

Phil Angelides: former state treasurer of California; currently head of the Financial Crisis Inquiry Commission

Jeffrey Arricale: portfolio manager at T. Rowe Price with a focus on investing in financial stocks

Sheila Bair: chairman of the Federal Deposit Insurance Corporation

Ben Bernanke: chairman of the Federal Reserve

Lloyd Blankfein: CEO of Goldman Sachs

Peter Blanton: veteran investment banker who has worked at a variety of large Wall Street firms and now works for a boutique firm

Brooksley Born: Washington securities lawyer and former head of the Commodity Futures Trading Commission; now a member of the FCIC

Richard "Dick" Bove: banking analyst at Rochdale Securities; a veteran research analyst

Lise Buyer: has worked on almost every part of Wall Street as an analyst, banker, and investor; served as director of business optimization at Google; and now has her own firm that helps coach companies through the financing process

Tom Caldwell: chairman of Caldwell Financial, a Toronto-based investment and trading firm; one of the largest shareholders of the New York Stock Exchange's parent company

Marshall "Marsh" Carter: deputy chairman of NYSE Euronext, former chairman of State Street Corporation, and a veteran commercial banker

Tom Casson*: a former Bear Stearns investment banker; since that firm's collapse, he has worked for two other Wall Street institutions

Jimmy Cayne: former CEO and chairman of Bear Stearns; he spent his professional life at the firm

Steve Cohen: manager of one of the world's biggest hedge funds; known as a ferocious and secretive competitor and an avid art collector

Gary Cohn: president and COO of Goldman Sachs

Leon Cooperman: former Goldman Sachs partner; now runs a large hedge fund group, Omega Advisors

John Costas: rose to head UBS's investment banking; after briefly running a hedge fund group for UBS, he was caught with short-term losses and resigned; launched his own trading and market-making group, Prince-Ridge, in mid-2009

Robert "Bob" Diamond: CEO of Barclays Capital and president of Barclays PLC; Diamond orchestrated the purchase of many of Lehman Brothers' investment banking operations after Lehman's bankruptcy filing; formerly worked for Credit Suisse, among other firms

Jamie Dimon: CEO of JPMorgan Chase, a former protégé of Sandy Weill whom the latter fired at Citigroup and who went on to have the last laugh as the heir to JPMorgan himself during the crisis

Mike Donnelly*: former Wall Street investment banker who spent most of his career at Morgan Stanley

Glenn Dubin: cofounder of Highbridge Capital, a large hedge fund group now owned by JPMorgan Chase

James "Jimmy" Dunne: CEO of Sandler O'Neill, a smaller investment bank that specializes in serving financial institutions

Ira Ehrenpreis: a general partner at Technology Partners, a Silicon Valley venture capital firm

Gary Farr: former Citigroup banker hired by KKR to build an in-house investment banking division to assist its portfolio companies

Niall Ferguson: professor of history and business at Harvard University and Harvard Business School; specializes in economic and financial history

Jim Feuille: partner at Crosslink Capital, a venture capital firm

Richard "Dick" Fisher: late CEO of Morgan Stanley; his name often surfaces when people talk about competitive yet principled Wall Street executives

*Indicates a pseudonym.

Martin "Marty" Fridson: veteran high-yield bond market analyst; founder of FridsonVision

Richard Fuld: former CEO of LehmanBrothers; a Lehman "lifer"

Timothy Geithner: Treasury secretary; formerly head of the New York Fed

Mike Gelband: former co-head of fixed income at Lehman Brothers

Lou Gelman*: former investment banker specializing in equity sales and trading at Morgan Stanley

James Gilleran: former head of the Office of Thrift Supervision who bragged about his willingness to cut red tape and make it easier to take risk

Lew Glucksman: Wall Street trader and briefly chairman and CEO of Lehman Brothers

Alan C. "Ace" Greenberg: former chairman of Bear Stearns, whose vision propelled it to the ranks of the "big five" investment banks

Robert "Bob" Greenhill: founder of Greenhill & Co., a merger advisory boutique firm, in 1996 after leaving Morgan Stanley, where he had run that firm's merger business

Ken Griffin: founder of Citadel Investment Group, one of the largest hedge fund groups in the world; now making a push into investment banking

Tony Guernsey: chief client officer at Wilmington Trust; has worked with many Wall Street figures over the last three decades

William R. "Bill" Hambrecht: former CEO of one of the "four horsemen" (boutique banks that played a decisive role in financing start-up companies), Hambrecht & Quist; since that firm was sold to Chase Manhattan in the late 1990s, has undertaken a variety of quests, all involved in improving financing access for fledgling firms

Nick Harris*: manager of a large hedge fund

Jeff Harte: banking analyst at Sandler O'Neill

Samuel Hayes: holds Jacob H. Schiff Chair in Investment Banking at the Harvard Business School; has been writing case studies about Wall Street since 1970

Mike Heffernan*: investment banker on Wall Street

Jaidev Iyer: managing director, Global Association of Risk Professionals; former senior risk manager at Citigroup and its predecessor institutions

Fred Joseph: late founding partner of Morgan Joseph, a boutique investment bank; formerly CEO of Drexel Burnham Lambert

Rob Kapito: president of BlackRock

Todd Kaplan: veteran Wall Street banker recruited by Ken Griffin at Citadel to launch the hedge fund's push into investment banking; resigned in early January 2010 for personal reasons

Henry Kaufman: the original "Dr. Doom" and a prominent economist at Salomon Brothers; now president of Henry Kaufman & Co.

Dow Kim: briefly headed the fixed-income investment banking operations at Merrill Lynch; tried but failed to launch his own hedge fund after Merrill began to take write-downs

Michael Klein: one of the first architects of a sponsor group of bankers catering to private equity clients; a former Citigroup banker

Bill Kohli: fixed-income portfolio manager at Putnam Investments in Boston

Richard "Dick" Kramlich: cofounder of New Enterprise Associates, a large Silicon Valley venture capital partnership

Henry Kravis: cofounder of KKR, one of the first large buyout firms

Sallie Krawcheck: former banking analyst and Citigroup chief financial officer; now runs the wealth management business at Bank of America Merrill Lynch

Ken Lewis: former chairman and CEO of Bank of America; negotiated the merger between B of A and Merrill Lynch but was ousted after revelations of large losses at Merrill and agreements to pay Merrill bankers big bonuses

Michael Lipper: architect of data and analysis firm Lipper Advisory Services (now part of Thomson Reuters, named Lipper Inc.)

John Mack: veteran investment banker who has worked at many of Wall Street's most significant firms; until 2010, CEO of Morgan Stanley; remains the firm's chairman

Jake Martin*: partner at a large New York–based buyout firm

Mike Mayo: veteran banking analyst and managing director at Calyon Securities (USA) Inc.

Larry McInnes*: veteran technology and telecommunications banker

Tom McNamara*: investment banker who works within a sponsor group at a Wall Street firm, putting together financing packages for private equity buyouts

Seth Merrin: founder of LiquidNet, a Wall Street trading firm

Michael Milken: at Drexel Burnham Lambert in the 1970s and 1980s, developed the high-yield/junk bond market into a real asset class, but violations of securities laws led to his being banned from the industry for life; now a philanthropist

Eric Mindich: youngest partner in Goldman Sachs history; left the firm to found a hedge fund, Eton Park Capital

Ken Moelis: began his career at Drexel Burnham Lambert; ultimately became president of UBS's investment banking division; left in 2007 to launch his own boutique firm, Moelis & Co.

Angelo Mozilo: chairman and CEO of Countrywide Financial until 2008; cofounder of IndyMac Bank; a symbol of the credit bubble, Countrywide is now owned by Bank of America; IndyMac collapsed

Duncan Niederauer: former partner of Goldman Sachs & Co., CEO of the New York Stock Exchange, and a pioneer in the world of electronic trading

Stanley "Stan" O'Neal: former CEO of Merrill Lynch & Co.; behind the firm's push into CDOs structured with subprime mortgages

Vikram Pandit: veteran banker and later a hedge fund manager; joined Citigroup and quickly became its CEO

Richard "Dick" Parsons: chairman of the board of Citigroup

Henry "Hank" Paulson: former Goldman Sachs leader who went on to become Treasury secretary in the administration of George W. Bush; an architect of the TARP plan

John Paulson: hedge fund manager who made billions betting that the housing bubble would burst; now betting on a turnaround in financial stocks

Pete Peterson: cofounder of Blackstone Group; previous posts included CEO and chairman of Lehman Brothers between 1973 and 1984

Anna Pinedo: partner at Morrison & Foerster specializing in corporate finance

Charles E. "Chuck" Prince: former CEO of Citigroup

Phil Purcell: former chairman and CEO of Morgan Stanley; ousted by firm dissidents unhappy with the company's lagging stock price, a reflection of its lack of risk taking

Leslie Rahl: founder of Capital Markets Risk Advisors LLC, a risk management firm that has handled a lot of derivatives debacles

Lewis "Lew" Ranieri: mortgage bond and securitization pioneer at Salomon Brothers

Clayton Rose: former banker at JPMorgan Chase; now an adjunct professor at Harvard Business School

Wilbur Ross: former investment banker and "workout specialist" at Rothschild Investments; founded his own private investment firm, WL Ross & Co. LLC, in 2000

Nouriel Roubini: economist and professor at New York University's Stern School; known as "Dr. Doom" for his pessimistic economic forecasts

Jeff Rubin: director of research at Birinyi Associates; has studied the way financial markets function

Robert "Bob" Rubin: former Goldman Sachs partner and Treasury secretary during the Clinton administration; went on to work as a director and advisor at Citigroup

Ralph Schlosstein: CEO of Evercore Partners; cofounded BlackRock, a major asset management firm

Stephen "Steve" Schwarzman: cofounder of Blackstone Group; formerly an investment banker at Lehman Brothers

Peter Solomon: veteran Wall Street banker and Lehman Brothers alumnus; now runs his own boutique investment bank, Peter J. Solomon Co.

Larry Sonsini: chairman of Wilson Sonsini Goodrich & Rosati, a Silicon Valley–based national law firm that advises start-ups and Fortune 500 companies

Mike Stockman: former risk management officer at UBS

Richard "Dick" Sylla: Henry Kaufman Professor of the History of Financial Institutions and Markets, Stern School of Business, New York University

James "Jim" Tanenbaum: partner at Morrison & Foerster specializing in corporate finance

John Thain: former CEO of Merrill Lynch; previously CEO of the New York Stock Exchange and a partner at Goldman Sachs

Leo Tilman: president of L. M. Tilman, a risk advisory firm; contributing editor of *The Journal of Risk Finance,* and former executive at BlackRock and Bear Stearns

Mark Vaselkiv: fixed-income manager at T. Rowe Price in Baltimore

David Viniar: chief financial officer of Goldman Sachs

Paul Volcker: former Federal Reserve chairman; named chairman of Economic Recovery Advisory Board by President Barack Obama; championed the idea of re-creating a division between risk-taking and deposit-taking institutions on Wall Street

Sandy Weill: financier who combined risk-taking and deposit-taking institutions on Wall Street with the formation of Citigroup; his view of a financial supermarket was largely responsible for the repeal of the 1933 Glass-Steagall Act that separated investment and commercial banking

The Chase

Does Wall Street owe the American people an apology?"

Tom Casson* heard the question—the one on the minds of every American taxpayer furious at the very idea of footing the bill for Wall Street's excesses in the shape of the $700 billion bailout package under debate in a Senate hearing room—from the television on the trading floor just outside his office. He saw himself as part of Wall Street—it was where he had spent nearly all his working life—so the

---

* Here and throughout the book, a name followed by an asterisk is a pseudonym for a Wall Street professional. Casson, as is true of many of his colleagues still working on Wall Street, does not have permission to speak openly to the press or book authors about what they see happening around them; while their CEOs do, it's rare to find them frank and forthcoming. In cases such as that—where speaking openly and honestly about what individuals on Wall Street witnessed and experienced would have caused trouble for my sources with their employers or investors, and where simply using an anonymous source would have made following the narrative unnecessarily difficult for the reader—I have chosen instead to gives these sources a pseudonym. In cases where that is done, their name is followed by an asterisk when they first appear. When senior Wall Street officials declined to be quoted on

very idea that some senator from who knows where thought he should apologize to the country piqued his curiosity immediately. "Why would I and the rest of my guys do that?" he wondered. Still, listening to either Treasury secretary Henry "Hank" Paulson or Federal Reserve chairman Ben Bernanke struggle to answer the question in a way that would keep the members of the Senate Banking Committee happy had to be more fun than just watching the lines on his Bloomberg terminal that signaled stock and bond market index levels inching their way lower and lower with every passing minute. In search of distraction, Casson got up from behind his desk and ambled toward the trading floor. Leaning against the glass wall that separated his small fiefdom from the hurly-burly of the floor, he waited for the answer.

It wasn't what he expected to hear. After a lot of hemming and hawing, Ben Bernanke finally replied that to most of America, "Wall Street itself is a . . . is a . . . is an abstraction." Casson felt as if he'd accidentally stuck his finger in an electrical socket. He stood upright, staring at the television in astonishment. *What did Bernanke just say? Can he really have just described Wall Street as an* abstraction? In Casson's eyes, Wall Street couldn't be *less* abstract—it's where businesses find

---

the record for this book, I have *not* given them pseudonyms, but simply cited them and referred to their roles on the Street, but not their firms. Reporting this book at the height of the crisis in the winter of 2008 and spring and early summer 2009 proved particularly challenging, as many of these individuals were focused on what was going to happen in the next twenty-four hours or the following week, not what happened in past decades or what might happen over the next decade. "How can you ask us to predict that?" said Fred Joseph, former boss of junk-bond king Michael Milken, who went on to cofound a boutique investment bank but who, sadly, died in late 2009. "We can't predict what we'll have to deal with in a month or two, and how that will change our options." This book reflects the views and thoughts of some two hundred individuals whose lives are tied to Wall Street in one way or another and who, like Joseph, made that effort.

capital, where investors with capital find places to put it to work in hopes of earning a return. Over the decade that he had toiled on the Street, Casson had raised money for some of those companies and helped others to negotiate multibillion-dollar mergers. Now the politicians were demanding that he and his colleagues apologize for what they spent their lives doing? Even worse, the head of the Federal Reserve—the individual who was the public face of banking regulation and monetary policy making—couldn't find a better word to describe Wall Street than *abstraction*. Months later, Casson was still bemused. "How could anyone say that Wall Street was an abstraction?" he wondered aloud. What had happened to make even the Fed chairman blind to Wall Street's real value?

The details of what happened during the weekend in September that preceded those Senate hearings, the weekend of frenetic deal making, hectic negotiations, and never-ending meetings within the Fed's fortress-like New York headquarters involving nearly every top figure on Wall Street, have by now been told and retold. We know that Merrill Lynch held its board meeting to approve the sale of the firm to Bank of America at the St. Regis Hotel in Manhattan; that Securities and Exchange Commission (SEC) chairman Christopher Cox accused a British counterpart of being "very negative"; that Hank Paulson commuted to the negotiations downtown from a suite at the Waldorf Astoria in midtown Manhattan. We even know the favorite route for the dawn runs by Timothy Geithner (then head of the New York Fed, who would succeed Paulson at the Treasury Department in the New Year) along the southern tip of Manhattan.[1] We know *what* happened—the names of the firms that failed, and those that rapidly returned to making money hand over fist. (We still don't know the names of those institutions saved from disaster by last-minute help from the Treasury Department, but if media organizations make a compelling freedom-of-information case to the courts, that information won't be long in coming.) We know the proximate causes of the crisis: too much leverage, too much risk, and too much subprime lending.

This book will take you on a different journey. Instead of rehashing every detail of *what* happened to Wall Street, I'll take you behind the scenes and show you just *why* our financial system came so close to falling over the edge of the abyss. How did we reach the point where Wall Street was in so much jeopardy that the staid and somewhat self-important Paulson was willing to go down on one knee in front of House of Representatives Speaker Nancy Pelosi—a Democratic politician most investment bankers distrusted and even roundly disliked—to beg for her assistance in passing a financial aid package for the surviving firms, including his own alma mater, Goldman Sachs? Above all, what had happened to Wall Street that Bernanke could describe it as an "abstraction" and be greeted not with howls of outrage or confused questions by his audience but rather with nods of acknowledgment and understanding?

Truth is, Wall Street isn't an abstraction but a kind of public utility. That's a characterization liable to make those who work on the Street bristle in indignation. But in many ways, the financial system of which Wall Street is a critical part bears an uncanny similarity to any power company or water system. When you come home at the end of the day, you count on being able to flick a switch and see your lights come on; in the morning, you rely on being able to turn on a tap and get clean running water for your shower. You almost certainly rely on Wall Street in the same unconscious way. Wall Street offers us an array of investment ideas for our retirement portfolios; Wall Street institutions finance our entrepreneurial dreams and lend us the capital we need to help us buy homes, cars, and even birthday gifts for friends and family. (Sure, they make money doing that—but so do the power company and the water company.)

From its inception Wall Street had been there to serve Main Street, and it took that role seriously. "It was valued; serving your corporate clients, if you were an institutional firm like Morgan Stanley, or investors, if you were a retail-oriented firm like Merrill Lynch, exceedingly well was the ticket to success on Wall Street," says Samuel Hayes, professor emeritus at the Harvard Business School. The problem is that from the 1970s onward, serving as a public utility and performing these intermediary functions for the people on both ends of the "money grid" (investors and companies needing capital) just wasn't as profitable as it used to be.

That's the starting point for this book, which will explain just how and why Wall Street drifted away from its core intermediary function and morphed from utility to casino, under pressure from those running Wall Street firms and from their investors. Both of those groups put a priority not on fulfilling Wall Street's role as a utility but on finding the most profitable products and business strategies, of which subprime lending and structured finance were only the latest—and, so far at least, the most toxic—manifestations.

Eventually, these insiders came to treat Wall Street as if it were any other business, only as valuable as the profits they could extract from it. Instead of turning to proprietary trading or structured finance only to supplement their returns from the less profitable utility-like or intermediary operations, many Wall Street firms deemphasized Main Street in favor of catering to Wall Street clients: hedge funds, private equity funds, and their own principal investing and proprietary trading divisions. Nor were there any incentives for Wall Street residents to question their collective transformation from quasi-utility to self-serving, risk-taking, profit-maximizing behemoth. Compensation policies across the Street rewarded bankers and traders for turning a blind eye to the needs of the money grid; regulators—agencies charged with ensuring that utilities operate in the public interest—ended up catering to Wall Street rather than trying to rein in its worst excesses.

When utilities come under too much systemic stress, they fail. Think of the electricity system, and what happens when its managers fail to plan for the hottest summer days, when everyone turns on the air conditioner full blast and the demand for power peaks. Like millions of others living in the northeastern United States, I experienced that firsthand one muggy August afternoon in 2003, when the power to everything from elevators in high-rise office buildings to streetlights on Manhattan's busy roadways flickered off—and stayed off for much of the next twenty-four hours. Suddenly, I realized just how important the power grid was to my life. I joined thousands of others who had to walk home along the darkened New York streets, through the heat and humidity. Eight miles and many hours later, there was no cold water to ease the pain from my blistered feet (the lack of electricity had caused a plunge in water pressure) and no food (there was no way to cook anything); I couldn't even find a cold drink to revive me.

Thankfully, the reasons for the blackout were relatively straightforward. Someone had decided to take a power plant offline, meaning that its output wouldn't be available to customers on one of the hottest days of the year. A bad call. When electricity demand spiked, that put a strain on the high-voltage power lines. Since electricity companies know that can happen, causing power lines to sag dangerously low, they make an effort to keep trees and foliage trimmed back. That didn't happen at one utility—another bad call—and the power lines brushed against some overgrown trees, triggering a series of failures that cascaded throughout the region's power grid.[2]

The 2003 blackout was an accidental phenomenon. But imagine if in the years leading up to the blackout, the power companies had been overrun by a new breed of managers, extremely bright and imaginative engineers armed with MBAs. Imagine that they had been given a completely different mandate by shareholders: blackouts don't happen too often (the last big one was in 1965), so if preparing for one consumes too much capital or limits profits too much, don't bother with it. And imagine that those engineers, in order to maximize profits, decided to use all the money they had saved by not investing in backup capacity and maintenance to build and operate a casino, or some other business that would generate a much higher return in the short run. Finally, imagine that regulators were asleep at the switch and let them do it. Happy shareholders would have richly rewarded the engineers for their efforts right up until the last minute. And even after the blackout (which would have been far more catastrophic and longer-lasting than that of 2003), while all of us were struggling in the dark, those investors and the engineers would have had more than enough money to buy their own generators to provide power to their mansions.

In a nutshell, that's what happened to Wall Street as it morphed from being an intermediary to being a self-serving, risk-taking machine for generating profits. As long as times were good, few participants stopped to ask questions about this transformation, including those who have today become some of the Street's harshest critics. And even now that we've experienced the near blackout of the financial system, the fingers of blame are pointing to individuals—Richard Fuld, at the helm of Lehman Brothers, for instance, or Christopher Cox, the chairman of the SEC, who looked the other way as Bernie Madoff ran his Ponzi scheme and as the investment banks his agency regulated teetered on the edge of disaster. If we ever are going to be able to devise wise policies for Wall Street and ensure the future health of the financial system, we have to take a hard look at more than just the proximate causes of the debacle, such as subprime lending or the activities of pot-smoking, bridge-playing Jimmy Cayne at Bear Stearns. We need to understand how to make the money grid work properly. Maybe just being an intermediary doesn't generate enough in profits to sustain the system anymore—but that doesn't mean that people running the utility should feel free to toss caution to the wind and start speculating on a host of new and risky businesses.

Bankers are trying to clear up the mess they have made, while in Washington, regulators and policy makers are running around in circles trying to analyze what went wrong and to put in place a new set of rules that will prevent the financial system from coming so close to the brink ever again. But none of these very smart people is either admitting or acting on the biggest problem of all: the fact that while Wall Street is as important to our economy and society as any other utility, it doesn't work like one. Let's say that Morgan Stanley decided, as a result of the events of the last two or three years, to pare back the amount of risk it is willing to take. It shuts down its proprietary trading desk, says it won't act as a principal and invest alongside its clients in businesses, and limits its involvement in risky products such as synthetic credit default swaps. It even decides to turn away underwriting assignments if its bankers conclude that the stocks or bonds the firm would be underwriting would add to the level of risk in the system. Instead, Morgan Stanley focuses on wealth management, on building a commercial banking franchise, or on market making (facilitating the two-way flow of trading in stocks or bonds). What would happen next?

Well, none of these is a high-growth business that will lead to big annual jumps in profitability. Before long, the impact of this decision would show up in the bank's quarterly earnings; with each fiscal quarter, the gap between Morgan Stanley and its rivals would widen, in both absolute levels of profitability and the rate of growth in profits. The bonus pool would shrink, and if this risk-conscious move was one that only Morgan Stanley had made on its own initiative (and not part of a government-mandated change affecting the entire industry), the bank's most talented and skilled employees would be lured away to work for competitors. Ultimately, the investors in Morgan Stanley, those who have purchased its stock in hopes of seeing the value appreciate, would stage a rebellion. It wouldn't take long before they'd protest to the bank's management team and demand that the managers do whatever it takes to keep up with the returns being posted by their peers. If those managers stick to their guns, the investors' next stop would be the offices of the company's directors. It's pretty easy for anyone to imagine what would happen next to the executives who had decided that shunning high-risk but profitable businesses was a good idea. "Give us a new management team, with some guts, that's willing to go out and do what it takes to capture whatever profits are going!" shareholder A would demand. Since the board's absolute duty is to maximize value for shareholders, it wouldn't take long for it to capitulate.

Do you think that couldn't happen? Well, it did, over the course of the last two decades. Over that period, Goldman Sachs emerged as the rival to beat, or at least to try to mimic. The firm seemed to have a Midas touch: in the decade leading up to the financial crisis, it generated an average annual return of 25.4 percent on shareholders' equity, while the four other large investment banks earned an average return on equity (ROE) of 15 percent annually in the same time frame. No wonder Goldman's rivals were furious as they fended off complaints from their own shareholders. It was clear to every other Wall Street CEO that chasing Goldman Sachs was the only way to boost their personal wealth and simultaneously keep their cantankerous shareholders pacified.

What Goldman was doing, however, was something very different from the traditional business of Wall Street. By 2007, the year that it posted record profits of $11.6 billion and distributed a bonus pool that was even larger ($12.1 billion) among its employees, Goldman was getting only about a third of those earnings from serving Main Street clients; the rest came from investing and trading for its own account. It had become commonplace for Goldman's rivals to refer to the firm, scornfully, as a hedge fund disguised as an investment bank, even as they scrambled to mimic the strategy. The problem was that they weren't moving into these businesses because they believed they had a competitive advantage or the most talented bankers and traders. They were doing it just to keep pace with the market leader. And while Goldman Sachs, as we'll see, managed to steer clear of some of the subprime mess, those firms that were just trying to chase Goldman Sachs didn't have the tools or the people to help them properly manage the new risks they were taking.

During those years, when everyone was chasing Goldman Sachs, there was every incentive to just keep doing so and not much encouragement to stop and rethink the strategy. John Costas, former head of investment banking at UBS and one of the Swiss bank's most powerful deal makers, says the system worked in such a way that everyone was under pressure to do whatever it took to grab the extra percentage point of market share or return on equity and to ride roughshod over naysayers. "For a decade, from 1999 through the middle of 2007, anytime you stopped participating, by *not* adding more risk or by *not* aggressively pursuing more transactions, you were wrong." In other words, chasing Goldman Sachs was a strategy that paid off for so long that Wall Street's leaders were ill equipped to recognize that it might not always continue to do so.

Nor was it possible to sit out the dance, to not try to emulate Goldman's golden touch. With the benefit of twenty-twenty hindsight, deciding back in 2003 or 2004 not to get caught up in the business of repackaging subprime mortgages into collateralized debt obligations (CDOs) looks great. At the time, it would have been untenable, says one former senior banker. "What was happening at the bank that did that? The investment analysts are downgrading it, the shareholders are unhappy, and the employees are unhappy because the bonuses aren't as fat as those their friends are earning. The press is all over the bank, saying it's not as well run as the other bank." That, he argues, is the kind of thinking that sealed the doom of some of Wall Street's most venerable names.

That kind of thinking is still alive and well on Wall Street today, even after the near apocalypse. The quest is already under way for the next "new new thing," the next product or strategy that will help firms such as Goldman Sachs and its rivals earn massive profits in the short run while creating new risks for the financial system. Perhaps it will be something that Goldman Sachs pioneers, or something that is launched by one of the new boutique institutions. The one certainty is that Wall Street's mind-set remains unchanged. Left unchecked, every firm will again overlook risk in hopes of gaining a dominant market share in that new product. The financial system has been saved from destruction, but as long as the mind-set of "chasing Goldman Sachs" lingers, it hasn't been reformed.

As the worst of the crisis recedes into the distance and Wall Street battles to return to business as usual, Goldman Sachs is once again the firm that all its rivals want to emulate, at least when it comes to financial performance. As David Viniar, the firm's chief financial officer, told a reporter in 2009, "Our model never really changed"[3]; by the end of 2009, Goldman was on track to reward its employees with one of the biggest bonus pools in its history and had rapidly returned to reporting astronomically high earnings. Once again, a relatively small proportion of those profits came from serving Main Street. Wall Street is still geared toward serving itself—its shareholders and employees—and as long as that collective mind-set endures, we run the risk of another systemic shock.

There is no point sitting around and waiting for Wall Street to apologize to us, individually or collectively. Nor can we content ourselves with the idea that bankers are twenty-first-century cartoon villains and demand that they get their just deserts. It's not even reasonable for us to indulge in bouts of nostalgia for the banking system of the past. True, in hindsight, the 1960s look like a golden age but we can't just wipe out innovations such as high-speed trading based on computer algorithms that didn't exist then. Nor can we force investment banks to return to the days when they weren't large publicly traded corporations but partnerships that valued long-term relationships over short-term quarterly profits. We can't turn back the clock to a time when hedge funds and private equity funds were a tiny sideshow on Wall Street. What we can and must do is understand the way Wall Street functions today and try to align that more closely with its special role in our economy and society.

This book isn't another anecdotal history of the subprime crisis of 2007 and 2008. Rather, it's the tale of how Wall Street's metamorphosis from a utility serving Main Street to a business that took extraordinary risks to maximize its own profits at the expense of that utility function set the stage for that crisis. It's an analysis of where we stand today and where we need to go next—to a world where, instead of blindly chasing Goldman Sachs in hopes of replicating its success, the players that make up Wall Street identify ways to *emulate* the strengths and avoid the flaws that lie within the business model of Goldman Sachs and seek out their own paths to success. Above all, those strategies must be based on their own competitive strengths and be pursued in a way that doesn't jeopardize Wall Street's core utility function.

The story is told through the eyes of those who lived it, such as Tom Casson—the bankers, traders, research analysts, and investment managers who have spent the bulk of their professional lives on Wall Street. Some of them can recall firsthand the events of the 1970s, when new technologies and new rules began to reshape the world they inhabited. It's the story of how Wall Street came to be seen, even by one of its devotees, as an "abstraction." With any luck, the next time Bernanke uses that phrase to describe the money grid, he'll be met with howls of outrage.

PART I

DANCING TO THE MUSIC

The financial markets had begun to feel the first shocks of what would become the worst market earthquake since the Great Depression when, in July 2007, then–Citigroup CEO Charles "Chuck" Prince came up with an unusual metaphor to explain why he and his team were forging ahead with business as usual, making loans to private equity funds to help finance the increasingly gargantuan buyout deals the latter were trying to structure. Sure, the credit markets were rocky, raising fears among some market participants that big banks like Citigroup—those that had been the most aggressive lenders to the LBO community and the biggest participants in the world of structured finance, marketing securitized products and derivatives to clients—would get stuck holding too many of those loans if there were no willing investors to take them off their hands. Prince, too, may have been worried, but he wasn't going to show it. Instead, he told the *Financial Times,* "as long as the music is playing, you've got to get up and dance." And, he added, Citigroup was "still dancing."[1]

That music came to a sudden and discordant end only months later, by which time Prince himself had been ousted as the giant bank's CEO. Citigroup was still paying the price for his philosophy years later. In order to prevent collapse, the bank had to accept government bailout funds, a portion of which was later converted into stock that gave the federal government an ownership position in Citigroup. Write-downs produced a gargantuan loss—$27.7 billion—in 2008; while the bank's 2009 loss of $1.6 billion was a lot smaller, it stood in stark contrast to the big profits being earned by the likes of JPMorgan Chase and Goldman Sachs.

How and why did one of Wall Street's premier institutions end up in such a pickle? The story of why Prince felt it necessary to keep dancing as long as the music played is one that has its roots back in the late 1960s and early 1970s, long before Citigroup existed or Wall Street had ever heard of collateralized debt obligations, credit default swaps, multibillion-dollar buyout funds, or any of the other instruments or players now often cited as culprits in the meltdown of the financial markets. The story of Citigroup—both its rise and near collapse—hinges on the changes to Wall Street's very structure. Without those transformations—some of them slow and almost imperceptible; others, like the collapse of the 1933 Glass-Steagall Act mandating a strict separation between investment and commercial banking, grabbing headlines worldwide—Wall Street could not have become as powerful a player in the U.S. economy as it did. Equally, it would not have endangered the entire money grid.

During the opening session of the hearings of the Financial Crisis Inquiry Commission (FCIC), Mike Mayo, a veteran banking analyst and now a managing director at Calyon Securities (USA) Inc., described Wall Street's member firms as being "on the equivalent of steroids. Performance was enhanced by excessive loan growth, loan risk, securities yields, bank leverage and consumer leverage. . . . Side effects were ignored, and there was little short-term financial incentive to slow down the process despite longer-term risks." But by the time the problems became so big that they began to nag at Mayo and many of his colleagues during the first decade of the new millennium, the trends that had led to those problems had been in place for decades. As I'll explain, the changes to Wall Street forced its financial institutions to rely on the most innovative and most leveraged products it could devise, because those generated the greatest profits. Similarly, the needs of "insiders"—Wall Street players like hedge funds and buyout funds—came to dominate the Wall Street landscape. As long as dancing to the music produced the profits that firms like Citigroup and its investors craved, they would continue to jig, two-step, or even produce a creditable Highland fling, if necessary. The first section of this book is the story of how that ethos became central to the way Wall Street functioned.

CHAPTER 1

From Utility to Casino:
The Morphing of Wall Street

Alan "Ace" Greenberg's firm may have collapsed underneath him, but even in the darkest days of 2008, the eighty-one-year-old investment banker's legendary chutzpah was visible on Bloomberg's business television network. "There's no more Wall Street," Greenberg, the former CEO of Bear Stearns, declared, adding that it had vanished "forever" in the rubble.[1]

It's fashionable on Wall Street today to talk wistfully—or in a tone of reverential awe—about investment banking as it was practiced during what is now seen as a kind of golden era. Greenberg's comments, though more hyperbolic than most, are one example.

The changes over the course of 2008 were so dramatic that Greenberg believed the Wall Street he helped forge no longer existed in any kind of recognizable fashion. Some nostalgic Wall Streeters view the investment banking landscape of the 1960s, '70s, and early '80s as a kind of utopia: investment banking as its purest, before the 1987 stock market crash, the collapse of the junk bond market, and Gordon Gekko made Wall Street seem slightly reckless and disreputable. To others, Greenberg among them, the golden era is the more recent past, when investment banks such as Bear Stearns saw their revenues and profits soar as they catered to the emerging powers on the Street, hedge funds and giant buyout funds, and watched their bonus payments and personal wealth climb even more rapidly.

The balance of power has certainly shifted on Wall Street, and new products, players, and technologies have transformed it. But Greenberg's comments were directed at the collapse of specific institutions: the shotgun wedding of his own firm with JPMorgan Chase, the bankruptcy filing of Lehman Brothers, and, the same weekend, the flight of Merrill Lynch into the arms of Bank of America. Greenberg most likely knew about the behind-the-scenes wheeling and dealing orchestrated by Ben Bernanke and Hank Paulson that involved every conceivable combination of every Wall Street firm with every one of its rivals (J.P. Morgan and Morgan Stanley? Goldman Sachs and Citigroup?). The desperate rush to save the financial system from utter collapse had resulted in the kinds of merger negotiations—however short-lived—that would have seemed laughable only weeks earlier. To Greenberg, still reeling at the collapse of his own firm (which had, after all, survived even the 1929 market crash and the Great Depression), that must indeed have felt like the end of Wall Street.

Wall Street, however, is more than just a set of institutions with big brand names, however old and venerable. At its heart, it is a set of functions, and those functions remained intact even in the midst of the crisis. Two days before Greenberg delivered his epitaph for Wall Street, a small Santa Barbara company, RightScale, raised $13 million in venture capital backing from a group of investors led by Silicon Valley's Benchmark Capital.[2] RightScale's secret? It was in the right business—cloud computing, a way for customers to reduce their IT development costs by using Internet-hosted services—at the right time. Despite the dramatic headlines focusing the world's attention on the plunge in the stock market and the deep freeze that hit the credit markets, parts of Wall Street's core business were still functioning, albeit in a more muted fashion. In the final three months of 2008, venture capital firms invested $5.4 billion in 818 different deals, bringing the total for the year to $28.3 billion. That was down a bit from 2007, when venture firms—partnerships that have made fortunes backing companies such as Amazon.com and Google and lost smaller amounts backing stinkers such as Pets.com—put $30.9 billion to work. But it's still more than they invested in any year from 2002 through 2006.[3] By the first anniversary of the collapse of Lehman Brothers, even the high-risk world of junk bonds was back in business. The sign? Beazer Homes, one of the worst-hit home-building companies in the entire industry, was battling not only the collapse in the real estate market but also a federal fraud investigation. Yet Wall Street found enough investors willing to close their eyes to those risks and invest $250 million in junk bonds issued by the company to help replenish its coffers.[4]

What Does Wall Street Do, and Why Does It Exist?

The reason for the Wall Street bailout—the explanation for Hank Paulson being desperate enough to literally drop to one knee in front of Nancy Pelosi in the White House and plead for her help passing the initial $700 billion rescue package—is that Wall Street's functions are essential to the economy. According to reports that were leaked to the media almost immediately, Paulson begged Pelosi not to "blow it up" (referring both to the bailout package and the financial system itself) by withdrawing the Democratic Party's support for the rescue effort. "I didn't know you were Catholic," Pelosi quipped, referring to Paulson's kneeling before her, in an effort to lighten the atmosphere before blaming the Republicans for the gridlock.[5]

By saving some of Wall Street's institutions—those viewed as the strongest or the most important to the system—the architects of the bailout and many of the subsequent reform packages hoped to preserve intact the system that enables capital to flow more or less smoothly through the economy the way power flows through the electrical grid or water through a municipality's water and sewer system. Regardless of what Main Street was thinking—and communicating to their members of Congress—Wall Street isn't incidental to what happens in the rest of the economy. Without Wall Street to perform its financial grid functions, it would prove almost impossible to raise capital to repair bridges, finance new companies such as RightScale, and keep others—such as Beazer Homes—afloat.

What we tend to think of as Wall Street—the stock market, the investment banks, and the newer entities such as hedge funds—is really only the visible tip of a much larger iceberg that is the entire financial system. Collectively, these institutions help ensure that capital continues to move throughout the rest of the "money grid." Sometimes they do this by providing a market for participants to undertake basic buy or sell transactions; on other occasions, they negotiate or devise solutions to more complicated capital-related questions, such as helping a company go public or sell debt (a process known as underwriting) or working with it to establish and achieve the best price possible in a merger negotiation.

That intermediary function is alive and well, most visibly at the New York Stock Exchange, which occupies not only the epicenter of Wall Street at the corner of Broad and Wall Streets but the heart of its role as a financial utility. On its sprawling trading floor, traders go about their business in much the same way their earliest predecessors did in the naves of Amsterdam churches, executing the purchases of blocks of shares for their clients, who these days could include an individual trying to sell 100 shares of General Electric or Microsoft inherited from a grandparent or a mutual fund manager trying to reduce his holdings in Amazon.com in order to buy a stake in

Alibaba.com, a Chinese counterpart. Exchanges trading stocks, futures, and options contracts as well as commodities remain one of the most heavily regulated parts of Wall Street because of the essential role they play in a large, geographically scattered, and diverse community.

Not convinced of the value of Wall Street's functions and processes? Imagine you are a retiree in your seventies, living off your investment portfolio. The wisdom of your decision to invest in Microsoft in the mid-1980s has become clear; now you're counting on being able to sell some of that stock at its current market value in order to cover your living expenses for the next six months. Wall Street's processes make that relatively simple—all you have to do is place an order to sell the stock at the market price with your broker or custodian (say, Charles Schwab) and ask for the money to be transferred to your bank account when the trade is settled in three days' time.

Now, imagine that there was no Wall Street. For starters, you'd have a hard time establishing a fair price for that stake in Microsoft without the stock market, with its countless numbers of buyers and sellers meeting in cyberspace to decide each minute of the day what value they ascribe to Microsoft's shares and thus what price they are willing to pay for your stock. Even if you thought you knew what your shares were worth, how would you find a buyer and persuade her that your analysis is right? Would you go door-to-door in Miami or Los Angeles? Put up an ad on Craigslist? (In Vietnam's over-the-counter market, that is exactly what happens; you then arrange to meet the buyer on a street corner to swap the shares for cash.) And if you found a buyer, could you be certain that you would be paid in full and on time, so that you could pay your own mortgage and purchase your groceries?

Money has existed for millennia, ever since people recognized that barter was an inadequate method of exchange. The stock exchange, just a few centuries old, was the next logical step as society's financial needs became more complex. The first exchanges were established in wealthy trading cities such as Hamburg, Antwerp, and Amsterdam. Here, by the early sixteenth century, there was a significant concentration of wealth in the hands of merchants and noblemen, all of whom had an interest in putting it to work in new and different kinds of enterprises in the hope of diversifying and making still more money. These communities traditionally were also home to cutting-edge commercial enterprises, ranging from new technologies such as printing to global trading ventures to the East Indies.

Investors willing to back these enterprises—most of which could take years to pay off—needed a secondary market: a place where people who were interested in buying or selling shares in ventures could meet each other or find an intermediary to help them with that transaction. For a while, Amsterdam's church naves served that purpose, along with the open-air wharves on Warmoesstraat near the city's old church, or Oude Kerk. The first formal stock exchange in Amsterdam opened its doors in 1610; between noon and 2:00 p.m. each business day, members were expected to show up and buy and sell on behalf of the general public—in other words, to provide liquidity to the secondary market.[6] By 1688, the Amsterdam exchange already looked a lot like the trading floor of the New York Stock Exchange in its twentieth-century heyday; seventeenth-century stock jobber Joseph de la Vega, in his dissertation on the financial markets of the time, entitled *Confusión de Confusiones*, famously described the scene as one in which "handshakes are followed by shouting, insults, impudence, pushing and shoving." (Perhaps it was this familiar atmosphere that led so many former professional football players to pursue second careers in the trading pits of the Chicago Board of Trade and the Chicago Mercantile Exchange.)

There probably has never been a time when people didn't complain about how the financial system worked—or failed to work. Nevertheless, the United States, as Alexander Hamilton, the country's first Treasury secretary, realized, would need a smoothly functioning financial system as part of its struggle to emerge as a viable nation-state.[7] Hamilton's initiatives included creating the country's first national or central bank, the First Bank of the United States, to replace myriad institutions within each of the thirteen original colonies, each of which had its own monetary policy and issued its own currency. Hamilton's goal was financial order and transparency, necessary if the new country was going to be able to repay its war debt and finance its growth by investing in new industries.

Wall Street, the narrow thoroughfare in lower Manhattan that owed its name to its former role as the northern border of the sixteenth-century Dutch colony of New Amsterdam, benefited from many of Hamilton's efforts to create the infrastructure of a national financial system and emerged as the heart of the new country's financial markets. It was here merchants chose to hang out on street corners to swap their ownership interests of government debt or the handful of start-up companies, such as canal construction ventures, that would form the core of the United States' new economy. (If you wanted to trade in the bonds newly issued by Alexander Hamilton's fledgling Treasury Department, you'd have to know which lamppost on Wall Street to stand under.) Eventually, the introduction of New York state regulations banning curbside haggling as a "pernicious" practice drove these early Wall Streeters indoors. Some two dozen dealers gathered under a buttonwood tree to sign a pact that served as the foundation of the New York Stock Exchange. First housed informally in a Wall Street coffeehouse, the exchange moved to a room at 40 Wall Street in 1817, paying $200 a month in rent, before relocating to the quarters it now occupies, just across Wall Street from Federal Hall. Today, the original Buttonwood Agreement, a tiny sheet of yellowing paper, is on display at the Museum of American Finance a few doors away at 48 Wall Street, the building that once housed the Bank of New York, also founded by Hamilton himself.

"You know, if Hamilton came back to life, I don't think he'd be all that surprised at the way the financial system has evolved," says Dick Sylla, the Henry Kaufman Professor of the History of Financial Institutions and Markets at New York University. A silver-haired, slightly built man, Sylla appears unruffled by the dramatic changes that have taken place on Wall Street, smiling wryly at a display at the museum featuring Citigroup's now-reviled leaders—Robert Rubin, Sandy Weill, and Charles Prince. But then, for him as for Hamilton (about whom he is writing a book), America's financial system was never about a single institution, however large. "It's all about the functions that the various institutions perform, rather than what names they go by or where their headquarters happen to be," Sylla explains. "Hamilton knew that there would be bubbles and periods of chaos. But if over the long run the system as a whole performs its function of allocating capital and allowing us as investors to diversify our portfolio, to not put all our eggs in one basket, it is doing what he wanted it to do."

The Nature of the Money Grid: The Intermediary

Wall Street, in its totality, involves more than what happens on the floor of the New York Stock Exchange or within the walls of any single investment banking institution. It has become a labyrinth of many different groups and institutions, all of which have one thing in common: they make the whole money grid work more smoothly and more efficiently. Many of them work hundreds or thousands of miles away from Wall Street itself. In Tacoma, Washington, Russell Investments devises stock indexes widely used by mutual funds and other big investors; in Kansas City, a firm called TradeBot uses computer-generated models to exploit tiny differences in the price of different types of securities and trades—in only milliseconds—on that information, making markets more liquid; Chicago's options exchanges make it possible for investors to bet not on the direction of a stock's price but on the rate and magnitude of change in that stock price and the time frame in which the change will occur.

All of these players perform functions that link the "buy side," those who have capital and want to invest it profitably, and the "sell side," those entities in need of capital. "At its heart, when it is doing what it does best, Wall Street is a superb gatekeeper, making matches between investors and businesses, governments, or anyone else who needs to finance something," explains Mike Heffernan*, a former Morgan Stanley banker. The sell-side client could be a regional bank trying to resell portions of some of the loans it has made, a credit card company looking for an investment bank to package up its receivables into asset-backed securities for resale, a town in Indiana trying to find an underwriter for the municipal bonds it must sell in order to finance new hospitals and schools, or a company trying to raise capital for expansion or to acquire a rival.

The sell side wants to get as much capital on the most favorable terms possible from the buy side—investors who range in size and importance from individuals to mutual fund conglomerates such as Fidelity, and include hedge funds, private equity funds, foundations, college endowments, pension funds, venture capital partnerships, and ultrawealthy individual investors such as Microsoft cofounder Paul Allen or financier George Soros. In a perfect world, the sell side would love free money—with no interest payable, no specific term for repayment, and no promises about increasing the value of the investment. It is the myriad institutions that collectively make up Wall Street that—in exchange for a fee—bring together the two parties and negotiate a compromise: the terms on which the buy side is willing to invest some of its capital and the sell side is willing to agree to in order to get its hands on that capital. Banks have been fulfilling that kind of function in more limited ways for centuries: the Bank of Venice issued government bonds back in 1157 to finance its war with the Byzantine empire in Constantinople, and by 1347, as the Medicis rose to power in Florence, there were no fewer than eighty banks making loans and doing business in that city-state; a few years later, the Florentine authorities started a special credit fund that would give interest-free loans to distressed *condottieri,* or soldiers of fortune.[8]

But as the sums got larger and the members of interested parties on the buy side (investors) and sell side (individuals or entities in need of capital) expanded in size and number and their needs became more complex, the process of bringing them together got tougher, and Wall Street–like intermediary institutions arose to facilitate the procedure. If you were a former *condottiere* who had lost an arm fighting for Florence against its neighbor and rival city-state Pisa in the fourteenth century, you knew which bank to approach for your interest-free loan. But what about financing a decade-long voyage to Southeast Asia in hopes of finding the mysterious Spice Islands and returning with a king's ransom in the shape of black pepper, cinnamon, and nutmeg in the sixteenth century, or funding the development of the latest gene-based cancer therapies in the twenty-first century? Both require the right kind of buy-side backer, or else the sell-side entity (the merchant adventurer or biotech engineer) would squander weeks or months it could ill afford trying to raise the capital it needed on its own. And it was only logical that these go-betweens—the investment banks and their predecessors, who made it their business to be familiar enough with all the deep-pocketed members of the buy side to quickly route the different investment opportunities to those they believed would have the most interest and the right risk appetite—should pocket a fee for that knowledge as well as for their skill in negotiating the terms of any investment.

Wall Street exists to help investors and those in need of capital find their way through the financing maze. Investment bankers still not only link the two sides but also help them sort out what terms are fair for the kind of capital being sought. Wall Streeters weigh in on the relative merits of different kinds of capital as well, advising corporate chief financial officers when it will be cheaper in the long run to issue debt on which the company will have to pay interest periodically, or when it might be a better idea to sell a stake in itself to investors in a stock deal. If they opt to issue corporate bonds, what kind of debt do investors want to buy, and what interest rate will the buy side demand in exchange for capital? Without the processes that Wall Street collectively oversees, it's hard to see how that vital function in our economy would be filled. The U.S. Treasury could still issue bonds and sell them directly to citizens, and municipalities might be able to raise at least some of the money they need selling muni bonds to their own citizens. But the latter, at least, won't raise all the capital they could at the cheapest possible price without an intermediary to help them identify the maximum number of interested investors.

If we were still back in the early 1900s, the prospect of the collapse of the investment banking system wouldn't be quite as apocalyptic as it is today, at least as long as enough of the commercial banks remained in business. That's because well into the 1920s, corporate finance was largely a matter of bank loans—if you could persuade your local bank manager that your business idea was sound and that you were a good credit risk, then he would lend you what you needed to get going and perhaps introduce you to some other folks who would invest in the fledgling company.

The earliest backers of auto pioneers Henry Ford and William "Billy" Durant (who founded both General Motors and Chevrolet) were local businessmen willing to risk some of their own money on two of the ambitious pioneers trying to build and sell the new horseless carriages. Durant even orchestrated a bidding war between Flint and Jackson, two midsized Michigan towns, to decide which would become the corporate headquarters of Buick, the company that would later become General Motors. Flint won the battle (along with the future tax revenue and jobs for its citizens) when its four banks and several carriage and wagon businesses, along with hundreds of other corporations and civic boosters, put up nearly $1 million in cash in exchange for stock in the fledgling company, more than double what Jackson's citizens were able to offer.[9]

Financing these entrepreneurs was both risky and nerve-racking: two-thirds of the more than five hundred car companies launched between 1900 and 1908 had either collapsed or changed their business within a few years.[10] Once a bank or a backer had committed its capital to a specific venture, there were few exit strategies—the stock wasn't publicly traded. This early version of the money grid was unsophisticated and underdeveloped. Even Durant—far easier to work with than the mercurial Ford, and a former stock trader to boot—couldn't penetrate Wall Street's establishment and get the money grid working for the benefit of his company. Discussing the possibility of forming a trust made up of the biggest automakers to design and build a car for the mass market with J. P. Morgan's minions, Durant couldn't persuade the great man himself of the virtues of the automobile. Much as he loved the idea of an oligopoly, Morgan seemed to love his horse-drawn carriage still more, dismissing automobiles as toys for the rackety younger generation and Durant as an "unstable visionary."[11] Durant was no more enamored of Morgan. "If you think it is an easy matter to get money from New York capitalists to finance a motor car proposition in Michigan, you have another guess coming," he wrote bitterly to his lawyer. Ultimately, Durant relied on local financing to get his new venture, General Motors, off the ground. Henry Ford managed to steer clear of Wall Street until the end of his life, relying on a steady flow of loans from banks such as Old Colony Trust Co.

Today's money grid is altogether a far more sophisticated and effective entity, having expanded geographically and evolved functionally. Wall Street is no longer a small clutch of giant investment banks, but includes a large and diverse network of venture capital funds whose specific function is to underwrite risky start-ups of the kind that Ford and Durant sought financing for a century ago and that a new generation of automotive industry entrepreneurs are trying to launch today. "This is what we exist to do," says Dick Kramlich of New Enterprise Associates, one of the venture industry's veterans. "Until the postwar period, and even for a while after that, if you wanted to start something completely new, your personal network needed to include people who had money or who could vouch for you to the bank. Now all you need is a great business plan that you can get in front of one of us. We've become part of the bigger, broader Wall Street system."

Indeed, during the Internet boom in the 1990s, Sand Hill Road, the long and winding thoroughfare that connects downtown Palo Alto, California, with the campus of Stanford University and other parts of Silicon Valley, became a kind of Wall Street west as the venture capital funds that set up shop there became more important to both the economy and the financial markets, financing start-up companies and generating big paydays for their own backers when some of those—eBay, Amazon.com, Netscape, and Google, to name a few—hit it big. Of course, just as many of the ships that sixteenth-century merchants financed in their voyages to the Spice Islands of Indonesia ended up dashed to pieces against the rocks on the coast of Africa, so many of the start-ups that today's venture capitalists back never live up to expectations or go belly-up. But the winners have been frequent enough that venture capital investors willing to wait five, six, or even ten years for their bet to pay off in their little corner of Wall Street can make just as much money as top-flight investment bankers or superstar hedge fund managers in theirs.

At the height of the dot-com boom in 1999, commercial real estate on Sand Hill Road was more expensive to rent than anywhere else in the world (including Manhattan and London's West End), reflecting the triple-digit returns some venture funds were earning.

That bubble popped in 2000, making it possible once again to find affordable office space in Silicon Valley. But the venture capital community continues to scour the landscape for the next "new new thing." To many VCs, one of the most exciting of these is green technology, with businesses built around environmentally friendly twists on the pioneering products of a century ago, such as new kinds of batteries and power generation technologies along with—yes, you guessed it— new kinds of automobiles. Detroit's executives might have had to grovel for a share of bailout funds after their financial prospects became so bleak that Wall Street east couldn't do anything to help. But on Wall Street west, some of Sand Hill Road's venture investors were eagerly backing companies such as Tesla Motors, founded by Elon Musk, the millionaire creator of electronic payments system PayPal.

"A few years ago, this was the lunatic fringe of the venture capital industry," explains Ira Ehrenpreis, a general partner at Technology Partners, one of Tesla's financial backers. Today, he estimates, as much as $17 of every $100 that venture funds collectively invest goes into clean-technology companies as a category, while half of all the capital Technology Partners raises is allocated to the industry. Ehrenpreis waxes rhapsodic about Tesla's first car, the $109,000 Roadster, of which 1,200 were on order by the end of 2008; 937 had been sold by December 2009. "It makes a Prius look like a gas-guzzling hog and drives like a Ferrari!" he exults. A couple dozen of the brightly colored sports cars, which can travel 236 miles on a single charge, can sometimes be spotted whizzing silently along Silicon Valley's highways and streets, Musk's among them. The Roadster, says Ehrenpreis, shattered the belief that going green meant abandoning style; the next step is to take the concept to the mass market, rolling out a more affordable Tesla sedan by 2011, and to raise capital for that through an initial public offering (IPO) of stock in the company.

Kleiner Perkins Caufield & Byers is one of Silicon Valley's most venerable venture firms; it has invested in most of the technology industry's landmark deals, now runs a $100 million "iFund" jointly with Apple in addition to its other portfolios, and has the same status in the venture capital universe that Goldman Sachs does on Wall Street east. But despite the motto on its website—"In Search of the Next Big Idea"—the firm passed up the chance to invest in Tesla. "All-electric cars probably aren't practical for a long time," argues Ray Lane, a partner at Kleiner Perkins and former president of Oracle Corp., the world's second-largest software company.

But Lane's resistance to the idea of investing in a next-generation kind of auto company didn't last long. Kleiner Perkins is now backing a more hybrid, less purist company, Fisker Automotive, launched by a designer who briefly worked for Tesla. "The Fisker cars are what I call a 'no-compromise' vehicle—beautiful and with a price point as well as features that will compare to a BMW," boasts Lane, who has a gray Fisker prototype in his garage at home that can run for fifty miles per battery charge. "To back these electric vehicle companies, you have to be as entrepreneurial within the venture world as the entrepreneur is within the corporate world—in other words, very, very willing to embrace risk." But, he quickly adds, Fisker will build some seven thousand electric vehicles in 2010. "GM can't seem to produce one."

By being able to reconceive itself and its role to include venture capital, Wall Street has proven itself, in the long run, more entrepreneurial than the Detroit-based automakers. It's not just venture capitalists that have spotted the potential of this new breed of automaker, however. Even with only a few dozen vehicles on the road, the fledgling green technology banking teams from Goldman Sachs, Morgan Stanley, Credit Suisse, and others were already making the trek to San Jose to check out Tesla and its rivals. So what if they are still guzzling capital faster than an SUV or Hummer can guzzle gasoline? Wall Street today doesn't need to be persuaded that it needs to be present from the very beginning if it is to capture all the business—and profits—it can. Sure enough, early in 2010, Tesla Motors filed to go public, with Goldman Sachs selected to lead four blue-chip underwriters.

How the Financing Life Cycle Works

There may be no better example of Wall Street's raison d'être than the role that venture capital—itself part of the money grid—plays in making entrepreneurial dreams a reality.

The same week that Lehman Brothers collapsed, the major figures of the venture capital community assembled at Microsoft's campus in Mountain View, California, a stone's throw from Sand Hill Road. The occasion was the National Venture Capital Association's thirty-fifth anniversary. They listened to presentations by three carefully selected venture-backed companies: Tengion, a firm developing biotechnology to build new human organs from cells; Digital Signal Corp., which is honing 3-D facial recognition software that can be installed anywhere from airports to shopping malls; and Tesla Motors. Formalities over, the crowd escaped gratefully to the reception room to quaff Napa Valley wines and buzz excitedly about the meltdown under way on Wall Street east. One of the most visible of those present was former star technology banker Frank Quattrone, who had spent the 1990s steering one promising technology company after another through the financing process, from the first capital infusions to the initial public offering (collecting hefty fees for his firms, which included Morgan Stanley and Credit Suisse, along the way). He became the banker most closely associated with the dot-com boom, but years after it burst, he was back helping start-up technology companies raise capital.

That evening he was talking up his new quasi-banking venture Qatalyst, and debating the impact the turmoil on Wall Street proper would have on start-up businesses in Silicon Valley and his own firm's prospects. "He was very interested, feeling that this might pave the way for a revival of the old West Coast boutique investment bank, like the Four Horsemen," said one venture investor who was on the receiving end of his pitch that evening.

The Four Horsemen were four small to midsized investment banks—Hambrecht & Quist, Montgomery Securities, Robertson Stephens, and Alex. Brown—that individually and collectively carved out both a niche and a reputation for themselves as the go-to guys for entrepreneurs in need of finance, venture capitalists hoping to take their portfolio companies to the next level, and investors hoping to get in on the ground floor of the next great business idea. "We didn't go into this wanting to be Goldman Sachs; we knew we'd end up as a marginal player trying to compete with them on ground that they owned, and that would be dangerous," recalls Bill Hambrecht, who founded the firm that bore his name and who now runs another boutique, W. R. Hambrecht & Co. "More than many of those larger East Coast firms, our model was very straightforward—we were there to help those companies move up the ladder to the next stage in their financial life cycle."

In 1981, the rest of the investment banking universe woke up to what was happening on the West Coast. "In a sixty-day period, we underwrote [the initial public offerings of stock in] Genentech, People's Express, and Apple," recalls Hambrecht. "I think we had sixty people in the firm; we made about $50 million that year and it changed everything." Hambrecht had attended college with the late Dick Fisher, then chairman of Morgan Stanley, who recognized what was brewing before the rest of the big Wall Street institutions. "He called me, then came to visit me, and told me, 'Okay, I want in on this business.' I asked him what companies interested him, and he mentioned Apple and a few others—he and his team had done their work and identified the best companies, not the biggest ones." Hambrecht & Quist would go on to co-manage multiple deals with Morgan Stanley, helping each other earn hundreds of millions of dollars more in fees for both firms before Fisher retired and Hambrecht & Quist's partners decided to sell their firm to Chase Manhattan in 1999, at the peak of the dot-com market.

The names of the institutions that help Silicon Valley's most promising companies move from one stage of development to the next by providing capital directly or introducing the company to potential backers are likely to continue to change, but the process itself remains intact. The earlier it is in a company's life cycle, the more informal that process is, as was the case with Google, now a corporate behemoth. One of the company's earliest supporters was David Cheriton, a Stanford professor who knew its founders, Sergey Brin and Larry Page. Cheriton also knew Andreas "Andy" Bechtolsheim, the cofounder of Sun Microsystems, and introduced him to the two would-be entrepreneurs at a gathering at his Palo Alto home. Bechtolsheim wrote Brin and Page a check for $100,000 on the spot even though the company hadn't yet been formed. He followed that with another $100,000 when the first formal venture financing round occurred the next month.[12] (One firm that passed on Google was Bessemer Venture Partners; offered the chance to meet the "Google guys," tinkering in the garage of a friend's home, David Cowan asked if there was a way out of the house that would enable him to bypass the garage.)

In the space of those few weeks, the Google guys had rounded up another $760,000 in start-up funding after Bechtolsheim introduced them to John Doerr, one of Sun's earliest investors and at the time the lead investor at Kleiner Perkins. Where Doerr went, others eagerly followed: the imprimatur of Kleiner Perkins was as valuable as that of *Good Housekeeping* or Goldman Sachs. Doerr roped in Jeff Bezos (he had also provided start-up funding for Bezos's Amazon .com), who in turn brought along Amazon colleague Ram Shriram; all invested in the fledgling company long before it was clear that Google was going to become, well, Google. At the time, it was just another speculative "angel" investment, one of scores that each of these individuals undertook between 1998 and 2000. But by the time the IPO had been sold and Google's stock was trading on the public market, Bechtolsheim's $200,000 was worth $300 million or so.

A typical venture firm, such as Kleiner Perkins, raises and provides capital at the earliest stages of the financing life cycle. That capital comes from other buy-side players, such as college endowments, pension funds, and very wealthy individuals whom the general partners know and trust, often successful entrepreneurs such as Bechtolsheim and Bezos. Venture funds make most of their money from their share of the profits of their funds (usually 20 percent) but also collect a fee from their investor base in exchange for their services bringing together those investors with bleeding-edge investment ideas at their earliest (and most potentially profitable) stage of development. Without venture funds and their vast networks, how would Verizon's pension fund know that two bright young Stanford students were about to put together a company that within a decade would dominate the technology landscape? And how would Brin and Page have navigated the Wall Street labyrinth in search of financing at such an early stage, while still working out of a friend's garage?

The next stage in the financing life cycle for venture-backed companies such as Google is something that will allow those early backers to realize the value of their investment. People such as Doerr and Bechtolsheim, like everyone else on the buy side, don't want to keep their capital tied up in the same companies indefinitely; at some stage they want it back, along with a healthy return, in order to put it to work somewhere else and repeat the process. In other words, they want liquidity, just as any of those sixteenth-century merchants wanted to be able to sell part of his stake in the East Indian trading vessel long before it returned home with its hold stuffed with nutmeg, cinnamon, and silks so that he could provide his daughters with dowries.

By the time Google was ready to go public in the spring of 2004, its team didn't need any help from Bechtolsheim or Doerr in finding an investment bank willing to serve as an intermediary between Google and its future stockholders. Every investment bank in the United States, as well as an array of foreign competitors, wanted a piece of the action. Unlike all the dot-coms that had crashed and burned just months earlier, *this* technology company could point to real revenues, not just an ambitious business plan. It was a jewel, and every bonus-starved banker wanted a place on the list of underwriters—preferably as lead underwriter or, even better, the book runner, the guy in charge of deciding which equally excited mutual fund managers, brokers, and individual investors would win a few Google shares at the IPO price and who would get to pocket the bulk of the underwriting fee in compensation for all the aggravation. This would be a multibillion-dollar offering, and in a typical IPO, the underwriters collectively could pocket as much as 7 percent of the proceeds as their fee.

Every banking team in the world began to chase the deal, and they all took it very seriously indeed. Morgan Stanley opened up a Silicon Valley war room, complete with a team of top bankers and analysts preparing pitch books and rehearsing answers to questions they expected to get from Lise Buyer, then Google's chief financial officer, and the other Google execs who would select the winners. "It was just like a presidential election campaign," recalls Hambrecht. Two weeks before the "bake-off" was scheduled to take place at the Palo Alto offices of Google's law firm, Wilson, Sonsini, Goodrich, & Rosati, pitting the finalists against each other, Morgan Stanley's team hired the key analyst that Hambrecht had assigned to prepare his own firm's pitch for the deal. "They wanted to find out what we were doing," Hambrecht says, shrugging. "All's fair in love and war."

And this *was* war, make no mistake about it. On a Saturday afternoon in early April, the finalists were scheduled to appear, one at a time, to make the final pitch to Google executives and board members, each explaining (with the aid of thick pitch books stuffed full of charts, diagrams, and other propaganda) why they were the only guys for the job. The Google folks knew what they were in for. Buyer had helped prepare pitch books herself in a previous life as a top technology analyst. Aware of the other tricks that Wall Streeters liked to play, she instructed the top bankers to stay home, decreeing that only the middle-ranking people who would actually do the grunt work on the deal should show up. (Few abided by that rule.) She also told them to be creative. "We wanted to be sure we'd be working with bankers who got our corporate culture, so I guess we kind of opened the door to a lot of the silliness that followed," she said.

One banking team brought beer, apparently assuming that a free-wheeling culture was synonymous with the liberal consumption of alcohol. Another tried to design a PowerPoint pitch incorporating Google's own search engine, which would spit out the firm's name when asked, "What is the best bank to underwrite Google's IPO?" (The technical challenge proved impossible, and the banking team resorted to a paper version of the same pitch.) Citigroup's technology bankers designed laminated place mats that spelled out the bank's achievements and creative strategies for marketing Google to the public, using Google-like design elements and layout. The place mats probably came in useful for the pièce de résistance. The banking team from Goldman Sachs, taking to heart Buyer's quip that, "given that we're all here on a Saturday afternoon, you can damn well bring me dessert," and learning through their own research that Brin and Page loved chocolate, ordered up a big chocolate cake, emblazoned with the Google logo, to bring to the pitch meeting. Stunts like that have been known to work, as Lisa Carnoy, who is now global capital markets co-head at Bank of America, knows from her days co-managing the same group at Merrill Lynch & Co. Pulling together a pitch book for the investment bank's presentation to Lululemon, a yoga clothing retailer seeking to go public, Carnoy included details of the favorite yoga positions of each member of the banking team in hopes of showing just how much the bankers understood their potential client's business. "They got a kick out of that and we got the deal," she recalled.

Winning an IPO is one matter; completing it to the satisfaction of all parties is something else altogether. However crucial the role played by Wall Street in bringing together and reconciling the competing interests of the buy side and the sell side, there is usually one group that feels it has given up too much in the process. A typical IPO investor, for instance, wants the largest allocation possible of a hot new issue. Many of those investors are also investment bank clients; they execute buy and sell orders and generate trading fees for Wall Street institutions year-round and aren't shy about telling the investment banks what they expect them to deliver in return. Fidelity, back in the days when it routed more than half of its immense trading activity through Wall Street trading desks, routinely threatened to "cut the wire" and trade with a particular investment bank's rivals if it didn't get an allocation twice that of its nearest competitor for an enticing IPO. The investment bank usually obliged.[13]

To make the buy side happy, the new stock should be priced at a level that will allow it to rise in value—preferably by 20 percent or more—in the days immediately following the IPO. That gives any mutual fund manager the chance to sell some of his shares at a quick profit—and can mean a big boost in trading revenues for the investment bank as trading volume in the newly public stock shoots higher. When Netscape went public in 1995 at $28 a share, it posted its first trade at $71. Those watching the electronic screens were convinced it was a typographical error or that they were hallucinating. An entrepreneur watching that kind of drama, however, is well aware that he may have just lost millions of dollars of new capital for his company and is left wondering whether Wall Street has just ripped him off. "Everyone was angry about that, and very vocal about" what they viewed as giving up that much in potential proceeds, says Buyer.

Google tried to ensure that it would capture as much of the proceeds as possible for itself and its backers. In fact, while the deal itself turned out to be messier and less profitable than anyone had hoped, it did at least leave all three parties—the buy side, the investment bankers, and the company itself—feeling equally dissatisfied. Morgan Stanley and Credit Suisse were told they had won the coveted co-lead-underwriting spots but that they would have to use Hambrecht's new method of capital matchmaking, a kind of auction that forces would-be buyers to bid against each other for the stock, disclosing the maximum price they will pay. That approach was anathema to both bankers and the buy side: it not only involves a much smaller fee for the underwriters (about 2 percent of the proceeds rather than the traditional 6 percent or 7 percent) but also in theory eliminates the possibility of a first-day pop in the price of the newly public company of the kind that investors cherish but that issuers such as Google had learned to loathe. Hambrecht's new firm, W. R. Hambrecht & Co., which had devised the auction methodology, won a co-manager slot due solely to Brin and Page's fascination with the auction idea rather than his four-page stapled pitch, which Buyer rated the worst she'd ever seen.

For their part, potential buyers were disgruntled at being asked to relinquish their traditional instant profit. Hambrecht remained unfazed. The auction process, he says, "means that Wall Street is really fulfilling its role as the intermediary because the proceeds are going to the company, not as instant, nearly risk-free returns to the bankers or investors who've owned the stock less than seventy-two hours." The rock-bottom fee took a toll on the process, banking analysts would later argue. Merrill Lynch walked away from the underwriting syndicate outright, unwilling to do all the work for what it saw as a measly return. The remaining underwriters later confessed to being reluctant to battle as ferociously as they might have done to combat buyer apathy, given the low fees. Buyers lowballed the deal, responding to the process and the deteriorating climate for technology stocks. Google had to settle for a price of $85 a share, instead of the $135 it had hoped to make from the deal.

The Troubled Heart of Wall Street

The process of underwriting an IPO or raising other kinds of capital for companies such as Google and providing exit strategies for their venture backers remains one of the core "utility" functions of Wall Street's big investment banks. "It's really not all that different today from the way it was back in the 1960s, when I wrote my first-ever case study about the IPO process," says Samuel Hayes, professor emeritus at Harvard Business School. Only the names of the issuers and the underwriters are different, while the dollar amounts are larger. But as the Google transaction illustrates, the relationships between Wall Street institutions and the two groups on either end of the capital exchange transaction that develop when a company goes public or otherwise raises new debt or equity capital aren't always smooth and straightforward. On the sell side, corporate clients such as Google don't always feel that their investment bankers are looking out for their best interests. Meanwhile, parts of the buy side—the investors— are just as skeptical.

The first part of the problem—the increasingly bumpy relationship between the investment bank and its corporate clients—Hayes attributes to changes on Wall Street itself. The mergers that have taken place over the last twenty years—all of the Four Horsemen were absorbed by national institutions, most of which in turn became part of still more massive financial behemoths—mean that doing the kind of smaller deal that is characteristic of what most companies need in the earliest days of their existence isn't cost-effective. Venture capital investors are well aware of this trend, and it worries them. "Unless I have another potential Google, these guys don't want to know," says one Silicon Valley venture capitalist bitterly. "They want the sure thing, the big deal that is going to be able to make a visible difference to their own profits at the end of the quarter. They are more interested in that than in building relationships with corporate clients that might generate a stream of fees over the years. They have betrayed our trust." He points to Goldman Sachs, which shuttered its Sand Hill Road outpost (in a building it had shared with archrival Morgan Stanley) a few years after the tech bubble burst. "They'll fly people in for things they consider important, but there aren't as many people competing to serve this space, which means that all the companies that we are starting to fund today are going to have a much harder time in the later stages of their corporate lives when it comes to getting financing."

This venture investor predicts that a greater number of venture-backed companies will wither on the vine, unable to get financing simply because of their size relative to that of the investment banks. That, he argues, may not augur well for the future of both entrepreneurial energy and Wall Street. Will some prospective entrepreneurs be deterred or some promising companies derailed? And what happens if Wall Street turns its back on its core function of helping promising businesses realize that promise by accessing capital? "We play our role; we want Wall Street to play theirs."

For now, at least, the venture industry is keeping its part of the tacit bargain and continuing to invest billions of dollars a year in start-up companies. Despite the market chaos, venture funds still want to back the companies that they believe have the potential to become next-generation versions of Genentech, Google, or Amazon. These days those companies will range from start-ups offering innovative ideas on managing power grids more efficiently to businesses based on new medical devices. But by 2009, the signals were becoming more mixed. Wall Street's recent aversion to doing what it saw as small-scale underwriting deals had remained, and had been exacerbated by the general chaos as banks focused on their own internal restructuring. That forced some venture companies to direct as much as 40 percent of their investment funds in 2009 toward existing, relatively mature companies still languishing in their portfolios and unable to find an exit.[14] In a normal year, says Jim Feuille, a general partner at Crosslink Capital, his venture capital firm invests in eight or nine new businesses. By late October 2009, they had selected only three new companies in which to invest, in order to preserve enough capital to be able to continue supporting those older businesses. The National Venture Capital Association reported that the same trend was being seen across the industry: by the third quarter of 2009 only 13 percent of all venture capital investment dollars were directed to first-time companies, the lowest percentage on record. Venture capital analysts such as Tracy Lefteroff at PriceWaterhouseCoopers began to fret that if this trend continued, it could create a "hole" in the pipeline of companies going public, doing a disservice to parties at both ends of the money grid.

This kind of breakdown in the relationship between Wall Street, as represented by investment bankers, and its corporate clients isn't confined to Silicon Valley—nor, as I'll explain later in the book, is the breakdown restricted to one part of the money grid. The relationship between Wall Street and its partners on both the buy and sell sides has been under threat for more than a decade, as Wall Street drifted further and further away from its core utility function and those clients generated a decreasing proportion of its revenues and profits.

From Gatekeeper to Casino Croupier?

Harvard Business School's Sam Hayes has studied the breakdown in the relationship between Wall Street and its corporate clients in real time. Hayes knows whereof he speaks. He holds the Jacob H. Schiff Chair in Investment Banking as a professor emeritus and has studied

Wall Street from the perspective of a scholar (he has published seven books and countless research papers and other articles about various aspects of Wall Street), a consultant (to the Justice Department, the Treasury Department, and the Securities and Exchange Commission, as well as many businesses), and even a participant (he chairs the investment committee at his alma mater and is a former chairman of the Eaton Vance family of mutual funds, making him a member of the buy side, while his role as a member of the advisory board of brokerage firm Edward Jones puts him on the sell side). When in 1970 he began scrutinizing the way Wall Street worked, it was performing its intermediary function adeptly; the relationships with clients, he says, were true long-term ties of importance to both parties. When a CEO wanted to sell bonds, raise new capital through a stock issue, or mull over other strategic issues, he'd pick up the phone and call his banker. That banker would be the same person, or at least someone at the same firm, year after year.

But Hayes soon began to detect signs that those relationships were crumbling, as they came under siege from both sides throughout the 1970s. A new breed of CEOs and chief financial officers with MBA degrees felt better equipped to pit one Wall Street firm against another in search of a way to cut financing costs. Wall Street firms were quite eager to poach their rivals' investment banking clients, adding fuel to the fire. To both groups, this breakdown seemed logical and even beneficial—why shouldn't corporations shop around for the best deal and investment banks compete to offer that deal? By 1978, *Institutional Investor* magazine had stopped publishing the annual "Who's with Whom" list documenting which firms "banked" which corporate clients. "Clients didn't like being labeled as 'belonging' to Kuhn Loeb," Hayes recalls.

The turning point came a year later when IBM wanted to add Salomon Brothers as a co–lead underwriter to a bond sale it was planning. When the company informed its traditional bankers at Morgan

Stanley of its wish to include Salomon because of the latter's growing importance in the bond markets, Morgan Stanley refused to share the spotlight. (At the time, Morgan Stanley, in an attempt to emphasize how exclusive it was in the clients it accepted, even insisted on using a special typeface in the newspaper "tombstone" ads announcing deals it had done.) Instead of backing away from the idea, as Morgan bankers had expected, IBM awarded the whole deal to Salomon Brothers, shutting out Morgan Stanley altogether. It wasn't until 1984, when Morgan Stanley agreed to share the lead underwriting role for Apple with Hambrecht & Quist, that the blue-chip New York firm conceded that it would have to relinquish part of the limelight on occasion in order to participate at all in the deals it wanted to do.

If IBM's decision to put its foot down was the turning point in the relationship between Wall Street and the sell side, the tipping point in ties between the Street and its buy-side clients came in 1995, when Netscape went public with the assistance of several leading investment banks. The transaction certainly was part of Wall Street's core function—the underwriters were raising money for a corporate client—but the company in question had a far riskier and less established business model than those that bankers were accustomed to introducing to the buy side. With Netscape, says Lou Gelman*, a former Morgan Stanley banker involved in the IPO, Wall Street was asking its buy-side clients to adopt a completely different approach to investing. Netscape wasn't earning a profit, and its business model was untested, relying on the then-new phenomenon of the Internet. "Until Netscape came along, Wall Street used to say a company had to have two years of operating profits in order to go public," Gelman says. But Morgan Stanley badly wanted a piece of what promised to be a very hot IPO. "Suddenly our top guys were tossing their own rules out the window in order to get this business."

Above all, the Netscape IPO opened the door to speculation as an investment strategy. It was now in Wall Street's financial interest to encourage its buy-side clients to toss away their concerns about investing in a relatively risky business. "We went from being a gate-keeper to [being] a croupier," says Gelman. Until that time, he argues, Wall Street had served its buy-side clients by helping them preserve and protect their wealth. Now the ethos seemed to have changed; Wall Street was becoming a casino, a place where people could create wealth rapidly by speculating. "It was with the Netscape IPO that the conviction we have today—that it's actually possible to get rich in a day by owning the right stock—took root," Gelman says. "It's corrupting."

Not only that, but for several years it was also exciting and dramatic; that drama would help swell Wall Street's own coffers as hundreds of Internet companies followed Netscape's lead and paid their 7 percent underwriting fee to go public. It all followed the success of the Netscape underwriting team, which, after overseeing the production of an IPO prospectus containing twenty-plus pages of risk factors, took the fledg-ling Internet company's management team on the road to drum up buying interest. The target stock price crept slowly higher, to $12 per share and onward, as public awareness grew during that "road show." The battle to acquire stock in the deal ended up bringing Wall Street and Silicon Valley to Main Street's attention; both captured the imagi-nation of ordinary investors who until then had never had a brokerage account. One caller to Netscape's headquarters asked what the IPO signified. "Essentially that means our company will be trading a cer-tain number of shares on the stock market, which will raise capital so we can expand our business," the operator informed him. "What's the stock market?" the caller inquired. Another caller had heard people talking about the deal in the grocery store and wanted more informa-tion. A third threatened to report Netscape to the San Jose police for "insider trading" when he wasn't allotted shares at the IPO price of $28 apiece. It's not surprising he was unhappy: the stock soared as high as $75 in its first trading day, before closing at $58 a share.

The external exuberance wasn't always matched inside Morgan Stanley itself, even after the deal turned into a runaway success story. "Some of us pushed back, but the argument came down to the reputation of our franchise against the potential revenue," says Gelman today. "Were we going to be the firm that doesn't do early-stage IPOs, when this is what the public wants to buy? No one, it turned out, was willing to walk away and leave that to our rivals." By the time the dot-com bubble was fully inflated, Gelman was convinced that the capital-raising process had undergone a fundamental change. "We weren't there to provide companies with the best long-term sources of capital to grow with; we were doing this to help our investor clients get richer faster." In his view, Wall Street had abandoned *both* of its core constituencies in pursuit of its own self-interest.

That approach gained momentum as the years passed, and extended into a variety of products, including higher-risk corporate bonds and collateralized debt obligations (CDOs), the bundles of mortgages (including those issued to subprime borrowers) that had been repackaged in the form of marketable securities. Caveat emptor, Wall Street declared—buyer beware. "Eighteen or twenty years ago, when someone [on Wall Street] showed us a bad product, we went crazy; we'd tell them, 'Don't ever show us that again,'" recalls Scott Amero, a portfolio manager at BlackRock, a major buy-side asset management firm. "At first we took the time to explain why something was a bad product, why it was risky or poorly designed." But eventually Amero found it impossible to provide that kind of detailed feedback: either the relationships weren't strong enough to permit it or the banker wasn't in a position to do anything about BlackRock's concerns, especially since there were other willing buyers. All Amero could do was go on a buyer's strike. In 2009, Larry Fink, one of BlackRock's founders and its chairman and CEO, gave voice to his fury with Wall Street for abandoning its traditional role as gatekeeper that took care to funnel only valid and viable products to the buy side. In the past, Fink told the *Financial Times*, firms such as BlackRock "relied on Wall Street to be the safety guards to the capital markets," winnowing out the poor-quality deals. Now, he added angrily, it seemed as if it was up to his firm and other buy-side institutions to protect the integrity of the parts of the market.[15]

The Core Function Becomes a Sideshow

The IPO market may be one of the best examples of Wall Street's core function at work, funneling capital from those who have it to those who need it. But Wall Street saw underwriting IPOs as less and less attractive with each year that passed. Most transactions were far smaller than either Netscape or Google, and the amount of work the investment bank had to do in order to drum up investor interest in a previously unknown company could be time-consuming. When that company planned to raise only $15 million or so, the fees were small. But being willing to work on an IPO was what a bank had to do in an era where relationships alone were not enough to win business. Some, such as Morgan Stanley's Dick Fisher, realized that technology companies weren't going to generate a lot of banking fees in the future. They didn't need much new equity after an IPO, typically, and almost never raised debt capital, since they didn't have the kind of fixed assets that bond buyers like to see. Unless the company decided to make acquisitions, the IPO fee might be the only banking revenue the underwriter ever earned. "Fisher told me he knew [companies such as Adobe and Apple] weren't going to be good investment banking clients," says Hambrecht. "He was right; Adobe had a $10 million IPO and then never raised another dime on Wall Street."

But Fisher's ultimate goal was to capture a different kind of business and a more secure stream of fee income for Morgan Stanley: he wanted to woo the newly wealthy executives as clients for Morgan Stanley's private banking team. "Sure enough, Morgan Stanley ended up managing about 90 percent of the wealth created in the Apple IPO, while Goldman Sachs did the same for their Microsoft millionaires," says Hambrecht. And when the $4.4 billion initial public offering of stock in UPS closed in November 1990, Morgan Stanley saw its $50.5 million share of the $191.5 million in fees paid by "Big Brown" to the thirty-five-member Wall Street underwriting syndicate as just the tip of the iceberg.[16] That evening, when UPS's top brass sat down to celebrate the first day of trading in their new stock (and its 30 percent pop in value), they were sharing their prime rib not only with the bankers who had sold the stock but also with the Morgan Stanley wealth managers summoned to woo them as clients for *that* side of the company's business. Yes, Wall Street was changing.

Some of those who felt as if the new Wall Street was leaving them behind as it drifted further away from its core function came from within the ranks of Wall Street itself. While one group of Wall Street bankers focused on helping companies raise new capital, another specialized in advising corporate clients on making a different kind of match: negotiating a merger with or acquisition of another business. Fees on these transactions may be a smaller percentage (from 1 percent to 3 percent) of the value of the deal, depending on the complexity and the players—but the deal sizes can be large. And a satisfied client can earn a banking team a series of fees year after year, as a business grows through acquisitions. JDS Uniphase, an optical networking company, forked over $30 billion in stock for big-ticket acquisitions in just a few years, each of which generated hefty deal fees—mostly in cash—for the matchmakers who helped orchestrate them.[17]

At any rate, this part of Wall Street tended to see itself as an elite group. Other members of their firms underwrote stock and bond offerings, handled sales and trading, or devised structured products such as CDOs and might generate high fees when their part of the business enjoyed its moment in the sun. But the mergers and acquisitions (M&A) advisory business, in their eyes, was the heart of what Wall Street was really about. "In my mind, the really sharp minds on Wall Street are not doing IPOs or debt financings; they're doing strategic stuff like M&A advisory work," says Mike Donnelly* bluntly. Donnelly, who lost his own job in the wake of the collapse of his firm, hasn't lost his awe for those he considers to be Wall Street artists. "Someone who is really great at this has a knowledge of the business, the industry and the company and the strategic issues that lie ahead. He has the technical knowledge, he knows the latest twists and turns in accounting rules and the law. He has experience and is never taken by surprise because he knows the kind of odd things that can happen," explains Donnelly. "And they can present everything to a board in a lucid and compelling way. I suppose they're a bit like a Pied Piper; people who hear them will end up following them anywhere. It's incredibly hard to find someone like that, and that's why they are so valuable."

Robert Greenhill, Morgan Stanley's president and Fisher's heir apparent back in 1992, has always been that kind of banker. Flying his own Cessna from one client meeting to the next, he and his team had propelled the firm to the coveted top spot in the league table rankings. (These widely scrutinized lists, published quarterly by data groups such as Dealogic LLC and Thomson Reuters, told the world which investment bank had underwritten the most deals in any specific area imaginable; the battle for league table credit and the bragging rights that went along with a top-three finish was fierce and remains so today.) Alas, merger volumes were down overall that year, and John Mack—whose own background was in sales and trading, the heart of the underwriting function—ended up elbowing Greenhill out of his way. Deposed as president in early 1993, Greenhill resigned shortly after, first joining Sandy Weill as the latter began to construct the behemoth that would become Citigroup and later founding his own boutique advisory firm. He left behind him what became known as the "Greenhill gap"—there was no one who was his equal as a rainmaker for the firm.[18]

To Gelman, the former Morgan Stanley banker, Greenhill's departure symbolized the final transition of power from the long-term strategic thinking characteristic of an M&A advisor to the emphasis on speculation and short-term profit maximization symbolized by the rising power of the trading desks and their chiefs within the power structure of many investment banks. "By the time Netscape came along, serving investors who were speculating and trading like crazy—and trading for our own account—had become what it was all about," he says. "Even in the IPO business, what had been a craft became an assembly line."

But by then, there was no way for Wall Street's investment banks to become purists, even when it came to fulfilling their gatekeeper role. Too much had changed in the world around them, and their responses to those changes had produced a series of unanticipated consequences. Long before the Netscape IPO was a gleam in the eye of the company's venture capital backers, it had become clear to investment bank CEOs that relying on the basic gatekeeping functions of yore was never going to generate enough profit to keep their ever-expanding empires afloat.

CHAPTER 2

Building Better—and More Profitable—Mousetraps

Long before the dawn of the twenty-first century, it was clear to Wall Street's leading investment banks that while being a superstar at raising capital or negotiating mergers might earn them kudos, it wouldn't keep their shareholders happy in normal or slow market environments. These publicly traded entities needed to deliver reliable, consistent, and ever-increasing profits to their investors, whether or not the cyclical financial markets cooperated. Fees tied to the process of raising capital for clients—which was, in its turn, dependent on those financial market cycles—weren't going to be enough to keep those investors happy. The future of Wall Street's biggest institutions lay not simply in helping Main Street clients navigate the liquid and transparent stock and bond markets but in generating newer and more exotic proprietary products.

The ugly end to the dot-com boom in early 2000 drove that message home to Wall Street decision makers like nothing else had done. They had spent the waning years of the twentieth century chasing the kind of fees that had been the bread and butter of Wall Street: taking start-up technology companies public, raising both debt and equity for the likes of WorldCom and AT&T Wireless, and pocketing merger advisory fees by helping companies such as Cisco and JDS Uniphase snap up innovative young companies. At least some of those who were part of that boom look back on it now with a degree of wistful nostalgia as the last golden age for the classic investment banker. "It was a period when we did what we were good at, more efficiently than ever before, and made more money for ourselves than ever before," says Larry McInnes*, a veteran technology and telecommunications banker.

Shareholders were happy; the average brokerage firm reported a 27.3 percent return on equity in 1999.[1] Goldman Sachs, which hadn't even had an investment banking office in Silicon Valley itself until that year, nevertheless managed to grab a commanding lead in technology stock underwriting, helping it capture a return on equity of 34.2 percent and making the firm—yet again—the envy of all the other chief financial officers on Wall Street. But that happiness could endure only as long as the market bubble kept inflating. Profitability on that scale came from making Wall Street's core process work overtime. After Netscape changed the game, Wall Street, eager to capture its share of the speculative frenzy in the shape of investment banking fees, was happy to fuel that frenzy by underwriting initial public stock offerings for increasingly risky companies, some of which had been in existence for just months and had no revenues, much less profits, to offer their investors. Goldman Sachs led the offering for Webvan, a grocery delivery service that rapidly closed its doors, while Merrill Lynch brought Pets.com to market; that company shut down ten months after the IPO. But Wall Street's priority was keeping its *own* shareholders content; as those transactions became more speculative and riskier for investors, they became increasingly lucrative for the investment banks.

In 1995, the fee per transaction (equity and debt underwriting as well as advisory fees) on Wall Street hovered around $1.19 million; it hit $1.48 million in 1998, $1.81 million the next year, and a high of $2.03 million in 2000.[2] The average Wall Street bonus nearly doubled between 1998 and 2000, topping $100,000 for the first time.[3] Goldman Sachs alone had pocketed $24.5 billion in fees for underwriting sixty-three IPOs during 2000. By the end of that year, two-thirds of all IPOs were trading below the price at which the stock had first been issued. Investment banks were not going to give back any of their fees, however.

Still, with the classic financing process in a cyclical slump and the average ROE for investment banks and brokerages plunging to between 12 percent and 13 percent in 2001 and 2002, it was time for Wall Street to play the card it had kept stashed up its sleeve for years. The fact was that Wall Street firms no longer needed to rely purely on the fees they earned for overseeing processes such as underwriting, sales and trading, or advising on mergers. These intermediary functions were profitable only when they could be done in tremendous volumes, as had happened at the height of the dot-com boom. The longer the slump that began in 2000 lasted, the more Wall Street needed to find an alternative source of revenue, preferably one with a higher profit margin.

Wall Street couldn't survive without fees, as veteran banking analyst Mike Mayo pointed out in the first round of hearings convened by the Financial Crisis Inquiry Commission (FCIC). Fees from Wall Street activities, Mayo noted, had generated no more than about 20 percent of bank revenues from the early 1950s right up until the early 1980s. But as other sources of revenue slid and banks found ways to create, package, and sell more exotic securities, that proportion rose—by the late 1990s, banks were earning some 40 percent of their revenues from fees. The answer, it became clear, was to develop structured products: the more complex the better, since the more sophisticated investment and risk management products commanded the highest fees from their clients.

As Federal Reserve monetary policy makers addressed the recession of 2000–2002 by slashing interest rates to the lowest levels most Wall Street bankers had seen in their lives, it made sense that many of these new products would be tied to two markets that are not only the country's largest but also closely linked to interest rates: the debt market and the housing market. Lower interest rates drove borrowing costs down for everyone, from the biggest leveraged buyout fund to the most cash-strapped home buyer. Not surprisingly, the level of borrowing skyrocketed, as did a host of new Wall Street debt products, from the relatively straightforward corporate bonds to leveraged loans and the now-infamous collateralized debt obligations (CDOs).

By 2005, the CDO had steered Wall Street back into extremely profitable territory. The focus on products (in the shape of CDOs) helped profitability per transaction jump back to $1.54 million and then to $1.91 million in 2006, by which time the CDO market was worth a whopping $2 trillion, according to research firm Celent. (Estimates are that Wall Street investment banks and other participants in the mortgage boom had pocketed the same amount in fees for originating, packaging, and repackaging the mortgage-backed securities in those CDOs during the five years from 2003 to 2008.) Wall Street was hooked, this time on a product—the CDO—rather than on a process such as IPO underwriting.

As profitability zoomed, so did the risk. As one unnamed subprime lender in California recounted, "The sales guys from the Street would come and talk to you and hype you up. They would try to get you to do something. From Monday to Thursday you would make the loans. . . . By Friday your mistake would be on the marketplace" in the form of a new CDO.[4] The subprime lender (a firm such as Angelo Mozilo's Countrywide, for instance) pocketed an origination fee for making the loans; the Wall Street institution begging for the raw material to turn into CDOs collected the fees for gathering the loans together, repackaging them, and selling them. The quantitative analysts on Wall Street, who used mathematical or statistical markets to analyze the financial markets and develop new trading and investment strategies and tactics (these "quants" would become known as the Street's rocket scientists), began pushing the boundaries of the possible still further. As margins on CDOs began to dip, they first sought to create CDO-squared products (made up not of packages of mortgage-backed bonds but of chunks of CDOs) and even CDO-cubed structures (made up of pieces of a few CDO-squared products in a different combination). These variants weren't even composed of real assets but were "synthetic" securities, built of derivatives designed to mimic what the real assets would do.

Ultimately, Wall Street came to rely on these exotic securities for its profits. At the end of the day, there are a finite number of blue-chip companies that need Wall Street's help to raise capital or complete a merger deal. Persuading any one of those to do one extra deal a year is time-consuming and the odds of success are low, as any Wall Street veteran will admit; corporate deal makers are well aware of the many studies showing that most mergers don't deliver the promised operational or financial benefits. Without a clutch of blockbuster deals—a few IPOs like that of Google, a series of multibillion-dollar takeovers on which to earn advisory fees—it was going to be hard to earn the kind of profit margins investors wanted. Wall Street needed help, and one of the places it found it was in the development of a new kind of deal machine, based on proprietary products. If the deal machine faltered, investment bankers knew, so would profit margins—and that just wasn't acceptable.

For all its fascination with correlations—market relationships, such as that between the price of crude oil and the value of oil and gas drilling companies, for instance—Wall Street seemed oblivious to one of the most significant correlations of all. Whenever its own fee income spiked to unusually high levels and its ROE levels surged well above average levels (by some calculations, around 15 percent), disaster seemed to follow. That had happened in 1999 and 2000. In 2006, the average ROE of the investment banks hit an average 23.3 percent, with Goldman Sachs again leading the pack with 33.3 percent. But Larry Sonsini, the Silicon Valley lawyer whose firm advises about four hundred public companies and thirty-five hundred privately held businesses, was watching with growing anxiety. "Month by month, year by year, I saw one investment bank after another drifting further and further away from their knitting, investing more and more in products rather than services," he says. Even the rhetoric changed, he observes. Instead of talking about Wall Street's role in the economy, the bankers he knew began to emphasize their role as profit-making businesses with no overarching economic mission. "They didn't even realize that they were moving outside the boundaries of what they had traditionally done; much less ask if it was a good idea for themselves, let alone the broader system. And as it turned out, they screwed up; Wall Street didn't understand what they were doing well enough to manage the risk associated with it. They felt they needed this business, and now we're all paying the price."

Mayday, Mayday, Mayday!

Wall Street's obsession with products and product innovation as a recipe for profits has roots more than thirty years old. May 1, 1975, has gone down in the history of the Street as "Mayday," the date the Securities and Exchange Commission had dictated would mark the end of fixed trading commissions in the stock market. Overnight, Wall Street's comfortable existence was shaken; its long-standing business model was turned upside down.

Until then, investors had been forking over 40 or 50 cents a share to place a buy or sell order for stock through their broker. "I was a big producer, because I'd do one trade in connection with a deal," recalled the late Fred Joseph, former CEO of Drexel Burnham (itself a victim of product-related risk-taking in the form of junk bonds), who went on to cofound a boutique investment bank, Morgan Joseph. "I could make a $500,000 fee without discussing it with the client" simply because the commission was fixed. Those fees, many paid by big institutional investors such as Fidelity and Capital Research and Management, earned massive profits for those who did nothing but execute the trades. Jimmy Cayne, then a rising broker at Bear Stearns (and later its CEO and chairman), pocketed up to $900,000 a year at a time when Bear's partners earned only $20,000 plus a share in whatever profits the firm made each year.[5] "Oh, that was a wonderful cushion," recalled Joseph. Those profits, he explained, helped subsidize all kinds of other businesses that were vital to Wall Street's core function but that didn't make much money in their own right, such as research.

When regulators dismantled the fixed commission structure, they weren't thinking much about the unexpected consequences that might follow. Their focus instead was on the rebound in trading volumes that took place as the bear market of the early and mid-1970s loosened its grip. A pricing system that seemed reasonable when the average daily trading volume in a stock might be a few hundred shares looked like Wall Street getting rich at the investor's expense when volumes climbed. After all, it didn't cost a brokerage firm ten times as much to trade a thousand shares as it did to buy or sell a hundred shares of stock, in terms of the salaries paid to staff on the New York Stock Exchange, telecommunications costs, and other forms of overhead. Commissions of 40 cents a share were simply too costly for Wall Street's buy-side clients—the investors—to sustain, and the SEC decided that the intermediaries should have to negotiate their fees with their clients, competing against each other to offer the best deal. At Goldman Sachs, bankers recall they expected those transaction fees to fall 10 percent or so during the first few months of the new pricing regime. It was one of the few occasions when

Goldman Sachs would be proven dead wrong. By the end of May-day itself, the first day of the new trading fee regime, Wall Street's largest and (until now) most profitable customers had used their clout to negotiate trading costs that were half what they had been the previous day. The trend continued. By the 1990s, trades that had once cost dollars to execute could be done for pennies; even the smallest individual investors were benefiting as discount online bro-kerages offered rock-bottom trading fees to win their business.

Initially, the end of fixed commissions won the moniker Mayday simply because of the date the new system began—the traditional May Day, celebrated for centuries as the beginning of spring. But per-haps the selection of a word that doubles as a radio communications signal for a life-threatening emergency wasn't all that coincidental. Mi-chael LaBranche, now head of one of the New York Stock Exchange's firms of specialists, recalls people walking around the trading floor la-menting the changes and proclaiming it was the end of their business.[6] In a way, it would prove to be just that. Even those firms who had supported it, such as Merrill Lynch (which hoped to use negotiated commissions as a way to nab a larger share of the trading business), couldn't have anticipated the long-term consequences, in particular the scramble to replace the now-vanished cushion of earnings.

Wall Street's Mayday "changed the whole nature of Wall Street; what we did and who we were," argues Wilbur Ross, a financier and private equity investor who at the time worked in an institutional bro-kerage that specialized in research. No longer did the large and lucra-tive trades by big institutions help investment banks and brokerages subsidize less profitable but systemically important businesses, such as executing trades for individual investors and providing investment research. "Research suddenly had no value in its own right and wasn't being subsidized," Ross contends. "So the clever people on the Street said, 'Okay, we'll use these smart and well-paid people to bring in in-vestment banking business.'" That led directly to one of the Wall

Street scandals of the last decade, the one that pointed out just how wide the gulf had grown between the Street and the investors who had previously relied on firms such as Merrill Lynch not only to execute their trades but to give them advice.

Henry Blodget, the former hotshot Internet analyst, had done a very good job picking winners for Oppenheimer's investment clients, suggesting that they snap up shares in Amazon.com when the online retailer was trading at about half of his price target of $400; it breezed through that level only weeks later. That forecast grabbed the attention of Merrill Lynch, which recruited him to make research calls that would be just as lucrative for their clients. But if Blodget was good (in the short term) at picking dot-com winners, he proved *great* at raking in investment banking fees and being a cheerleader for the speculative Internet stocks. Even when their prospects soured, Blodget remained publicly upbeat. After the bubble burst, regulators began to question just why supposedly smart people had advocated that the rest of us do stupid things. They discovered that Blodget had sent internal e-mails to Merrill Lynch colleagues, griping about having to talk bullishly about overvalued and risky stocks just to help Merrill land investment banking deals. Blodget later forked over $2 million in fines (Merrill itself paid $100 million) and was barred from the industry for life, but he was far from the worst offender. And to this day, no one has figured out how to make independent and substantive investment research a paying proposition for a Wall Street firm.

For his part, Wilbur Ross simply shifted gears, forging a career first as a turnaround specialist and investor in distressed assets at Rothschild Investments, then launching his own specialized buyout firm in 2000. In his new position, Ross rarely had to worry about dealing with the pressures that Mayday had unleashed—particularly the push to produce a constant stream of high-margin new products that could help (temporarily, at least) fill the void left by the disappearance of fixed commissions. But he was aware of them nonetheless. "I was performing a specialized function and collecting a fee for it," he says of his work restructuring bankrupt companies. "But elsewhere on Wall Street, people were substituting balance sheet strength for brains" whenever the new product pipeline slowed.

The Beginning of the End of the Old-Model Wall Street

Even before Mayday struck, the world had begun to change for Wall Street's investment banks and brokerages. The old-style partnership structure limited the amount of capital available and was increasingly proving inadequate for the new environment that was emerging. The capital belonged to the partners: they brought it with them and invested it when they joined the firm, and they contributed to it as the deals they did generated profits that caused the firms' profits to swell. And when partners retired, they could take it with them. Even the biggest partnerships chafed at the limits that this structure imposed on their ability to compete for big underwriting deals.

There were tremendous upsides to the partnership structure as well, especially when it came to managing risk. The partners all had a say in how to deploy the investment bank's assets—what deals to underwrite, what back office investments to make, whom to invite to join the partnership. The thinking was that no partner in his right mind (and they were all men) would take outsized risks that might jeopardize the health of the financial system, because in doing so he would destroy not only his professional reputation and his firm but also his financial security and that of his family. "When a partner put his capital on the line, he knew it was his right and responsibility to ask questions," says investment banking veteran John Costas, a former head of UBS's investment banking operations who launched his own boutique, PrinceRidge, in 2009. "If I'm involved in mortgage-backed securities, and someone else wants to do a big oil trade that I'm not comfortable with or don't understand, I'm going to raise my hand

and say so, and tell them they need to explain it to me, because it's my money that's at stake."

Peter Solomon, chairman of his own boutique investment bank, Peter J. Solomon Co., recalled the scene at his former firm, Lehman Brothers, for the benefit of FCIC commissioners during the latter's first round of hearings in January 2010. "The important partners of Lehman Brothers sat in one large room on the third floor of . . . the firm's headquarters," reminisced Solomon, who later became vice chairman of Lehman as well as co-head of its investment bank and head of its merchant banking operations. "The partners congregated there [but] not because they were eager to socialize. An open room enabled the partners to overhear, interact, and monitor the activities and particularly the commitments of their partners." There was a reason for any eavesdropping and snooping that took place, Solomon pointed out. "Each partner could commit the entire assets of the partnership" to a transaction.

The cons began to outweigh the pros of this system during the 1960s. That is when the capital constraints of the traditional partnership structure collided headlong with a surge in investor interest in stocks and a corresponding explosion in the trading volume on the New York Stock Exchange, which doubled between 1960 and 1965 and then more than doubled again by 1968. Drowning in the paperwork associated with each trade, Wall Street firms couldn't keep up. For a while, the stock exchange had to shut down every Wednesday, just to give its member firms a chance to balance their books. Even that didn't help; scores of brokerage houses simply collapsed, running afoul of net capital rules when they couldn't prove they had enough capital to support the trading positions that they had taken on behalf of clients. Technology was part of the answer, and so was hiring additional staff to deal with the flood of paperwork—but both would require large, long-term infusions of capital. And as Don Regan, then CEO of Merrill Lynch & Co., pointed out, with the partnership structure "you were never really sure what your capital was going to be."[7]

Dan Lufkin and his two partners, who had cofounded Donaldson, Lufkin & Jenrette (DLJ) in 1959, were determined that their fledgling firm wasn't going to be among the casualties. Although the NYSE's rules at the time required that its member firms be private partnerships, Lufkin believed that survival required major change. So in early 1970 he showed up at a meeting of the New York Stock Exchange Board of Governors, to which he had just been elected, and calmly informed his peers that his firm would file to go public the next day, in order to raise a permanent capital base and put the business on a firmer footing. The reaction, Lufkin later recalled, "was pretty nasty, old men screaming."[8]

Chief among the opponents was Felix Rohatyn, one of Wall Street's most revered deal makers and managing partner of Lazard Frères, who snarled at Lufkin, "You are Judas."[9] Despite furious opposition from Rohatyn and others (Lazard itself wouldn't go public until 2005, after Rohatyn had left the firm to become U.S. ambassador to France), Lufkin and his partners prevailed, completing their IPO in April 1970, at a price of $15 a share. Although they raised less than they had hoped in the IPO, and although the stock's price languished well below that level during the bear market of the early and mid-1970s, the firm and its partners had pointed the way to an entirely new business model—the publicly traded investment bank, whose executives deployed investors' capital (aka other people's money) in search of the highest possible return.

The pressures on other banks to follow suit increased over the coming years. During the 1970s, new computer technology made markets faster-moving and more efficient, which in turn caused the spread between the bid and ask prices on any given stock (the difference between the price at which investors were willing to buy or to sell) to contract. Mayday knocked one prop out from underneath the old model of investment banking profitability; the computer would do the same to another, since those spreads represented another big chunk of Wall Street's earnings. To stay profitable, investment banks would have to become more active traders, making up in the number of trades what they could no longer capture in profit margin per trade. But that would require capital investment, and one by one, the other Wall Street powerhouses followed DLJ's lead and filed to go public in the 1970s. Some moved rapidly—Merrill Lynch in 1971—and others dragged their heels, worried how the transformation might affect their culture. (The last major player to move was Goldman Sachs, which completed its long-contemplated IPO in 1999.) The results of this shift from partnerships to public ownership—and the wave of mergers that would follow—would prove dramatic. In 1955, the ten largest investment banks had about $821 million in equity (and subordinated debt) on their balance sheets; by 2000, that had ballooned to about $194 billion.[10]

Donaldson, Lufkin & Jenrette's open challenge to the Wall Street status quo was just the tip of the iceberg. There were other factors at work that would reshape the way Wall Street worked, notably the bear market of the early 1970s. Why do business at all? Wall Street's largest clients asked themselves. Why not just sit on the sidelines and wait it out until the extreme market volatility became a more manageable environment? Individual investors, who had flocked to Wall Street, savings in hand, during the 1960s, promptly pulled back. Wall Street's fee income from its traditional businesses—buying and selling stock on behalf of its clients and underwriting their debt and equity businesses—was threatened once more.

The solution? New products that would address new concerns, such as how to hedge against market slumps or volatility. Options were one possibility; these gave their purchasers a way to bet on the future price of an underlying stock (and, later, on the movement in indexes and other assets) for a fraction of the cost of buying the stock and with less risk than selling it short. (A short sale, in which investors borrow the stock from a broker and sell it in the hope of repurchasing it at a lower price to return to the lender and pocketing the price difference as their profit, has potentially unlimited risk. If a stock sold short at $10 soars to $100 a share instead of falling to $5, an investor is out $90 a share rather than making a $5-a-share profit.)

Until 1973, options had been used mostly by speculators, but that year a new mathematical model offered a seemingly perfect solution to the problem of how to understand the volatility and risk of a stock and therefore determine the correct price of an option. Devised by MIT professors Fischer Black and Myron Scholes (and immortalized as the Black-Scholes model), the formula gave dealers in the new and rapidly proliferating options products on the fledgling Chicago Board Options Exchange a relatively straightforward way to make a profitable market in options and helped investors use the products with greater comfort. (The model's limitations would become apparent only with the passage of time and in periods of market stress, as I'll show when it comes time to discuss risk management.) Black-Scholes opened the door for Wall Street to begin selling options-based strategies to their clients: investors could, for instance, own a stock but use options to hedge the risk that its price would succumb to the bear market. Best of all, in addition to proving that they were paying attention to their clients' needs and wants in a time of stress, brokers could actually earn higher fees from options transactions than they could by executing more plain-vanilla stock and bond trades. It was a win-win situation—at least for the time being.

Globalization also created new market opportunities. In 1971, the United States abandoned the Bretton Woods system of fixed exchange rates, creating a thriving market for options and futures contracts on foreign currencies, such as the British pound, Japanese yen, and Swiss franc. The Eurobond market was another attractive new opportunity. Born in London's financial markets in the 1960s, it involved issuing dollar-denominated debt outside the United States, meaning that the issues didn't need to be registered with the SEC and that the companies selling debt didn't need to abide by U.S. accounting rules.

The Eurobond market was one of the fastest-growing capital markets around—and, like options, it was a lucrative alternative to plain-vanilla bond deals, rewarding underwriters with higher fees. But trying to build a Eurobond business drove home, yet again, the need for a large and stable base of capital. Not only did trying to grab market share in Eurobonds mean establishing a presence in London, but players such as Morgan Stanley and Goldman Sachs (among the early arrivals) would need to compete with giant commercial banks such as Deutsche Bank and Credit Suisse, institutions that, unlike their U.S. counterparts, faced no domestic rules against using their giant commercial banking balance sheets to help them muscle in and grab investment banking business. (The 1933 Glass-Steagall Act, passed in the wake of the 1929 crash and mandating the separation of commercial and investment banking, was based on the belief that this kind of risk taking on the part of commercial banks had led to the collapse of the U.S. banking system during the 1930s.)

Long before the 1987 crash, all the ingredients required for Wall Street to become a higher-risk environment were solidly in place. "When we went from private partnerships that were the bread and butter of Wall Street's success for many years to publicly traded entities, we may have gained financial capital, but we lost one of those important checks and balances" that stops participants in the financial system from piling on the risk, says John Costas. Moreover, publicly traded investment banks found that their new shareholders had a slightly different view of what the institutions' priorities should be than the former partners had had. Both wanted to maximize market share, but one of the trade-offs for access to capital was the demand by new shareholders that the firms also maximize profitability. If Goldman

Sachs could earn an ROE of 20 percent or more, why couldn't Merrill Lynch, Citigroup, or Morgan Stanley? That's the kind of question that Wall Street's chief financial officers found themselves being asked year after year, with increasing heat, indignation, and exasperation. Soon they began to share that perspective. "Look, if we're going to be honest with ourselves, we need to admit that we wanted it all," says Lou Gelman, the former Morgan Stanley banker. "We wanted to keep making fat fees, posting high profit margins on relatively straightforward kinds of business. And after 1975, the writing was on the wall: that was never going to happen again." Wall Street, as it had functioned for decades, had undergone an irrevocable change, one that made its core utility function take a backseat to its ability to devise new and exotic products.

From Cornflakes to Raisin Bran

In Marty Fridson's view of the world, today's Wall Street has drifted far afield from its roots as a utility, driven there by the winds of change blowing through the financial system and originating outside it. He sees clearly through the rhetoric that the investment banks still put forward when describing their role, to the heart of the matter: Wall Street's real focus is profits, not its utility function. And after a quarter of a century spent warning investors when one of Wall Street's cherished junk bond deals is nothing more than a pig dolled up in lipstick, Fridson is willing to speak his mind. It is no longer about the process, he insists; it's about the products. "I tell anyone I meet who's starting out in banking or research today, Wall Street is really the breakfast cereal business," Fridson says bluntly. "Forget the idea of having a big mission. They're selling stuff to people, and after a while, that stuff becomes a commodity, like cornflakes. And then it's time to come up with a new, better idea, something that will become the financial equivalent of peanut-butter-flavored Cap'n Crunch."

How did fees earned from selling "stuff"—whether it's junk bonds, CDOs, or exotic derivatives—come to replace the fees captured as a result of the process of bringing together investors with those in need of capital? It all dates back to the changes that began in the 1970s. Wall Street's investment banks had always battled ferociously for the top spot in the league tables, the monthly, quarterly, and annual rankings of which firms dominated the underwriting of what kinds of securities for what kinds of companies. The turmoil caused by Mayday introduced a new, cutthroat element of price competition to that already feverish competition. Most institutions that survived the 1960s and 1970s, whether through some kind of strategic planning or through trial and error, ended up devising several different ways to try to boost their bottom line in a world of perpetual downward pressure on profit margins. A failure to replace trading revenues lost to technological innovation and deregulation could mean the institution's collapse, they were all well aware.

Sallie Krawcheck, who studied the investment banking business first as a research analyst and head of research at Sanford C. Bernstein and later as chief financial officer at Citigroup, notes that every year for thirty years after Mayday, the revenue that Wall Street collected in the form of trading fees declined. Every year, investment banks needed to generate more—not less—income and profit. The only solution? "You had to start running faster and innovating," says Krawcheck. "The best way to increase profits in that environment was, firstly, through innovation or by increasing the amount of leverage on your balance sheet."

The need for product innovation was made more pressing by the breakdown in long-term client relationships. The House of Morgan had ties to AT&T that dated back to a 1906 bond underwriting; Morgan Stanley inherited the investment-banking portion of those ties after the passage of the Glass-Steagall Act forced the venerable banking institution to separate its commercial bank from its investment banking operations. Between 1936 and 1968, AT&T steered $4.68 billion of underwriting business to Morgan Stanley, yielding lucrative fees.[11] And AT&T was just one of the forty-one major corporate clients that used Morgan Stanley as their sole lead manager on deals like this; 80 percent of their top clients would deal with no one but Morgan Stanley. So when one loyal client, IBM, decided to turn to Salomon Brothers to handle its 1979 bond deal, the writing was on the wall: client loyalty was becoming a matter of the question "What have you done for me lately?"

Sure enough, clients began shopping around for the best deals. That, in turn, put more pressure on investment banks to go public, since part of offering a client the best deal increasingly required the investment bank to put its own capital on the line first, by doing "bought deals" (buying the securities for resale to investors), and later, by providing bridge financing. But clients weren't only shopping for the best deals; they also wanted the brightest ideas. To return to Fridson's breakfast cereal analogy, Main Street was no longer content with being served cornflakes every day of the week. If a company needed capital, it wanted the right kind of capital, and if the increasingly sophisticated capital markets meant that was a highly structured customized transaction, well, so much the better for both the company and the investment bank, which could pocket a larger fee on the deal.

The cornflakes era had survived so long not just because it worked (it had helped the government finance wars from the Revolutionary War right through to Vietnam, assisted states in building canals for transportation, and created extraordinary wealth for the railroad barons and others) but because Wall Street's clients didn't realize that there were—or that there could be—alternatives to cornflakes that would meet their needs or cater to their tastes more precisely. To stretch the analogy further, as long as consumers can rely on cornflakes to be readily available at a reasonable price and to get them fueled up for the day, they may not actively hunger for alternatives. But as soon as a smart researcher discovers that a significant minority of those cornflakes consumers love eating raisins atop their cereal, and realizes that that group might pay much more for a specialized product that satisfies their craving for raisins, bingo—Kellogg's Raisin Bran is born, and the world changes. Consumers flock to the exciting new product; to keep their market share, cornflakes producers slash prices and profit margins.

On Wall Street, Salomon Brothers was one of the firms playing the role of the manufacturer of Kellogg's Raisin Bran. As a firm that had specialized in bond trading, it watched its profit margins shrink and plotted ways to escape its allotted role in the Wall Street scheme of things. Through a combination of price cutting and innovation, Salomon parlayed its bond market trading prowess into more underwriting mandates from firms such as IBM, chipping away at the market share of their white-shoe rivals in a process that Pete Peterson, a financier and onetime secretary of commerce who became chairman and CEO of Lehman Brothers in 1973, referred to as "de-clienting."[12] The firm, whose dominance of the bond market was matched only by its ambition to capture an ever larger share of Wall Street fees, became an expert innovator. Developing successful new products— even entirely new markets—would, Salomon's leaders calculated, be one surefire way to escape the "muddle in the middle" in investment banking and catapult a second- or third-tier financial institution to the top of the heap, alongside the likes of Goldman Sachs.

One of Salomon's chief bond gurus, Lewis Ranieri, originally had dreamed of becoming a chef in an Italian restaurant. When his asthma made it impossible for him to survive long days in smoky, steamy kitchens, he went to work in the mailroom at Salomon Brothers. It was the first step on his way to being anointed by *BusinessWeek* in 2004 as one of the greatest innovators of the last seventy-five years— and, later, to being referred to as one of the chief architects of the

2008 market meltdown. Unable to craft mouthwatering confections in a kitchen, Ranieri set about designing equally appetizing products for investors' portfolios: mortgage-backed securities.

The idea of taking homeowner mortgages, bundling them together, and selling them had been introduced in 1970, with the launch of the first Ginnie Mae (formally known as the Government National Mortgage Association) securities. The concept was very simple: the financial institution (or issuer) trying to sell the securities rounds up enough mortgages, pools them in a special-purpose vehicle (such as a trust), and then underwrites bonds issued by that special-purpose entity. To all intents and purposes, it was like any other underwriting, except that the issuer wasn't a real company, and the investors were getting a stake in a portfolio of some bondlike securities rather than a corporation. The cash from the sale goes right through the trust and back to the originator(s) of the mortgages, typically a bank or savings and loan institution. The way the bonds were priced and traded would depend on the kind of assets they contained—what kind of mortgages (commercial or residential) or the credit quality of all the home buyers taken in aggregate.

"No new product succeeds unless it's in the interest of investors," argues Michael Lipper, president of Lipper Advisory Services. In the more than thirty-five years since Lipper first created a series of indexes to track the performance of mutual funds, he has watched the Wall Street innovation juggernaut produce a seemingly endless series of new products, or new twists on older products, all in hopes of gaining at least a momentary edge in the constant battle for market share and fee income. "Chuck Prince's comment about keeping dancing as long as the music was playing got him a lot of hostile feedback, but what people often overlook is that it takes two parties willing to dance together," says Lipper, referring to the former Citigroup CEO's comment. Any product that succeeds, such as mortgage-backed securities, Lipper believes, does so because it meets a need for both the issuer (the banks and savings and loan institutions) as well as the investor. "Wall Street doesn't go around trying to invent things just for fun, and they couldn't sell them if the product didn't meet some kind of need on the part of the investor. Wall Street institutions don't go around holding guns to the heads of investors or their other clients, and insisting that they buy this structured note or the other derivative contract."

Indeed, it's pretty much impossible for Wall Street to do anything like that in the earliest stages of a new product's development. When Ranieri began to turn the fringe business of mortgage securitization into a money spinner for Salomon and for Wall Street as a whole in 1977, mortgage-backed securities were legal investments in only fifteen states; even where legal, they weren't necessarily respectable. But it became clear, as Ranieri fought a two-front war to win investor understanding and legal recognition of asset-backed bonds, that the new products filled needs on both sides. The 1970s were the era of market volatility, but also the decade in which the first baby boomers began purchasing homes. Banks were overwhelmed; every loan they made was a fresh inroad into their capital base, and demand was such that they couldn't cope. But if they could originate the mortgage loan and then sell it to another nonbank investor—well, that instantly removed any artificial constraints to issuing a mortgage. A home buyer in Boise, Idaho, wouldn't be turned down for a loan simply because that city's financial institutions—the only lenders directly available to him or her—had already made too many home loans.

The advent of the mortgage-backed securities market meant that home buyers indirectly had access to the entire money grid known as Wall Street. The banks were happy—they could keep collecting their fees for originating mortgages and maintain their other relationships with their clients. Home buyers were happy—they got their mortgages, often at a lower cost. (Ranieri figured that the evolution of the mortgage-backed securities market helped shave two percentage points off the cost of a typical mortgage simply by creating a more efficient market.) Investors eager for bondlike investments with higher returns than Treasury securities began snapping up the securities once they became more familiar with the structure itself. And the issuers— the Wall Street institutions such as Salomon Brothers—were the happiest of all. With an investment of time, money, and brainpower, they had created a viable new product, one that would become central to the financial system, earning them lots of fees. And while it wasn't as venerable a business as underwriting or trading on behalf of corporate clients, it was just another way of fulfilling the same core function of Wall Street, bringing together those who needed capital with those who had it—in this case, home buyers and their banks with outside investors such as pension funds and mutual funds. It was just doing so with an emphasis on a proprietary product that happened to generate heftier fees than the traditional process had done.

Innovate or Die

At a lavish dinner celebrating the fortieth anniversary of *Institutional Investor* magazine in 2007, Henry Kravis, a cofounder of the giant buyout firm KKR, was one of the evening's honorees—the forty "Legends of Wall Street." (That group also included John Gutfreund of Salomon Brothers.) In his speech, Kravis chose to laud Michael Milken, the investment banker who had popularized the "junk bond" during the 1980s. Without Milken, Kravis told the audience, KKR couldn't have done the gargantuan deals that made it famous, and the entire buyout business (which had generated $357 billion in deals in the United States alone the previous year, each of which produced massive fees for Wall Street investment banks) would have been stillborn. Kravis called for Milken to stand up and be acknowledged. With the Wall Street audience applauding and even whooping and cheering, Milken, sitting at a table in the midst of the crowd, rose to acknowledge the acclaim.

By the 1980s, innovation became the way for every investment bank aspiring to be ranked alongside Goldman Sachs and Morgan Stanley to achieve that dream. That is what Rainieri had shown with securitization at Salomon Brothers and Michael Milken would demonstrate at the firm that became known as Drexel Burnham Lambert. The venerable Philadelphia-based firm was still Drexel Firestone when Milken arrived there as a bond salesman in 1970. It had been in partnership with the House of Morgan until the passage of the Glass-Steagall Act in 1933, but like many of its peers had since undergone a long, slow slide. Three years after Milken joined Drexel, I. W. "Tubby" Burnham, head of a smaller but profitable investment bank, purchased the firm; when he learned that Milken, one of the smartest of Drexel's traders, was on the point of leaving because his bosses wouldn't give him any capital to use to trade, Burnham promptly handed over $2 million. In a single year Milken doubled it, and Burnham raised the capital available to him to $4 million.[13] The two men then struck what would become one of Wall Street's most infamous compensation agreements: Milken would collect 35 percent of his group's revenues, after the costs of running the business were deducted. "It was a good deal for us, and a good deal for him," recalled Fred Joseph, who later became Milken's boss. "Yes, it led to one year where he ended up doing so much business that he made $550 million personally, but he made even more for the company."

Milken's coup wasn't the invention of junk bonds; in one form or another they had been around since at least 1909, when Moody's began rating bonds issued by railroad companies and found that the credit quality of some wasn't high enough for them to be described as "investment grade," in the Wall Street jargon of today.[14] Milken transformed the market, realizing that to sell these lower-quality bonds, an investment banker needed to woo investors with the company's story, in the same way that a stock salesman would pitch the potential for future growth of a business. On the surface, the bonds were indeed junk—their credit ratings signaled that the company carried a heavy debt load or its business was troubled. But Milken could see that on a risk-adjusted basis, the prices for these bonds were too low, partly because there wasn't an active secondary market (there's no equivalent of the stock market for bonds) and partly because investors weren't evaluating them the right way.

Milken persuaded investors to look past the ugly credit rating to the underlying potential of the business. It was only natural, he argued, for some companies to have a lower credit rating, but the risk that they'd default on that debt, given the underlying business story, was far lower than the market price of the debt suggested. Milken succeeded so brilliantly that by the late 1970s, a host of companies that previously had been shut out from selling bonds because of their less-than-pristine credit rating were now able to issue debt—through Drexel Burnham, of course—to a growing coterie of investors that Milken had cultivated. "The first year that new issuance hit $1 billion was 1977," recalls Marty Fridson, who in a few years' time would decide to specialize in analyzing junk bonds. When Fridson made that move, his colleagues thought he was a bit nuts; the products were new and the move was risky. "But it was a great career maker, because too few people were really studying these products, and the lack of understanding" created opportunities that Fridson believed trumped the risks.

Junk bonds, like mortgage-backed securities, were, in their earliest and simplest form, great for both investors and issuers. Investors able to do their credit homework got access to a whole new pool of higher-yielding bonds, while the availability of the capital in this new market helped jump-start a host of new businesses in the gaming, telecommunications, and media businesses. Multibillionaire Steve Wynn relied on junk bonds to build his casino empire, as did Ted

Turner in expanding his broadcasting business (including CNN). As these and other moguls caught on to this new type of financing, the early days of the junk bond revolution were good for everyone. The sheer newness of the junk bond market and the fact that no one but Milken and his team of specialists seemed to understand it meant that Drexel could charge an astonishing 4 percent of the proceeds of a junk bond issue in fees, compared to 1 percent for an investment-grade corporate bond issue. And there were more junk issues coming every year, as a new breed of financiers such as Henry Kravis used junk bonds to finance their buyouts.

That meant hefty profits. In 1977, Drexel reported about $150 million in revenue; by 1985, that had soared to about $2.5 billion, and the book value of its stock (which didn't trade publicly) had increased more than tenfold. By 1986, when its revenue hit $4 billion, Drexel's estimated net earnings were $545.5 million, making it the single most profitable investment bank in the country. None of its rivals could sell a billion-dollar deal in hours, as Milken boasted he could; the network of investors he had carefully cultivated was the ace in the hole that allowed his group (known as "the Department") to dominate Drexel, and Drexel to dominate Wall Street. Meanwhile, Salomon, the other upstart firm, had parlayed its dominance in other parts of the market (including the burgeoning world of securitization) into the position of Wall Street's second-most-profitable firm, earning about $516 million (although it took twice as much capital to generate that kind of profit, making for a much lower return on capital).[15]

But every successful innovation carries within it the seeds of its own potential destruction, and Drexel's junk bond empire would be no exception. First, the product itself became less cutting-edge with every year that passed, and, as competitors became more adept (or hired some of Drexel's pros), the firm slowly but steadily lost market share. Profit margins also shrank; in the case of junk bonds, the average fee an investment bank could demand for underwriting a junk

bond issue fell steadily, to 2.1 percent by 2003 and a low of 1.5 percent in 2006. As with any hot new product, from the pocket calcula-
tor to the DVD player, on Wall Street the passage of time and greater
sophistication makes it easier for rival manufacturers to offer the
same product profitably at a lower cost. "The increasing complexity
of products is a direct result of the fact that you can't get a patent or
copyright for your innovations on Wall Street," explains Sallie Krawcheck. "So if you make something so complicated it will take your
competitors a long time to figure out and replicate, well, that's great.
The longer it takes, the longer your advantage lasts."

The awareness that fees are falling (or about to fall) puts the
pressure on an investment bank to compensate for lost revenue. If
the margins are shrinking, then, as Krawcheck points out, it's up to
the investment bank to somehow replace that revenue, whether by
boosting volumes or adding complexity. In the case of products such
as junk bonds (or CDOs), the logical first option is to ramp up the
number of transactions. And that's exactly what happened at Drexel.
Fred Joseph, named president of the firm in 1984 and CEO in 1985,
had promised Tubby Burnham that within the next decade he would
use Drexel's junk bond prowess to transform it into a firm that was
even more powerful than Goldman Sachs, already considered the
gold standard on Wall Street. "If we'd been asked publicly if we
wanted to be Goldman Sachs, we'd probably have denied it, but se-
cretly a lot of people coveted what they saw as Goldman's cachet,"
said Joseph, comparing this "Goldman envy" to the same feeling
that hits a bright kid with a blue-collar background who makes it to
Harvard or Yale only to find himself among privileged prep school
grads who take their advantages for granted. "It wasn't that we had a
chip on our shoulder; just that many people figured they were just as
bright as anyone at Goldman, but even then they and Morgan Stanley were the firms that got the automatic respect of every potential
client. All they had to do was show up, some people would complain,

to knock us out of the running for a deal." That's what Drexel's junk bond prowess helped change.

But Joseph couldn't reshape Drexel's culture, which was now dominated by Milken's group. And that group, it seemed, was playing fast and loose with the rules to drum up deals and profits. No one could figure out all that they were doing or get them to toe the line. Milken and others created a number of limited partnerships of dubious legality that allowed them to make even more money than Drexel itself and of which even Drexel's top executives and board members weren't aware. Ultimately, Milken refused to cooperate with Drexel's own internal investigation into the possible involvement of the department with insider traders Ivan Boesky and Dennis Levine. To settle the case, the firm forked over what was then the largest securities industry fine in history—$650 million. Milken, indicted on a variety of securities offenses, ended up serving nearly two years of a ten-year sentence after pleading guilty to six felonies. By the time that Milken emerged from jail in early 1993, Drexel had been gone for years. Joseph himself was barred from actively running the new investment boutique he co-founded; until the day of his death in November 2009, he remained restricted to the role of co-head of corporate finance.

The roots of the problem, of course, were Milken's excesses and the risk management and governance failures those revealed. "Frankly, while I feel bad for people who worked at Drexel and had nothing to do with the high-yield bonds and lost their jobs and life savings, I don't feel bad that the firm collapsed," says Fridson today. "Any other firm could have done the same thing that Drexel did by committing almost all its capital to that one ultrasuccessful product line, but they didn't—and they were right, because that's too risky." And that's another reason it is perilous for any investment bank to rely on any single new product as a steady source of profits. In the case of junk bonds, by the time that Milken ran afoul of regulators, the junk bond cycle was coming to an end—a prospect to which he and others at Drexel seem to have blinded themselves. "Well, we only realized it in theory," Joseph admitted only a few months before his death. Interest rates jumped, the economy slumped, and suddenly companies that had issued junk bonds began to default, at a rate of one in ten. The buyout kings, including Kravis, put their deal making on hiatus, cutting off the flow of fees to Drexel. Even if Drexel hadn't run afoul of the securities laws, its heavy dependence on a single product that was about to hit a cyclical slump, coupled with the fact that it was using its own capital to buy back some of those distressed bonds from unhappy investors, likely would have wreaked havoc on its profits and balance sheet. In 1990, Drexel filed for bankruptcy.

As Drexel's experience with junk bonds illustrates all too clearly, success requires more than one brilliant idea. To succeed at the innovation game, an investment bank needs a string of them, carefully developed so that as one is flagging or hitting a cyclical low, the next is ready to appear on the horizon. But how many "new new things" are there on Wall Street, really? In practice, Wall Street ended up turning to other, more dangerous ways to artificially prolong the profitable life span of its innovations, such as leverage and doing lower-quality deals. As Mike Mayo told the FCIC, the world of banking and investment banking became "an industry on steroids," whose loan volumes grew at about twice the rate of the underlying economy. "[Banks] pushed for loans that should never have been made," Mayo said. Rainieri's brainchild fell victim to this, as investment banks took the mortgage-backed securities he had pioneered and turned them first into CDOs, then into subprime CDOs, then into more complex CDO-squared or CDO-cubed structures. Ranieri began warning investors publicly about the problems with these later, high-risk incarnations of his creation around 2006. (In a 2008 interview, he would describe the increasingly exotic features of CDOs, conceived as a way to keep the fees flowing and the profits climbing, as "loans [that] need the tooth fairy to keep up their values.")[16] The more successful a new product or strategy is, the harder it becomes for an investment bank to stay disciplined, and Salomon (which would be caught up in a Treasury-bond trading scandal in 1991) and Drexel were no exception to that rule. Salomon would survive, although not as an independent firm (it became part of what is today Citigroup); Drexel's deal makers moved on to try to work their magic at other investment banks and its alumni can still be found scattered across the Street.

Chasing Goldman Sachs

One of the reasons most of Wall Street's investment banks have spent the last two decades chasing Goldman Sachs—or at least lusting after and trying to replicate its profitability—is the fact that Goldman is one of the few firms that has managed repeatedly to get the innovation process right. Part of the reason, rivals say now, is that the firm didn't place all its bets on a single product or even a single strategy. "They were about the only firm on the Street that saw the kinds of changes that were coming and planned for them strategically," says one former senior figure from another investment bank. "Of all the firms on the Street, Goldman Sachs is the one that behaves most strategically, nearly all of the time. When it doesn't know what kind of new business model will emerge, it puts a bet on everything, in order to be sure it will be part of whatever emerges the winner." That's what happened in the late 1990s, when the SEC ordered some of the most sweeping changes to the way stock trading took place on Wall Street. That meant that the New York Stock Exchange lost its control of trading in the stocks listed on its own exchange to rival start-up electronic networks. Goldman had taken a stake in a number of these; ultimately it used its clout to arrange a merger between one of the winners, Archipelago, and the venerable stock exchange. Today the

combined entity is run by a former Goldman Sachs managing director. "That's just what they do," says the former rival with a shrug.
"Their approach to innovation is opportunistic."

That approach dates back to the 1980s, when two of Goldman's
former leaders, Robert Rubin (who would go on to become Treasury
secretary for the Clinton administration before returning to work on
Wall Street, this time at Citigroup) and Steve Friedman, realized that
they had two options if their white-shoe investment bank was to
retain its elite status. Midsized firms were doomed, they concluded;
either they would collapse or become acquisition targets. That left
Goldman with the choice of either being a great boutique investment
bank or making the leap and becoming a giant global financial institution. Rubin and Friedman decided on the second course of action.[17]
(In the 1990s, faced with the same dilemma and reaching exactly the
same conclusions that being stuck in the middle was a recipe for disaster, Bill Hambrecht's successor at the head of Hambrecht & Quist,
Dan Case, decided that even survival as a boutique was doubtful in a
world now dominated by giants; he decided to sell the firm to what
was then Chase Manhattan Bank, a predecessor of today's JPMorgan
Chase.)

Goldman recruited quantitative analysts—known as quants—such
as Fischer Black to help them come up with new products and fresh
approaches to trading, and tried to identify new business opportunities wherever they could. The firm needed to devise new products
and business lines—and it needed to be the first to launch them,
Stephen Friedman believed. "If we're not leaders in innovation, we
won't be fast enough to reap the really good profits that the innovators get—and deserve."[18] The 1970s bear market had left many companies with depressed stock prices and discontented shareholders,
making them vulnerable to hostile takeovers by a growing array of
corporate raiders who were beginning to make their names on Wall
Street. Goldman's bankers began offering what they labeled "tender-

defense" services to actual and potential targets. The first few times their bankers called on a target company, their offer of help was politely declined. They persisted, and beleaguered executives quickly realized how useful it could be to have Goldman's financial markets know-how on their side in a battle for control of their companies. Ultimately Goldman managed to parlay this into a business that generated a steady stream of income each year. CEOs, reassured by the fact that Goldman refused to work for any of the raiders, were apparently quite happy to fork over annual retainers to the investment bank in exchange for the right to call on its team of defense specialists should a raider come calling. (In contrast, many of Goldman's rivals seemed more like mercenaries, working on an ad hoc basis for either raiders or targeted companies, depending on who was willing to pay a fatter fee.)

In addition to creating its tender-defense business and its push into overseas markets, Goldman Sachs acquired J. Aron, a veteran commodity and futures trading business. As Rubin and Friedman had recognized earlier, and as Dan Case would later, Herb Coyne of J. Aron saw Wall Street was changing; his firm wasn't likely to survive if it remained a stand-alone business. Coyne's willingness to sell gave Goldman a toehold in these high-margin businesses (J. Aron's business lines generated a third of Goldman's profits with only about 5 percent of the staff) and helped the company prepare for a still more significant change, one that the next chapter will explore in greater detail—the transformation of Goldman from a firm that simply executed transactions for its clients to one that used its own base of capital to take risks, investing or trading on its own behalf.

Collectively, those innovations resulted in the creation of a business model that increasingly appeared to the rest of Wall Street like an unbeatable juggernaut. Between 1996 and 2008, Goldman Sachs's return on equity averaged 24.4 percent, dwarfing those of its rivals. Lehman, its nearest rival for most of that period, managed to earn

19.2 percent, while Morgan Stanley came in third, with an ROE averaging 18.6 percent. That was a wide gap, and one the outside investors in the now publicly traded investment banks badly wanted to close. It was now that the IPOs of the investment banks proved to be a double-edged sword. They provided Wall Street investment banks the capital base they needed to expand globally and to innovate as well as giving partners the ability to lock in their profits and reduce their risk. (The Goldman Sachs IPO alone created hundreds of instant paper millionaires out of all its partners.) "It was very, very tempting to sell to the public," says Sam Hayes of the Harvard Business School. "The claim was that they needed the capital, but to this day I think it was just as much about greed. An IPO gave partners in an investment bank the opportunity to sell, or at least value, their ownership of the firm at a multiple of book value."

The IPOs had made bankers richer and helped them expand their business, but they had also made that business more accountable to outsiders, whose definition of success involved generating the biggest return on equity within the industry and boosting profits quarter after quarter, year after year. Large shareholders, including mutual fund managers, would meet with the CEOs of large publicly traded investment banks and challenge them—not always politely—to do whatever it took to boost the firm's return on equity to match that of Goldman Sachs. How would they get the extra 5 or 10 cents in earnings per share that investors wanted this year? What business could it come from? What product could be created and sold, rapidly and profitably? And what could they do to maintain those profits over the long haul, when the newness wore off and rivals started to imitate them?

The pressure filtered its way down the food chain. "Every quarter, we'd get some kind of note about how this would be the biggest or most important quarter in the firm's history, asking us to keep focused and deliver the results," recalls Peter Blanton, whose career as an investment banker has taken him to Citigroup, Credit Suisse and Lehman Brothers, among other firms, and who now works for a boutique firm. Bankers found it harder to say no to a piece of new business, even if it looked a bit risky or otherwise unappealing. The scramble for market share and a bigger ROE came to look almost like the cold war arms race, with Wall Street firms rolling out one innovation after another—the block trade, zero-coupon convertibles, PIPE (private investments in public companies) deals. Then, as the financial markets struggled to recover from the aftermath of the dot-com collapse of 2000, came the CDO revolution. Not only were these new products part of the largest and most liquid markets out there—the bond market and the real estate market—but financial wizards could make them even more profitable and strip out the risk as well (or so they claimed).

Innovation, says Tom Caldwell, had finally gone too far. Caldwell runs a Toronto-based investment firm and owns stakes in stock exchanges globally; his career as a trader and investor dates back to the early 1970s, just as Wall Street began its metamorphosis. "I watched this happen, but I didn't get alarmed until banking started becoming exotic," he says. "Banking should be boring." To Caldwell, Wall Street's role remains all about providing capital to growing companies—and withholding it from others, as it has done recently in the case of the automakers or companies such as Kodak, when their leaders showed an inability to manage or to innovate. "The business of Wall Street isn't innovating, or creating some flashy new product to boost its own profits; it's providing the wherewithal for corporate innovation," he argues. Whenever financial innovation—the kind Wall Street indulges in—ends by making capital *less* available to corporate innovators, that is when Caldwell knows Wall Street has drifted too far from its mission. "That's what happened when the credit markets froze; it was the last sign of that trend."

Indeed, at the height of the exotic product innovation craze in 2005 and 2006, fueled by the need of Wall Street to keep dancing while the music played, few products were being developed to help improve access to capital for companies. "It goes in cycles," says Rob Kapito, president of BlackRock. "When we started out in this business, oh, 150 or so years ago, if we developed a new security, it had to have a purpose and it had to work the way we thought it would. It had to be something that was good enough for your mother to buy. But over time, there's a tendency for things to go crazy, for innovation for innovation's sake to take over." Kapito agrees with Caldwell that Wall Street lost its way. From his years working at an investment bank before moving to the sell side (joining the ranks of those who invest in the products Wall Street creates or underwrites) at BlackRock, he figures he can identify a bond-based security that serves a purpose for the investor, as did the first mortgage-backed securities or junk bonds. The innovative products being pitched to buy-side firms such as BlackRock by 2006 didn't qualify, he says. "If we had created a security like some of those [that are collapsing and causing large losses], we would have been fired, and the firm would have done whatever it took to make reparations to their clients," Kapito insists.

Ultimately, innovation for innovation's sake put Wall Street in peril when investment banks began packaging lower-quality, higher-risk deals into these complex mortgage-based securities, and then using leverage to make the transactions more profitable still. As Lloyd Blankfein told the FCIC hearings in early 2010, the average annual growth in new mortgage loans was about 6.3 percent between 1985 and 2000, but between 2001 and 2006, it had jumped to 10 percent. And subprime loans were making up a greater and greater portion of all the new lending: from 2 percent in 2002, new subprime loans jumped to make up 14 percent of all new mortgages in 2008, Blankfein testified.

But then, to keep the deal machine whirring, Wall Street and its mortgage suppliers—firms such as Angelo Mozilo's Countrywide—simply overlooked the fact that they had lent all that was prudent to creditworthy buyers and moved further down the quality spectrum.

They began lending more than was prudent, offering loans for 100 percent of the purchase price of a home, and reaching out to buyers with limited incomes or poor credit ratings. About 7 percent of all the mortgages repackaged into asset-backed mortgage securities in 2000 were subprime loans, or about $74 billion. By 2004, subprime lending made up 22 percent of the market, or about $608 billion by some estimates. True, Wall Street CEOs such as Chuck Prince, Stan O'Neal, or Richard Fuld weren't themselves signing off on subprime loans or undertaking risky, highly leveraged buyouts. But their willingness to embrace that risk and their reluctance to adopt a cautious attitude toward the products on which so much of their revenues and profits now depended ensured that firms such as Countrywide had every motivation to push their own sales forces to generate more and riskier home loans.

That kind of reckless competition should have made it clear that a balance sheet blowup was looming, says financier Wilbur Ross. "When Salomon Brothers started out, they made their money trading [Treasury bonds]. Well, there's a risk in trading them, [but] it's a market timing risk, not a credit risk." When Wall Street branched out and began to rely on junk bonds and securitization to generate profits, that meant new risks, Ross adds. Every innovation brought new risks to Wall Street. "The whole thing was getting bigger and bigger and bigger, but the basis on which people were competing wasn't innovation anymore, because that didn't go far enough. But you can be the biggest deal maker in the world if you don't care, if you go far enough down the food chain." By the autumn of 2008, Wall Street had only a handful of very large and highly innovative deal makers, most of which seemed to the best-informed insiders to be teetering on the verge of bankruptcy and could only be saved by an unprecedented government-organized bailout.

Wall Street, at its best, had proved to be a very good innovator, spotting opportunities and turning them into creative products that their clients needed and wanted and that generated lucrative enough fees for themselves to not only survive the dog days of the 1970s but grow dramatically during the 1980s and 1990s. But chasing after fees, it was becoming increasingly clear, could be a dangerous pastime. Indeed, the more that Wall Street firms managed to collect in fees, the more risk lurked in the system. The wizards of Wall Street may have been very adept at devising ever more exotic and profitable twists on all kinds of classic products, but like the sorcerer's apprentice in Goethe's poem, they failed to realize the risk and danger associated with that financial alchemy.

Later, Wall Street observers would begin to focus on the role that innovation played in the cataclysm. Paul Volcker, the former Federal Reserve chairman, was among those who spoke out; describing the biggest useful financial machine as the automated teller machine, or ATM, he told a conference of bankers at a luxurious country house hotel in England that he wished "someone would give me one shred of neutral evidence that financial innovation has led to economic growth—one shred of evidence."[19] Testifying to the FCIC a few weeks later, Mike Mayo was even more blunt. "Wall Street has done an incredible job at pulling the wool over the eyes of government and others," he declared. Not only did the economy work just as well *without* CDOs, the risk "was more obvious and easy to see." Certainly, as financial market innovation ran amok in the early years of the new millennium, the risks only increased, as new Wall Street players displaced those on Main Street as principal clients of the investment banks, causing the Street to drift further still from its traditional role in the economy.

CHAPTER 3

What's Good for Wall Street Is Good for . . . Wall Street

How Wall Street Became Its Own Best Client

Over the years that Mark Vaselkiv and Dave Giroux had worked on Wall Street's buy side as portfolio managers at T. Rowe Price, selecting investments for an array of bond mutual funds, they had become accustomed to having Wall Street bankers call or show up on their doorstep to pitch the latest structured product or market a hot new deal. So it was with a sense of something being slightly askew that the two men boarded the high-speed Acela train in Baltimore one morning in the early spring of 2005. Their destination: the New York head office of JPMorgan Chase, where they would meet with Nils, the salesman the bank had assigned to cover their account.

Vaselkiv and Giroux wanted to talk to Nils about the leveraged loans that investment banks such as JPMorgan Chase were issuing at an ever more rapid clip to help private equity funds finance their ever-growing string of buyout transactions. Loans of this type are the least risky investment to own since they rank above bonds or stocks in a company's capital structure; in the event of a bankruptcy, lenders have first claim on assets. But the Federal Reserve's commitment to fighting a recession in the wake of the dot-com bust and the 9/11 terrorist attacks meant that interest rates had remained at rock-bottom levels for so long that the world was awash in money. With every day that passed, it was becoming harder for investors such as Vaselkiv and Giroux to find bonds to buy that offered a yield high enough to offset the potential risk of the investment. Vaselkiv thought that leveraged loans just might be part of the answer to this conundrum.

The T. Rowe Price managers were hardly minnows in the fixed-income world. Together, the two men managed about $25 billion of investor funds; Vaselkiv figured that that should help them win a share of some of the leveraged loans. Even better, he calculated, was the fact that T. Rowe Price bought bonds and other products and held on to them for longer-term returns; the firm's investment managers didn't try to capture profits by trading them rapidly, as hedge funds tended to do. Historically, being an owner rather than a trader has been a desirable trait in the eyes of Wall Street when it has been trying to match up companies in need of capital with the right kind of investor. Still, Vaselkiv couldn't quite shake a sense that all was not quite right with the picture. What was he doing, boarding a train to visit a salesman to *ask* for access to a product that in prior years the same salesman would have been pleading with him to purchase?

It was odd, especially since Vaselkiv calculated that JPMorgan Chase probably could use some new buyers for these loans. The recent buyouts had left companies carrying outsized amounts of debt on their balance sheets, and the economic environment was starting to wobble amid sky-high energy prices and rising interest rates. "The buyouts were getting larger, the loans were getting bigger, and we all anticipated that at some point defaults would rise," Vaselkiv says. "No question, the cycle would come to an end." That was just why he was interested in owning the loans, rather than the more readily available junk bonds: in that kind of scenario they would hold their value better. "By the same token, we figured that the investment bank would be interested in us as a new client."

On their arrival in New York, Vaselkiv and Giroux traveled across town from Pennsylvania Station to JPMorgan Chase's Park Avenue offices. They sat with Nils, their salesman, and made their pitch: T. Rowe Price, one of the largest mutual fund investment groups in the country, was eager to become an investor in leveraged loans. It should have been the answer to a Wall Street salesman's prayer. Vaselkiv, however, was left dumbstruck by the response. "I'll never forget this, to my dying day; he looked at me and said, 'We don't need you,'" Vaselkiv recalls. This was no pleading Wall Street salesman: The shoe was now on the other foot. Vaselkiv realized now what had been bugging him about the idea of the trip to New York in the first place: He and his firm, which managed hundreds of *billions* of dollars of assets, had had to bang on the bank's door and ask humbly to be considered as a worthy buyer. Not only had he done so, but he and T. Rowe Price had been rejected out of hand.

Wall Street had changed: Giant investment firms such as Fidelity and T. Rowe Price were now less important to an investment bank than were smaller but more profitable hedge funds, which generated more trading fees and made buy decisions faster than the old-style mutual funds. Nils explained to Vaselkiv that JPMorgan Chase had about twenty-seven collateralized loan obligation (CLO) products in various stages of development. "Each and every one of those [leveraged] loans would go into those products, which in turn would be resold," Vaselkiv recalls. "He said there wasn't going to be any product for people who asked as many questions about a deal as we did." T. Rowe Price, the seventy-year-old $400 billion behemoth, had just been royally dissed by a mere salesman.

But Nils was right. JPMorgan Chase didn't need the traditional buy-side clients nearly as much as it had a few years earlier; neither did the other Wall Street institutions. Nor did these investment banks rely nearly as much on their classic corporate finance clients, companies such as Coca-Cola or Verizon that were on the other side of the money grid from investors like T. Rowe Price. These Main Street clients still called on Wall Street firms to help them raise capital or advise on merger transactions, but their significance paled when compared to that of the giant buyout funds. In 1997, only about 2.3 percent of the IPOs Wall Street firms underwrote were done on behalf of a buyout firm. A decade later, in 2007, nearly 30 percent of the IPOs completed were done for companies held in the portfolios of buyout funds such as KKR that were using the IPO as a way to begin to sell their holdings in the company. KKR, the Blackstone Group, and other such firms also turned to Wall Street to raise capital to finance their leveraged buyouts; as the buyout industry's deal making exploded, so did junk bond issuance. In 2000, the average junk bond deal brought in a mere $881,300 in fees for its underwriter; by 2007, the average deal was worth $2.45 million to bankers. In 2005, the year that Vaselkiv and Giroux made their pilgrimage to JPMorgan Chase in search of leveraged loans, those transactions—nearly a thousand of them across Wall Street as a whole—generated an average of $3.5 million in fees.[1]

Only later, in revisiting the events of the decade while testifying to the FCIC, would Nils's ultimate boss, Jamie Dimon, concede that the bank got carried away. "We should have been more diligent when negotiating and structuring" leveraged financing commitments for clients, Dimon said, referring to those loans themselves. "We allowed the lending terms to create too much leverage and assumed too stable a market appetite for these types of loans." Or perhaps they were simply targeting those leveraged loans at the wrong part of that market? But then, back in 2005 and 2006, the buyout funds seeking the leveraged financing, and the hedge funds that bought the CLOs containing the loans, were the bank's biggest clients. Why would that change?

"Let's face it, if you asked J.P. Morgan or Goldman Sachs who their best and most profitable clients were in 2006 or 2007, well, the answer you'd get wouldn't be Lockheed Martin or General Electric," says the manager of one large hedge fund. "The names you'd hear would be KKR or Citadel. Because how many deals or different kinds of deals is a Lockheed going to do in a year? Whereas KKR, well, they do a deal and they'll be back in a few weeks to do another one." And underwriting the junk bond and leveraged loan issuance to finance those deals was just the tip of the iceberg by that point. In addition to those fees, a private equity fund could generate bridge financing fees, deal advisory fees, and, down the road, IPO fees when the buyout firms exited their portfolio companies (at a profit). In between, there was plenty of opportunity for an investment bank to step in and grab a few million more in fees here and there, in exchange for advising a buyout portfolio company on how to pay out a special dividend to its new owners (a quick way for the latter to book a return on their acquisition) and then for executing that transaction.[2]

Hedge funds, it was also clear by the beginning of the new millennium, could generate similarly lucrative fees for Wall Street in exchange for different products and services. These "go anywhere, buy anything" investment vehicles had become increasingly popular during the 2000–2002 market slump, and their assets under management exploded from the late 1990s onward, despite the collapse of hedge fund Long-Term Capital Management. By 2007, a study by Greenwich Associates, a consulting firm, showed just how important they had become to Wall Street. Hedge funds, unlike mutual funds, usually weren't long-term investors looking for steady sources of return; rather, with hedge fund managers pocketing their fees (20 percent of every dollar of profit earned goes straight to the fund's managers) at the end of every year, they preferred short-term gains and didn't care how many trades it took to earn those returns, as long as the turnover didn't erode returns.

Although hedge funds made up only about 20 percent of all buy-side assets under management (other players included pension funds, college endowments, and mutual funds such as T. Rowe Price),

Cambridge Associates calculated that the group was responsible for nearly a third of all trading in the bond markets by early 2007, double the level of only a year earlier. That meant that hedge funds were generating a disproportionate amount of the fees Wall Street trading desks were earning. (Vaselkiv's pledge to be a buy-and-hold investor of leveraged loans was probably the last thing that any Wall Street firm involved in trading wanted to hear.) They were even more important to Wall Street in the smaller parts of the bond market, areas where the market is less liquid and trading harder to do, meaning that investment bank trading desks could command higher fees for facilitating those trades. Cambridge Associates reported hedge funds accounted for 55 percent of the trading in both investment-grade derivative products and bonds issued in emerging markets.[3] When it came to distressed debt and derivatives with low credit quality and high yields, hedge funds ruled the roost, accounting for 80 percent to 85 percent of the trading volume.

No wonder, as Greenwich Associates pointed out, that Wall Street was now trying to devise products that would appeal directly to hedge funds. The leveraged loans that Vaselkiv had been eyeing were the result of the Street's efforts to attract not one but two important new constituencies: the buyout firms, who needed to issue them to finance their deals, and the hedge funds, who found the loans interesting and profitable to buy and trade. Nobody really needed Mark Vaselkiv.

Turning Wall Street on Its Head

At times, it almost seemed to some bankers that private equity funds and hedge funds had been sent to them by the gods of finance to meet their insatiable need for fee income. Why would anyone be at all surprised that hedge funds were getting red carpet treatment? wonders Leon Cooperman, a former Goldman Sachs partner who set up his hedge fund business, Omega Advisors, back in 1991. "It's

like Willie Sutton said when he was asked why he robbed banks—
that's where the money was. Why did Wall Street get all excited about
this business? That's where the money was!"

Certainly, Cooperman wasn't surprised to see Wall Street begin
to tweak its business model to better accommodate these new and
very lucrative clients. Investment banks, led by Bear Stearns and
Goldman Sachs, packaged up all the services that hedge funds
needed under the umbrella of new, dedicated teams that were known
as prime brokerage groups. (The name of these groups came from
the idea that it made sense for a hedge fund to have one "primary"
banking relationship; to rely on one bank for services such as tracking its positions, monitoring its collateral, clearing, and other services.)
Most of the largest investment banks, led by Goldman, JPMorgan
Chase, Citigroup, and Morgan Stanley, also created sponsor groups.
These teams of generalist bankers were dedicated to serving buyout
funds with whatever they needed to put a deal together, coordinating
all the specialist bankers and financial wizards who could structure
deal terms.

In the early 1990s, very few investment banks had prime brokerages; by 2000, they were ubiquitous and nearly as many had sponsor
groups working with their buyout fund clients. Now that the banks
didn't make these big private equity clients run from one industry
banking team to another, depending on whether their next deal involved an industrial conglomerate or a new computing venture, they
could vie for the loyalty of this attractive group of clients more effectively. "There was a need," explains Tom McNamara*, who works
as a midlevel banker at one large bank's sponsor group. "The day-
to-day business of these guys was doing deals. Serving them is going
to be different from serving a widget maker who is only going to
do a deal once a decade. There's a big difference between a widget
maker's strategic deals and the opportunistic ones that a sponsor
will do."

Ever since the 1980s, Wall Street had been in the habit of paying more heed to the needs and wishes of investors than to those of the widget makers on the other side of the transactions that it helped to execute. "It was, has always been, and always will be a case of he who pays the piper the most gets to call *all* the tunes," says former Morgan Stanley banker Lou Gelman. The pattern was set when Michael Milken priced junk bond deals in a way that rewarded his group of dedicated investors rather than the companies that needed to raise capital; companies were just pleased to have been able to complete the financing. The logic behind this buy-side power was solid: there were relatively few specific deals that a mutual fund manager or pension fund manager *had* to buy, and companies such as Netscape or Google were the exceptions that proved the rule. So while companies trying to raise capital needed their Wall Street underwriter slightly more than the latter needed them, the same wasn't always true of money managers. Wall Street couldn't annoy a Fidelity, or even a T. Rowe Price, without feeling some pain down the road. "It was very critical to have a very high market share in those institutions, because 80 percent of your business was being done with 20 percent of your clients," says Rob Kapito, president of BlackRock.

Right up into the 1990s, it was firms such as T. Rowe Price that were still paying the piper and calling the tune. That's one reason so many of the IPOs of that decade were priced with plenty of room for the price to pop a few dollars on the first day of trading. When that happened, it was an instant winner for the investors who had just paid $15 a share to acquire the stock in the IPO, and who could now sell it for $18 or so the next day, a strategy referred to as a flip. That was great for buy-side clients, but, as noted earlier, at the height of the dot-com boom it left more than a few of the companies feeling as if they had accidentally handed a cabbie $50 on a $10 fare, and not been given any change.

The buy-side client—the investor—was the Wall Street client

who was there day in and day out, generating fees for investment banks through their trading. Even before the days of hedge funds, the buy side knew how to throw its weight around: a company such as Fidelity wouldn't even promise to hold on to newly issued stock for any length of time, reserving the right to flip some of their shares in a particularly successful IPO for a quick profit. So when Wall Street investment banks began bending over backward to keep the new group of power players—hedge funds and private equity funds—happy, no one was too surprised. But these power players were different. Often run by former bankers and traders, they were really part of Wall Street itself, and had developed business models that relied on deal making alone to generate profits. Buyout firms were consuming capital not to make cars or finance biotechnology research but to acquire companies that they would try to resell for a profit later on. Hedge funds weren't investing the retirement savings of the average American citizen for the long haul but instead were trying to make as many quick bucks as possible. These were more than just new names; they were an entirely new breed of client who knew how to extract every ounce of value from Wall Street. "You knew when you were sitting across the table from a [buyout firm executive] that you are about to negotiate with someone who used to be a banker," says McNamara. "And you know that his repeat business is going to be so valuable to the next guy on his list that you'll do whatever it takes to accommodate him."

Jeff Arricale, a T. Rowe Price portfolio manager who invests in financial stocks such as insurance companies and investment banks for the firm's mutual funds, understands this trend intellectually. But that doesn't mean it's easy to cope with. "The investment banks know very well that we're never going to call them up and say, 'Thanks, you did a great trade for me, here's a check for $50,000,'" he says, laughing at the very idea. "But a hedge fund manager will do just that—and be back the next day for more. And to get hold of that guy, the dude on the trading desk at Goldman or Morgan Stanley or wherever just has to make a single phone call." In contrast, getting a T. Rowe Price portfolio manager to act on a trading idea might require multiple phone calls and a lot of patience and effort on the part of the Wall Street trader. "Realistically, what we might pay him months later would never be enough to get this guy promoted," Arricale acknowledges. "We keep a close eye on those expenses." In contrast to hedge funds, firms such as T. Rowe Price are doing all they can to reduce their reliance on Wall Street and its endless demands for fees, building their own trading desks and research divisions.

So the fact that with each year that passed Wall Street was paying more and more attention to its hedge fund and private equity fund clients was little more than the financial markets version of Henry Kissinger's realpolitik, akin to the former secretary of state's decision to open diplomatic relations with Mao's China. That kind of pragmatism is what Wall Street is all about, and T. Rowe Price's managers understand and accept the logic that led Nils at JPMorgan Chase to reject them out of hand as potential investors for the leveraged loans. What did worry them was the combination of the nearly monomaniacal focus by Wall Street investment banks on their Wall Street clients and the investment banking industry's constant need to boost revenues and profit margins. If carried to extremes, this could mean that Wall Street's role as the money grid would take a backseat to the pursuit of profits for their own sake.

Increasingly, Wall Street's newest products fit the needs of the banks issuing them or the Wall Street players, such as the hedge funds, that bought most of them. Many mutual funds didn't want to touch some of the securities that Wall Street was devising; unlike classic bonds, the new products didn't have terms that required the issuer to maintain certain minimum credit standards. In some cases, the company issuing the bonds had the option to finance its regular interest on that debt by issuing *more* debt, a feature known as a pay-in-kind option and about as appetizing to a mutual fund manager as a dose of cod liver oil. (Indeed, by mid-2008, rating agency Standard & Poor's was already predicting that investors in these securities were likely to recoup only 10 cents on the dollar.) And how, critics wondered, could ordinary individuals saving for retirement be considered logical buyers of highly structured CDOs? By 2007, however, Wall Street firms such as Bear Stearns and their hedge fund partners— firms such as Highland Capital Management—had begun spinning off some of the least attractive CDO structures in products aimed at just those mom-and-pop investors, hoping that they would overlook the warning signals contained in the prospectuses.[4]

Meanwhile, mutual fund managers such as Arricale could see deals in which they *did* want to invest going to other, more favored Wall Street clients. "There was a company whose stock we had owned for four or five years; we were the third-largest shareholder," Arricale recalls. "They came back and raised more equity through a follow-on stock offering, and obviously we wanted to participate. Then we get the call from the underwriters telling us, 'Congratulations, you got 6 percent of the shares you requested.' And you know in your heart that wasn't a good deal for anyone except the bankers."

Arricale insists that he doesn't feel entitled to stock in deals he likes. "But when I saw the list of where the new stock went, and saw that nearly all of the top ten accounts on that list were the names of hedge funds, well, there's no way that's in the issuer's interest, either," he says, thumping his desk with his fist. "Come on! This is a *hedge fund*! What are the odds they'll be around in four weeks, much less four months or four years? They're looking for a quick flip! But they're also the guys waving the big stick. Not only do they generate the trading fees, but if they don't get what they want, they'll move all their prime brokerage business over to Lehman Brothers."

Working on stock underwritings and other corporate finance transactions at a series of investment banks, Peter Blanton found that his corporate clients weren't any happier about this trend. Often he'd have to break the news to clients that even if they didn't want hedge funds to end up as their biggest shareholders, there wasn't much that he or they could do about it. "The clients would tell me, 'I just want the [buy-and-hold] guys, like the mutual fund managers or the pension funds,'" says Blanton. "But the hedge funds were making their way into the new issue market as buyers, and that was just reality." Hedge funds came to completely dominate the market for convertible securities, in particular, thanks to the special characteristics of these "converts." A convertible security is faster and easier to sell to investors than stock; it looks like a bond (because it offers regular interest payments), but down the road investors can exchange it for shares at a set ratio of so many shares per $100 convertible security. Those features—the income and the ability to swap it (convert it) for stock—make convertible securities particularly intriguing to hedge funds. With their trading expertise, hedge fund managers could place complex but profitable bets involving both the convertible security and the stock; the most common of these arbitrage strategies involved selling the stock short. Owning the convertible securities gave them an indirect stake in the company's stock; selling the stock short outright was simply a way for the hedge fund to manage its risk and maybe capture a bit more profit.

But companies that had issued convertible securities in order to raise new capital weren't happy about the unintended consequences. They didn't want hedge funds to buy these securities if it meant that the funds' next move would be to sell the company's stock short. After all, an increase in short selling not only put downward pressure on the stock price but was tantamount to a public declaration of lack of faith in the company's business or prospects; only very well-informed or sophisticated investors would figure out that the short selling had nothing to do with a lack of confidence and that the hedge funds were merely hedging the exposure associated with owning the convertible security. "There was a period where we'd have to soft-talk the issuer, point out that they'd need hedge funds" to make the deal a success, Blanton says. It took time for the companies to accept the inevitable, although the fact that hedge funds were willing to accept lower interest payments and to quickly commit their capital to a deal helped; companies could now raise capital more rapidly and cheaply.

In the eyes of Wall Street, classic buy-side managers such as Arricale, Vaselkiv, and Giroux were small fry compared to buyout and hedge funds, nitpicking over trading fees and increasingly trying to squeeze already razor-thin trading margins even more. These mutual fund buyers that companies claimed to want as investors could take days or weeks to commit to a deal. Wooing them also meant taking the underwriting client on a four-day road show to visit key investors in cities such as Boston, Baltimore, and Los Angeles in person, an expensive and time-consuming proposition. Why bother, irritated investment bankers wondered, when the hedge funds were willing to just sign on the dotted line?

"Wall Street got to the point, eventually, where it figured it didn't need Main Street, except for the firms like Merrill Lynch, which could use their retail networks as a way to get products out the other end," muses Harvard Business School's Sam Hayes. Although his students have included some of the biggest architects of the buyout and hedge fund universe—including the late Bruce Wasserstein, Joseph Perella, and the Blackstone Group's Stephen Schwarzman—Hayes isn't blind to Wall Street's errors of judgment in catering too slavishly to this group. "There's a kind of social contract that is implicit in the relationship between Main Street and Wall Street," he argues. "Wall Street has to produce a sense of financial well-being in the shape of a rising stock market, or it will generate a terrible sense of envy [on Main Street] of what will be seen as the obscene profits and compensation that Wall Street is earning for catering to these other groups who *aren't* seen as part of Main Street."

Dealogic data show that by 2005, when Vaselkiv and Giroux called on Nils, about a quarter of Wall Street's investment banking fees were coming from private equity deals, while 40 percent of the trading fees Wall Street institutions were earning came from executing trades for hedge fund clients. By some estimates, there were now more than eight thousand hedge funds in existence, double the number of only five years earlier, and their managers were in charge of more than $1 trillion in assets, more than three times the level estimated five years previously. Both hedge funds and buyout funds had been important Wall Street clients since the 1980s—firms such as KKR and Blackstone on the private equity side and hedge funds run by veterans with impressive long-term track records, such as George Soros and Julian Robertson. But by the dawn of the twenty-first century, these players were not only more numerous but more significant. Wall Street, in the form of these entities (most run by former bankers and traders), had become its own most important customer, generating the lion's share of investment banking fees and using that influence to even dictate the shape and nature of the transactions that were done.

"In 2003, when I started my MBA program, everyone in the class wanted to be in mergers and acquisitions when they graduated," McNamara says. "By the time we finished, everyone was eager to work for a sponsor group or, as a second best, the prime brokerage group." Today, thanks in part to the havoc wreaked by the toxic combination of cheap capital, innovation run amok, and overaggressive deal making by a Wall Street that had forgotten its traditional client base, McNamara admits that he and other bankers just want a job—any job at all.

Leaving Goldman Sachs?

With the benefit of twenty-twenty hindsight, one can identify the first sign that a fundamental change was in the making. That was the year that thirty-six-year-old Kevin Conway turned down the offer to become a partner at Goldman Sachs, becoming only the second person to do so in the firm's 125-year history. Goldman had been confident enough that Conway would join the partnership to include his name in the list of all the new partners in a newspaper ad. But two days later, Conway left egg on the face of Goldman's management when he announced that, rather than take up the partnership, he planned to leave the investment bank and join the ranks of buyout firm Clayton, Dubilier & Rice.

The gossip spread like wildfire. Turn down a partnership at *Goldman Sachs*? That was akin to deciding that you'd rather stay in the minor leagues than take a job as a starting pitcher for the New York Yankees. Who in his right mind would do such a thing? Contemporary newspaper accounts explained the move as a result of Conway's concern about the personal risk he would be assuming in becoming a partner at any investment bank: joining the partnership at Goldman, which wouldn't go public for another five years, meant that Conway, like his peers, personally would take on a share of the firm's liabilities. But that had never frightened anyone away before; after all, partnership had almost invariably proven to be a ticket to the top of the investment banking world, and to wealth.

But 1994 was a bumpy time in the financial markets, one of those years proving that life on Wall Street wasn't always a bed of roses. A series of surprising and surprisingly large interest rate hikes in the early spring and summer had wreaked havoc on financial markets; later in the year came a crisis in emerging markets that culminated in the devaluation of the Mexican peso. Goldman Sachs partners were defecting at a record rate—by the end of the year, about a third had left for greener pastures. But Conway's decision still astonished Wall Street. It was one thing to leave Goldman and go off to do something else—politics, say, as Bob Rubin had done and Jon Corzine would do later, or philanthropy. It was also understandable and acceptable to move on to start a new business, as Leon Cooperman had when he launched Omega after retiring as chairman and CEO of Goldman Sachs Asset Management. But to curtail a career at Goldman so early on, voluntarily, in favor of moving to a private equity firm? Wall Street gave an almost visible shudder of alarm.

For most of the Street's existence, investment banks had been admired and respected institutions; the young bankers who got a toehold on the bottom rungs of the ladders at the top-flight firms were envied by their peers who had to settle for a regional or second-tier firm such as Jefferies & Co. Premier institutions such as Goldman Sachs had become career destinations in their own right. But Kevin Conway's decision to bolt from an elite firm and go to a private equity firm, of all things, would signal the beginning of the end of Wall Street's ultra-elite status. Increasingly, for the Kevin Conways of Wall Street, working for a top investment bank was no longer an end in itself but simply a stepping-stone to something still better. And what was better? In the eyes of aggressive young bankers and traders, more and more that was defined as working for an elite private equity firm (KKR, say, or Blackstone, or even Clayton, Dubilier) or joining a top-flight hedge fund.

By the new millennium, the goal was to be the next Eric Mindich. Mindich was Wall Street's version of Doogie Howser, the lead character in a television comedy whose plot revolved around Howser being both a normal teenager and a genius who, before he gets his driver's license, has already become a surgeon. After becoming the youngest partner at Goldman Sachs in that firm's history (at the tender age of twenty-seven) in the same year that Kevin Conway departed for the world of private equity, Mindich stuck around at Goldman for another nine years before leaving to start his own hedge fund based on the risk arbitrage tactics that he had learned at Goldman (in the group formerly headed by Bob Rubin). Mindich raised what was then a record of $3 billion for a start-up fund, despite his insistence on relatively onerous terms: to get access to the fund, his limited partners had to be willing to tie up at least $5 million of their capital for nearly five years (at a time when investors in most funds could get their capital back on a few weeks' or months' notice).

Mindich is what all savvy young traders want to be—a multimillionaire who hangs his hat in a Park Avenue co-op building with neighbors such as newsman Mike Wallace. Certainly Mindich couldn't have done that well that quickly toiling away in the (relatively) bureaucratic world of Wall Street. In 2007, his personal share of his new hedge fund's profits was nearly three times what his former boss, Goldman Sachs CEO Lloyd Blankfein, took home—about $200 million, compared to Blankfein's $68 million in salary and bonus. And Blankfein was Wall Street's most richly paid CEO ever that year.

As the years passed, former Morgan Stanley banker Lou Gelman observes, "The best people tended increasingly to see Wall Street as a great place to learn and to forge relationships, and then to leave." (Gelman himself bolted for the hedge fund world in the late 1990s.) "Wall Street, instead of being the folks cracking the whip in the relationship with everyone else, would become more and more under the control of these new Wall Street clients. You just couldn't afford to say no to them." Perhaps not coincidentally, it was also in 1994 that Goldman set up its own dedicated sponsor group to serve the buyout funds.[5]

The increasing prominence and, ultimately, dominance of both hedge funds and private equity funds can be traced to the concept of alpha. In finance, the Greek letter becomes a word that signifies an investment return that is due only to the manager's skill rather than to what the broader market is doing. A portfolio manager who earns 11 percent in a year when the major stock indexes are up from 10 percent to 12 percent is said to earn a return that is mostly beta; she is benefiting from the rising tide of the markets lifting all the portfolio managers' boats. But in a year where an index is up only 5 percent and a manager succeeds in posting a 15 percent return—or whenever the broader markets post losses but an investor generates a positive return—that is alpha. And by the end of the 1990s, the pursuit of alpha made the quest for the holy grail look like child's play.

Chasing Alpha

Investors of all stripes, it turned out, were in dire need of alpha. The biggest among them—pension funds such as CalPERS, the behemoth that oversees the retirement savings of California's state employees, or Yale University's endowment—were run by managers whose all-encompassing goal was finding a stable, steady source of investment returns not tied to what stocks and bonds were doing in any given calendar year. In search of investments that would zig when the U.S. stock market zagged, these powerful players had begun investing in emerging-market bonds, timberland, Chinese stocks, oil well partnerships, real estate in Dubai, and commodities: they were all in quest of alpha returns. Every stock market slump—in 1987, in 1989 and 1990, again in 1994, and briefly but violently in 1997 and 1998—reinforced the importance of having exposure to assets that didn't behave the way the broad market did. The larger and longer-lasting three-year bear market of 2000 to 2002 was when hedge funds, for instance, really caught fire: during that period, their number jumped more than 25 percent, while their assets under management surged 42 percent. While mutual fund managers struggled, many hedge fund managers continued to post positive returns. Hedge funds had an edge over many other "uncorrelated" investments—in contrast to, say, five hundred acres of farmland, the investment in the hedge fund was liquid (at least initially) and relatively easy to value. If an investor wanted to leave, all he had to do was request his money back at the prevailing market value. (As hedge funds became more powerful, however, managers followed Mindich's lead by imposing more onerous lockup periods that meant that liquidity proved more illusory in practice.)

For investors, the allure of hedge funds lay in their go-anywhere approach to financial markets. Their name implies that these managers spent their time hedging, or finding ways to limit the risk of one investment by taking another market position. (One example of a hedge might be investing in the stock of a company that makes most of its money producing crude oil; to address the risk that a slump in crude oil prices will hurt the stock, an investor might sell crude oil futures short. If crude falls, he would hope to make up in profit on the oil futures what he would lose on the stock bet.) In practice, the thousands of hedge fund managers today pursue far more varied and complex strategies than simply hedging. Some structure complex positions revolving around actual or potential merger transactions involving public companies, shorting one company involved in a deal while owning the stock in another, a strategy known as merger arbitrage or event-driven investing. Others use convertible securities, which combine elements of stocks and bonds, and employ different strategies to capture any difference in value between these and the stock of the company that had issued them. Increasingly, a hedge fund manager was simply an investor who acknowledged no restrictions on where he could invest, how much he could borrow to try to magnify his returns, the extent to which he could use derivatives, or how much he could put to work in a particular stock or industry.

This go-anywhere, do-anything approach was appealing to investors, who felt that skilled managers able to anticipate twists and turns by financial markets should be able to use whatever products and strategies were available to make money regardless of what asset class was winning. Relative outperformance was appealing only in a bull market. Who wanted to own the best large-cap mutual fund in a year when stocks as a whole were in the doldrums? As the Wall Street saying has it, you can't eat relative returns. While mutual funds were restricted to buying, owning, and later selling a specific kind of stock (say, small-cap value shares), a hedge fund manager could do anything he wanted with his investors' money, as long as he spelled out his general strategies in advance. He could invest at home or abroad; he could focus on stocks, bonds, or more exotic instruments; he could buy and hold or sell short; he could borrow to buy and generate leveraged returns; in short, he could be a real master of the financial universe.

"The first time you saw this pattern develop was in the commodity trading advisor [CTA] world during the eighties," says Glenn Dubin, cofounder of Highbridge Capital, a hedge fund empire that he and childhood friend Henry Swieca built and later sold to JPMorgan Chase. (Dubin and Swieca still run the show.) In the mid-1980s the two partners teamed up to create a series of portfolios combining CTA multistrategy funds with funds that invested in stocks and bonds. "The first big eye-opener for investors probably came during the 1987 crash," Dubin muses. "Soros, [Bruce] Kovner, and all the other guys who were short stocks and long bonds when that happened made a killing, while the long-only guys got pummeled."

Then in 1990 came the first Gulf War; that and the recession that followed seemed to prove that hedge fund managers could make money from anything, in any environment. "You could [own] crude oil futures in the months leading up to the Gulf War, as the supply fear drove prices higher, then short it when the guns started going off, for instance," says Dubin. "Suddenly stocks are plunging and traditional asset managers are losing their shirts, but the global macro hedge fund guys like Soros and Paul Tudor Jones and Kovner are all up enormously as a result of their positions."

The "lost decade" for stock and bond market investors in the first part of the new millennium just confirmed that hedge funds provided alpha, in the eyes of some data providers. The Hennessee Group, one of those market analysis groups, proclaimed that while the S&P 500 Index had plunged 23.33 percent over the course of the ten years between January 2000 and December 2009, the Dow Jones Industrial Average had lost 9.3 percent, and the NASDAQ Composite Index had nosedived 44.24 percent, its proprietary hedge fund index had *gained* 88.3 percent in the same period. Skeptics may point to the flaws associated with performance tracking in the hedge fund industry, such as survivor bias, but to advocates of alternative investments, results like that spelled one thing: seeking alpha in the form of alternatives, like hedge funds, is the way to go.

By the time hedge fund managers were attracting widespread attention, private equity funds were already well established. One of the first firms into this new business was KKR. As a corporate banker at Bear Stearns in the 1960s and 1970s, Jerome Kohlberg devised debt-financed exit strategies for small to midsized family-owned companies, deals he referred to as "bootstraps." When Bear Stearns was reluctant to give Kohlberg and his protégés Henry Kravis and George Roberts the capital to establish an in-house fund dedicated to these new transactions, the trio bolted to form KKR in 1976.

The rest is history. KKR landed its first institutional investor (an Oregon state employee pension fund) in 1978, and by the mid-1980s the partners were conducting multibillion-dollar management buyouts of companies such as Safeway and Beatrice. The battle royal for ownership of RJR Nabisco in 1988 proved to Wall Street just how attractive private equity clients could be; the $31.1 billion deal, the outcome of a titanic battle between KKR and a rival group led by RJR Nabisco's CEO along with an investment bank, earned the numerous Wall Street firms involved an estimated $1 billion in fees.

Both private equity funds and hedge funds raised funds privately, from what regulators like to call "accredited investors" and what the rest of us tend to refer to as rich people and sophisticated institutional investors. In other words, unless you have at least a million or two in investable assets (realistically, much more, since even the smallest of these funds likely won't even take your phone call unless you're worth $15 million or more and can spare at least $1 million for their fund), don't bother trying to get inside the golden circle. Investors, referred to as limited partners, tie up their capital in a private equity fund for a decade or so. In the early years of a fund's life, its general partners (the managers at funds such as KKR) spend their time hunting for deals and investing and then find ways to exit at a profit. (As of this writing, KKR has raised about fourteen different private equity funds over its life span.)

The long-term secular decline in interest rates throughout most of the 1980s and 1990s fueled a boom in the leveraged buyout business, making financing relatively cheap and helping private equity funds reward their investors with outsized returns. By mid-2008, KKR estimated it had invested about $43.9 billion and earned $60.1 billion in profits from those fourteen funds; another $27.5 billion of profits were still on paper because the investments hadn't yet been sold. It also revealed that its average annual internal rate of return (IRR, the most commonly used measure of investment returns used by private equity investors) was a whopping 26.2 percent during a period when investing in the Standard & Poor's 500 index would have earned the same investors about 8.8 percent a year.[6] With that kind of track record, it was little wonder that investors didn't balk at the fact that it could take years before KKR and other buyout funds would achieve those returns and pay them their share of the profits. In fact, while once investment managers who had run portfolios stuffed with illiquid assets that couldn't be quickly sold for a price close to their fair value—like those of a private equity fund—charged their investors lower fees to compensate for the lack of liquidity, now the magnitude of those returns (all that alpha!) meant that firms such as KKR could command premium fees. While a mutual fund might charge a flat 1.25 percent management fee, KKR could levy a 2 percent fee—and collect 20 percent of any profits, to boot. In the eyes of investors, illiquidity was no longer a risk, but simply the price one paid for alpha.

Hedge funds adopted a similar compensation scheme. But while private equity investors didn't get their 20 percent share of the profits until after the investments in their portfolios were sold, hedge fund managers could become very wealthy very quickly through what is known as mark-to-market accounting. At the end of every fiscal year, the assets in the hedge fund are valued, and the manager pockets a fee equivalent to 20 percent of those paper gains without having to liquidate the portfolio. (That compensation scheme is, in the eyes of some private equity investors, responsible for some of the aggressive risk taking on the part of hedge funds; as long as the transaction worked in the short run, hedge fund managers could become wealthy regardless of what happened to their investors over the longer haul.) By the mid-1990s, the prospect of easy riches enticed a steadily growing procession of bored, frustrated, or fed-up traders to walk away from their investment banks and set up shop on their own.

At first, explains Patrick Adelsbach, a principal at Aksia, a hedge fund advisory group, who has studied hedge funds since the early 1990s, these traders invested their own money, the fruits of years of big bonuses, and brought in some family and friends as fellow investors. Those who were successful quickly earned a reputation as stars and went on to establish a more formal structure. By 2000 or so, skilled traders with an idea for a new niche strategy were leaving investment banks at a rapid clip to set up their own shop; Goldman's IPO in 1999 spawned a particularly large batch of new hedge fund managers, including, ultimately, Eric Mindich. "It seemed almost as if these guys were afraid of being left out of the biggest party around if they didn't leave and start a hedge fund," says Anna Pinedo, a partner specializing in securities law at Morrison & Foerster, a national law firm. With each year that passed, the new funds became larger;

in the late 1990s, a significant debut fund could have $100 million to $200 million in assets, but by 2002 or so, a manager needed to have $300 million to even get the attention of Wall Street's traders and the burgeoning prime brokerage industry.[7]

Wall Street had long recognized the potential for hedge funds to become a big new source of fees. Bear Stearns was one of the first, using its expertise in the relatively unglamorous business of clearing trades (making sure that they are properly executed and documented) to move up the food chain and provide other services to hedge funds, including record keeping and lending them the stocks they needed in order to sell short. Other firms caught on quickly; by the early 1980s, Morgan Stanley was providing one-stop shopping for Julian Robertson's Tiger Fund as well as for George Soros, while Goldman Sachs dealt with the needs of another top hedge fund manager, Michael Steinhardt, within what was known as their personal client services division. These ad hoc services formed the basis of the prime brokerage groups.

The earnings power and clout of Goldman's new prime brokerage business, Global Securities Service (GSS), grew in tandem with the hedge fund industry itself. The business was so profitable that soon employees in GSS without MBA degrees were outearning those who did possess the graduate degree but who toiled away in higher-profile but less profitable parts of the firm.[8] The good times only got better in the coming years as the hedge fund industry's explosive growth continued, peaking at 9,550 funds managing a cool $1.535 trillion in assets by mid-2007. Best of all, because hedge funds needed the services so much—and were raking in so much money in management and incentive fees—they didn't balk at paying the bill for prime brokerage services. Finally, it seemed, Wall Street had found a product that couldn't be easily commoditized and that maintained its profit margins. Despite the growing competition from the mid-1990s onward, Goldman Sachs, at least, found that its prime brokerage fees slid a relatively modest 20 percent, an amount it could easily recoup from the massive growth in volume.[9]

Using these new prime brokerage businesses, investment banks set out to do everything they could to smooth the path for traders hoping to launch a hedge fund, facilitating the industry's explosive growth. "The average bank had a turnkey solution for any manager who wanted it; he'd show up at one of the more sophisticated prime brokers like Goldman or Morgan Stanley, and the guys there would find him office space, help him set up his computer technology, even help him order his office furniture," says Adelsbach. They'd also introduce the fledgling manager to potential investors, offering what they dubbed "capital introduction services." The pitches walked a narrow line between what was legal and ethical and what wasn't; funds would be invited to attend high-profile conferences where they could set up booths in the exhibit halls or brokers would help a new manager arrange a series of meetings with potential investors—but without taking an explicit fee for raising the capital in the same way they would have if they had been underwriting a transaction. The very fact that Goldman or Morgan Stanley was willing to stamp the Wall Street equivalent of a *Good Housekeeping* seal of approval on a start-up hedge fund was enough to set the new manager apart from the crowd. The bank might charge a fee for that particular service, but the tacit quid pro quo was that the manager would direct all his trading and other prime brokerage business to the firm that employed his capital introduction team.

The stock market slump and the economic recession that followed the collapse of the dot-com bubble in 2000 rang the death knell for old Wall Street relationships. As they had in past slumps, hedge funds outperformed the stock market during its three-year slide (in their worst year, 2002, the average fund fell only 2.89 percent).[10] Unhappy investors pulled money out of the stock market and directed it to the portfolios run by the go-anywhere gurus. Pension funds, facing future payout obligations to retirees and blindsided by large losses, found the allure of alternative asset classes and alpha to be almost magnetic; they hoped hedge fund gains could help them recover their losses as rapidly as possible. The stock market's malaise meant that stock underwriting was difficult and far from lucrative for investment banks; after raising $300 billion in equity for companies in 2000, Wall Street institutions collected fees on a measly $97 billion of deals in 2003.[11] Nor were there many M&A advisory fees to be pocketed: few corporations were interested in making strategic acquisitions in the midst of economic uncertainty when they couldn't compute the value of what they planned to buy. While the private equity funds weren't immune to the market slump of 2000 to 2002, they still had funds to invest and a big incentive to do deals. KKR alone raised another $6 billion in capital in 2002, a sum that could finance $35 billion or more in buyouts, given how low interest rates had fallen and how easy it had become to obtain debt financing even for risky transactions. But if Kravis and his colleagues didn't put that money to work, they wouldn't even earn the 2 percent management fee.

The "Saviors" of Wall Street

By 2002, it was clear the balance of power had tipped away from Main Street institutions—investors such as T. Rowe Price and corporations that relied on Wall Street to meet its capital needs—in favor of these new players. "New prime brokers were calling us every day," says Nick Harris*, manager of a large hedge fund. "They were offering us access to their balance sheet—if we needed to borrow to trade or otherwise generate fees for them, well, they were going to do whatever it took to make sure that happened." His fund's average leverage level was around 1.5, meaning that for every $1 billion he invested of the firm's own capital, he would borrow another $500 million from one of those eager prime brokerages and invest it, too. But Harris's prime brokers were urging him to go further, to raise that borrowing to $1 billion. "When I started in the business in the early 1990s, you could lever up three or four times what you had on your balance sheet," Harris recalls, meaning that for every dollar of capital, a maximum of $3 or $4 could be borrowed. "At its most extreme level, leverage of 20 times became at least theoretically possible."

On the surface, borrowing was tempting; it was certainly cheap, since interest rates had fallen and so had the cost to hedge fund managers to borrow. At the end of 2001, Harris says, his interest costs were 170 basis points above the international interest rate benchmark, known as the London Interbank Offered Rate (LIBOR). That meant that if institutions borrowing money on London's interbank market paid 2.5 percent, he would be forking over 4.2 percent. By 2005 or 2006, he says, those costs had plunged to 30 basis points above LIBOR; a 2.5 percent LIBOR rate would have meant he was now paying a mere 2.8 percent to borrow the same amount of money. Had Harris increased his borrowing, he would have had a lot more firepower to put behind his trading strategies and investment ideas, making it possible for him to earn exponentially higher returns. But he was also aware that if a trade went sour, the borrowing could backfire.

The Wall Street prime brokers didn't seem worried about that risk and even downplayed it, he says. Of course, the more leverage they could persuade Harris and his fellow hedge fund managers to take on, the higher the fees they could generate for their firm. And even the ultralow borrowing costs weren't set in stone, Harris says. The prime brokers' original role was handling back office functions for the thinly staffed hedge funds, keeping track of trades, clearing them, and keeping custody of the assets, carefully segregated from those of its other clients. The profit margins on this business might be low, but it was a consistent earner for the prime brokerage. "Our firm alone was large enough that we could generate $10 million to $20 million just in custody and back office fees these prime brokers charged" every year, Harris says. The prime broker also tended to handle a lot of trades for its hedge fund clients, collecting fees on those as well. Those fee streams were important enough in their own right that hedge funds could use them as a way to negotiate even lower financing costs. The more Wall Street firms jumped into the prime brokerage business, "the more we had carte blanche," he adds.

If Wall Street's prime brokerages were helping to drive up the level of risk taking in the financial markets by making ultracheap financing available to hedge funds, its investment banking operations were about to play their own part in making the financial system riskier. Once it had seemed at least possible for an investment bank to take the moral high road and not participate in a deal that might jeopardize the firm's reputation or long-term profits simply in order to capture a fee. That's what Goldman Sachs had done when it chose not to advise corporate raiders and others making hostile takeover bids. But as competition to woo the notoriously fickle private equity firms became fiercer and as clients grew more cutthroat by the day, the investment banks themselves rejected the mere idea of leaving anything behind on the table that a rival might be able to parlay into a penny of profit. By 2006, private equity firms, encouraged by the availability of cheap capital and their ability to raise larger and larger funds from alpha-hungry investors, were doing new deals at such a rapid clip that at any given time, a bank's sponsor team could be working on four or five multibillion-dollar takeovers simultaneously, recalls Tom McNamara.

The deals were sometimes happening so quickly that it was nearly impossible to conduct proper due diligence. "On a Friday afternoon at 5:00 p.m., Blackstone or someone would call and want a commitment from us to finance a deal that would require $15 billion in debt—and they would want it by Monday," McNamara says. Credit research was being conducted by associates, the junior members of the team fresh out of business school, because there weren't enough experienced credit analysts to go around. When something struck one of them as not making sense or being too risky, McNamara says, "the response was that if we didn't do this, someone else was going to—one of our rival institutions. Then whoever had asked the question would be told, 'Are you going to be the guy that didn't get the commitment okayed, and the guy who let that business and all its fees go to a competitor?'" Naturally, nobody wanted to be that guy.

The business of financing buyouts proved nearly as addictive as crack cocaine. Banks could collect a series of fees from these private equity funds and didn't have to spend millions of dollars wooing them or presenting them with deal ideas that would never be acted on, as they did with corporate clients who didn't do deals for a living. The first revenue might come in the shape of an advisory fee, or in exchange for a financing commitment. Another fee could be levied on providing interim financing or bridge loans. More fees could then be charged for selling the junk bonds and leveraged loans that replaced that interim financing. And then there was the 7 percent fee that the bank could collect on the IPO of the company in a year or two.

Lloyd Blankfein, CEO of Goldman Sachs, admitted that his institution, like others, "rationalized" pushing the risk envelope during the credit bubble years. But he also insists that these rationalizations for the relaxation of lending and credit standards were completely justified. In his January 2010 testimony to the FCIC commissioners, Blankfein says bankers would cite reasons such as the power of the emerging markets and the ample liquidity in the financial system to justify the risk taking. But he undermined his own argument when he concluded that the rationalizations were the result of the fact that "a firm's interest in preserving and growing its market share, as a competitor, is sometimes blinding—especially when exuberance is at its peak."[12] In other words, while every other firm on Wall Street may have been chasing Goldman Sachs, Goldman itself was afflicted with just the same kind of hypercompetitive urge, and feared losing even a fraction of a percentage point of market share to its own rivals.

These sponsor-backed IPOs weren't the tiny, $100 million or $200 million deals that came from taking start-up companies public; the IPO of private-equity-backed Hertz, the large car rental company, was a $1.32 billion affair that raised an estimated $90 million in fees for its underwriters—Merrill Lynch, Goldman Sachs, and JPMorgan Chase. Anyone who wanted a piece of those fees down the road had to be prepared to play ball with the private equity funds when the latter first structured and sought to finance those takeovers, says Peter Blanton. Blanton himself wasn't involved in putting together the packages of bridge and longer-term buyout financing, involving multiple layers of loans and bond issues, but he'd hear about them when it came time for the bankers to try to win the lead underwriting job on the IPO. "Writing the pitch books, we'd always note that we put up some of the original money, so we should be part of the deal." That turned into a vicious circle; the next time the same private equity team needed financing for a deal, they'd use the same argument to the bankers: they had just paid out millions of dollars in underwriting fees and so had earned some generous terms on the next financing. "A lot of sponsors looked at Wall Street and saw a honeypot full of money and felt that was their money, because it had come out of their pockets when they paid the IPO fee," Blanton says. "Now they wanted some of that back in concessions on the cost of the deal financing. The Wall Street firms had no backbone; all anyone could say was yes. The answer was never no." Wall Street institutions knew they might be getting squeezed on the terms of any single deal by their ultra-aggressive clients. But they could make up for that on volume, they reasoned.

Some bankers chose not to stick around. Gelman, the Morgan Stanley banker who had helped bring Netscape public even as he saw it as an example of Wall Street's transformation into a casino that encouraged short-term speculation rather than long-term investing, left early, before the market reached its most extreme levels. He didn't want to go through the whole dot-com experience again, this time with junk-bond-financed buyouts. "Over and over again, I'd find that the client whose stock issues I worked on wasn't a corporation raising capital for a new plant, but an IPO that would get a buyout firm a fast profit," he says.

Private equity funds argued that the way they earned their hefty returns was by taking a poorly managed company private, restructuring and overhauling its operations, and then selling the new and improved version, either back to public shareholders in an IPO or to another private buyer. But the time frame that elapsed between when the buyout was done and the IPO that marked the buyout fund's exit shrank steadily. Often, the private equity managers might have bought the company less than a year before the IPO, not enough time to make fundamental operational changes, much less for those improvements to pay off in higher earnings or a higher valuation. A transaction like that "was a classic flip," Gelman says. The stock underwriting business, once a craft, had become an assembly line, he laments. "It was all about 'How many deals can we price this week?'" Gelman left, he says, "when it became impossible to be an effective conscientious objector to these deals."

Others stayed but became increasingly worried by the deals that were being done. Some voiced concern about the pattern of one buyout company selling portfolio companies on to another one, a phenomenon that became known as secondary buyouts. Why, they wondered, would a company that supposedly had already been through the private equity wringer—costs slashed, business revamped and refocused—be attractive to another buyout firm, one that presumably would try to make money by doing exactly the same things? If there was any fat left to be trimmed, that meant that the first firm hadn't done its job properly, which meant it wouldn't be able to extract the maximum sale price and thus the maximum return for its investors. On the other hand, if the first firm had done its job properly, then the second buyer was making a foolish investment; there would be no way for its managers to generate a return for their own investors. Private equity investors were openly skeptical, but the deals got done: by the end of 2004, the Simmons mattress company had been acquired by no fewer than five different buyout firms—the latest, Thomas H. Lee Partners, had paid $1.1 billion for the company.

Deals, Deals, Deals!

Secondary buyouts were just the tip of the iceberg, bankers and private equity funds agree today. By 2005, dividend recapitalizations had arrived on the scene as a way for buyout firms to generate quick profits on deals they had done only a few months earlier. Think of these a bit like refinancing a mortgage: the homeowner takes advantage of the increase in her home's value (or at least the increase in its paper value) and increases the size of the mortgage. While homeowners were doing just that in the mid-2000s, private equity firms were doing the same with the companies in their portfolio in order to lock in profits for themselves and be able to provide returns to their investors more rapidly.

"What I think happened was that bankers weren't gatekeepers, thinking about the quality of the transactions they were financing for their buyout clients," says Jake Martin*, a partner at one large buyout firm. Investment banks were shuffling the assets they underwrote off their own books as rapidly as possible and into the portfolios of other investors. "The question became not whether it was an attractive deal for buyers so much as 'Is it structured right, so that I can push this stuff out the door?'" A lot of lipstick was being applied to make a lot of pigs look more appealing to buyers, he figures. With interest rates at such low levels, buyout firms had an incentive to put smaller amounts of capital into each deal they did—perhaps 10 percent or even 5 percent of the total value—and finance the rest. That was great news for all concerned. The buyout firms could put more money to work in more deals, and have less cash at risk in each one; the greater the number of deals done, the more fees the Wall Street bankers could collect. Because investors were starved for securities that offered even slightly higher yields than those on Treasury notes, they held their noses and bought.

Martin admits that his firm was probably one of the beneficiaries of this phenomenon, able to finance its transactions more cheaply than otherwise would have been the case. But he adds that the new dynamics of the market—particularly the fact that increasingly the only investors who would buy the relatively low-yielding and higher-risk debt used to finance the later-stage buyouts were hedge funds—ultimately made his life more difficult. "We would rather know who is going to own our paper," Martin says. "In the old days, you'd know who your lenders were and you'd have a relationship with them, and if something went wrong, you'd go and you'd sit down with them and work it out. Now I go and look at the list of people who hold my paper and it's like alphabet soup. It's XYZ hedge fund, or JJB, or GBX, all weirdly named hedge funds that I've never heard of before. If I have a problem with a company and try to talk to them, they basically look at me as if I'm a criminal, and I can see them wondering, 'What kind of pound of flesh can I get out of you? What extra return from your misfortunes can I get?' That is just the reality of today's Wall Street."

Wall Street Joins the Party

Watching their clients rake in profits hand over fist beginning in the late 1990s, Wall Street firms found themselves envying the apparent ease with which these firms made money. Serving these clients was great; working with hedge funds meant that they not only earned big fees but also picked up valuable market intelligence that helped in other parts of their business. But across Wall Street, investment banks as well as banking giants such as Citigroup began to wonder how they could get a bigger slice of the pie for themselves. Wouldn't the best way to maximize profits for their own restless shareholders be to just become their own clients?

A growing number of firms took stakes in hedge fund businesses; JPMorgan Chase's acquisition of Highbridge was the biggest deal, but Morgan Stanley spent $1 billion to purchase pieces of Avenue Capital, FrontPoint Partners, and Lansdowne. Citigroup paid $800 million for Old Lane Partners, a hedge fund founded by former Morgan Stanley banker Vikram Pandit, as part of a bid to convince Pandit to join the company's team of top executives. (That turned out to be a particularly controversial deal when, less than a year later, Citi shut down Old Lane.) Lehman Brothers acquired stakes in firms such as Ospraie Management, run by high-flyer Dwight Anderson, an alumnus of Julian Robertson's Tiger fund, but also backed former employees who decamped to start hedge funds; after all, one of them might become the next star, like SAC Capital's Steve Cohen. Among its other investments, Lehman acquired a 45 percent stake in R3 Capital Partners, started by a former proprietary trader at Lehman, Richard Rieder, as late in the game as the spring of 2008. (By the time that interest was sold in October as part of Lehman's bankruptcy proceedings, it had lost half its value.)

Still, Wall Street CEOs wondered whether it wouldn't be even better if their firms could just go and make money for themselves in the financial markets, using their capital to do deals and place bets in the markets through proprietary trading desks. Why not become deal makers in their own right? The logic was impeccable: turning themselves into their own client would be so much simpler . . . and it wouldn't require that much of a leap. Ever since Wall Street had begun its transformation back in the 1970s, investment banks had been looking for ways to put their balance sheets to work profitably. "All Wall Street CEOs have two traits in common," says Marsh Carter, deputy chairman of NYSE Euronext and former chairman of State Street Bank and Trust Corp., who has worked closely with most of the current crop of these individuals. "They are very, very, very optimistic. And they all have an undying, unquenchable thirst to do something unique."

To Pete Peterson, who headed Lehman Brothers from the early 1970s until the early 1980s, *unique* meant looking back in time to the days when banking meant merchant banking, buying and owning businesses rather than just serving as an intermediary for others. Financing other people's deals was inherently perilous, Peterson worried, since blips in the market or the economy could cause a stream of fees to vanish overnight. Why not use Lehman's capital to do its own leveraged buyouts or invest in other businesses, such as real estate, where no one else put a limit on how much they could earn by telling them what kind of fee was acceptable?[13] Lew Glucksman, Peterson's co-CEO, had a different vision for the firm, however. A street-smart trader, Glucksman was aware that trading the growing array of products available—options, futures, and commodities, as well as stocks and bonds—generated two-thirds of Lehman's profits by the early 1980s.[14] Why shouldn't the firm build on those strengths and put its capital to work accommodating its trading clients and taking proprietary positions?

Both co-CEOs had a vision of the future that went well beyond Wall Street's classic role as an intermediary and involved Lehman using its own capital and becoming its own client. The difference in the nature of their vision, however—Glucksman believed Lehman should become more like a hedge fund, while Peterson preferred a private equity model—resulted in an epic battle for control of the firm in 1983. Glucksman triumphed briefly, ousting Peterson and ruling the company for another ten months before the partnership collapsed under the weight of the internecine battling. It is perhaps not surprising that Peterson went on to cofound the Blackstone Group with fellow Lehman alum Stephen Schwarzman in 1985, a company that the two men turned into one of the largest buyout firms in the world. (Glucksman went on to work with Sandy Weill as the latter began building what became Citigroup; he died in 2006.)

At Goldman Sachs, partners were also debating how best to make use of their own balance sheet. As Wall Street's transformation got under way in the 1970s and 1980s, a growing number believed that the recipe for long-term survival and success involved more than simply acting as an agent for its clients: Goldman Sachs should do business as a principal, to take risks with its own capital and pocket 100 percent of any return. Steve Friedman and Bob Rubin battled to get their partners' assent to a $5 million investment in one of KKR's first funds over the objections of colleagues who griped that they didn't want their profits going to support the business launched by Jerome Kohlberg, Henry Kravis, and George Roberts. But the investment was made, clearing the way for more direct investments in operating businesses by Goldman itself. Goldman veterans still fretted that this time KKR would see them as rivals instead of bankers. ("Yes, but they'll get used to it," Friedman retorted.) Finally, in 1991, Goldman opened what would become the first in a series of private equity funds carrying the Goldman Sachs brand name.[15] The $1 billion GS Capital Partners I, with $300 million of Goldman's capital invested in it, set out to compete directly with the big guys. In less than two decades, Goldman Sachs *was* the big guy, raising a $20 billion fund that even dedicated buyout firms such as KKR and Blackstone would find hard to match in size.

Goldman was slower to set up its own hedge fund, although Leon Cooperman had proposed doing so at a partners' meeting in the same year that GS Capital Opportunities made its debut. "The other partners were reluctant, because the hedge fund might short stocks of companies who were also investment banking clients of the firm," Cooperman recalls. "They worried that if that happened and the clients found out, there would be hell to pay. They just weren't progressive enough to see that in a few years this would become mainstream" and that even though those corporate underwriting clients *didn't* like it, they didn't have enough clout to punish the increasingly powerful Wall Street institutions. Cooperman left to set up his own hedge fund, to which other Goldman alumni have flocked. Meanwhile, Goldman quickly overcame its qualms and rolled out proprietary hedge funds. It also allocated a steadily increasing stream of capital to its proprietary traders, who were charged with using that money to generate profits for the firm in much the same way that the hedge funds would.

Both the hedge fund and proprietary trading businesses exploded in the 2000s. "Within ten years after I failed to convince them, suddenly hedge funds were all they were selling to their [investment] clients—these premium products," says Cooperman. Indeed, so great was Goldman's dependence on these principal activities—private equity investing, its hedge funds, and its proprietary trading business—that among the cognoscenti it had become almost a cliché to refer to Goldman Sachs as a hedge fund disguised as an investment bank. That's a description still guaranteed to cause Goldman Sachs executives to sputter in outraged indignation. Gary Cohn, the company's president, insisted in a 2009 interview that "the vast, vast majority of our revenue and income comes from our client facilitation" activities.[16] Many see that as posturing; others nod knowingly at the almost Clintonesque precision of Cohn's choice of words in describing Goldman's activities.

Ultimately, it became hard to figure out whether a Wall Street investment bank was operating as an intermediary, helping clients finance transactions; as a partner, investing alongside them; or as their rival, competing with them for trading ideas or access to deal flow.

"It became very situational," says Jim Tanenbaum, a partner at Morrison & Foerster, who has worked closely with Wall Street clients of all stripes; the answer would vary depending on what day of the week it was or even the time of day. If Goldman Sachs met with the board of directors of a company thinking of going public, there was no guarantee that the investment bank would agree to underwrite the deal, for reasons Tanenbaum says had less to do with the IPO candidate's appeal to public investors than with Goldman's own interests. "What would have happened? Goldman's bankers would have gone to the first meeting, said, 'That's very interesting. Let us introduce you to some of our colleagues,'" he observes. "And then at the next meeting, they'd be there with managers of their proprietary funds, because they had decided that rather than be the conduit for you to raise capital and earn a fee, they'd rather compete with their peers by buying you outright or investing in you." Instead of acting as an agent, the banks had themselves become principals in the financing transactions.

Is that better or worse for the hypothetical company looking for new capital? It's impossible to know if the company would have been better off following the traditional path of going public and selling stock to a number of mutual funds rather than selling itself to a private equity firm. Blanton is forthright in assessing the kind of analysis that was being made by his bosses. "Who is to say that this is wrong? You're a public company; your duty is to make money for your shareholders. And if everyone else is doing it too, why would you be the one firm to become holier than thou? It's just inconceivable." What was significant was that, increasingly, it was harder than ever for midsized or start-up companies with respectable revenue and profit track records to go public. Meanwhile, venture investors and bankers note that the same investment banks who turned them away as underwriting clients would often return with acquisition offers, sometimes emanating from themselves, on other occasions on behalf of buyout funds. Wall Street firms, which once saw their role as facilitating access to public markets, increasingly seemed inclined to block it, say a number of corporate lawyers and venture capital investors.

Part of this shift, Wall Street veterans agree, stemmed from the fact that investment banks and the growing numbers of commercial banks vying with them for capital markets transactions were almost all publicly traded businesses by 2000. Only a handful of firms remained partnerships, including Lazard, Greenhill & Co. (the boutique launched by former Morgan Stanley rainmaker Bob Greenhill) and Evercore Partners, another boutique launched by a group of veteran bankers (many of them Blackstone alumni) including Roger Altman, who had also worked at Lehman Brothers. (By 2008, all of these firms would also be publicly traded, following an IPO.) "When I started practicing on Wall Street, none of this could have happened, because people owned their own firms," remarks Tanenbaum. "The idea of using capital to pay traders based on the volume of the business they did would have been viewed as an absurdity."

Now that they were publicly traded, investment banks faced two conundrums: the perennial challenge of finding new and profitable business lines in order to deliver a stream of steadily rising profits to shareholders; and finding ways to deploy their constantly expanding balance sheets to generate those profits. "When any company raises new capital, they need to invest it in a business that will make even more money than what they are already doing," says Jimmy Dunne, CEO of one of Wall Street's boutique investment banks, Sandler O'Neill. "It's no good raising capital if it goes into a business at which they aren't as good as they were at the core business. That's a bad use of capital." Not coincidentally, Sandler O'Neill remains a private partnership.

By early 2006, some of Wall Street's more thoughtful insiders were questioning what was happening. How much of the record earnings that investment banks were posting could be attributed to their wisdom and deal-making prowess, and how much to the fact that they were benefiting from record low interest rates and investors' seemingly insatiable appetite for risky investments? What was unquestioned was that by 2006, the definition of success for Wall Street had changed. Once, the masters of the universe were those who could navigate the money grid most adeptly, generating the biggest benefit for their corporate clients while earning hefty fees for their firms. Now success was about not only serving a new breed of clients but trying to emulate them. Financial alchemy was the magic ingredient; if they could find the right ways to structure and hedge their financial innovations, the world, they were sure, could be their oyster.

And killjoys? Well, they didn't last long on the new Wall Street. No one had to look further than Phil Purcell, the Dean Witter executive who had risen to the top spot at Morgan Stanley in the wake of the two firms' merger in the late 1990s, only to be ousted in 2005 in a bloody battle for control of the investment bank. "In a lot of ways, the smartest guy out there was Phil Purcell," comments Nick Harris, the hedge fund manager. "He took few balance sheet risks, he said no to that special bottle of Château Leverage 2003. And he got fired for it."

That was only part of the story, of course. Purcell was widely disliked within Morgan Stanley, and during his time at the helm a number of top bankers had fled the elite investment bank. Still, under Purcell, Morgan Stanley hadn't taken the same kind of big balance sheet bets as its competitors—and that showed up in the company's profit margins and return on equity, which compared unfavorably with those of rivals. Shareholders were already concerned by news of the defections, and, backed by bankers inside the firm eager to delve further into the world of principal investing and proprietary trading, they ended up ousting Purcell. "He just didn't get what it meant to be a banker in the twenty-first century," says Gelman, the former Morgan Stanley banker. "I don't know why he seemed to be surprised that people weren't happy." Purcell's replacement was John Mack, who promptly went where Purcell had feared to tread. When Morgan Stanley reported its first-quarter earnings in 2007, the company announced a $1 billion profit made by shorting subprime securities in the first stage of their slump; investors beamed with delight at one-upping Goldman Sachs.

The lesson of Purcell's ouster wasn't lost on anyone. It wasn't that people lamented his absence as a person or even as a leader. But to many Purcell stood for an old-fashioned way of thinking about what Wall Street did and how it worked. "His Wall Street was a customer-focused place, not a place where people chased after business as a principal," Gelman notes. So Purcell's departure was symbolic; if he could be driven out of Morgan Stanley for failing to maximize profits at all costs, the thinking went, then consciously walking away from business opportunities just because they might involve a bit of risk was likely to be a career-limiting move for anyone else on Wall Street. "We watched, we listened, and we all learned from that," says another Wall Street veteran. "The message was clear: the question we were supposed to be asking ourselves wasn't whether a piece of business was prudent, it was whether it would help us beat Goldman Sachs."

CHAPTER 4

To the Edge of the Abyss—and Beyond

Flying Too Close to the Sun

Richard Fuld didn't like naysayers or killjoys any better than anyone else on Wall Street, especially when they came from inside the ranks of Lehman Brothers, the firm that had been his home his entire professional life. As CEO, he struggled daily to win the respect he felt Lehman deserved after clawing its way to the position of Wall Street's fourth-largest investment bank. Occasionally Lehman even managed to earn a larger return on equity than Goldman Sachs did, as happened in 2000 and again in 2003. Fuld, say some former Lehman bankers, was obsessively competitive and focused on beating Goldman Sachs on a consistent basis, and that meant emulating Goldman's risk-taking culture and taking on even more leverage. While Goldman Sachs borrowed about $25 for every dollar it put to work in proprietary deals or other high-margin undertakings, Lehman, by some calculations, borrowed more than $30. To continue earning those returns, Lehman devoted a lot of that capital to buying mortgages and repackaging them into CDOs as fast as it could, billions of dollars at a time. The 1 percent fee on creating and selling CDOs was a windfall that flowed straight to Lehman's bottom line.

When Mike Gelband, Lehman's new co-head of fixed income, began questioning the health of the real estate market in the summer of 2005, he was directly challenging the resolute optimism of Fuld and his closest allies at the top of the firm about one of the most profitable parts of their business. According to Lawrence McDonald, a Lehman banker who went on to chronicle the collapse of the investment bank in a book entitled *A Colossal Failure of Common Sense*, Gelband was a studious kind of person, as bankers go. But, McDonald added, "to this day I've never met anyone who could grab and comprehend a difficult new idea faster than Mike Gelband."[1] The "difficult new idea" that Gelband was focusing on in June 2005 certainly wasn't a welcome one for many at Lehman. It had nothing to do with the invention of a new way to make money but instead questioned the rationale for the profits the firm was already earning. Gelband prepared a thirty-page report spelling out just why he thought the real estate market was a bubble about to pop and do far more harm to Wall Street and the economy than the Internet bubble had done only a few years previously.

Gelband presented his evidence to McDonald's group early one morning at the beginning of June 2005. To the tense group of bankers and traders assembled in a conference room at Lehman's midtown Manhattan headquarters, he argued that the real estate industry "was pumped up like an athlete on steroids, rippling with a set of muscles that did not naturally belong there," McDonald later recalled. "Those muscles gave a false impression of strength and in the end would not be sustained."[2] With almost oracular ability, Gelman identified everything that would go wrong and ultimately cost Fuld his post and Lehman its very existence—the rise of the shadow banking system of which Lehman was a part, the leverage, the poor quality of the mortgage loans that Wall Street was churning into CDOs. He even predicted the timing of the debacle: the chickens would come home to roost in 2007 and 2008, he said.

Not surprisingly, this kind of analysis was unwelcome to those toiling within Lehman's mortgage banking and trading division. Gelband just didn't get it, they argued; he was too conservative. And Fuld tended to agree with them. Why did Gelband want to kill the proverbial goose that was laying golden eggs at a very rapid rate? The buzz, McDonald said later, "was that Mike Gelband had developed some kind of an attitude problem, and it needed to be changed real fast."[3] As Gelband's anxiety grew about Lehman's exposure to what he saw as a catastrophe in the making, so did the worry among Lehman's top brass about Gelband and his inability to be a cheerleader for the business that was generating big profits for the firm.

In 2006, the volume and value of CDO deals hit another record, $552 billion—generating about $5 billion in profits for the Wall Street firms packaging the securities. But Gelband's anxiety grew just as significantly. That spring, some four million homes were for sale across the United States, double the number at the same time of year in 2000; CDO issuance was now more than three times the level of 2003. Gelband tried on several occasions to communicate those worries to Fuld and his chief lieutenant, Joe Gregory. At a year-end review in late 2006, Fuld openly told Gelband he was being too conservative. Ultimately, the naysayer had to go: by March, Gelband had been forced out of Lehman Brothers.[4] Only weeks after his departure, however, Gelband's predictions began to come true. Fuld may have won the battle, but Lehman would lose the war.

In the life cycle of every bubble, there is a point where it becomes clear that what looked like a boom is really a bubble—one, moreover, doomed to explode violently in the near future. By the early summer of 2007, that point had been reached. True, regulators such as Fed chairman Ben Bernanke could burble reassuringly about the problems associated with the subprime mortgage crisis being "contained," while Wall Street investment bankers remained publicly upbeat. But if the summer of 2007 was a tipping point, it is by studying the eighteen months that led up to it that we can begin to appreciate the extent to which Wall Street was afflicted with a kind of willful blindness or magical thinking. Each of the Street's five large investment banks, together with the investment banking divisions of giant global banks such as Citigroup and UBS, was fixated on doing whatever it took to maximize its short-term profits. If one risky deal was highly profitable and thus good, then doing ten such deals had to be even better, they reasoned. With their gaze focused on their own bottom line, they neglected to consider the implications for the entire financial system of each step they took. "We talked ourselves into complacency," Blankfein later admitted during his FCIC testimony.

By the time Gelband began to warn his colleagues at Lehman Brothers about the impending storm, it was already on its way. At first it looked like nothing more than a single, distant cloud marring an otherwise perfect sky, or a small snowball rolling down an Alpine slope. But as the months passed throughout 2006 and early 2007, the number of clouds grew in number and became darker and more ominous; the snowball became a giant boulder and, moving faster and faster, threatened to trigger an avalanche that would crush everything in its path. At the time, few seemed to realize just what was brewing, yet the signs were everywhere. Nine of the ten largest leveraged buyouts proposed in the industry's history were negotiated in 2006; subprime lending reached a peak along with CDO creation and leverage levels. Wall Street was drunk on cheap money and oblivious to the inevitable hangover.

The period that elapsed between two IPOs that, in different ways, signaled just how greatly Wall Street had changed over the last few decades proved to be the period in which that avalanche became unstoppable. The first of those transactions was the decision in the final days of 2005 by the New York Stock Exchange to merge with electronic trading network Archipelago and become, in the process, a publicly traded, for-profit entity. The second was the June 2007 initial public offering of stock in the Blackstone Group. The private equity group hoped to leverage its own decades-old brand name and its status as one of the linchpins of the "new" Wall Street into another successful nontraditional IPO. By now, however, the cracks in that new financial system were beginning to show up, and only days after the Blackstone IPO was completed, the financial apocalypse had begun. The fifteen months that followed would prove to be just as ugly and traumatic as the fifteen months that lay between the two IPOs had been filled with euphoria. Wall Street would never be the same again, the pundits proclaimed.

The Big Board Goes Public

In the final weeks of 2005, the New York Stock Exchange's 1,366 members prepared to vote on the most dramatic change to the centuries-old institution they ever expected to witness. Enough yes votes, and the Big Board would end 215 years as a member-owned nonprofit utility. Merging with electronic trading firm Archipelago Holdings Inc., the exchange would become a publicly traded for-profit entity whose activities revolved not around the venerable trading floor but around increasingly sophisticated computer networks.

To the exchange's new leadership—Goldman Sachs banker John Thain had just replaced Big Board veteran Dick Grasso at the helm in the wake of a scandal surrounding Grasso's lavish compensation package—the deal was a slam dunk. The exchange may still have been a symbol of American capitalism and the financial markets themselves, visited by every head of state that flew into New York to attend United Nations events. But, they argued, it was stuck in the twentieth century at a time when all of its major competitors at home and abroad had thrown themselves into the world of electronic trading. Its best clients—hedge funds and the trading desks of buy-side and sell-side firms alike—demanded execution in milliseconds, not seconds, especially for the vast majority of trades that simply involved buying or selling blocks of stock. The NYSE had taken a relatively slow and haphazard approach to computerized trading, and its ability to execute client trades cheaply and rapidly was in question even as the SEC forged ahead with plans to level the playing field still further. Supporters of the Archipelago merger argued that the deal wouldn't just make members rich—they would get, collectively, $400 million in cash and 70 percent of the shares in the new company—but also would save the centuries-old institution from becoming about as irrelevant as, say, a quill pen in the computer era.

Few Wall Street culture clashes are as visible as the one between the old and new Wall Streets that surfaced in the months after the transaction was sprung upon the world in the spring of 2005. The proposed merger had been negotiated in a matter of weeks, after Archipelago was rebuffed in its attempt to acquire the Big Board's largest competitor, Nasdaq. Not a word of the negotiations—in which both sides were advised by Goldman Sachs—leaked out. On the day of the announcement, Archipelago executives attending the press conference snuck in a side door of the NYSE and up a back staircase to reach the room where the media was assembled in order to keep the news secret until the last possible second. "Rarely do you get to completely shock the Wall Street world, and we did," recalls one of the participants in the negotiations, gleefully.

Shock was the appropriate word. One NYSE member loyal to ousted exchange CEO Dick Grasso and angry about Goldman Sachs's increasing clout at the exchange (Goldman also owned a stake in Archipelago) tried to launch a rival offer. He argued that the deal didn't compensate seat holders for the value of the exchange's real estate at the corner of Wall and Broad Streets, much less its brand. On the floor of the exchange itself, a coterie of traders quietly mourned what they believed was the end of a long tradition. "I had always taken great comfort in the idea that the Big Board was above the fray, a kind of disinterested, nonprofit thing where our focus [as an institution] was to keep the wheels turning rather than only making money," one trader mused. "Obviously, we all wanted to make money for ourselves, but we also thought that the system within which we were making money was one that thought first about that system and only then about profiting for itself. I suppose we felt as if we had a kind of trust to discharge."

But the future lay with a new breed of player, such as Tom Caldwell, a Toronto financier who thirty-five years earlier had stood beside George Washington's statue outside Federal Hall, just across Wall Street from the exchange, and vowed to himself that one day he would own a seat on (and thus a stake in) the NYSE. By the time of the vote, Caldwell, now head of a multibillion-dollar investment empire, owned forty-nine seats on the NYSE and cast his own ballots in favor of the merger and the IPO. "When an exchange is public, when people are willing to own it, it's a sign of a stable financial system," argues Caldwell, who also owns shares of publicly traded stock exchanges worldwide, from Europe to Latin America. "By having a publicly traded exchange, you give investors a way to participate in the growth of the economy and the region, and you give the exchange a currency that it can use to invest in itself to make sure it remains a competitive force." The kind of push that comes from shareholder-investors to become more competitive and efficient is the best way to make sure an organization is as effective as possible, he adds. The NYSE just couldn't afford to cling to its nonprofit status in a new world of intensive competition among stock exchanges for market share. It was this "new" Wall Street, with its emphasis on technology, innovation, and maximizing fees and revenues, that triumphed in the December vote. At least 85 percent of the exchange's members (95 percent of those who cast their ballots) voted in favor of the transaction, Caldwell among them.

Three months later, shares of the new New York Stock Exchange

Group began trading on its own exchange. Tiny ceremonial bells were handed out to all who showed up for the traditional party accompanying the first day of trading in any new listed company, and as the moment approached when exchange officials would ring the opening bell, members-turned-shareholders and hundreds of assembled guests began ringing them in celebration. The celebration was even louder at the end of the first day of trading, after the exchange's shares rose from $67 to $80 apiece.

Nonetheless, everyone was well aware that this was an entirely different kind of IPO; for two centuries, the exchange had been a member-owned organization that wasn't just a part of the financial system but one of its hubs. Even its location, at the corner of Broad and Wall, had given its name to that financial system—Wall Street. The reason for its existence was to give everyone a chance to access the secondary market for stocks. Unanswerable questions were everywhere. Some wondered what effect the fact that the exchange's single largest holder was now a private equity firm—General Atlantic LLC— would have on governance.

It was early days for the merger, but even as the bells rang out joyfully, a chorus of boos was also heard on the trading floor. Some came from disgruntled floor traders who hadn't had seats to sell and who thus hadn't been made rich in the transaction, but who knew that significant upheaval lay ahead. Others, on and off the exchange floor, were wary for different reasons, and continued to voice their unease at the idea of a for-profit exchange. "Look, I think it's great that the NYSE is competitive and innovative, but I don't know how much thought has gone into finding a way to be both a utility that has to serve all of us who are market participants and a for-profit company that has to maximize shareholder returns," says one investment manager who has served on exchange committees in the past. "They had struggled with these conflicts even before they were public, earning profits for the exchange by selling the right to trade in certain stocks [specialist listings], even though they acknowledged those listings belonged to everybody who participated in the markets, not the exchange itself. I don't know how they'll cope with this over the long haul."

Cultural clashes such as these likely will recur for many years to come. Exchange insiders, on the other hand, point out that a separate regulatory company reports to an independent board of directors, while the exchange as a whole is still overseen by the SEC. And the risk is worth running, they argue. "If the exchange was a public utility, which implies being a kind of monopoly, then there would be no incentive for it to become better, faster, or more efficient; the competitiveness of our markets would suffer," says one former senior executive at the exchange. In other words, the profit motive was necessary; without it the exchange couldn't discharge its responsibilities to the system properly. Certainly, without the public listing the NYSE never could have taken its next step. Only a few months later, it signed a deal to merge with Paris-based Euronext, forming the first transatlantic stock exchange company and setting the NYSE on course to having a global footprint. The only way the NYSE could outbid Deutsche Boerse, its rival to acquire Euronext, was its ability to use its stock as the "currency" in the €8 billion offer.

Blackstone Cashes In

Little more than a year after the NYSE's debut as a public company, in June 2007, armies of television cameras showed up again at the New York Stock Exchange for another unusual kind of IPO. This time the company going public wasn't an exchange but an entity from another part of the Wall Street labyrinth: private equity giant Blackstone. Only a month before the IPO plan was announced, Blackstone's CEO, Stephen Schwarzman, had called the public markets overrated and not really worth it when it came to raising capital.[5] Now, it seemed, Schwarzman was willing to eat his words (which had been directed at hedge fund firms and rival private equity companies that had filed for IPOs) if it meant that he could raise nearly $700 million by selling part of his interest in the company he cofounded to other investors, and put a $7.7 billion valuation on the rest of it. It would quantify the magnitude of his achievement in the eyes of everyone— and make him even wealthier to boot.

On the surface, the deal looked appealing; it was pitched to potential investors as a way for them to get a piece of the private equity action that was usually confined to the deal makers themselves, their closest (very wealthy) allies in the finance and business worlds, and blue-chip institutional investors. The only problem was that owning Blackstone's stock wouldn't give ordinary investors access to the same riches they might have enjoyed as real partners in the private equity firm's deals. What Blackstone was offering to the public were shares in its management company, not participation in its deals. Moreover, investors would have limited voting rights, giving them little to no say over the way Schwarzman and his board decided to run the business. In the eyes of some potential investors, the Blackstone folks were hanging on to their cake even as they ate it.

The success of the NYSE's debut as a public company hinged on the ability of a centuries-old brand name to overcome worries that the newly merged company might not be able to reinvent its business model and compete successfully in the twenty-first-century era of computerized trading. Blackstone now faced its own set of obstacles. Despite its status as a different kind of icon—a symbol of the riches that came from being a success on the "new" Wall Street—Blackstone's IPO bid raised eyebrows. After all, the firm had made that money for its partners and investors in its funds from *private* equity. Indeed, Blackstone's entire business model relied on the premise that the public markets it now sought to tap for its own benefit were inefficient. Only by taking publicly traded companies private (using debt to finance the deals) and overhauling and streamlining them could the true value of a corporation be unlocked, private equity investors argued. Of course, the public markets would come in handy eventually, when Blackstone needed an exit strategy to turn its investors' paper profits into cold hard cash. But an IPO wouldn't take place until Blackstone's partners had extracted as much value as possible from the company, leaving little on the table for subsequent investors. In other words, for Blackstone, the stock market had served traditionally as a dumping ground for its leftovers.

Nonetheless, Citigroup's Michael Klein, co-head of investment banking, felt the time had come for Blackstone itself to go public; the fascination with private equity as a source of fees for Wall Street had reached its logical extreme. It was time to turn those private equity profits into cash for the buyout firm's owners—and into fees for Citigroup. Klein, one of a small handful of bankers who pioneered the concept of sponsor groups within the investment banking world, had helped Blackstone finance so many of the firm's buyouts that Citigroup became known as Blackstone's bankers in much the same way that midtown Manhattan's Four Seasons restaurant, around the corner from the private equity shop's offices, was referred to as the Blackstone cafeteria. Klein broached the idea of an IPO for Blackstone itself not in Manhattan but over lunch at Schwarzman's recently acquired $34 million estate in the tony Hamptons.[6]

It was obvious that Blackstone had a better track record than many more conventional companies that seek to raise new capital through an IPO. In the nearly twenty years that had passed since it launched its first fund, Blackstone's assets under management had grown at an average rate of 34 percent. Even after paying Blackstone's fees, clients of its core private equity funds had pocketed an average annual return of 22.8 percent, a figure that dwarfed stock market returns in the same period.[7] Klein argued that Blackstone's managing partners could hang on to what mattered to them—control over the management of the funds and the ability to continue raising new ones—while generating a permanent capital base for the parent company and—not coincidentally—turning some of the wealth that Schwarzman, Peterson, and other partners had generated into cold hard cash. "It was very astute," says junk bond analyst and money manager Marty Fridson. "They seemed to realize that the market would never be at these levels again; a smart investor knows that the time to sell is when the market is at the peak and about to head south again. It was as if they'd said, 'Well, if people are willing to give us capital very cheaply, if they are willing to pay a premium—why not?'"

A Study in Contrasts

Aside from the timing and the nature of the deals—two parts of the Wall Street system for raising capital, raising capital for themselves through that system—the two IPOs could not have been a greater study in contrasts. The NYSE remains in many key ways a symbol of "old" Wall Street, despite the fact that 95 percent of the trading now takes place via computers rather than on the venerable trading floor. In contrast, Blackstone is the epitome of the "new" Wall Street. Even the purpose of the two IPOs was different. While that of the NYSE was simply a way to get the stock publicly traded (no fresh capital was raised), the Blackstone IPO was a way to help cofounder Pete Peterson (the former Lehman banker) make his wealth liquid: when the IPO was over, Peterson had sold all but 4 percent of his stake in Blackstone in exchange for $1.88 billion. Steve Schwarzman kept a 24 percent stake in the firm but still made nearly $700 million from the IPO.

Peterson and Schwarzman both rejoiced in lavish displays of their wealth, with Schwarzman sometimes taking it to extremes. For his sixtieth birthday, celebrated on Valentine's Day 2007, Schwarzman commandeered the Park Avenue Armory; comedian Martin Short was the evening's master of ceremonies, Patti LaBelle sang a song written especially for the master of the universe, and Rod Stewart performed in an evening that—lobster, filet mignon, and all—cost $5 million, by some estimates. That was just slightly more lavish than Schwarzman's annual holiday parties, the 2007 version of which had an orchestra playing themes from James Bond films while models dressed as the various "Bond girls" mingled with hundreds of guests. He's also a property junkie, owning lavish homes in Manhattan, Jamaica, Florida, and Saint-Tropez, in addition to the Hamptons estate.

In contrast, Duncan Niederauer, the former Goldman Sachs banker who replaced John Thain at the helm of the stock exchange, plays down his own wealth in a more "old" Wall Street way even as he continues to urge the Big Board forward into a new era. He and his family live in a relatively modest New Jersey suburb and, until the exchange's security people put their feet down and insisted he agree to a car and driver, preferred to drive himself to work early every morning in a pickup truck. Schwarzman attends galas for high-social-impact institutions such as the New York Public Library; Niederauer prefers to work for Habitat for Humanity and an array of autism non-profits. (His son was diagnosed as autistic as a toddler.) Still, Blackstone's IPO was "new" Wall Street, and the high-octane private equity business had, in the eyes of investors, a lot more pizzazz than the stodgy business of facilitating trades. While the exchange's stock had dipped below its $31 IPO price by the summer of 2007, Blackstone and its underwriters were confident that all that glamour would command a premium valuation.

Certainly the buyout business seemed white-hot, with several veterans speculating openly that 2007 or 2008 would see what many bankers and analysts had believed to be impossible: a $100 billion buyout. "That November 2006, we were working on three or four deals all at once, and then we got a call to work on structuring what would have been an $85 billion buyout," says one Citigroup banker. (By way of comparison, the largest buyout to date had been the $33 billion purchase of hospital chain HCA in the summer of 2006.) The bankers figured out ways to sell no less than $35 billion of term loans and worked through different strategies for financing the rest of the transaction but—to the poorly hidden relief of at least some of the bankers—the transaction fell apart. "Someone made the comment, 'I think we just flew too close to the sun.'"

Even for those who believed in the fundamental strength of the private equity model, the rapid-fire pace at which new buyouts were being done, the enormous deal sizes (seventeen of the twenty largest deals in history were announced in the eighteen months that preceded Blackstone's IPO), and the equally gargantuan valuations and levels of debt aroused unease. "Why would I want to buy stock in Blackstone if a guy like Steve Schwarzman is selling?" was the question heard across Wall Street. Those qualms didn't stop the underwriters (led by Morgan Stanley and Citigroup) from rounding up more than enough interest to price Blackstone's shares at $31 apiece, at the high end of the range. Behind the scenes, the level of nervousness was growing, say people who were involved in the underwriting and the road show. "Steve decided to accelerate the pricing by two days," says one of the bankers. "He saw the environment deteriorating."

In Washington, Senator Charles Grassley (the ranking Republican member of the Senate Finance Committee) was "stomping around," in the words of one private equity deal maker, introducing, along with his Democratic counterpart and committee chairman Max Baucus, a proposal that would tax the 20 percent share of profits earned by partnerships such as private equity, venture capital, and hedge funds at the rate applied to corporate profits rather than at the much lower capital gains tax rate. Meanwhile, the leveraged loan market—on which Blackstone and other private equity funds relied to help finance their deals—was beginning to crack. "In 2005, a normal backlog of paper that banks had committed to finance and waiting to be sold would be about $70 billion, but by June of 2007, it was $380 billion," says Tom McNamara, the private equity banker. "The tidal wave of

paper in search of a home was so overwhelming that almost overnight we started to hear investors starting to say no to deals and commenting that they didn't need to buy everything, especially at the
prices being asked." Schwarzman's instincts were right. Within days
of the Blackstone IPO, shares of the newly public company (trading
under the symbol BX—pronounced "bucks," as in cash) were falling;
by March 2010, the stock was changing hands for $15 a share, less
than half its IPO price of $31, although three times its 2009 low.

Flying Too Close to the Sun

Before the Blackstone IPO had been completed, the pendulum reached
one extreme and began, slowly, to swing back in the other direction,
gathering speed as it went and culminating in the Wall Street debacle
of 2008. During the months that elapsed between the two IPOs,
nearly everyone on the Street—from veteran regulators to the greenest
traders—recalls experiencing some kind of eureka moment: a point in
time where they stopped what they were doing and reflected to themselves that the good times they were experiencing were unsustainable.
For some, the warning signal was a particular deal that made them realize just how much risk their institution and the rest of the market was
accepting without question. For others, it was an offhand remark by a
colleague, or being confronted with the kind of careful research presented by a handful of Wall Streeters such as Mike Gelband to their
colleagues and bosses.

In the early spring of 2006, during the celebration of the stock
exchange's IPO, the warning signs were subtle and articulated only
by those willing to be provocative and challenge the status quo. Even
months later, few were willing to listen to Gelband and others like
him, those whom Wall Street CEOs such as Fuld were quick to label
as false prophets of doom and professional worrywarts. After all, fee
income and profits at investment banks and other firms hit record

levels in 2005, for the fifth year in a row; so, too, did compensation. Collectively, Wall Street firms pocketed $34.1 billion in bonuses in 2006. At the annual Robin Hood Foundation gala that December, the hedge fund managers who had founded the antipoverty charity took from the rich (themselves) and gave a record $48 million to the poor of New York City.

As the weeks passed and the clock ticked down to the Blackstone IPO in mid-2007, the warning signs became more pronounced. Crude oil prices had been rising, putting a crimp in the budgets of those who, unlike Schwarzman, didn't have billions in spare cash to cover the increased costs of heating even one home. But with twenty-twenty hindsight, one would have to say the real party pooper was the Federal Reserve, which had begun raising interest rates back in June 2004. Until then, policy makers had spent some three years flooding the American financial system with cheap capital in hopes of staving off a sustained period of recession and deflation in the wake of the stock market crash that had begun in 2000. That prolonged period of readily available, ultracheap debt fueled the boom in private equity deal making that made private equity firms such as Blackstone so superficially appealing, as well as generating all kinds of other trading and underwriting fees for fixed-income bankers across Wall Street.

It also distorted the perception of the risk of many transactions. Why worry that many of the new asset-backed securities being repackaged by Wall Street involved so-called subprime credit card receivables and mortgages—debt owed by borrowers with tattered credit histories? Low interest rates would cover a multitude of sins, and in the meantime, there were rich fees to be harvested. Until there was evidence that Wall Street's hubris, in the shape of its quest for more and more profitable fee-generating business, had collided head-on with the forces of gravity, no one on Wall Street wanted to worry. "Why would we borrow trouble?" says one former senior Wall Street executive. "We had to keep making money, keep our shareholders happy."

The Quest for ROE

Keeping shareholders happy had been the name of the game on Wall Street ever since the first big wave of investment bank IPOs culminated in the decision by Bear Stearns to go public in 1985 and Morgan Stanley to follow in 1986. By the early 2000s, a tidal wave of consolidation and the collapse of the regulatory barriers that had once separated investment banks and commercial banks had reshaped the competitive landscape dramatically. Just as the changes in the 1960s had pushed many firms out of the business, the trends of the 1990s caused bank and investment bank CEOs to question their ability to go it alone. Technology costs were soaring; paying key employees enough to stop them from jumping ship and heading off to work at hedge funds or buyout shops also drove up expenses, as did maintaining a global footprint. Meanwhile, profits from traditional businesses, such as trading, were continually under pressure.

For many Wall Street institutions, the answer seemed to be joining forces with a giant global institution. The U.S. division of UBS, the Swiss powerhouse bank, acquired PaineWebber in 2000, ending the latter's 120 years of independence. (The PaineWebber brand name vanished three years later.) Credit Suisse, UBS's rival at home in Switzerland and overseas, had become an aggressive investment banking competitor to firms such as Goldman Sachs and Morgan Stanley in the late 1980s, when it snapped up First Boston and its powerhouse M&A division, which employed two of the biggest buyout bankers around, Bruce Wasserstein and Joseph Perella. (Wasserstein died suddenly in late 2009 at the helm of Lazard, while Perella now runs his own boutique, Perella Weinberg Partners.) It followed that up with the purchase in 2000 of Donaldson, Lufkin & Jenrette.

The big U.S. banks were just as interested in getting a share of Wall Street profits that, in good years, dwarfed the skimpy margins they could earn from commercial banking operations. Sanford

"Sandy" Weill got the ball rolling by forming a new financial services behemoth, Citigroup, which would bring together a major bank (Citibank) and an insurance company (Travelers Group). Back in 1997, Wall Street's Salomon Brothers ended nearly eighty years of effective independence when it agreed to be acquired by Travelers Group; when Weill created Citigroup, he brought together a commercial and a major investment bank for the first time since the Depression-era passage of the Glass-Steagall Act. Weill's 1998 deal forming the future Citigroup violated that law, but Weill was given a two-year waiver; sure enough, in 1999, an obliging Congress officially repealed the crucial parts of Glass-Steagall and opened the door to the creation of other financial conglomerates. J.P. Morgan became JPMorgan Chase; other players, including Bank of America, became viable competitors to the traditional stand-alone investment banks on Wall Street. One after another, small investment banks sold out or were acquired by their larger rivals, with Deutsche Bank picking up Alex. Brown. Chase had acquired Hambrecht & Quist before its own purchase by J.P. Morgan. NationsBank purchased Montgomery Securities and later merged with BankAmerica to become Bank of America.

Now traditional Wall Street firms such as Morgan Stanley, Bear Stearns, and Lehman Brothers found themselves jostling for deals and profits with new or suddenly stronger players in the investment banking arena, such as Citigroup, UBS, and J.P. Morgan, all of which had vast amounts of capital at their disposal. It didn't matter whether they had originally been commercial banks or investment banks; all were now engaged in a relentless battle to maximize their return on equity. "The higher the ROE, the higher the book value of the investment banking operations and therefore the higher the stock price can climb," explains Jeff Harte, an analyst at Sandler O'Neill who has been studying the investment banking universe for many years. "It tells you how hard the bank's managers have been making the capital work, and how good they are at doing their job."

A bank can boost its ROE by moving into higher-margin products or into business areas that don't require it to use a lot of its own capital (one reason so many institutions are eager to move into wealth management), or by using leverage, which is borrowed money. Between 1975 and 1984, securities underwriters reported an average after-tax ROE of about 16.2 percent. Commercial banks had a smaller return on equity because their equity base tended to be much larger; in the same period the ROE of commercial banks averaged 12.3 percent.[8] By 2000, average ROEs had crept higher, even as traditional high-margin businesses came under pressure. Three years later, as both the financial markets and the investment banking industry began to recover from the dot-com blowup and the Enron and WorldCom governance scandals, a gap started showing up in the ROE data.

Goldman Sachs was pulling ahead of the pack decisively: in 2004, it generated an ROE of 19.8 percent while perennial rival Morgan Stanley earned 17.2 percent, Citigroup investors were rewarded with 17 percent, and Bank of America posted an ROE of 16.5 percent. Bringing up the rear was Merrill Lynch, with an ROE of 15.7 percent. Among the major Wall Street players, the only institution able to challenge or surpass Goldman in the ROE sweepstakes was Bear Stearns, which, thanks to its aggressive use of leverage and willingness to put its capital to work on its proprietary trading desk, earned an ROE of 19.1 percent.[9]

"The call went out around the Street—we had to beat Goldman's ROE," says one former top banker who worked for a rival firm. "Every quarter, there was a debate over how we could reduce equity and increase leverage to make the ROE look better, over ways to squeeze an extra penny or two out of each of the business units." The pressure on Wall Street's CEOs and CFOs made them look, once again, at the fate of Phil Purcell at Morgan Stanley. Overlooking Purcell's shortcomings, they focused on the fact that it was discontented shareholders who had spearheaded the coup d'état. Had Morgan Stanley posted a higher ROE in 2004 (when it trailed all but one of the four other top investment banks), they figured those investors wouldn't have been quite as eager to oust Purcell. "It was very, very apparent to every CEO on Wall Street that Phil Purcell had been run out of Morgan Stanley because he couldn't keep up with the ROE that Goldman had, because he wasn't using leverage enough and taking enough risks," the former banker adds.

The pressure on the rest of Wall Street to keep pace with Goldman Sachs continued to grow as Goldman's ROE increased and the gap between its performance and that of its rivals widened. In 2005, Goldman reported an ROE of 21.9 percent, climbing to 33.3 percent in 2006 and again in 2007. At Bear Stearns, meanwhile, 2005's ROE actually fell, to a measly 16.5 percent, as did that at Morgan Stanley, which hit 15.9 percent. At Merrill, it rose to 15 percent and up another fraction to 15.7 percent in 2006; Citigroup saw ROE rise to 17.5 percent in 2005 and then 17.9 percent in 2006. Wall Street was motivated to catch up with Goldman, since a hefty ROE performance was usually matched with an equally large payday for employees. In 2007, for instance, when Goldman paid an average of $661,490 to each of its employees, those at Lehman Brothers earned about half that, or $332,470.[10]

Chasing Goldman Sachs was a risky proposition. "Goldman was posting those kinds of returns because of decisions it had made years ago. When, after the downturn in 2000, all the other investment banks really cut back their exposure to risk and walked away from their risky business lines, Goldman Sachs didn't," Harte points out. In other words, they had been thinking strategically when their rivals hadn't been focusing on the long-term opportunities at all.

Elsewhere on Wall Street, the perception was that Goldman had relied solely on risk taking—borrowing to finance proprietary trading and investments—and that firms that hadn't kept up had failed to do this as thoroughly or as adeptly as Goldman. That implied that the problem could be quickly reversed if Goldman's rivals just hired the right people, focused on the right products, and pursued the right strategies. Some of Goldman's rivals, like UBS, hired consultants to advise them on how to keep up with Goldman. "Part of the reason that didn't happen the way they expected was that they missed out on the fact that Goldman had been investing in things like building up commodity trading in Asia long before 2003," when commodity markets ignited, Harte adds. When Goldman's ROE surged and investors in its rivals demanded that they do what it took to match those gains, taking two or three years to design and implement a long-term strategy wasn't an option. "The only way to accomplish what investors wanted as rapidly as they wanted was [by] taking on more leverage and getting more deeply into riskier businesses, or at least businesses that, if you were evaluating them properly, had more risk in them than might appear on the surface."

Chasing Market Share

By the spring of 2006, the battle for market share was at its most feverish. Across Wall Street, bankers deciding whether to undertake a new piece of business never asked themselves whether that transaction was good value for investors or even their clients over the long term. Nor did they seem to question whether the short-term rewards (the fees, higher profit margins, and higher ROE) made sense in light of the longer-term risks to the investment bank, its clients, or the financial system. The only question that mattered was whether the deal could be done and how much the institution could earn from it.

The risks associated with the securities the banks were packaging or underwriting were less important than the bank's ability to shift that risk off to someone else—specifically, to transfer it to an investor. Buyout banker Tom McNamara knew he would be viewed as less than a team player when he questioned his boss about a large private equity transaction that took place in the autumn of 2006. In the same way that subprime borrowers were buying homes with a 5 percent down payment rather than the traditional 20 percent, the buyout firm proposed to invest only a fraction of the equity typically committed to deals of this sort. McNamara's boss, he recalls, looked at him and asked, "What's your problem? Can't you sell the [junk bonds and leveraged loans]?" McNamara, in a bid to explain his concerns, began to reply, "Yes, but—" only to have his boss cut him off. "That's all I need to know. If we don't do the deal, [our biggest rival] will. So do it." McNamara never again questioned a borderline deal, however risky it looked to him.

That pattern was the same across Wall Street. "How can a loan officer who is under pressure to produce loans realistically say, 'Maybe we should sell less loans?' and keep their job," said Mike Mayo in his FCIC testimony. Even Mayo, theoretically an independent analyst, had experienced the backlash. When he wrote critically about compensation issues within the banking world in the late 1990s, some of the Wall Street institutions he was charged with monitoring began to block his access to the data he needed to do his job. "The reaction . . . was that these issues were none of my business." He began disclosing the lack of access to his clients and testified to Congress about the problem. "If I face a backlash even after I testify to Congress on backlashes," then why expect more from someone at the heart of the system? Mayo queried.

Certainly, none of the clients questioned the readiness to make a deal on the part of Wall Street. "We examined each deal in a vacuum," admits Jake Martin, the private equity firm executive. Looking back, he says, it's easy to understand why buyout fund managers such as himself and their bankers never moved beyond thinking how to do each individual deal long enough to consider the effect on the financial system of all that low-cost, high-risk borrowing. "It's a flaw of human nature." Martin says no one stopped to think about the cumulative effect of all this leveraged lending. Now, he acknowledges, it should have been obvious that those large and risky loans were going to make any downturn far worse than it otherwise would have been. "When everybody is doing exactly what you're doing, that is the time to stop and question what it is you are doing," he now says.

In 2006, the cumulative impact of all that frenzied deal making was showing up in the profit statements posted each quarter by Wall Street's investment banks. One after another, they announced big jumps in revenue, earnings—and, of course, ROE. Back in 1996, Morgan Stanley had earned $22.1 million in fees handling a dozen mergers for private equity clients, and a total of $52.1 million from all of the investment banking mandates those funds had awarded to it. In 2006, the firm earned $271.7 million in M&A fees alone, and $520.7 million from sponsors in all kinds of investment banking fees. Not only were those private equity transactions growing in number, but the rate of growth in profitability (and thus contribution to the ROE) dwarfed that of conventional transactions. In 1996, advising on an investment banking transaction for a sponsor earned Morgan Stanley an average of $1.3 million; a decade later, the average fee had soared to $3.35 million. No wonder McNamara's bosses didn't want to stop and question the deals they were working on, any more than a buyout manager wanted to discover that his bankers were suddenly insisting they would only finance his deals on more conservative terms. By comparison, the rate of growth in fees paid by clients for routine investment banking transactions was far more modest: the average transaction earned the bank only $1.9 million, up from $1.35 million in 1996.[11]

The Thundering Herd Runs Amok

The hunt for ROE would prove to be particularly dramatic at Merrill Lynch, the ninety-two-year-old investment bank best known for the strength of its vast retail brokerage network dubbed the "thundering herd." While Morgan Stanley and Goldman Sachs had earned their investment banking chops by working with corporate clients to underwrite stock and bond issues and advise on mergers, Merrill traditionally demonstrated its clout by selling those issues via its horde of brokers. The problem was that simply acting as the middleman or gatekeeper in plain-vanilla transactions was no longer the best way to earn a respectable ROE. Merrill's board of directors had handed CEO Stanley O'Neal a clear mandate to make the firm competitive, by which they meant generating a higher ROE. At the end of 2005, Merrill's ROE was only 15.7 percent, compared to the average for the investment banks of 18.4 percent.[12]

And that's when directors approved a new compensation policy: the more O'Neal and his chief lieutenants could boost the firm's ROE, the more generous their compensation packages would become. Now O'Neal had an explicit incentive to do what he wanted to do anyway—transform "Mother Merrill" into an elite Wall Street institution that could be spoken of in the same breath (without irony) as Goldman Sachs. O'Neal was convinced that the way to do this was to push Merrill into new business areas, away from its traditional reliance on the now stodgy business of underwriting and selling stocks and bonds. He told everyone on Wall Street that he intended to take Merrill in the direction of becoming a principal player in the world of trading and as an investor. In 2006 he demonstrated just how to do so and hit the ROE targets set for him.

Even as the compensation committee was drawing up its new rules the previous year, he and his senior executives had begun to take the first steps to deliver what investors and directors wanted. They started by carving out a role for Merrill in what would become (as of that date) the second-largest leveraged buyout in history, the $15 billion purchase of car rental chain Hertz from Ford in December 2005. It collected fees for advising buyout firms Clayton, Dubilier & Rice and the Carlyle Group on the deal, and pocketed more fees for underwriting the billions of dollars of loans and bonds needed to finance the transaction.

But Merrill Lynch also became an investor alongside the two private equity firms, which collectively invested only $2.3 billion of their own money in the transaction, using the debt that Merrill raised to pay for the rest. Within ten months, Merrill had recouped $400 million of its $748 million share of that equity stake, thanks to a series of "special dividends" that Hertz paid its new owners. One of those special dividends was paid out of the proceeds of Hertz's IPO in November 2006, which also generated (not coincidentally) more underwriting fees for Merrill. By the end of 2006, one analyst calculated that the firm had already doubled its money on the Hertz investment—even without taking into consideration the value of all those fees. Merrill beat out every investment bank except Goldman Sachs for the title of most profitable firm on the Street that year, and generated more profits than it had in its history.

Merrill began investing more aggressively alongside private equity firms in other buyouts. When its bankers visited executives at HCA, America's largest for-profit hospital chain, in early 2006, they arrived with a decidedly different kind of pitch, one that HCA wasn't accustomed to hearing from bankers. Instead of suggesting that HCA buy some more assets or even bid for a rival, Merrill proposed that it would put together a "club" of buyout funds—itself chief among them—to take HCA private in a leveraged buyout. After recovering from their astonishment, the HCA honchos agreed to be acquired by a group that brought Merrill together with Bain Capital and KKR. The $31.8 billion deal would finally eclipse the KKR-financed acquisition of RJR Nabisco in 1989 and become the largest-ever such transaction. That's what grabbed the headlines; left unanswered was the question of just how the buyout investors would add value.

"This deal was a real red flag," recalls Marty Fridson, who analyzed the junk bonds being sold to finance the transaction. "What was the plan for improving HCA? Nothing." There were whispers of a secret plan to sell a bunch of hospitals and restructure the company, but nothing was announced or materialized, he says. "Really, they were just buying a company that was selling at a fifty-two-week low and using borrowed money. Basically, they were saying to their own investors, 'There aren't any more beaten-up or battered companies that need us to help fix them. . . . So we're going to buy stocks in the public market with borrowed money and, knowing that stocks go up over time, count on that to help us earn a good return.'" Fridson points out that investors could have done the same thing for themselves by purchasing HCA stock on margin—and they wouldn't have had to pay a 2 percent fee or 20 percent of the profits to the buyout funds. "But that wouldn't have had the allure of being invested in a top buyout firm," Fridson adds with a dash of cynicism. Sure enough, one of the partners—KKR—had marked down the value of its stake in HCA by a third by early 2009, according to a regulatory filing.

Still, in the short run, O'Neal's team was finding other ways to make all these new fees and other earnings from deals such as the HCA buyout generate a bigger bang on the bottom line that had more to do with accounting than investment banking. One logical strategy to boost ROE and make it look more impressive was to reduce the amount of equity on the investment bank's balance sheet; the smaller the number of shares over which those earnings must be divided, the higher the ROE. So the firm spent $9 billion to buy back stock and borrowed to add assets to its balance sheet. Instead of selling its own stock at the top of the market—Blackstone's strategy—Merrill was buying it back.

Rivals and risk managers understood why O'Neal and the board had signed off on the plan. Still, some questioned the wisdom of the strategy, despite the record-breaking earnings Merrill posted quarter after quarter in 2006. "They were counting on the good times keeping going, and that their ability to unwind the risky, high-leverage deals they were doing would always be there," says one hedge fund manager who says he decided to sell Merrill Lynch stock short, betting that its price would decline, after hearing of the stock buyback plan. "Okay, so they maximized their ROE in the short term, but then they took away the capital cushion they might have used to cover any losses when things went wrong." Anyone with any sense, he adds, knew that a reckoning was just a matter of time.

But within Merrill's executive suite, no one seemed to be looking further ahead than the next three-month earnings announcement, at least when it came to risk. As well as the profits and fees associated with the investment in Hertz and other transactions in which it was a principal rather than an intermediary, Merrill had made $7 billion using its own capital to make trading bets, up from $2.2 billion in 2002. In January 2007, a triumphant O'Neal reported "the most successful year in [Merrill Lynch's] history": the investment bank had earned a record $7.5 billion and its ROE hit 20.7 percent, beating Citigroup, Bear Stearns, and even Morgan Stanley. If the company needed its own fleet of Brink's trucks to haul away its gains for the year, so would O'Neal. Although his salary for the year was a relatively paltry $700,000, his total compensation package soared to $48 million. Few within the firm seemed to be concerned that by the time the Blackstone IPO was priced, Merrill was sitting on a record $1 trillion in assets, more than double the level of four years earlier.

Working more closely with private equity firms wasn't the only high-risk business that Merrill Lynch had pursued as part of its quest for a higher ROE. Another source of hefty profits in 2006 and into the first half of 2007 came from a corner of the banking world that was still further away from Merrill's traditional area of expertise and Wall Street's core functions. Merrill had joined what was becoming known as the shadow banking system, moving beyond assisting buyout managers to saddle their portfolio companies with artificially cheap debt loads to help America's homeowners saddle themselves with artificially cheap debt in the shape of mortgages and home equity lines of credit. Drawing on new technology as well as their sales network—they could resell their structured products to clients in the same way that they marketed stocks and bonds—Merrill could earn outsized fees for packaging and repackaging home mortgages and other income-generating assets for resale to yield-hungry investors.

The market for residential real estate had hit $18.4 trillion by the end of 2004, and the mere idea of finding a way to link such a gargantuan market with the ultraliquid debt markets was alluring. Making it possible was the fact that investors were fed up with the low returns that accompany low interest rates and were clamoring for bondlike investments that generated higher yields in much the same way that investment bank shareholders were clamoring for higher earnings and an ROE to match that of Goldman Sachs. Maybe a push into structured finance could keep both groups happy?

The Mortgage Machine

In the summer of 2006, as one team of Merrill bankers and investors prepared the way for Hertz's IPO in a few months' time, another group was negotiating the $1.3 billion purchase of First Franklin, a San Jose, California–based mortgage origination "machine" that had underwritten some $29 billion of home loans the previous year. The motivated seller was National City Corp., a bank based in Cleveland, Ohio; perhaps its executives, like those of Blackstone, were relieved to be getting out of at least part of the mortgage business at what already seemed to be the peak of the market. For its part, Merrill Lynch was an equally motivated buyer. Its mortgage bankers were relieved to have another way of feeding its securitization habit, one the firm had acquired early on in Stan O'Neal's tenure as part of his push to boost risk-taking businesses and ROE.

Securitization was one of the first-generation innovations on Wall Street in the post-Mayday environment, pioneered by Lew Ranieri and his colleagues at Salomon Brothers. "Like all innovations, it started out as a great idea and ended up in craziness, with loans structured in ways that only a few Ph.D.'s can understand, and where there's no obvious purpose for its existence," says Rob Kapito of BlackRock.

Kapito was one of the next-generation innovators in the securitization market during his years at First Boston (later absorbed by Credit Suisse), where he worked for BlackRock's founder, Larry Fink, to develop what was then referred to as the collateralized mortgage obligation (CMO) market in the early 1980s. The CMO was another way to put together a pool of mortgages and make them appealing investments by splitting them into tranches, or slices. The topmost tranche—the senior layer—would pay less in interest but would be of lower risk or higher quality, or perhaps be shorter term in length; in one alternative structure, one tranche would consist of bonds that sold at a discount and paid no interest (zero-coupon bonds), while the other would be an interest-only tranche that would fluctuate in value along with interest rates (as investors prepaid their mortgages, the flow of interest income would taper off). "The whole idea was to give investors a security that met their specific needs— low risk, or high yield, or shorter duration," notes Kapito. By the late 1980s, he adds, the CMO market was starting to run amok. "All of a sudden there were structures out there that didn't make sense, Ph.D.'s making bonds look better than they really were—and they blew up. And we all said, 'Okay, let's get back to something simpler.'"

In the era of rock-bottom interest rates that began in the fall of 2001, when the Fed started slashing interest rates, and reached its peak in June 2003, when key lending rates fell to 1 percent, it made sense for both sides of the market—and for bankers—to take another look the way home mortgages were securitized; at this point, new mortgage origination had hit a record of $3.9 trillion. Many homeowners wanted to refinance their properties, while new buyers were being lured into the real estate market by the combination of ultra-cheap financing and ample liquidity, thanks to the de facto national financing market that securitization had created during the 1980s. Not surprisingly, issuance of mortgage-backed securities soared. They also became more complex, and thus more profitable for the Wall Street firms who were buying these mortgages from savings and loan institutions as well as the growing array of nonbank institutions that had set up shop explicitly to make these loans.

In 2000, mortgage-backed-security-related transactions generated only $690.7 million in fees; by 2006, that had climbed to $2.3 billion. And the average transaction generated $1.8 million in fees in 2006, up from $1.3 million six years previously.[13] Even trading in these securities was becoming a money spinner. All that home-buying activity sent housing prices soaring: the median house price jumped 27.6 percent in the three-year period between 2001 and 2004, when Federal Reserve policy makers decided to begin pulling away the punch bowl full of cheap money. In contrast, for more than a century, housing prices had risen less than 1 percent a year. That rise in valuation triggered still more activity for mortgage originators and parts of the shadow banking system, as borrowers refinanced their mortgages or took out lines of credit secured by the equity that had suddenly appeared.

Merrill Lynch wanted a piece of that business, and O'Neal hired Christopher Ricciardi from Credit Suisse to get it for them. Ricciardi was an expert in collateralized debt obligations, around which the latest incarnation of the mortgage finance market was built. In the latest twist on the CMOs that Kapito and Fink had structured at First Boston in the 1980s, CDOs were divided up by risk level, with higher-risk pieces carrying a higher yield; some tranches carried a triple-A credit rating, awarded by Moody's and Standard & Poor's, and offered a small but still appealing premium over other top-grade securities. Part of Ricciardi's job was to make sure he could get the mortgages he needed in order to structure the mortgage-backed bonds and then the CDOs.

Under Ricciardi, whose efforts ultimately propelled Merrill into first place in the CDO league tables, Merrill Lynch was a particularly aggressive bidder for the mortgages that mortgage originators were churning out at an increasingly rapid rate to meet the insatiable Wall Street demand. By 2004, those mortgage originators were convinced that Merrill was buying market share—in other words, it was paying more than its rivals believed the mortgages were worth just in order to obtain the loans to stuff into their CDO creation machine. By the end of 2005, CDO issuance had nearly doubled from 2004 levels, hitting $271.8 billion.[14]

But 2006 and the first few months of 2007 would mark the peak of this bull market and deliver some of the first major warning signs of the apocalypse that was taking shape here just as in the private equity arena. At least it did for those who, like Lehman's Gelband, were looking for any signs that the boom was really a bubble in disguise. Fitch Ratings, a credit rating agency, slapped an alert on one subprime lender as early as the final months of 2003. By early 2004 the Federal Reserve system (which regulates banks) began picking up signs that the quality of the loans being made by banks, nonbank mortgage originators, and others was deteriorating. That year CDO issuance would peak at $520.6 billion and subprime lending would also reach new highs, five times the level of five years earlier. Lenders were scrambling to feed the Wall Street mortgage machine, even if that meant lending money to people who could present no evidence that they earned enough to keep up payments on the loan or whose credit ratings were wobbly. They developed new structures to enable them to rationalize signing off on these risky mortgages, including "no-doc" loans (also known as liar loans), which didn't require any proof of income, and interest-only loans. Among the most toxic were mortgages with ultralow teaser rates that would reset later at much higher levels that the unwary borrowers often could not afford.

Wall Street itself was doing whatever it could to keep the mortgage machine chugging along. In October 2005, Merrill Lynch had purchased a 20 percent stake in Ownit Mortgage Solutions, one of the growing coterie of nonbank mortgage originators, to keep the mortgages flowing onto its books. Within a few months, Ricciardi had left to launch a specialized CDO investment boutique of his own; he wasn't around to see the value of the mortgage-related assets on Merrill's books spike to a high of $52 billion from a mere $1 billion back in 2002.

The CDOs being structured with those mortgages carried increasingly exotic names that gave no hint of the risky nature of the underlying assets; some hinted at prosperity (Golden Key) or the good life (Costa Bella). All generated lavish fees for the Wall Street firms. Every time another $500 million or so of mortgages were repackaged first into mortgage-backed bonds and then into CDOs, the underwriters picked up $5 million in fees. BlackRock portfolio manager Scott Amero could boycott the deals when he realized what was happening, but that was it. "Look, I couldn't stop the market; I couldn't stop Wall Street from doing what it was doing," Amero says now. "All I could do was stop participating in this Wall Street–style food fight as everyone demanded higher yields."

By the fall of 2006, even Ranieri, the godfather of the mortgage-backed securities market, had sent out an edict banning anyone who worked for him from touching the increasingly poor-quality CDOs.[15] By then, Merrill was negotiating the acquisition of First Franklin, described by the firm in a press release as "one of the nation's leading originators of non-prime residential mortgages" (aka a big subprime lender). Dow Kim, president of Merrill's investment bank, who had taken over the business on Ricciardi's departure and publicly pledged to the team of mortgage bankers that he would keep the good times—and deal flow—rolling, proclaimed his view that owning First Franklin would enhance "our ability to drive growth and returns" higher.

It should have already become clear that subprime lending, whatever it had done for the ROE of Merrill Lynch and other investment banks in earlier days, was more likely to be a source of losses than profits in the years to come. Merrill announced the First Franklin transaction in early September; by December, when they forked over the purchase price and celebrated the closing, the investment bank was in the midst of a spat with its 20-percent-owned mortgage provider, Ownit. Some of the loans that Ownit had fed to Kim's banking team were going sour within months of origination, just as Amero had discovered, and Merrill was pushing the firm to buy back the loans.[16] Ownit, balking, closed its doors in December, just as First Franklin became part of Merrill Lynch. While CDO issuance would keep climbing until the late spring of 2007—about the same time that Blackstone completed its IPO—and would peak at $178.6 billion in that three-month period, it was becoming increasingly clear that hyperaggressive risk taking on Wall Street was no longer a recipe for quick and outsized profits.

The love affair between Wall Street and extreme banking had been intense, exciting, and highly lucrative during the fifteen months that separated the IPO of the New York Stock Exchange and that of Blackstone the following summer. Everyone had been eager to keep the music playing and to continue dancing. But in their mania to generate ever higher returns on equity, Wall Street institutions had succeeded in distorting the financial grid beyond all recognition as they pursued one fee-generating opportunity after another. There was no possible reason for any banker to create a CDO-cubed, as bankers acknowledged in the calm that followed the Wall Street storm of 2008. "But we did it anyway," one former Citigroup banker admits somewhat sheepishly.

The Chickens Come Home to Roost

For centuries, the coronation of a new pope in the Roman Catholic Church was accompanied by an odd custom. As the new pontiff, arrayed in all his glory, walked toward St. Peter's Basilica, the master of ceremonies would halt the procession three times, fall to his knees, and raise a small silver platter on which burned a piece of cloth. "Sic transit gloria mundi," he would intone, urging the new pope to remember that all worldly glories vanish in time. Unfortunately, no one was on hand to remind Wall Street that the laws of nature and the rules of gravity still applied to them. While rising interest rates and the perils of reckless lending to homeowners and leveraged buyout deals alike would be slow to register on the minds of Wall Street bankers (Gelband being one of the rare exceptions), within days of the Blackstone IPO being completed, it was clear that Wall Street was in for trouble.

Wall Street's investment banks and their leaders would end up paying a heavy price for their obliviousness. In March 2007, Bear Stearns proudly proclaimed in a proxy filed with the SEC that its ROE was among the highest of its key competitors. A year later, its ROE had slumped to 1.9 percent and JPMorgan Chase stepped in at the behest of the Federal Reserve to prevent the entire financial system from having to pay too great a price for the risks that Bear Stearns had taken to beat its rivals in the ROE sweepstakes. "I guess, in hindsight, you could say that was a bit of hubris," admits former Bear banker Tom Casson. By the summer of 2007, Merrill Lynch had $31 billion in leveraged loans sitting on its books that it needed to sell, while Citigroup had another $57 billion—but there were no willing buyers. They were stuck owning securities that they had hoped to be able to sell to yield-hungry investors; now that the music had stopped, they were on the banks' balance sheets. "We did eat our own cooking, and we choked on it," John Mack later admitted to FCIC commissioners. One by one, buyout deals—some announced, some still being negotiated—began to fall apart.

The most dramatic change occurred on Wall Street itself. Bear would be absorbed by JPMorgan Chase, Lehman filed for bankruptcy, and Merrill sought refuge in the reluctant embrace of Bank of America, whose top executives reeled at the size of the losses they were expected to absorb along with Merrill's operations. (Eventually, Merrill's losses would be so large as to effectively erase the investment bank's profits for the last eleven years; those at Fannie Mae eradicated twenty-plus years' worth of profits, according to calculations presented by Kyle Bass of Hayman Advisors LP to the FCIC.) Only later did it become public that Bank of America CEO Ken Lewis wanted to use those enormous write-offs as a reason to walk away from the deal, which undoubtedly would have led to Merrill's filing for bankruptcy protection. Only thinly veiled threats from Bernanke and Treasury secretary Hank Paulson kept him onboard, and by the fall of 2009 he had been fired as chairman of the company (by shareholders, at the company's annual meeting) and forced to step down as CEO (by the board of directors).

Lewis wasn't the only casualty. John Thain resigned after negotiating the sale of Merrill, although he soon returned as CEO of CIT Group, a commercial lender that had filed for bankruptcy in 2009. John Mack, exhausted by the effort to save Morgan Stanley, announced his decision to retire as CEO, although he stayed on as chairman. Across Wall Street, bankers whispered that the chaos of the previous two years had contributed to the sudden death at age sixty-one of Lazard's Bruce Wasserstein. The legendary deal maker died two days after being admitted to the hospital with an irregular heartbeat in October 2009. And as for Richard Fuld, who had ousted Mike Gelband for not being a team player? Months after his firm collapsed, a sleepless Fuld spent the evenings wandering through his mansion in Greenwich, Connecticut, a community that was also home to many of the hedge fund managers who were among his firm's biggest and most lucrative clients. "How did it all go so disastrously wrong?" he wondered.[17]

There would be no more record-setting deals from which the surviving institutions could reap big fees. Among the last to collapse was the massive $48.5 billion proposed buyout of giant Canadian telecom concern BCE Inc. by a group that included the veteran buyout firm KKR. Announced only days after the Blackstone IPO, the transaction would have become the largest leveraged buyout in Wall Street history. Instead, it staggered along, half alive, as bankers and buyout firms tried frantically to pull off the deal in the months that followed the demise of Bear Stearns. The events of September 2008 were the last straw; the BCE deal was formally laid to rest two months later.

"Old" and "new" Wall Street suffered equally in the downturn and in the subsequent market chaos that accompanied the "deleveraging," as the process of unwinding all the complex debt instruments and structures was referred to. At the New York Stock Exchange, the lack of leverage started to show up in the shape of declining trading activity by hedge funds, the exchange's most lucrative group of clients. Thanks to that trend (as well as ongoing concerns about competition at home and in the exchange's new European business), NYSE Euronext's shares were trading at $36.62 at the time of this writing, down from their $81 first-day price. Blackstone, for its part, was changing hands for a mere $14.95 by the spring of 2010. Citigroup, a stock worth more than $50 a share in early 2006, could be picked up for less than $1 a share in early 2009. Veteran bankers were fleeing to join start-up firms, fearful of regulation that would limit the scope of their activities or even—heresy!—the size of their bonus checks. Wall Street was on the verge of yet another transformation. What remained unclear was perhaps the most important question of all: whether this would return the Street to its roots as an intermediary or carry it further away from its core function as the money grid.

PART II

GREED, RECKLESSNESS, AND NEGLIGENCE: THE TOXIC BREW

On Tuesday, September 16, 2008, the major players in the unfolding financial crisis gathered in the Oval Office at the White House in order to brief President George W. Bush on the magnitude of the catastrophe that was looming. Treasury secretary Henry Paulson warned the president that, only days after Lehman Brothers had filed for bankruptcy and Merrill Lynch had sold itself to Bank of America in a deal arranged over the course of a weekend to prevent itself from following suit, insurance giant AIG was now teetering on the edge of collapse. "How have we come to the point where we can't let an institution fail without affecting the whole economy?" Bush wondered aloud after listening to his economic and market advisors lobby in favor of a bailout for AIG.[1]

The answer lies in a toxic blend of three elements, all of which were part and parcel of Wall Street by the beginning of the twenty-first century and all of which flowed from the same cultural breakdown on Wall Street itself. Individually, each could have damaged the ability of Wall Street to fulfill its core function effectively and created immense stress on the financial system as a whole, and each is addressed in a separate chapter in this section. But they evolved and reached an apogee almost simultaneously. Together, they would prove to be a recipe for disaster.

All three revolve around human behavior, more specifically on the kinds of incentives that are present on Wall Street to take foolish risks and the disincentives that *should* be in place to keep that risk taking within reasonable limitations. "The mixture of unlimited capital, limited liability, and incentive compensation inevitably led to testing the levels of risk," veteran banker Peter Solomon told FCIC commissioners. "It might be argued that public ownership and the compulsion to increase earnings per share propels employees towards greater risk." Especially when risk taking is so lavishly rewarded: Wall Street's pay packages rapidly became one of the biggest and easiest targets for its critics, not least because they made bankers who often were no more than moderately intelligent human beings into multimillionaires. "I know my limitations; I know I'm bright enough, but I'm no genius," says one former senior banker who toiled at Lehman Brothers and other firms. "Certainly, many of the top guys were only just of average intelligence. But they were being paid for being ruthless and taking on as much risk as possible. The goal was to beat Goldman Sachs at its own game. It was clear to us all that the closer we could come to doing that, the more likely we were to walk away with tens or hundreds of millions of dollars, rather than just become single-digit millionaires."

Even if Wall Streeters were encouraged to behave with reckless abandon, as long as they generated higher and higher returns on equity, it was still possible for the CEOs and directors of any of the investment banks or institutions such as Citigroup to apply a counterweight to any irrational exuberance that might bubble up as a result. Risk management had been a buzzword across Wall Street for decades. The 1998 collapse of Long-Term Capital Management should have highlighted the vital role that risk management could play in helping a financial institution avert catastrophe, both for itself and for the financial system. Alas, while Wall Street firms paid lip service to risk management, in practice they tended to rely too much on models that even their architects admitted were full of flaws. And too often they massaged those models to produce the results that were needed.

Jaidev Iyer now is the managing director of the Global Association of Risk Professionals; his former job was as head of operational risk management at Citigroup. In that role, he watched leaders at Citigroup develop risk management models that produced results showing that the bank's capital was adequate to cover all possible scenarios, with a 99.97 percent confidence rate. "Think about that. What they were really saying was that the capital was adequate for all but three years out of every ten thousand years!" Iyer understands the reason for Citigroup's arrogance. "To get a double-A credit rating from Moody's meant that you had to have that much confidence that your capital was enough to ride out any shocks, and Citigroup wanted that rating" because it would ensure that the company was seen as a stable, solid institution. The problem was that Citigroup was basing its high confidence level on only four or five years' worth of data. "That doesn't begin to be enough to tell you what will or could happen, especially when you are dealing with markets and products and strategies that didn't even exist a decade ago," Iyer says.

Still, just as it was in the interests of Wall Street's bankers and traders to take as much risk as possible in hopes of earning outsized bonuses, so it was in the interests of their top managers and even their boards of directors to egg them on rather than rein them in. When Bear Stearns went public in 1985, Wall Street's investment banks had an average of $258,677 of capital for every employee. If that figure were merely adjusted for inflation, by 2000 it would have been about $540,000. In fact, by that year Wall Street had more than $1 million in capital for every employee, and as much as $3.5 million at some firms.[2] The pressure was on for those employees to make all that capital pay off by finding new ways to earn returns. And the way to do it wasn't by becoming more cautious and risk-averse. Behaving like that wouldn't help Lehman, Merrill Lynch, or Citigroup become the next Goldman Sachs. Rather, they needed to out-Goldman Goldman by taking on *more* risk.

None of that would have mattered had Wall Street had any effective adult supervision. What the money grid needed in order to protect it from the consequences of the greed, ineptitude, and folly within Wall Street's institutions was a team of well-compensated, intelligent, and aggressive outside regulators monitoring what those people were getting up to. And those regulators needed backup from legislators willing to give them both the resources and the political capital they needed to get the job done.

Instead, the money grid got a regulatory mess: a cat's cradle of agencies with responsibilities and mandates that sometimes overlapped and sometimes clashed. All too often, that web of regulatory supervision left large and increasingly significant parts of the markets, such as derivative securities, almost entirely uncovered. And their staff members—whose ambition, in some cases, was to stop guarding the henhouse for less than $100,000 a year and quintuple their annual income by joining the foxes in devising new ways to raid it—too often lacked motivation, direction, or support from their political masters.

"Perfect storms happen when you create the opportunity for them to do so," says Iyer. Teaching future risk managers, he likes to use as a case study the *Titanic*—the "unsinkable" boat that sank less than three hours after hitting an iceberg in the North Atlantic, taking more than 1,500 passengers to a watery grave. Had *Titanic*'s builders and captain not been so convinced that their vessel was unsinkable, had there been enough lifeboats, had the weather been better (enabling the lookout to spot the iceberg), or had the iceberg not brushed alongside *Titanic*'s hull (damaging multiple watertight compartments), the death rate might have been much lower. While it is unclear how many actual deaths can be attributed to the disastrous Wall Street events of 2008 (many bankers tell stories of acquaintances who opted to commit suicide when their firms collapsed or they were laid off as a result of the cost cutting that eliminated more than 300,000 jobs in less than a year), the Street's great meltdown has certainly had a disastrous impact that has stretched well beyond its boundaries, all because the checks and balances that should have prevented the disaster either weren't functioning or weren't even in place to begin with.

Everyone was focused on what Wall Street could do for them, rather than on what they needed to do to maintain the health and integrity of the money grid. The bankers wanted more interesting jobs and career paths, punctuated with lavish paydays. Reaching the corner office, they needed and wanted to beat Goldman Sachs by generating bigger and better returns. Meanwhile, the regulators wanted a peaceful and uncomplicated life; the politicians wanted votes. Collectively, they displayed a reckless indifference to the extraordinary risks that had become obvious before the credit bubble finally began to burst.

To prevent it all from happening again, like a bad nightmare that we can't escape, we need to do more than get angry about how much Wall Street bankers take home each year in their bonus checks. We need to understand how each part of this behavioral dynamic contributed to the crisis, and find a way to re-create effective checks and balances that encourage the right kind of risk taking but discourage some of the rash excesses of recent years.

By the time the final bill is presented to Congress, the cost of the financial industry's bailout may top $2 trillion, by many estimates. The immediate catalyst for that massive rescue attempt may have been fear of what would happen if those who should have protected the money grid allowed it to sink like the *Titanic*. But the reason the bailout, however distasteful, was unavoidable is the same reason that it behooves all of these interested parties to find real solutions to the problems presented by compensation policies, risk management failures, and regulatory shortcomings. In all three, participants placed their own interests ahead of those of the financial system. If Wall Street—the money grid—is to survive future shocks, we can't afford to have that happen again.

CHAPTER 5

"You Eat What You Kill"

At first glance, David Rubenstein and John Whitehead seem like unlikely party poopers. Both men had made billions of dollars by rising to the top of the heap on Wall Street and had overseen two of its most powerful institutions. But as the Street celebrated its record-breaking 2006 and plotted how to earn still more fees and proprietary trading and investing profits in 2007, both Rubenstein, cofounder of the Carlyle Group, one of the largest private equity firms, and White-head, the former senior partner of Goldman Sachs, were worrying publicly about Wall Street's addiction to easy money, particularly in the form of multimillion-dollar bonus days. "Greed has taken over," warned Rubenstein at a private equity conference in the spring of 2007.

The eighty-five-year-old Whitehead was even more forthright in an interview with Bloomberg News reporters that May. He blasted the lavish pay packages at his former firm, where the average em-ployee had pocketed $621,800 in 2006. Goldman's top traders walked away with tens of millions of dollars apiece, and even secre-taries could count on a yearly bonus worth a few thousand dollars. That was double what Goldman employees had earned a decade earlier, before the firm had gone public, and 20 percent higher than 2005. It flew in the face of the fact that Goldman traditionally had been more restrained when it came to compensation than many of its Wall Street peers: its bankers were told firmly that a large part of the value they generated was because of Goldman's brand name rather than their individual efforts. Until they became partners, they learned, they would have to reconcile themselves to viewing the firm's high status as part of their "compensation."

But by 2006, even Goldman seemed to have joined the bonus party. Not only were the denizens of Wall Street—and Goldman Sachs in particular—already far richer than their counterparts on Main Street (the national wage grew an average of 2 percent that year), they were getting even richer at a far faster clip. Whitehead said he was "appalled" that Goldman was leading the way "in this outrageous increase" in Wall Street compensation. He tried to convince Goldman's board to donate $1 billion of its record $9.5 billion earnings for the year to charity; he had even turned to the Bill & Melinda Gates Foundation for help devising some specific proposals about how such a philanthropic donation could be deployed. Goldman's active partners weren't interested, however: their priority was on maximizing returns to shareholders, and a massive philanthropic donation would harm, not help, that cause. Besides, why run the risk of losing its top producers to rivals by donating part of their bonus pool to charity?[1]

Whitehead's concerns were the exception rather than the rule in 2006. Few on Wall Street demurred when they were handed six-, seven-, or even eight-figure bonus checks that year. Anyone outside the Street who voiced concerns about investment banking compensation policies or levels was largely dismissed as an envious crank who either didn't have what it took to survive on Wall Street or had chosen a field that wasn't as lucrative or glamorous as investment banking. Certainly, Dow Kim, co-head of investment banking at Merrill Lynch, likely wasn't second-guessing his own 2006 Wall

Street pay package any more than were the lavishly paid Goldman Sachs bankers of whom Whitehead complained. That year, Kim pocketed a salary of $350,000 for his efforts, a comfortable sum, if modest by Manhattan standards. But Wall Street salaries are just the tip of the iceberg; in gratitude for his 2006 performance, Merrill's compensation committee awarded Kim a cash bonus of $14.5 million and another $20.2 million worth of stock in the investment bank. His total compensation package was worth $35 million, *one hundred times* his nominal salary.[2] But then, Kim was a particularly valuable employee for Merrill Lynch; it was he who, after the departure of Christopher Ricciardi (the man who had pushed Merrill into the forefront of the CDO league tables), kept Merrill's CDO creation machine churning at an ever-faster rate.

The Rainmakers Rake It In

As Wall Street's transformation proceeded during the 1980s and '90s, investment bankers who could dream up products and generate outsized profits were increasingly valuable to Wall Street institutions. According to one study of Wall Street compensation, bonuses and salaries became "excessively high" in the mid-1990s and stayed that way until 2006.[3]

Wall Street put a premium on creativity and innovation, at least within those firms that were intent on beating their rivals and maximizing their profits. The result was a jump in demand for investment bankers with more sophisticated skill sets—the ability to structure, evaluate, and trade junk bond transactions, say, rather than just handle the lower-risk Treasury bond trades. However much Wall Street's elder statesmen might lament the fact, the relentless quest for innovation and new sources of growth inexorably had created a war for talent and fueled runaway growth in salaries and bonuses. Taking a hard line on compensation would have required an investment bank to tacitly acknowledge that they were prepared to forfeit growth—an unacceptable alternative.

At Merrill Lynch in 2006, few employees were more important than Dow Kim, who promised to do whatever it took to keep Merrill ahead of its rivals in the battle to capture the largest possible chunk of the ever-growing market for spinning mortgage securities into CDOs.

In 2006, Merrill created $147.2 billion of new mortgage securities-backed CDOs, up from $90.3 billion the previous years; some of the more complex structures could earn Merrill fees of as much as $15 million for each $1 billion CDO. "Every time we went to meet with someone at Merrill, they would speak in hushed, reverential terms about this guy, Dow Kim," says Mark Vaselkiv of T. Rowe Price. "He and guys like him were leading their firms and Wall Street as a whole into the brave new world of mortgage-based derivatives, and his team worshipped the ground he walked on, it seemed, at least in part because he was making them so much money."

It was only a matter of months before problems surfaced. Even as Kim pocketed his gargantuan bonus, he must have been aware that his CDO assembly line was working almost too well. Kim's division was turning out more mortgage-backed securities than the firm could structure into CDOs and creating more CDOs than it could sell quickly. As a result, more of the increasingly risky securitized assets were left sitting on the investment bank's own balance sheet; by the end of 2006, Merrill had $44.5 billion in mortgages, CDOs, and other related assets sitting on its balance sheet, up from $29.2 billion the previous year and only $15 billion at the end of 2002.[4] At the same time, it was becoming harder and harder to find a counterparty willing to let Merrill hedge the risk that the value of those assets would slump before they could be sold to investors. In May 2007 Kim left the CDO-creation machine he had structured to others to run, and set out to launch his own hedge fund.

Everyone involved in creating, launching, and marketing the CDOs knew that the size of their bonus depended on keeping the machine humming as rapidly as possible. There was no incentive to holler stop.

Outsized Pay and Outsized Losses

But by late summer 2007, it was clear that the securities on Merrill's balance sheet contained a lot of subprime mortgage assets on which the firm would have to record large losses as their values plunged. Sure enough, in October 2007, Merrill slashed the value of the CDOs and subprime mortgages still on its books by an astonishing $8 billion, nearly double what it had estimated only a few weeks earlier. By year-end 2007 it had announced another $11.5 billion in CDO-related write-downs, leaving Merrill with the largest loss in its ninety-three-year history, and the first it had recorded in nearly two decades. In only months, any gains Kim and his team had made for Merrill over the years they had toiled there while pocketing small fortunes for themselves had evaporated. Ultimately, Merrill's losses would be large enough to swallow eleven years' worth of profits.[5]

Not surprisingly, the outsized paydays reported by Kim as well as Wall Street CEOs such as Merrill Lynch's Stan O'Neal—who walked away with $160 million or so of deferred compensation, stock options, and other goodies as well as years of lavish pay packages after presiding over the carnage—touched off outrage and protest that has stretched from the Oval Office right down to the folks in the streets. How could Wall Street folks be paid so well for doing so badly? And what does any banker do in a single year that is worth a $14.5 million bonus—at least, what that is legal?

But the incomprehension is mutual. In the Wall Street view of the world, its inhabitants put in long hours doing increasingly complex jobs that few others have the ability to handle, even if they are willing to tolerate the extraordinary stress and the complete absence of any kind of work-life balance. Naturally, the argument goes, they are well paid for those efforts. Even long after Wall Street's compensation policies became a hot-button issue, some prominent individuals were still willing to defend them. Thomas Donohue, president and chief executive officer of the U.S. Chamber of Commerce, admitted that the bonus payments made by Goldman Sachs and other firms in 2009 may seem "obscene" to the average person—and perhaps even to himself. But Donohue still believed they were justified, he said in early 2010. After all, those lavish pay packages were awarded to "very unique kinds of people," he explained to a reporter. "They are like mad scientists. They are all mathematicians and they are very mobile. They can go to private equity and hedge funds."

One of those financiers, Jake DeSantis, an executive vice president at AIG, spent a year helping to dismantle the company in the wake of its toxic derivatives blowup. When he discovered that Congress, President Barack Obama, and Andrew Cuomo, New York's attorney general, to name just a few, were determined that he shouldn't receive the bonus AIG had promised him, DeSantis blew his stack and published his resignation letter in the *New York Times*. "[We] have been betrayed by A.I.G. and are being unfairly persecuted by elected officials," he railed.

The response was both immediate and predictable. On the *New York Times* website, where DeSantis's letter had been published in its entirety, a steady stream of responses flowed in. Why, wondered a reader named Rob, did DeSantis fail to grasp why his "retention payment" (undisclosed, but potentially around $750,000) was "so offensive to taxpayers in a country where the median family income is approximately $48,000 [?] . . . Please clean out your desk. Security will take your key and show you to the door." Another respondent, Tim Burke, pointed out the flaws in DeSantis's comparison of himself to a plumber who is penalized when an electrician burns down the house that they have both been working on. If both the plumber and electrician were hired by the same contractor and the plumber was present when the electrician "laid a trail of flowing gasoline between all the homes in the neighborhood, then the plumber might reasonably expect his own payment might be at risk." And someone called only IW took a jab at the lifestyle of the rich and (in)famous bankers. "Even if this guy was not in the CDS [credit default swaps] business himself, where does he think that the money was coming from to pay for his 10 cars and house in the Hamptons? . . . I am sure you can survive on $80 a bottle champagne rather than the stuff you are used to, Jake."[6]

DeSantis wasn't alone in triggering public outrage. After bankers lost so many billions of dollars so rapidly, their lavish lifestyles came under closer and harsher scrutiny. In one spectacularly ill-considered move, John Thain, after replacing O'Neal at the helm of Merrill Lynch, cheerfully signed off on a now-infamous $1.2 million redecoration of the firm's CEO suite of offices; the payments included $1,400 for a parchment "waste can" and $13,000 for a chandelier for a private dining room. Then, only weeks before the emergency takeover of Merrill Lynch by Bank of America was completed, Thain rushed through $4 billion in bonuses to Merrill executives, to prevent them from fleeing to a better-capitalized rival, bolting to a hedge fund, or starting their own boutique.

No one on Wall Street doubted Thain's abilities; after all, he won partnership at Goldman Sachs and reinvented the New York Stock Exchange before snatching a kind of victory from the jaws of defeat for Merrill by negotiating the Bank of America deal. And it's certainly true that many Merrill executives—like those elsewhere on Wall Street—had managed to generate profits for their firms despite the extraordinarily difficult market environment and by Wall Street standards deserved some kind of reward. But jaws dropped when word leaked out that Thain wanted Bank of America to recognize his achievement in pulling off the merger by awarding him a $10 million bonus. Few of Merrill's massive problems had occurred on his watch, of course, but Thain had earned $84 million in compensation the previous year; Merrill had even reimbursed him for a bonus that he had forfeited by walking away from his prior job at the New York Stock Exchange to join Merrill. Was Thain tone-deaf to the degree of public outrage? It certainly seemed so; word leaked out that he had calmly informed Bank of America executives, in connection with the proposed bonus, "I really think I'm worth that."[7] (In the end, he didn't get it; belatedly recognizing the degree of public outrage, he waived his bonus for the year.)

Had Wall Street gone insane? Possibly. Certainly the Street's compensation system had gone badly awry, although the problem had less to do with the sheer magnitude of the salary and bonus checks than those on Main Street might have believed. True, those *were* exorbitant, and some people on Wall Street sheepishly admit they had a tough time explaining their jobs and their compensation to family members even before the subprime debacle—and not just because the world of finance was so complex. The real problem was that as Wall Street investment banks had morphed from closely held partnerships into publicly traded entities, their compensation structures had remained stuck in the past. Paying out 40 percent or more of each year's revenue had been the norm within a partnership, and remained standard within the new publicly traded entities. But that compensation model didn't take into account the changes that had occurred within the financial services industry.

Wall Street had once been a fragmented business, with a large number of firms vying with each other for market share and none of them in a position to shake the system to its foundations on its own. But by the late 1990s, Wall Street had become a business dominated by global behemoths formed through a series of mergers. Even when the businesses themselves remained relatively small, as Bear Stearns and Lehman had done, they became critical to the financial system because the linkages between those firms and the rest of the system grew exponentially. At the time of Lehman's collapse, for instance, the investment bank had more than a million derivatives trades outstanding; at the other end of each was another financial institution of some kind.[8] All but the smallest and most isolated Wall Street firm is now "systemically critical," as Fed chairman Bernanke has phrased it; each one plays a much greater role in the health of the system than ever before. In other words, Wall Street institutions had become too big to fail, a phrase that is now repeated endlessly by everyone discussing the future of the financial system. In that environment, risk taking wouldn't be restricted by the usual concerns of collapse—there was no moral hazard. Even firms that publicly proclaimed that they didn't believe a financial institution should be so systemically important were quietly confident that their bank was among that elite group that would receive some kind of assistance from the powers that be should it become necessary.

But while Wall Street had changed, increasing the level of systemic risk, the compensation system was set up in such a way that it encouraged players such as Dow Kim to boost that risk level even further by using leverage or putting a firm's own capital on the line in hopes of generating higher returns for shareholders. "We lost the checks and balances, a system that provided a kind of curb on excessive risk taking, when we moved away from the partnership model," argues John Costas, the former UBS investment banking head. Once, even those who hadn't yet become partners in a firm, the deal makers and traders such as Dow Kim, would have been very conscious of the risks they were running, since it was their own capital—past, present, and future—that was on the line, argue Costas and other Wall Street veterans. In contrast, today's bankers were largely employees, with every incentive to maximize risk taking and few, if any, to curb that risk.

True, many Wall Street employees, from the top all the way down the line, did get a majority of their annual pay in the form of stock, options, or restricted stock, or opted to keep the bulk of their savings in their own firm's stock. At Bear Stearns, for instance, some 30 percent of the company's stock was owned by employees, whether in the form of stock grants made during the annual bonus payment season or direct or indirect investments. Owning stock didn't give bankers the sense of being the company's owners, however. The capital that they were using to place their bets—structuring riskier leveraged loans for private equity clients and riskier CDO structures that would sit on their own balance sheet until they could find a willing buyer—didn't belong to them, they felt. "There was no question that we saw it as other people's money," says one former senior banker.

In fact, employee ownership may have backfired. Just as had occurred at companies such as Enron and WorldCom in the 1990s, employees were motivated to take on more risk rather than curb their risk appetite as the market environment became more difficult. "We wanted to boost the share price" so that their holdings were worth more, the banker says. "The risk managers were the guys that tried to stop us from doing that." Aggravating the problem, that banker adds, was the fact that Wall Street firms increasingly began to see themselves as being more accountable to the demands of shareholders than to the needs of clients, at least at the top levels of the company, where policy was made. "Who were our clients? They were ourselves first—because half the revenue goes to us—and then the shareholders."

Swinging for the Fences

In a nutshell, Wall Street's compensation policies rewarded traders, investment bankers, and even CEOs for taking enormous risks in exchange for enormous profits rather than for keeping an eye on whether the risks they were running made sense for either the firm itself or the financial system as a whole. "It's that asymmetry that's at the heart of so much that has gone wrong," says Seth Merrin, cofounder and CEO of Liquidnet, a next-generation trading system. Merrin began working as a trader when he graduated from college with a political science degree and couldn't even find a job as a waiter. Within a few years, he was running a risk arbitrage desk and pulling down a Wall Street–sized salary, but already he was aware of the gap between the sums he and his colleagues were paid and the value they delivered to customers. "There was such a mystique to Wall Street; everyone saw it as so automated and efficient, as if it were a supermarket," Merrin observes. "But it wasn't, because it didn't have to live on supermarket profit margins. And people on the Street there were paid for generating wider profit margins, not for lowering costs to customers."

In the late 1980s, Merrin decamped from mainstream Wall Street to launch his first "alternative" trading network, an electronic order management and routing system. He assumed that as Wall Street firms came under pressure to cut trading costs, that new discipline would spread to other areas of the business, including compensation. Instead, he saw the rate at which bonuses climbed escalate still further and become more out of whack with compensation policies on Main Street. "Everyone is their own profit center within a Wall Street firm and you eat what you kill," he explains.

Compensation has little to do with how well the investment bank's clients fare, much less how the risk taken by the investment banker to earn those hefty profits affects the financial system. Sometimes it doesn't even matter how the investment bank itself performed, as was the case with Merrill Lynch in 2008, when hundreds of employees pocketed million-dollar bonuses in a year in which the company and the financial system nearly collapsed and were saved only by drastic action. A federal judge who later refused to sign off on a deal between the SEC and Bank of America (which acquired Merrill Lynch and whose top brass agreed to the bonuses) regarding these bonuses wondered aloud, incredulously: "Do Wall Street people expect to be paid large bonuses in years when their company lost $27 billion?" The answer was yes. "There's a big incentive to swing for the fences," says Merrin. "Should they pull it off, they are compensated extraordinarily well." The only people who suffer are those whose direct actions cause the losses. Even then, "if they lose a couple of billion the next year, well, they don't give back what they earned the previous year. All they are is fired and rich."

It's normal in American society for those who are successful to be well paid and for those who become stars in their field to be lavishly rewarded. True, some gripe when a major league baseball team promises a superstar pitcher the equivalent of thousands of dollars for every ball he hurls from the mound during the next three years. But by and large, Americans feel that if someone has performed well, she deserves whatever the going rate is for her services. As long as the pitcher hurls strikes, the grumbling remains muted.

Most of us have few problems when a successful cardiac surgeon makes millions or billionaires such as Bill Gates and Warren Buffett earn a place on the Forbes 400 list of the richest Americans. Perhaps we find that acceptable, or at least tolerable, because it reassures us that if we work hard and succeed, we too will be rewarded with mansions, yachts, art collections, fast cars, and $6,000 shower curtains or lots of whatever money can buy that we hanker after. But the ultra-wealthy can squander that tolerance: all that is required is for the average American to believe either that the wealthy individual has achieved those riches through some kind of fraud or deception or at the expense of the little guy on Main Street. Just ask a corporate CEO convicted of cooking the books or a star baseball player accused of taking steroids. And Main Street's tolerance for Wall Street's riches has always been a bit more fragile than is the case in the entertainment industry, sports, or even the rest of the business world, perhaps because so few people understand why packaging up mortgages and redistributing them is worth so much money. Like him or loathe

him, at least we can all gape at Donald Trump's buildings and understand where the money comes from to fuel his flashy lifestyle. When
it comes to the bankers who structure—and restructure—Trump's
loans, however, the value of their services is harder to grasp for anyone outside Wall Street's magic circle.

But while populist outrage focuses on the dollar amounts involved,
it is actually the incentives at the heart of the compensation system
that produce lethal results such as the near-total collapse of the financial system in 2008. If our hypothetical well-paid cardiac surgeon has
a 90 percent success rate among his patients, saving lives daily, then
most Americans would agree he's entitled to every dollar he earns.
But if he charges more than his peers and has a lower survival rate,
grumbling and outrage will follow, logically enough. And if half his
patients are dead at the end of a year, odds are he won't even be able
to retire to enjoy the income he has earned so far. The families of those
patients will sue him, the medical association may yank his license to
practice and, depending on the degree to which he was negligent, he
could even face criminal charges. There is, built into the medical system, a series of incentives and disincentives that link hard work, skill,
and the results of the surgeon's work to compensation.

Now, let's assume that the compensation policies that prevailed
on Wall Street in 2006 were the rule in medicine. That hypothetical
surgeon would have been paid more for every operation he performed, regardless of the risk to the patient's life. Indeed, the higher
risk the surgery, the greater the fee he could have charged, as long as
the patient survived for at least a few months and as long as he could
convince more patients to go under the knife. Should half of those
patients die the next year, the hospital might fire him, but he'd probably leave with a golden handshake; the odds that he would be sued
or face criminal charges would have been minute. In many cases, he
could move to another hospital or set up his own medical practice
and attract new patients. The problem with Wall Street's asymmetrical

compensation is actually worse. A surgeon has to buy malpractice insurance, footing the bill for his own errors and those of his peers; when successful plaintiffs drive him into bankruptcy, they can collect the balance of any sums owing from the insurer. Alas, Wall Street doesn't have to purchase malpractice insurance; there isn't even a sense that there is a duty of care to the "patient"—whether that patient is the client or the financial system. And so, as we have just witnessed, taxpayers end up footing the bill for Wall Street's errors of judgment.

Of course, there was the FDIC, which was responsible for "insuring" banks and thrifts—or at least their depositors—against the collapse of an institution. But that covered depositors' assets only up to a certain sum; it wouldn't affect banking counterparty relationships. And even so, as an irritated Mike Mayo pointed out to the FCIC in early 2010, FDIC members—the banks—hadn't had to pay anything in the way of premiums for the ten years leading up to 2006, since the insurance fund was believed to be robust enough. That, he said, is "analogous to an auto insurance company not charging premiums until somebody had an accident or a life insurance company not charging premiums until somebody dies."

On Wall Street, most bankers and traders begin doing the bonus math toward the end of the year. But their calculations aren't based on such macro issues as the strength of their company or their earnings relative to the risks they have taken, much less how well their customers have fared after consuming (purchasing) the products they have created or their role in maintaining or hurting the financial system as a whole. They are looking at a far simpler equation: how much money did their business division make, and how much of that did they themselves contribute? "If someone generated $10 million in fees last year and got paid $800,000, they expect that ratio to stay pretty much the same year over year," explains one former senior banking executive. "If that guy goes to $20 million the next year, he expects to be paid $1.6 million at least. And he gets really irritated if his boss tells him he's only going to get $1.1 million."

That compensation system creates a series of perverse incentives, the executive explains. If it costs that individual $2 in (company-paid) expenses to make $1 in revenue, he doesn't care, because he's being paid not to control costs but only to generate revenue. "And if someone tells him he can't spend that much, he'll probably fight for the right to run his business division as he sees fit." Similarly, if half of the business he generates is higher risk and lower quality, that also is irrelevant: every dollar of fee income is treated the same for the purposes of computing compensation. "I used to tell everyone I met that whatever they were earning, if they were on Wall Street, they were automatically overpaid," says the executive. Not surprisingly, he says, few of those he worked with agreed with him, his personal assistant (who took home $100,000 a year plus a bonus) among them.

In that context, it's not shocking that Dow Kim was so well rewarded for boosting Merrill's exposure to CDOs, even as the percentage of those packaged securities containing riskier mortgage loans to subprime borrowers increased every quarter. Joseph Stiglitz, a professor at Columbia University, summed up the conundrum in his testimony to the House Financial Services Committee in October 2008. "The problem with incentive structures is not just the level but also the form," he warned. As they stand, he pointed out, they are "designed to encourage excessive risk taking and shortsighted behavior."

Bonus Junkies

It wasn't always this way. Once upon a time, working on Wall Street was about as lucrative as any other profession that demanded an advanced education and a hefty time commitment from its practitioners, such as the law or medicine. Only a handful of people at the pinnacle—such as J. P. Morgan himself, who was as much a user of the system as a financial industry tycoon than a part of it, earning massive profits from restructuring businesses and entire industries—found Wall Street a ticket to great riches. At Morgan Stanley, bonuses rarely added up to more than a month or two's worth of salary for lucky recipients; a fraction of their annual salary.[9] For every J. P. Morgan, there were thousands of bankers toiling on Wall Street in relative obscurity, well paid but not lavishly so. In the words of former Morgan Stanley partner Fred Whittemore, the goal of investment bankers was to become "respectably rich in a respectable way,"[10] a phrase that was in tune with the 1930s pledge by Jack Morgan (J. P. Morgan's son) to Congress that the House of Morgan was committed to doing "first-class business in a first-class way."

By the 1980s, that approach to compensation seemed to be as much of an anachronism as Morgan Stanley's insistence on being the sole lead underwriter on any deal it did for clients. When Bob Greenhill's merger advisory group began generating hefty profits for the firm, resentment began to build among other partners at what they perceived to be Greenhill's arrogance. "Greenhill should remember that whatever success he has comes from the franchise," one of the firm's partners griped.[11] Increasingly, however, that wasn't true; a star banker, analyst, or trader could become his or her *own* franchise, as Greenhill and later figures such as the controversial technology banker Frank Quattrone proved, hopping from one firm to another with full confidence that their clients would follow them.

Loyalty shifted from the firm and the franchise to the department. Ultimately, at many firms the individual banker or trader owed his loyalty to that department only as long as it was profitable to do so. (The exception was at firms that retained a strong culture, such as Goldman and, until recently, the old J.P. Morgan.) As that process continued, Lou Gelman, the former Morgan Stanley banker, reflects wryly, Wall Street became more about doing *any* class of business for first-class pay, while bonuses had become multiples of annual salaries rather than fractions. "Nobody on Wall Street gets paid for turning down a deal," he says. "What are you going to say at the end of the year when your buddies ask what your bonus was? No one says, 'Oh, I turned down these five deals because I didn't think they were good for our franchise'! Because what was good for the franchise wasn't turning deals down, it was making more money." And that franchise wasn't always the institution itself, but some subgroup within it, from proprietary trading to telecommunications banking. In years when the newly public companies lost money and saw share prices plunge, employees in profitable subgroups still pocketed bonuses. Indeed, it was the payment of just that kind of bonus in 2008 that sparked such outrage.

And as the 1980s drew to a close, the value of those bonuses began to move into nosebleed territory. In the first stages of the bull market, during the late 1980s, the average Wall Street bonus remained less than the average salary—ranging between $14,000 and $15,500 a year. It wasn't until 1986 that researchers studying Wall Street compensation found that the average annual earnings of an investment banker began to exceed those paid to another group of professionals where skill and experience is also prized—engineers.[12] That gap continued to widen. Suddenly, in 1991, the average bonus doubled to $31,100, and continued to climb before peaking (for now, at least) at $190,600 in 2006. Over a seventeen-year span, bonus payouts to Wall Streeters grew at an average annual clip of 11.7 percent; during the same time frame, the rate of growth in the average wage declined from around 4 percent to as little as 2 percent. Interestingly, the total bonus pool grew more rapidly than the average bonus, signaling that the benefits were going to the higher-compensated employees.[13]

The growing Wall Street pay packages both contributed to the soaring cost of living in New York, and then, in a vicious circle, kept increasing to keep pace with that cost of living. By the late 1980s, in Manhattan at least (given sky-high real estate prices and the soaring cost of private school tuition), it was difficult for a senior banker to maintain his or her standard of living on salary alone, especially as it tended to stay relatively flat when compared to bonuses. Back in the 1970s, a Morgan Stanley partner could earn about $100,000 a year and financier Saul Steinberg bought one of the costliest apartments in Manhattan at the landmark building at 740 Park Avenue (formerly occupied by Mrs. John D. Rockefeller Jr.) for a mere $250,000. Today, only a Wall Street CEO or a handful of the industry's top producers can expect to earn the inflation-adjusted equivalent of $100,000 ($525,000 in 2009 dollars) in salary. At Merrill Lynch, for instance, the salaries of the six top executives in 2006 ranged from a mere $275,000 to $700,000 for CEO Stan O'Neal.

The apartment at 740 Park Avenue remained one of the city's most expensive, but someone such as Dow Kim would have had to pay out not two and a half times his annual salary (adjusted for inflation) but closer to a hundred times to purchase such a trophy property. In 2000, when Steinberg sold his apartment, a member of Wall Street's new elite, Blackstone Group's Steve Schwarzman, paid $37 million for it. (Adjusted for inflation, the 1971 purchase price would have been closer to $1.1 million.) Few on Wall Street were even in a position to fork over two and a half times their bonus payment to acquire the apartment. Years of outsized paydays at investment banks, hedge funds, and private equity funds meant that only a few investment bankers were now wealthy enough to contemplate the purchase. (One of Schwarzman's newest neighbors is John Thain, who spent $27.5 million for his own duplex in 2006.)

Why have bonus payments and compensation grown so exponentially? Ask anyone on Wall Street, and you'll get a list of reasons (today likely to be delivered in a rather defensive manner) that sound a lot like those advanced in Jake DeSantis's resignation letter. Bankers, they say, *earn* every penny of their money, thanks to their hard work, skill, and expertise. It's certainly true that the professional life of a

Wall Street banker, like that of a professional athlete, tends to be a Hobbesian one—nasty, brutish, and short. Walk onto a Wall Street trading floor and you won't see too many gray heads among those bent over computer trading terminals. Trading is simply a young person's game (and still largely a young man's game); people burn out at a relatively young age. Even in the world of investment banking, if you're still at it in your mid-fifties, it's either because you're a genius and on the fast track to the CEO suite, or because you don't have anything else in your life that you'd rather be doing.

Tony Guernsey of Wilmington Trust points to another reason for the magnitude of the pay packages. "People want the best service, period; it's no different than having the best plastic surgeon or a barracuda lawyer. If you want to sell your company, you want to maximize the price. You don't care what *he* makes as long as *you* get more than you thought you would." In the late 1990s, one of Guernsey's wealth management clients approached him for help selling the magazine publishing company he owned. Guernsey and his client picked Steve Rattner, then the acknowledged chief deal maker at Lazard and a star media banker, to handle the sale. Rattner sat down with some twenty potential bidders, including S. I. Newhouse of Condé Nast, to discuss the company and the potential deal.

"The first lot of bids came back at between $60 million and $90 million, and Newhouse was the low bidder," recalls Guernsey. Rattner, orchestrating an auction among the five most likely buyers, sent a draft contract back to them with instructions to alter it as they wanted, warning them that any changes they made would represent their final bid. "Four bids came back—and Si [Newhouse] won it with the highest bid of $175 million!" Guernsey says, grinning at the memory. "And that is why Steve Rattner has always earned the big bucks—he brings home the premium valuations for his clients."

Unfortunately for their clients, bankers like that may be harder to find on Wall Street these days. (Rattner himself decamped in 2000 and set up his own private equity firm before becoming President Obama's "car czar.") And as Wall Street has increasingly turned away from agency business—doing business as an intermediary for clients like Guernsey's—in favor of proprietary deal making and trading, it has become more difficult to point to excellent client service as a rationale for such enormous paychecks, especially since many of the bankers who still served clients did so at firms that were ramping up those proprietary activities at a far greater rate.

Tom Casson, the former Bear Stearns banker, still argues that he and his colleagues earned their bonuses by slaving, day in and day out, to deliver excellent results. "I would tell the new guys that anything less than perfection in a spreadsheet or a PowerPoint presentation earned them an F; it's the same standard of success as surgery," he recalls. But would Casson and his peers have had the platform to build a banking business on—much less had the opportunity to be richly rewarded for their undoubted efforts—if it hadn't been for the fact that Bear itself was, as Casson acknowledges, a giant hedge fund? And even if Casson had recognized the degree of leverage on his parent firm's balance sheet, would he have questioned either that or his compensation? "Probably not," he admits. "I would have drawn comfort from the fact that it was the standard across the investment banking industry; everybody was doing it."

In fact, the real reason for the hefty paydays came to have as much to do with the need to retain their top performers as with client service excellence. (Certainly, the very common comparison to other professions, whether surgery or the law, doesn't hold water: although the jobs can be just as grueling and all require advanced education, only exceptional lawyers and surgeons will be able to earn seven-figure compensation packages, and then only after a decade or two of experience.) Increasingly, private equity and hedge funds were cherry-picking the top performers at investment banks and inviting them to move to their corner of Wall Street, where bureaucracy and regulation was less arduous and where, when it came to compensation, the sky was the limit. After all, while Wall Street CEOs were making tens of millions—and suffering lots of headaches—hedge fund managers were raking in billions a year in profits for their firms, and up to hundreds of millions for themselves.

SAC Capital's Steve Cohen, one of the most famous of hedge fund investors, lived in a modest home in Greenwich, Connecticut, for several years, even after leaving Gruntal & Co. in 1992 to set up his own hedge fund. (Early visitors to that home recall that Cohen and his first wife would bring plastic patio chairs into the living room to accommodate overflow guests.) But Cohen's lifestyle changed as his earning power increased exponentially; he pocketed first tens of millions, then hundreds of millions of dollars a year in both management fees and as his share of profits earned for investors in his hedge fund empire. (In December 2009, Cohen's first wife, Patricia, filed a lawsuit claiming that he had hidden millions of dollars of those riches from her during their 1990 divorce. A spokesman for Cohen, whose net worth is now estimated to be around $6 billion, called the allegations "patently false.") That was a lot more than he would ever have been able to make at Gruntal, where he likely would have remained earning single-digit millions. In 1998, Cohen and his second wife, Alexandra, bought a 35,000-square-foot home in Greenwich that gets bigger with every year that passes (the couple requested permission to add an extra 1,100 square feet in late 2008) and offers its inhabitants and guests still more amenities.

Visitors report the Cohen mansion now includes not only an indoor swimming pool and an outdoor ice rink but its own Zamboni machine to keep the ice in pristine shape for impromptu hockey games. Indoors, the plastic chairs have given way to Cohen's art collection, which he has already spent close to $1 billion accumulating. Most famously, that includes a fourteen-foot-long tiger shark pickled in formaldehyde, for which Cohen paid artist Damien Hirst some $8 million; he is said by those who know him to have dismissed the costs associated with renovating and then replacing the molting shark (some $100,000) as the equivalent (in Cohen terms) of a cup of Starbucks coffee. Just as startling as the flaking shark is a work that Cohen has displayed in a frozen container in his own office: a sculpture of a human head made out of freeze-dried blood by the artist Marc Quinn.[14]

Meanwhile, Cohen's protégé David Ganek had already become a second-generation hedge fund wizard. Founding Level Global Investors in 2003, Ganek pocketed more than any Wall Street CEO in 2007 (between $70 million and $100 million, according to estimates by *Trader Monthly*) despite the relatively small size of his $2.5 billion fund. He is one of the new breed of Wall Streeters gravitating to 740 Park Avenue; he paid $19 million for the duplex that ITT chairman Rand Araskog once called home, making him a neighbor of Schwarzman and Thain. These days, 740 Park was looking more like a building designed for Wall Street; it boasted fewer captains of industry and scions of wealthy families among it residents.

For star traders at Wall Street investment banks, Cohen and Ganek were the guys to emulate. They could make far more money doing their own thing than those working at a Wall Street investment bank could hope to do over the course of their working lives. The investment banks were hardly oblivious to the threat: if they hoped to continue not just serving but competing with the biggest hedge funds and private equity funds, they realized they would have to fight to keep their most skilled traders and deal makers within their own walls. That meant rewarding promising newcomers and boosting salaries for a critical mass of veterans, and making sure they had as much capital as they needed to generate profits from proprietary deals and trades. After Vikram Pandit and two other senior bankers left Morgan Stanley to form the Old Lane hedge fund, and top M&A bankers Joseph Perella and Terry Meguid, among others, set up Perella Weinberg Partners LP, the firm's new CEO, John Mack, offered an array of incentives to keep other employees from following their example. (Among other perks, Morgan Stanley's employees were now allowed to invest part of their annual bonuses in the firm's own hedge funds and buyout funds.) John Whitehead, at least, would have preferred Goldman Sachs to call the bluff of employees threatening to decamp to greener pastures. "I would take the chance of losing a lot of them and let them see what happens when the hedge fund bubble, as I see it, ends."[15]

Whenever Wall Street's compensation policies have rewarded short-term profit generation at the expense of the longer-term interests of the firm, its clients, or the system, it has led to abuses, risk managers and other analysts argue. Behind any rogue trader, from Nick Leeson (who brought about the collapse of Barings Bank in the 1990s) to Jérôme Kerviel (who cost French bank Société Générale $7.9 billion in a trading scheme not uncovered until 2007), you'll find a bank employee who had hoped to make a big profit for his bank and a big bonus for himself by taking a big risk, they point out. Instead, the rogue lost control of his trading positions and covered them up, often aided either by colleagues who hoped to protect themselves or by a lack of internal controls at the bank in question.

The controversy surrounding Wall Street investment research is just as dramatic as any rogue trading scheme and shows how compensation policies that offered rich rewards to employees for inappropriate behavior easily became an accepted part of Wall Street. Research analysts working for investment banks knew from the 1980s onward that their output—the analysis of various stocks, bonds, or investment strategies—was valuable to their employers only insofar as their recommendations generated either trading fees or investment banking revenues. A sell rating on a stock could be a career-limiting move for an ambitious analyst if it led to the company's management steering all their business to another firm.

As trading margins shrank, the pressure grew for analysts to help bankers win lucrative underwriting or merger advisory deals. And the analysts seemed eager to play along, realizing that since their rec-ommendations no longer helped the firm make trading profits, they needed to find an alternative way to demonstrate their value. Richard Braddock, CEO of Priceline.com, publicly declared that his firm picked Morgan Stanley to underwrite its 1999 IPO because of Mary Meeker, the firm's influential Internet and technology analyst. Meeker obligingly slapped a buy rating on Priceline.com and kept it there even as the firm lost 97 percent of its value over the next three years. At Merrill Lynch, Henry Blodget didn't downgrade a stock that he privately acknowledged to be a "piece of junk" until after the com-pany in question had completed an acquisition on which Merrill earned advisory fees. At the end of 2000, Blodget sent an e-mail to his bosses at Merrill trumpeting his role in earning some $115 mil-lion in banking fees that year; he was rewarded with a big boost in his bonus, earning a total of $5 million.

That e-mail, along with thousands of others, were accumulated and studied by then New York attorney general Eliot Spitzer and his staff during their probe of the investment analysis business in 2001 and 2002, revealing a pattern of questionable judgment on the part of the analysts and their bosses. Perhaps the most dramatic example was the case of Jack Grubman, the star telecommunications analyst at Salomon Smith Barney (a division of what is today known as Citi-group). Grubman earned as much as $20 million a year in salary and bonus and helped his firm pocket at least $1 billion in fees arranging mergers or underwriting stock and bond issues for the companies he followed. But a CEO who couldn't generate lucrative deal fees for Salomon Smith Barney found it hard to get Grubman to pay attention, much less communicate the company's story to potential investors, al-though that, theoretically, was the heart of Grubman's job. "I tried to go to Jack and say we're the best of our peers and we're solvent, but I couldn't get in his office," Howard Jonas, chairman of IDT Corpora-tion, told a *New York Times* reporter at the time the research scandal finally surfaced. "If you had big merger-and-acquisition opportunities, then you had a chance."[16]

A host of the companies that Grubman *did* pay attention to and give buy ratings to—including Global Crossing, McLeod USA, and, famously, WorldCom—ended by filing for bankruptcy protection. (Until Lehman Brothers filed for bankruptcy six years later, World-Com would remain the largest U.S. bankruptcy in history, involving $41 billion in debt and $107 billion in assets.) Grubman, along with other Salomon Smith Barney bankers, had advised WorldCom CEO Bernie Ebbers—now serving a twenty-five-year prison sentence for fraud and conspiracy—on dozens of deals, reaping fees for the investment bank. He continued to recommend the stock to investors right up until days before the company reported a $3.8 billion accounting error. Those on Wall Street may have been blasé about Grubman's ongoing bullishness when it came to telecom stocks—they knew that his firm wouldn't have stood a chance of winning the lucrative banking mandates had he cooled off—but even they blinked in astonishment at Spitzer's ultimate disclosure: a series of e-mails demonstrating a link between a sudden about-face when it came to AT&T's stock (just in time for Salomon Smith Barney to win a top spot in the underwriting syndicate for stock in the wireless phone division, about to be spun off as a separate business) and his own personal financial interest. Specifically, Grubman agreed to raise his lukewarm rating on AT&T to a buy in exchange for help getting his toddler twins into the top-tier preschool at the 92nd Street Y—that help, it turned out, involved a $1 million donation from his firm.

Nearly everyone was happy. The toddlers were admitted to preschool, the Y got its donation, AT&T got its buy recommendation, and Salomon Smith Barney won a place alongside Goldman and Merrill as a lead underwriter for the AT&T wireless transaction, and thus a share of the fees that would help boost its status in the year-end league table rankings of each investment bank's market share.

Grubman and other exorbitantly well-paid Wall Streeters who have run afoul of specific securities laws, such as Mike Milken, will never work on Wall Street again. But they still got to keep the majority of their compensation for the years they spent there, and can, if they choose, parlay their experience into other jobs in the corporate world.

When Dow Kim left Merrill Lynch in early 2007, it was to set up his own hedge fund. Normally, that would have been simple; even raising $3.5 billion in assets would have been relatively straightforward had Kim opted to leave midway through 2006 and waived his massive bonus. But his departure came just a few months too late; by the time he began trying to raise money, the problems with the products he had constructed for investors and that now were stuck on Merrill's balance sheet were apparent. Merrill itself, which had promised to back Kim's fund at the time of his departure, quickly reversed that pledge only months later. As of early 2010, Kim hadn't raised enough from outside investors to formally announce the formation of his fund or begin deploying capital. On the other hand, he hasn't had to sacrifice any of the profits he made by structuring subprime CDOs, except for the value of any stock in Merrill Lynch that he still owned. (Kim was an active seller of Merrill Lynch stock in the year or two before his departure as his compensation levels climbed, according to insider-trading filings with the SEC.)

Efforts at Reform?

Several Wall Street firms began to tweak their compensation packages in late 2008 in response to the public outrage, introducing the concept of the clawback to investment banking pay packages. The first and most obvious step was for CEOs and other top executives to waive their bonuses for the year, and one by one, the announcements appeared. In some cases, those announcements were accompanied or rapidly followed by new pay policies, such as John Mack's proclamation at Morgan Stanley that in the future compensation would be tied to "multi-year performance and each employee's contribution to the Firm's sustainable profitability."

The ten-page brochure published by Morgan Stanley the following spring spelled out the basic tenets of this new approach to pay, including a commitment that 75 percent of compensation would be in the form of stock and that those stock awards to senior executives would be "at risk" for three years and would depend on the firm continuing to earn a solid return on equity, generate profits for shareholders, and perform well compared to its peers. Moreover, an employee who "engages in certain conduct detrimental to the Company or one of its businesses—causing, for example, the need for a restatement of results, a significant financial loss or other reputational harm"—up to three years after the compensation is first awarded could have any bonuses clawed back by the firm.

Before 2009 was over, Goldman, embroiled in a public relations nightmare that had a lot to do with plans to pay out what might be record bonuses to its own team, announced something roughly similar. Goldman's top managers wouldn't get a penny of cash in their bonus checks, only stock. Moreover, those shares would remain "at risk" for *five* years, longer than those issued by Morgan Stanley as bonus payments. Other firms devised even more creative new policies. At Credit Suisse, illiquid assets such as leveraged loans and commercial mortgage-backed securities were placed into a $5 billion fund, shares of which were then awarded to executives as part of their bonus. The fund, set up in January, had already gained 17 percent by August 2009, Credit Suisse told its banking team. (The bank's stock, however, had soared 86 percent on the Swiss stock market in the same period.)

To a large degree, these initiatives recognize and respond to the degree of public outrage at Wall Street's lavish paydays of the kind displayed during congressional hearings when Representative Henry

Waxman displayed a chart showing the growth in the pay packages awarded to Lehman Brothers CEO Dick Fuld. Fuld, sitting at the witness table, quibbled with Waxman's calculation that he had earned $484 million between 2000 and the firm's collapse in 2008, arguing that it was closer to $250 million, mostly in Lehman stock. "Is that fair?" Waxman demanded (largely rhetorically) of Fuld. While getting rich, Fuld and his colleagues "were steering Lehman Brothers and our economy towards a precipice." Overblown and hyperbolic statements on the part of other representatives and senators—many of whom had been quite happy to accept donations from Wall Street during its glory days—followed thick and fast. Proposals for salary caps at firms that had accepted bailout money that they hadn't been able to repay were adopted; regulators and legislators were kept abreast of all bonus payments.

To some on Wall Street, the actions and rhetoric emanating from Washington were entirely logical. "I say this as a citizen: I think that what is going on is fair," argues Leon Cooperman, the hedge fund executive and former Goldman Sachs partner. "If business looks to government to moderate and control the downside risk, then the government has the right to control and moderate the reward. So we now need to get used to living in a world where that kind of stuff will happen and where government is going to be more interventionist." To others, it was an overreaction. "I grew up without much money, and my goal in being on Wall Street was to make $15 million or so over a number of years and then leave," says Casson frankly. "If anyone had tried to put a lid on how much I could earn in exchange for all my work, I would have looked for somewhere where my earnings weren't limited."

Most of the compensation reform schemes that were proposed or announced overlook the fact that past efforts to rein in greed have had all kinds of unintended consequences. After a Chinese wall was created between investment banking and research, as part of the reforms the followed Spitzer's investigation and the Grubman scandal, bankers no longer had a voice in which companies analysts covered or even which analysts were hired. Not surprisingly they balked at subsidizing the research division. Analysts' compensation was cut in half; many fled to hedge funds.[17] Those reforms, while theoretically creating less-biased research, didn't result in the creation of better quality research, at least not in a way that was easily accessible to the general public. "Come on, Mr. Obama, how are you going to attract anyone of the right caliber who wants the headache of running these firms, if you put these salary curbs in place?" wonders Guernsey, a private banker who has worked with many of Wall Street's top deal makers. "I have never overpaid for someone who is a top performer. Pay is how those top performers are recognized, traditionally."

Address the Cause, Not the Symptoms

The biggest problem with the various compensation reform initiatives is that they tackle the surface issues, not the root causes of the problem. Salary caps, for instance, are likely to be effective only in driving the most skilled Wall Street veterans out of those parts of the financial markets that are now being most rigorously monitored by lawmakers and regulators and into overseas institutions or other segments of Wall Street over which the government has little control. Those hedge funds that have ridden out the storm so far, for instance, continue to reward their employees as lavishly as ever. In the spring of 2008, Fortress Investment Group gave thirty-eight-year-old Adam Levinson $300 million in stock in the publicly traded hedge fund to persuade the star trader to stick around, despite the fact that the massive stock grant diluted the value of the holdings of other, public investors.[18]

True, in some cases investors have succeeded in pushing back management fees from 2 percent of assets to a more modest 1 percent and "persuading" managers to accept a smaller chunk of profits than the traditional 20 percent or 30 percent. In London, the three top executives at GLG Partners voluntarily cut their own salaries to $1 each, although they remain investors in their own funds and will continue to collect a share of any profits. One of the top hedge fund groups, Renaissance Technologies, is waiving its 1 percent fee on a newer fund that has performed poorly, people familiar with the industry say. Another large hedge fund group plans to collect its "incentive" fee at the end of three years on the net result of that three-year performance, rather than at the end of each year on what the fund had earned that year, says Patrick Adelsbach, a principal at the hedge fund research and advisory firm Aksia LLC. That is a big departure from the classic hedge fund compensation model that rewarded its managers at the end of each year for what had happened in the previous twelve months, which saw managers transform paper profits into cash fees thanks to the wonders of mark-to-market accounting. "Marking," or putting a market value on a hedge fund portfolio on December 31 of each year, gives hedge fund investors an idea of how their managers are performing. But the manager collects 20 percent or more of any gains in the value of that portfolio as a performance reward, regardless of whether or not that increase in value proves lasting.

Even when a risky transaction in that hedge fund portfolio later went sour, there was no way to claw back what had already been paid out in fees. All that investors could do was limit future manager paydays until the fund had recouped those losses. "A lot of managers found a way around that, too," says a grim-faced Cooperman. "A lot of them, rather than working to make that money back, just say, 'I quit,' and hand the capital back to investors. If you tell me as an investor that you're going to work for nothing and then when you do have losses just quit on me, that's just not right." Cooperman takes an even dimmer view of the increasingly popular strategy of shutting

down one money-losing hedge fund partnership, only for its manager to reopen for business under a new name in less than a year.

If salary caps succeed only in driving the most talented bankers
to parts of the market that government edicts don't reach, they won't
get to the heart of the problem. Nor do policies that end up discour-
aging bankers and traders from taking any kind of risk whatsoever
by making it too risky from a career and compensation standpoint.
And while clawbacks are at least a step in the right direction, it's a
retroactive approach to solving the compensation conundrum. Of
course it would be wonderful to be able to recoup past bonuses paid
to people whose poor decisions and lack of attention to the risk associated with what they were doing end up bringing the financial
system to its knees. (After all, murderers can't collect life insurance
premiums or otherwise inherit anything from their victims.) But it
would be better still if the bright minds on Wall Street and in Washington could combine to devise a compensation system that rewarded the denizens of Wall Street for avoiding such catastrophes in
the first place.

Part of doing that boils down to defining more clearly who their
clients are. Ever since investment banks began going public, they
have emphasized the degree to which their interests are aligned with
those of their investors by pointing out the large stock holdings of
their senior executives and the degree to which bonuses are paid out
in stock. Having at least some "skin in the game" is seen as the goal,
as Peter Blanton, a veteran banker, recalls from his days at Credit
Suisse. "When the merchant banking team put together a deal, the
folks that blessed it had to put some of their own personal capital
into it as well as putting their names on the due diligence. It was a
policy. There was a sense that without having skin in the game, we
were just agents, without a long-term stake in the outcome." That attitude wasn't confined to the deals the bank did, but applied to their
governance policies more generally. Gary Cohn, president of Goldman

Sachs, told the *Wall Street Journal* in a 2009 interview that in his opinion, paying employees in Goldman Sachs stock is the "ultimate clawback." "When I got paid three years ago in $240 stock and it was trading [at] $54 or $53 ... it certainly felt like a clawback to me," Cohn insisted. "We have always had ... the ability to withhold stock or take it away for anything ... done illegally [or] immorally."[19]

But if a heavy reliance on stock ownership was the foundation of a healthy compensation policy, then why did Bear Stearns and Lehman Brothers collapse? In both firms, from the CEO's suite down to the most junior bankers, ownership of the company's stock was encouraged and viewed by all as the best way to build wealth. And yet at both firms, groups of traders and investors were taking the same kind of outsized and risky bets as Dow Kim, who also collected more than half of his salary in the form of stock in Merrill Lynch.

By the time that bankers across Wall Street received their record pay packages at the end of 2006, interest rates had been climbing for nearly two years and the rate of economic growth had begun to slow amidst concerns about sky-high energy prices. The subprime lending cloud had begun to take shape overhead. And yet Wall Street, in the early months of 2007, was cranking out *more* mortgage-backed securities in the form of highly structured CDOs, not fewer. And those CDOs were packed full of securities that carried *more* risk, not less. "To all intents and purposes, whether you got paid in cash or stock, the principle remained the same," says one former senior banker. "You were earning bonuses for maximizing fees, and the higher the fee income, the higher revenues and profits rose, and the better the ROE looked compared to your rivals, and the better the stock price did. It's all the same thing: pay was tied to profits." And at the end of 2007, the compensation on Wall Street hadn't fallen nearly as fast as some of the investment banks' stock prices. It's a cliché on Wall Street to say that financial markets are all about greed and fear; compensation, however, had become a matter of fearless greed in the mental calculus of at least a significant minority of traders and bankers eager for another record bonus day.

As long as compensation remains tied to competitive metrics—how much Bank A's return on equity exceeded Bank B's, or whether Bank B's share price grew more rapidly than that of Bank C—it won't matter whether an employee's bonus is 50 percent or 75 percent in stock. "One of the problems is that people lost sight of who their customers are, because there were so many of them, and instead focused only on delivering what their shareholders demanded of them," says a former senior banker who has now left the industry. "But do shareholders always know best? Is a rising stock price always the answer to every question?"

An asymmetrical compensation scheme that lavishly rewards excessive risk taking but fails to effectively punish failure is toxic in any environment, but when it isn't balanced by some broader consideration—the risks to the company, to investors, and to the financial system's health—then it becomes even more lethal. What happens, for instance, when a banker or trader is rewarded for his or her success in passing on a risky investment to a customer? Unless the problem is systemic—spread across Wall Street as a whole—the odds of such a problem wreaking long-term havoc on an investment bank's stock price are low. And if that banker or trader is otherwise a star, generating lots of fees from risky products of which only a few blow up (even though many others fare far less well than the banker or salesman had promised), the odds of that individual facing a clawback—especially in a more normal Wall Street environment— are slim. After all, only a minority of mergers and acquisitions end up being successful, generating long-term value for shareholders of the companies doing the deals, and yet the bankers who propose, structure, and help to execute these transactions are rarely held up to scorn.

One of the most novel proposals for revising Wall Street compensation revolves around an attempt to bring back the spirit, if not the reality, of the era of partnerships when, as Lehman alumnus Peter Solomon recalled, the partners of a big investment bank sat around in one large room, literally or figuratively peering over each other's shoulders to ensure that their peers weren't taking too many risks. It may not be possible or even desirable to transform today's publicly traded financial institutions back into private partnerships. In a paper written for a conference held at the University of Seattle Law School, two law professors from the University of Minnesota put forth the proposal that any banker earning more than $3 million a year should be required to sign a joint venture agreement with their employer. "That would make them personally liable for some of the bank's debts," Claire Hill and Richard Painter conclude in the paper—and hopefully instill in them a greater awareness of the consequences of their risk taking. The duo point out that reckless risk taking is a Wall Street tradition, and one that has claimed the "lives" of veteran firms before. "Michael Lewis's description in his 1989 book of the term used for a star trader—a 'Big Swinging Dick'—reflected . . . an ethos in which investment bankers engaged in risky conduct and were no longer personally responsible for their actions."[20] Sure enough, a rogue trading scandal followed shortly after Lewis's book was published. Despite a boost from Warren Buffett, Salomon Brothers' brand name was damaged beyond repair.

The two law professors point out that most of the existing proposals already out there—whether the prospect of vanishing bonuses or tying pay to the performance of not just the banks but also its debt securities—don't go far enough. By and large these still involve "no risk of loss for bankers—only forgone gains." What is needed, they argue, is a proposal that is based on a different perception of banking as a "type of socially useful yet potentially 'ultrahazardous' activity that should involve . . . some measure of strict personal liability.[21] The limited partnership proposal is just part of their suggested reforms, which also include the proposal that bankers can shield only $1 million of their annual compensation from creditors in the event of their firm going bankrupt—the rest would be "assessable." That means that if a banker is paid a $3 million stock bonus and his firm later goes bankrupt, $2 million of that stock—valued at the time it was granted—would be assessable, meaning the banker would have to pay its full market value at the time of issuance, or $2 million, to the firm's creditors.

Another proposed solution involves an approach that the Credit Suisse initiative hints at—putting Wall Street firms on the same side of the table with *all* their clients, not simply their shareholders or those that pay them fees. "If you're going to make a loan, or package some mortgage-backed securities and sell it, shouldn't your rewards be tied to the long-term success of the securities that you put your company's name on and sell to clients?" suggests private equity manager Tom McNamara. "You get paid when the things you sell pay off for the people that buy them, not when you sell them."

Paying out employee bonuses on the basis of deals that have only just been completed—long before it is possible to determine whether or not they were as rewarding for investors and other clients as they were lucrative for the institution selling or structuring them—is at the heart of the problem, in the eyes of many Wall Street veterans. Investment bankers shouldn't be richly rewarded unless their clients also make money, and certainly shouldn't be compensated when deals prove disastrous, whether for a client, the investment bank, or particularly for the financial system as a whole. One lawyer points to a structured product created within one part of an investment bank: the desk that created it earned a fee, but then another group of traders created a derivative structure atop the original product that blew up, generating a big loss for another part of the same firm: "No one was tracking what happened across the various desks, so this product generated fees for people, even though it was utterly dysfunctional," the lawyer says.

McNamara, like many of the investors who have been consumers of the products that Wall Street generates, argues that investment banks should find some way to tie the success of the banker or trader not just to fee generation or corporate profits but to the success of their clients and the system's well-being. It's a view that is shared by Columbia University's Joseph Stiglitz. "Those who originate mortgages or other financial products should bear some of the consequences for failed products," he argued in his congressional testimony. Specifically, he recommended that the institutions originating mortgages be required to hang on to 20 percent of any transactions they undertake. Stiglitz and others suggest that if that philosophy was extended to all of the transactions across Wall Street, with investment firms being required to retain a stake in every leveraged loan, junk bond transaction, or structured product that they sell, Wall Street would have a greater interest in maximizing not only the dollar value of the deals it does but the quality of those transactions. In 2008, many of the products that caused meltdowns within Wall Street's investment banks were those that they had hoped to sell on to other investors but which ended up stuck on their balance sheets with no buyers in sight. "Isn't it ironic?" muses BlackRock's Rob Kapito. "These were the same securities that they wanted to sell to us, the buy-side institutions. If they'd succeeded, everyone would be talking about how well they'd done and how successful they had been." And the buy-side institutions and their own investors—401(k) plan participants, pension funds, individuals—would have faced even larger losses.

Questions of Value

Wall Street's core function may be that of a utility, but it is an unusual sort of utility. Rather than transmitting clean water or reliable electricity supplies, it redistributes money throughout the financial system—and money is a far more exciting commodity than water or electricity. If you're running a power-generating station, it's easy to accept that what has value is the company you work for, rather than the commodity you are transferring from point A to point B. Certainly, if your bosses offered to pay you in kilowatt-hours, odds are that you would decline politely. But Wall Street transmits money, and a bit of every dollar that flows through the financial grid sticks to different players—the investment banks, trading firms, brokers, money managers, et cetera—in the shape of fees. Given that money is the one commodity that can be readily exchanged for any other tangible good someone might want, from food and shelter to a pickled shark by Damien Hirst or a trophy apartment on Park Avenue, it's hardly surprising that for those who live on Wall Street, life revolves not just on transferring money but on finding ways to scoop up a bit more of the stuff for themselves.

Greed is an emotion as old as time, and it's asking too much of human beings to expect that those on Wall Street should take as detached a view of the commodity that they see pass through their hands as the manager of a power-generating station takes of kilowatt-hours. The Archbishop of Canterbury, the spiritual leader of millions of members of the Anglican Communion, suggested that investment banking bonuses should be capped, and called on their recipients to repent, arguing that "people are somehow getting away with a culture in which the connection between the worth of what you do and the reward you get [is] obscure."[22] But turning bankers into individuals who look down on money may be not only impossible but undesirable— after all, the money grid's job revolves around how to make the flow of capital more efficient and profitable for *all* concerned. The key word is *all*—while the bankers can't corner those profits, they also shouldn't be totally disinterested. Perhaps the appropriate strategy is to bring financial professionals to think of their jobs in the same way that lawyers view the law, or doctors the profession of medicine. Those groups certainly hope to earn large sums as a reward for years of education and training, but they recognize and acknowledge that their self-interest goes hand in hand with a higher public and social

interest, one that is explicitly acknowledged in medicine's Hippocratic oath and its cornerstone, the pledge to "do no harm." Placing
one's own financial interests ahead of the interests of a patient or client can get a lawyer disbarred and force a doctor to relinquish her
medical license.

The solution isn't to take a hammer to the current model, as de-
fective as it may be, by imposing salary caps or punitive tax regimes.
Rather, if Wall Street is to reach a point where its practitioners abide
by their own version of a Hippocratic oath, what's needed is a longer-
term strategy to tie compensation more closely not only to returns—
whether short-term or long-term—but also to success in generating
risk-adjusted returns and success in bolstering the health of the financial system as a whole. A first step in that direction is to be sure
that even if Wall Street's firms pay out record sums in bonuses in the
future (bonuses rose to $20.3 billion of the financial industry's esti-
mated 2009 profits of $55 billion, the New York State Comptroller's
office announced), Wall Street compensation committees are taking
risk as well as return into the equation when designing policies and
fixing annual bonus levels. Of course, that assumes that those boards—
and Wall Street—have a firm handle on what risk really is and how
best to measure and control it.

CHAPTER 6

The Most Terrifying Four-Letter
Word Imaginable

There are known unknowns. That is to say, there are things that we know we don't know. But there are also unknown unknowns. There are things we do not know we don't know."

When then Defense Secretary Donald Rumsfeld delivered that cryptic pronouncement at a February 2002 press briefing, he was commenting on the instability in Afghanistan, not Wall Street. And yet within a few years, the phrase "unknown unknowns" had become one of the most popular ways to summarize all that had gone wrong in the investment banking world. Somehow it was all the fault of the "unknown unknowns": Wall Street CEOs, individually and collectively, had misperceived, misunderstood, and mismanaged the risks associated with their business and the financial markets because of factors that no one could have anticipated, much less avoided. Yes, these apologists agreed, Wall Street had failed the ultimate risk management test, but that was due not to greed or arrogance but just to the extreme nature of the risks themselves. No one on Wall Street, surely, could have imagined and planned for the sequence of events that followed the endless and constantly escalating quest for fees, they argue. Certainly, that's how Lloyd Blankfein characterized the events, in a verbal sparring match with FCIC chair Phil Angelides. But when he defined them as being akin to a hurricane in their ability to be predicted and controlled, an exasperated Angelides (himself the former head of a large California pension plan) shot back, pointing out that while hurricanes were defined as "acts of God," the financial crisis was the result of actions and inaction by human beings. That's convincing, but it raises one more question. Is Wall Street's conviction that they couldn't have prevented what happened to be blamed on self-deception, wishful thinking, or blindness?

In Chuck Bralver's eyes, it comes closer to being the latter. The very idea of flawless risk management makes him laugh out loud—in his opinion, this would require an infallible crystal ball. Still, he remarks, Wall Street appears to be oblivious to the ways that the changing nature of its business created new kinds of risk. Bralver, a former senior banker with Oliver, Wyman & Co., now oversees the Center for Emerging Market Enterprises at the Fletcher School, Tufts University's graduate school of international affairs. In both of those roles he has spent a lot of time thinking about the nature of risk and the discipline of managing risk. "True, each separate event that led to the crisis, or that happened as a result of it, had an extremely low probability of ever occurring at all," Bralver says. "Then they all happened—and they all happened simultaneously."

But that doesn't give Wall Street a get-out-of-jail-free card. Even if bankers can't be blamed for their failure to predict this perfect storm, they still could have developed robust risk management policies to protect their institutions and the financial system from the "unknown unknowns," Bralver argues. One of the justifications for the increasingly lavish pay packages awarded to Wall Street executives was the increased complexity and scale of the businesses they were running. "It's not an accident that this happened after the changes that had transformed Wall Street [into a place] dominated by very, very large institutions that were no longer owned exclusively by the same people making the decisions about what risks to take," Bralver says. "It's possible that some of these organizations had become too large and complex for the kinds of risks they were taking, or that the risk management processes hadn't kept pace with the risk."

But why not? Describing the market cataclysm as a "perfect storm" is a great sound bite and helps the folks on Wall Street convey both the nature and the magnitude of the events for critics on Capitol Hill and Main Street alike. But surely the same giant leaps forward in computing power and financial wizardry that made possible the creation of instruments such as a synthetic CDO-cubed structure or a credit default swap also made it feasible to ensure that those products were doing what they were supposed to and distributing risk more broadly throughout the financial system. At the very least, shouldn't it have been possible to gauge when these new products were being used in ways that *increased* the risk Wall Street was taking to dangerous levels? Or if the markets had become too fragmented, too complex, and too fast-moving to make that possible, then shouldn't someone somewhere have been prepared to step in and say, "Wait a minute—we can't accurately gauge the risks associated with what we're doing"? And then to ask the next logical question: If we can't grasp the nature of those risks, should we be courting them in the hope of earning returns?

LTCM and Systemic Risk

The events surrounding the collapse of Long-Term Capital Management (LTCM) in 1998 gave Wall Street an early warning of the perils associated with "unknown unknowns." No one at the beginning of 1998 had expected a series of unexpected and nearly simultaneous events culminating in the Russian government defaulting on its bond obligations; because no one considered such a string of events to be at all probable, no one seriously pondered what might happen to LTCM as a result of the bets it was making and the degree of leverage it was using if those events occurred. As it turned out, LTCM's losses were so gargantuan that they threatened not only the firm (that would have been only normal) but all of its counterparties—which included nearly every major investment bank in the United States—and the financial system itself. Many of those firms didn't realize the magnitude of the risks they had been running until it was far too late.

In the wake of the LTCM crisis, which should have delivered a salutary lesson about the dangers posed by excessive leverage and "contagion," Wall Street didn't take a step back from the daily hubbub to do a forensic audit of the risks to the financial system that the hedge fund's problems had exposed. The immediate danger over, Wall Street returned to maximizing its fee revenue, profits, and bonuses and too often shrugged off the concerns of those who, like Lehman's Mike Gelband or New York University professor Nouriel Roubini (who began warning of the real estate bubble as early as 2004), saw a new "perfect storm" taking shape on the horizon. When it came to managing risk, it was the risk of losing fees or market share rather than the risk of a blowup that weighed on the minds of most bankers and traders. Worrying about risks that seemed remote was in no one's interest.

In early 2008, UBS produced a report chronicling a series of errors of omission and commission to explain to its shareholders how it managed to lose a record $18.7 billion on its subprime structured product businesses in the previous year. UBS management set the stage for the debacle by deciding to act on the advice provided by external consultants; the best way to catch up to and overtake its largest competitors in key business areas—notably Goldman Sachs—was by expanding its activities in structuring and trading products based on subprime and adjustable-rate mortgages. What neither the consultants nor UBS management took into consideration were the extra risks associated with following those recommendations or how the bank might manage those risks.[1]

The report lays out in chilling detail the myriad opportunities that UBS bankers at all levels had to gain insight into the looming credit crisis, all of which were overlooked or ignored. In one case, UBS created the position of senior risk manager in the bank's fixed-income division in 2006. Would that individual have been able to perceive the risks that were looming? Could he have convinced superiors to rein in their risk taking? Would the bank have acted quickly enough to avoid large losses? The questions are academic: as of the summer of 2007, the position remained vacant and the bank's managers behaved as if the risk management function didn't matter.

In a mid-2009 survey, Capital Market Risk Advisors, a New York risk management consultancy, found that only 70 percent of the investment banks, commercial banks, investment management firms, and hedge funds polled had a chief risk officer. Of those chief risk officers, only 25 percent have a say on issues such as how much capital a group can risk, or other such specific rules and policies, but do not create firm-wide policy. More worrying still, the vast majority of those chief risk officers report not to the company's board but to senior management, who have a vested interest in maximizing profits at all costs. The board, which should have access to as much crucial information as possible about risk taking and risk management, may be in a poor position to rein in excessive risk taking, since a third of survey respondents only allow their top risk management officials to attend board executive meetings once a year, if at all.

No Adult Supervision

Even when risk management procedures are in place, Wall Street is littered with examples of bankers running roughshod over them. At UBS, for instance, bankers were supposed to seek approval for new CDO products up front. In practice they delayed doing so until their division had already purchased and warehoused many of the asset-backed securities that would be included in the new CDO. Saying no to a deal at that point was possible only in theory; the costs of unwinding those holdings made it unfeasible in practice.

Often UBS bankers didn't even know what assets lay beneath the subprime loans that they were eagerly repackaging into CDOs. Were they first or second mortgages? What was each borrower's credit score? That kind of due diligence was being conducted by some investors, such as BlackRock's Scott Amero, but not by the product vendors. Instead, UBS and others on Wall Street placed blind confidence in the ratings; after all, they reasoned, credit analysts at Moody's and Standard & Poor's wouldn't give a coveted triple-A rating to anything that didn't deserve it.

Crucially, nowhere within UBS did anyone try to understand the importance to the market of liquidity and what might happen to the bank if something caused that liquidity to evaporate. (They didn't have to predict *what* might cause such an event; all they needed to do was simply consider the fact that it *could* happen.) Similarly, until UBS began writing down the value of the subprime securities on its books in the spring of 2007, senior managers simply relied on the assurances of the people running the business divisions that everything was hunky-dory.

Those rank-and-file bankers had their own incentives to downplay the risks associated with subprime asset-backed securitization and the booming CDO market, even as it became a bigger part of UBS's business. Basic risk management principles suggest that any booming business should automatically be given more scrutiny, especially as its revenues and profits become vital to the firm's financial health and even its solvency. But Wall Street's mix of incentives didn't reward that behavior; rather, bankers were rewarded for downplaying any risks, for being courageous and aggressive. That, CEOs such as Stan O'Neal and Richard Fuld were sure, was the only way they could ever succeed in catching up with Goldman Sachs and matching the latter's enviable return on equity.

On Wall Street, "success" was defined in terms of the rapidity and magnitude of the growth of the business for which an individual was responsible, rather than prudence. Indeed, as the UBS report makes clear, at some institutions there was an incentive to deliberately take on more risk and not to look too closely at the potential fallout; the riskier the mortgage loan they agreed to underwrite and repackage, the bigger the fees. The UBS team responsible for structuring CDOs could earn fees of perhaps 0.5 percent, or 50 cents for every $100 of value in the CDO, by buying only high-grade CDOs containing top-quality securities. Or they could earn at least double and perhaps triple that in exchange for structuring a mezzanine CDO containing higher-risk securities. It was a no-brainer: they pursued the riskier option, which offered the best short-term rewards for both themselves and their division.

Since UBS's compensation policy rewarded bankers and traders based on how much profit they generated, there was no incentive to look too closely at the source of that profit. Was employee A really smarter than employee B because he generated more profit? Was he making more money because he was better at capturing alpha, returns that had nothing to do with what was going on in the broad markets? Were his returns due solely to the ultralow cost of capital? Was he jeopardizing the bank's health in order to enrich himself, taking risks that might pay off for him in the short term in the shape of a gargantuan bonus but that would hurt the institution over the long haul?

No one at UBS could begin to understand which employees were generating the best returns on a risk-adjusted basis. The data weren't there because all that mattered to those who had designed the reporting and compensation system was the bottom line. Thus UBS, like its peers on Wall Street, paid out hefty bonuses on the basis of earnings gains that proved ephemeral. The bank itself was oblivious to "the quality or sustainability of those earnings" until it was too late.[2]

At best, bankers and traders assumed that someone else higher up in the food chain was doing the worrying for them; that someone would come and tell them if they were taking unacceptable risks. On Wall Street, however, there was no "risk police" to rein them in. As in most of the business world, every business division tends to operate with a large degree of autonomy. Why would the head of mortgage origination check in with the head of fixed-income trading? Their overall objectives may be the same—to maximize revenue for their institution—but they go about it in different ways and they compete with each other for access to the firm's capital to accomplish that. Wall Streeters reason that this would be about as logical as the product manager for Colgate toothpaste making sure that someone selling Hill's Science Diet pet food or Ajax cleanser isn't creating problems for the company that employs them all, Colgate-Palmolive. "Look, we were all just doing our jobs, in our little silos," says buyout manager Jake Martin*. "It's hard to blame people for doing their job, or to suggest that they should have been doing more than their job—or even more so, doing someone else's job."

Unfortunately, the comparison between Wall Street and a consumer products company (or other nonfinancial business) isn't as clear-cut as Martin and others would like to believe. They weren't selling toothpaste or even breakfast cereal. At the end of the day, all the myriad parts of Wall Street still were engaged in operating the money grid and making sure that capital moved smoothly from point A to point B. That function may have accounted for a smaller part of the industry's revenues and profits with every year that passed, but Wall Street, however ruthlessly it might seek out profits for itself and however dispassionate its users could be in allocating capital only to those who would use it efficiently and provide a solid return on their investment, ultimately operated in the public interest.

Were the interests of clients and of the public as a whole best served by organizing a Wall Street firm by product line? Several veterans argue against that approach. "The various products are really just tools that somebody can deliver to their client," argues one former senior Wall Street executive. He believes that had Wall Street firms focused on the client and the client's needs as a way to maximize fees, instead of setting up a structure within which each product group battles to maximize its own revenues, the result would have been a healthier financial system. "A derivatives desk sells products that are great; they are tools, really powerful hammers," the executive explains. "But when a derivatives salesman or manager talks to a client, the solution they propose always involves the hammer that they happen to have available and want to sell. Let's use this hammer to pound in the nail, to pound on this screw, to pound on your computer when it's not working. As long as they can make a case that the hammer might be a solution and can keep selling hammers, they are rewarded." An investment bank that divided its business by type of client—hedge fund, private equity fund, pension fund, endowment, mutual fund manager—rather than by product wouldn't have ended up in the same pickle, he suggests.

Others on Wall Street—a majority—reject such revolutionary ideas. Instead, they take an odd sort of comfort in Wall Street's long history of booms and busts. That was Jamie Dimon's worldview, even after the hurricane had blown through Wall Street. In testifying to the FCIC, he sought to explain his view of what had happened by relating a story involving his daughter, who had called him from school to ask him what a financial crisis was. When Dimon told her that it was a market event that occurred every few years, she then asked why everyone was making such a big deal about it. (This anecdote was one of the rare occasions when Dimon—who has emerged from the crisis with a reputation that has been burnished rather than stained—appeared to be afflicted with the same kind of tone deafness and foot-in-mouth disease that afflicts some of his peers.)

In every market cycle, traditionalists point out, investment banks take big risks and many end up making bad deals. Wall Street is a Darwinian place: only the very fittest individuals or firms survive. So no one is surprised when every so often one of those investment banks takes a step too far and goes belly-up. Even Drexel Burnham went from being the most profitable firm on Wall Street in 1986 to filing for bankruptcy in 1990. Sure, it's sad for the guys who work there, but the good ones, Wall Streeters reassure themselves, will find another job eventually. (Indeed, a number of Wall Street firms today still are full of Drexel veterans.)

So even as subprime-related losses mounted and investment banks scrambled to find emergency cash infusions from overseas to help fill the holes in their balance sheets that had suddenly appeared, Wall Street prepared for little more than another Drexel-like event, something that would be painful while it lasted but that could be contained without posing a systemic risk. When the Federal Reserve forced Bear Stearns into a shotgun wedding with JPMorgan Chase in March 2008, there were some thinly veiled sighs of relief in a few corners of Wall Street. This was the moment of capitulation, they reasoned; Bear Stearns would be the subprime meltdown's Drexel, the sacrificial victim of the latest round of Wall Street excess. The real estate market would bottom out; there might even be a recession. But, they reasoned, the rescue of Bear showed that the risks could be contained.

But the closer bankers were to having an overview of the system, the more anxious they became. It was increasingly clear that to the extent they had pondered the issue of risk at all, they had been addressing the wrong set of risks. They hadn't factored into their sometimes perfunctory deliberations the degree to which the financial institutions had become intertwined, so that the collapse of one automatically became a problem for others who had agreed to be counterparties in myriad financial transactions with the now-defunct firm. As the long, hot summer of 2008 unfolded, it also became clear that they had underestimated liquidity risk. Investors were becoming

cautious, fearful, and unwilling to buy; they saw values as too un-
certain. When buyers weren't willing to buy, how could the owners of securities understand what they were *really* worth?

Within weeks, liquidity—the lifeblood of financial markets—had
begun to drain away, a process that would culminate in the massive
credit crunch that fall, after the collapse of Lehman and the $85 bil-
lion AIG bailout signaled just how great the market catastrophe was.
It was a chain reaction, and one that revolved around the level of
confidence Wall Street institutions had in each other. The first to
suffer were the investment banks, which relied on short-term financing to keep afloat. First Bear Stearns and then Lehman Brothers discovered that their usual financiers in the commercial paper and the
overnight repo financing market had begun to perceive that the quality of the assets put up in order to obtain that funding had declined.

Liquidity risk was one of the most contagious of all forms of risk,
as soon became clear. When Lehman Brothers collapsed, the plunge
in value of the company's commercial paper led to an old-fashioned
run on one of the oldest money market funds in the United States.
The Primary Fund, managed by the Reserve Management Co., had
about 1.2 percent of its $63 billion in assets invested in Lehman's
securities, or $796 million. That triggered demands from sharehold-
ers in the fund for the repayment of $20 billion, more than the fund
could provide quickly however rapidly they sold other, creditworthy
securities to meet those demands for redemption. The chaos spread:
other money market funds boycotted the commercial paper market,
unable to value securities in the midst of a liquidity crunch. The
money grid stopped working—in part because of Wall Street's failure to understand the nature of the risks it was running, and liquidity
risk specifically.

Wall Street, it seemed, had disregarded the possible impact of a
string of "unknown unknowns" on increasingly complex and fast-
moving financial markets that were more reliant on leverage than

ever before. "It was all about denial, and every day one more person would realize that they couldn't stay in denial any longer," says private equity manager Martin. Wall Street had spent too many years embracing returns and closing its eyes to risk; now it was more vulnerable to a "perfect storm," while at the same time less prepared to survive the havoc such a storm would bring. "Some of us knew that something nasty was inevitable; in a way, we were all waiting for our comeuppance, for our cavalier attitude to risk to come back and bite us on the ass," one senior Wall Street executive recalls of the summer of 2008. "We were waiting for the next shoe to fall."

Understanding—and Misunderstanding—Risk

Everyone thinks about risk and return every day, whether consciously or unconsciously. When you wake up in the morning, there is the decision to get out of bed and go to work. The return is pretty straightforward: you keep your job and earn a salary to pay your mortgage and cover the grocery bill. Sometimes you accept greater-than-usual risks because you see the reward as also being above average. How many men who normally wouldn't dream of speeding aren't tempted to do just that when they are driving their pregnant partner, now in labor, to the hospital?

What happens on Wall Street isn't all that different; it's just a bit more intense due to the fact that financial markets revolve very explicitly around the dual concept of risk and reward. An investment manager takes risks—buying stocks, bonds, or other securities—in hopes of earning a return for her clients; if those risks don't generate profits, it's because she has misjudged either the investment's return potential or the risks associated with it. Similarly, every time a trader on a Wall Street bond desk takes a bullish or bearish position in Treasury notes ahead of the employment data released on the first Friday of every month, he is assessing how much he could earn if the data show that 300,000 new jobs have been created the previous month or how much he might lose if it shows that 150,000 jobs were lost. Different data will have different consequences for the value of his Treasury notes. A skilled trader needs to be able to judge the myriad risks associated with his conclusion about the data and the Treasury position he chooses to establish. If he gets it right, how much might he earn? If everybody else in the market agrees with his assessment of the risks and potential returns, it's like betting on the favorite in the Kentucky Derby: the return will be minimal unless the trader makes the bet riskier by borrowing the money—in other words, unless he can use a lot of leverage. Betting on an outside chance, in contrast, offers more upside potential but carries a lot more risk of a different kind.

One of the biggest problems with risk is that its *real* level and nature are clear only with hindsight. Consider two hypothetical money managers, both of whom buy Google stock at the time of its IPO and hold on to it for the next four years. Now assume that one of those managers invested 20 percent of the assets she managed in Google, while the other invested only 2 percent of her fund in Google stock. At the time of the investment, the first manager would be called reckless and foolhardy by her peers and probably also by some of her clients; few self-respecting professionals would choose to keep so many investment eggs in a single basket. But by the end of 2008, it is likely that manager's bet on Google, however risky it looked at the time, would have paid off. Now, let's suppose that she did something even riskier by investing the remaining 80 percent of the assets she managed in Treasury securities. The risk here is a different one; she's not running much market or credit risk, since Treasury bonds are among the safest investments around, but she risks dramatically underperforming her peers because the tradeoff for that low risk is a tiny annual interest payment. Of course, what is seen to be risky behavior in one context may look prudent or benign in another, as

Treasury bonds outperformed every other asset class, except cash, throughout 2008.

It's often hard to correctly identify or understand the risk that you are actually running. Wall Street veteran and risk analyst Leo Tilman points out that even as the fees investment banks earned from their traditional businesses slumped and Wall Street institutions turned to "active risk taking" to generate returns for their shareholders, they were lulled into a sense of false security about the level and nature of risk.[3] "When the environment that you're doing business in is very benign, the risk management models start telling you the level of risk is declining, so you feel comfortable taking on more risk," Tilman explains. Whenever investment banks alter their traditional business model in the pursuit of higher fees, higher returns on equity, and higher bonus packages, they automatically take on more risk, he says. The commoditization of traditional businesses—as discussed in chapter 3—forced Wall Street firms to focus on new kinds of business, most of which involved new kinds and often higher levels of risk, Tilman believes. "The paradigm of risk management never caught up with reality," he argues.

In Tilman's eyes, the CDO business, which produced so much of the carnage on Wall Street in 2007 and 2008, is prima facie evidence of the Street's misunderstanding and mismanagement of risk. To the likes of Merrill Lynch and UBS, buying up mortgage-backed securities and repackaging them into these new structured CDO products (the CDO would then be sliced up into tranches on the basis of different risk and return characteristics) was simply a new way to earn the same kind of fees they had always earned. It wasn't really a new business, they reasoned, especially in a low-interest-rate environment. They saw it as "a riskless fee business," Tilman says.

In the eyes of Wall Street, a business that generates a fee is inherently far less risky than one that requires a long-term investment of capital and where returns come in the form of profits following the sale of an asset some time in the future. So even as the Wall Street firms committed more and more capital to the CDO business, they could tell themselves they were still acting as intermediaries between the mortgage originators and the ultimate investors. That gave them an artificial sense of security. Tilman argues that such behavior bordered on the delusional. "If you're gathering CDOs together in a warehouse and packaging them up, and the market suddenly freezes, well, that's a big risk," he says. "It doesn't matter that you would have eventually earned a fee from the transaction. If you believed it was a plain and straightforward transaction and if you didn't hedge the risk of keeping all those [mortgage-backed securities] on your balance sheet while you packaged the CDO, well, you didn't understand the risks you were really taking."

Tilman watched the debacle take shape and then unravel from positions at BlackRock and later as an investment strategist at Bear Stearns advising the firm's pension fund clients and other institutional investors. In his view, this pattern showed up across the whole array of Wall Street's most popular and most profitable new business lines. "Opening a proprietary trading desk, providing short-term financing for leveraged buyouts, serving hedge funds, starting an in-house hedge fund—none of this is as low-risk as people convinced themselves it was."

Of course, everyone on Wall Street knows that their business revolves around risk. But when you ask them about it, they'll tell you it's not about Wall Street taking risks, it's about Wall Street helping its clients offload what they consider to be unacceptable risks to another player. It's about risk transfer. (The classic example of this is one of the most basic derivative securities, the swap: in its original form, this was a way for a company to exchange debt on which it had to pay a variable interest rate for fixed-rate debt, making its finance costs more predictable.) Still, as big investment banks became more complex and placed more emphasis on using their capital to generate returns, they admitted it was time to hire in-house risk managers.

Ideally, Wall Street risk managers should play the role of circuit breakers. They should be able to force the bankers and traders at the various investment banks and other institutions to pause to consider whether they really understand the risks they are about to run and whether the potential return seems worth it. Unfortunately for everyone, Wall Street's relationship with risk managers hasn't always been healthy or productive. Financial institutions have pushed risk management to the sidelines and overlooked it entirely just when they needed it the most: when the level of greed is rising to new heights.

The Least Popular Guys on the Street

Wall Street loathes a party pooper—the guy who arrives on the scene and shakes his head solemnly while everyone else is having fun. The most unpopular subspecies is the kind who wants you to walk away from a deal that is going to generate hundreds of millions of dollars in fees, especially when it's going to cost you a zero on the end of your annual bonus check.

Risk managers on Wall Street are about as popular and welcome as a sensible spouse or cautious bank manager whispering words of reason to a Vegas gambler about to bet the ranch at blackjack. The last thing that a Wall Street banker wants is for that risk manager to acquire enough power internally to *force* him to listen and limit the risk he's taking. Bankers see risk as a way to make profits for themselves and the firm's shareholders; risk managers, meanwhile, want to be sure the institution survives long enough to book those profits. Not surprisingly, those interests clash, and finding a compromise is hard because both have logic on their side. Play it too safe, and the bank won't make money; take too much risk, and the bank won't exist much longer.

On Wall Street, however, the political power is in the hands of those who want to take more and more risk, not those who advocate caution. That's because the bankers and traders who generate the heftiest profits over the longest time periods (and who also have the diplomatic skills to win the support of large numbers of other big revenue producers) are the people who rise to the positions of power within investment banks and other financial institutions.

That's what happened at Goldman Sachs, which once had maintained a balance of power between trading and investment banking within its leadership. (One odd couple was Bob Rubin, a veteran trader, and Stephen Friedman, known for building the firm's merger advisory business, who were co-chairmen of Goldman in the 1990s.) But by the new millennium, the leadership was coming under the control of the traders, such as Blankfein and Gary Cohn, the firm's president, both of whom had begun their careers at J. Aron, the commodities and futures trading business Goldman had purchased. Their trading operations were driving profits, and they were comfortable with risk; still, their priority was clearly on maximizing returns. That's how any banker gets to a position of power and influence in the first place, and it's what they need to keep doing in order to keep shareholders happy and retain their jobs. Anyone who wonders if it might be wiser not to push the risk envelope just has to recall the fate of Phil Purcell or Mike Gelband.

Jaidev Iyer, now head of the Global Association of Risk Professionals (GARP), learned the lesson about the balance of power between risk managers and reward seekers firsthand during the twenty-eight years he spent at Citigroup. From GARP's offices in New Jersey, Iyer now has a panoramic view across the Hudson River to the gleaming office towers of Manhattan, including the skyscraper where he toiled as head of operational risk for Citigroup. He has an equally panoramic view of what went wrong on Wall Street. "Everyone is to blame," he says flatly. "No one is exempt, and I include risk managers in that." But risk managers carry a different burden and thus a different kind of blame, he argues. "Their primary failure was a failure to understand or communicate the risks."

Think of the old legend of the turtle and the scorpion. The scorpion, who needs to get across the river but can't swim, asks the turtle to carry him. The turtle initially scoffs at the idea. "Are you mad?" he demands. "You'll sting me while I'm swimming and I'll drown." The scorpion points out that if he did, he'd drown, too. "Where's the logic in that?" he inquires. The turtle, convinced, tells the scorpion to hop aboard, and starts swimming. Halfway across, the scorpion stings the turtle. As they start to sink to the bottom of the river, the turtle turns resignedly to the scorpion and asks, "Why did you do it? You said there'd be no logic in you stinging me." "It has nothing to do with logic," the scorpion answers sadly. "It's just my character."

On Wall Street, the turtle is the risk manager who knows full well that the nature of the bankers and traders is to take as much risk as they can in pursuit of profits. Failing to find an effective way to communicate the potentially toxic consequences of loading up the bank's balance sheet with subprime loans is the equivalent of the turtle agreeing to ferry the scorpion across the river. The risk manager becomes complicit, indirectly, in the subsequent losses and write-downs.

Iyer says managing risk on Wall Street is easier said than done, since risk managers don't generate profits for their firms and can even recommend actions that would curb short-term gains. "The guy who is always forecasting Armageddon is never going to be the guy anyone wants to listen to; if you listened to him all the time, you'd never do anything," Iyer says. "You have to do that without becoming a wet blanket."

Still, Iyer admits that during his years at Citigroup he found it difficult to always practice what he preaches. At a 2007 meeting of the bank's risk committee, he annoyed Tom Maheras, the powerful co-head of investment banking, by suggesting that the latter hadn't set aside enough capital to provide for some operational risks Iyer had identified. Maheras, a bond expert and a veteran of Salomon Brothers and its high-risk, high-return culture, was an aggressive banker who had risen to the top ranks of Citigroup. Transforming the bank into the dominant global fixed-income trader and propelling it toward the top of the underwriting league tables meant taking on more risk, he was convinced. Sure enough, Citigroup's average value at risk (VaR, pronounced as one word to rhyme with *car*), a measure of how much the bank could lose in a single day if its strategies fell apart or the markets turned sour, soared from $63 million in 2001 to $105 million by 2005.

Perhaps Maheras's track record made him comfortable with risk taking. Bankers who worked with him agree that to Maheras, risk equaled returns. Setting aside more capital to guard against future losses, as Iyer suggested was prudent, would mean less was available to put to work generating the all-important return on equity. Not surprisingly, Maheras was angry; Iyer's suggestion promptly died. More surprising, Iyer was told not to attend further risk committee meetings. Most surprising of all, it wasn't Maheras who had banned him but the bank's senior risk managers. "They wanted to keep Tommy happy," says Iyer with a shrug.

Maybe it shouldn't have been all that astonishing. However important the risk management function seemed to be to those performing it—they knew their activities helped keep their institutions from large losses or running afoul of regulators—risk management didn't generate profits. And profits are all-important on Wall Street, whose icons are bankers such as Maheras, Joe Perella (now out on his own again after leaving Morgan Stanley), or Jimmy Lee at JPMorgan Chase. This list would include some hedge fund managers and buy-out investors. But ask the average investment banker the name of Wall Street's smartest risk manager and you'll likely get a blank stare in response. Even the most successful toil in anonymity.

The UBS forensic analysis of the causes of its massive losses confirms that risk managers had trouble getting their message across. In some cases, they had become too eager to please the more powerful bankers. The UBS report cites one example after another of occasions when managers at all levels silenced points of view that conflicted with their own. UBS bankers complained that the bureaucracy associated with risk management caused them delays in earning revenue from new businesses; their logical response was to find ways to bypass the risk management team or to co-opt them. When bankers explicitly requested more favorable treatment for pet projects, risk managers listened agreeably. In one case the report concluded that if the risk team had been more alert to their circuit-breaker role, such a request could have pushed the bank "to rethink the rationale for the business model as a whole."[4]

Some on Wall Street did listen to what their gut was telling them: that when things seem too good to be true, there is usually something amiss. Whether or not the increasingly popular quantitative risk models captured it, risk-conscious bankers and their analysts knew instinctively or had learned from experience that when it seemed as if nothing could go wrong, it was time to look around for the hidden iceberg ready to rip a hole in the side of the vessel. But to be able to ask the right questions and draw the right conclusions required not only common sense but also the willingness to be a contrarian, even in the absence of evidence that there was a real reason to be alarmed.

Asking Questions, Challenging Models

At Sandler O'Neill, a boutique investment bank catering to financial institutions, CEO Jimmy Dunne was aware that he had a few hundred million dollars' worth of trust-preferred securities (a kind of low-cost financing favored by financial companies) sitting on the firm's balance sheet in the spring of 2007. That was routine; Sandler O'Neill was warehousing the securities while awaiting the right time to repackage them and sell them to investors. But Sandler O'Neill's balance sheet was much smaller than those of firms such as Merrill Lynch, making Dunne nervous. He started looking into the firm's risk.

It all boiled down to just one question, which Dunne asked in the summer of 2007. He wanted to know how much collateral the firm had on its balance sheet in connection with the trust-preferred securities. Hearing the answer, and realizing that the figure was out of whack with the historic average, Dunne reacted instantly. "I told them to get out [of the positions in the trust-preferred securities], forget what the models said [about value], to just sell everything. I had to assume the worst-case scenario, for the sake of the firm."

Dunne had learned over the years that following closely in the footsteps of bigger Wall Street institutions wasn't necessarily prudent. More than a decade earlier, his closest friend and the head of investment banking at Sandler O'Neill, Chris Quackenbush, had pointed out that just because a firm is bigger doesn't mean its behavior or attitudes are worth emulating. They had both learned that lesson when Sandler O'Neill underwrote a new stock issue for a client alongside Salomon Brothers (now part of Citigroup). Quackenbush cautioned Dunne that the SEC rules required underwriters to stay out of trading activity in the stock for two days after the issue was priced and sold. The next morning, Dunne spotted Salomon's trading desk busily making a market in the stock and raking in fees. He stormed into Quackenbush's office, furious at losing potential profits to a rival firm. "I said, 'Look, pal, don't tell me they don't have lawyers and risk guys all over at Salomon. Come on, we're losing money!'"

Quackenbush—one of the sixty-six Sandler O'Neill employees killed in the 2001 terrorist attack on the World Trade Center—stood up to Dunne. "He said he didn't give a hoot—only he didn't use the word *hoot*—about what another firm was doing," Dunne recalls. What mattered was that Sandler O'Neill should do the right thing and not take foolish risks. Dunne says those events taught him a lesson he would later recall as he watched Merrill Lynch, Citigroup, and others accumulate massive exposure to subprime CDOs. "The big guys may build the system that the rest of us have to live in, but we don't have to follow what they are doing blindly," he says today.

It would have been far harder for Citigroup to sell or hedge the $43 billion in subprime securities sitting on its balance sheet than it was for Sandler O'Neill to slash its much smaller exposure. But in the summer of 2007, Citigroup's CEO, Chuck Prince, didn't seem to be asking the same questions that Dunne was. Indeed, it wasn't until he convened a meeting in September to discuss the market meltdown that was already under way that Prince grasped the magnitude of the bank's exposure. His once-blissful ignorance would cost him his job before the year was over. At Merrill Lynch, Stan O'Neal had built a culture revolving around his dream of transforming the firm into the next Goldman Sachs; now he too was put out to pasture. (Nearly simultaneously, and perhaps not coincidentally, Merrill finally created and filled the position of chief risk officer.)

Wall Street investors were much more alert to subprime-related risks. They watched with concern as Wall Street's CDO creation machine churned out more and more of these structured products, each containing a higher proportion of subprime loans than its predecessor. But then, they were looking at the market from the point of view of an investor, and had long had concerns about the extent to which ultralow interest rates failed to reflect the real levels of risk. "The pricing became ridiculous," says Bill Kohli, a fixed-income manager at Putnam Investments in Boston. "The more risk you took, the better your performance was; [bond] yields got so low that in order to generate the same returns you had a few years earlier, you had to take a *lot* more risk."

If Wall Street's investment banks and the mortgage companies who were providing them with their raw material didn't get the trade-off between risk and return, investors did. For them, buying CDOs was a long-term investment, in contrast to Merrill Lynch or

Citigroup, which planned to pass the CDOs to someone else, along with their risk. To compete with their rivals, investment managers need to offer superior returns, but to keep their own investor base satisfied, those returns have to be steady and consistent. Taking too much risk raised the odds of losses, which would in turn cause fund investors to demand their money back.

By 2006, it seemed to Kohli and many of his peers that whichever way they turned, they saw only risk. Many bond managers recognized that yields being offered on corporate bonds were ridiculously low by historical standards; since bond prices and yields move in the opposite direction, for investors to make money by buying those bonds, the yields would have had to fall still more, an improbable scenario. Yield levels were so low that just pocketing a bond's income stream wasn't an attractive option, either. And anyway, how many of those securities might run into trouble if the economy stalled and borrowers struggled to make payments?

Another risk was that an increase in bond yields would send the bond's price, and therefore its value, plunging. Many still decided to hold their noses and buy higher-yielding products, reasoning that many of those structured CDOs had been assigned triple-A credit ratings by Moody's or Standard & Poor's. Others began to balk as the products became increasingly complex or opaque, or valuations reached what they considered to be extreme levels. Some, including BlackRock's Scott Amero, did the due diligence into the loans that underpinned these securities and recoiled in horror at what they found. "Buyers of CDOs are given a take-it-or-leave-it deal; the investor isn't at the table participating in the discussion of how to structure the CDO alongside the issuer and the guy from Moody's or S&P," says Ed Grebeck, CEO of Tempus Advisors, who teaches courses on structured finance at New York University. "For fixed-income managers, this was what was available—end of story." And fixed-income managers were encouraged to put their trust in those ratings; after all, they were limited as to what they could own by those ratings.

Aware that the CDO vendors are in the business of boosting their own bottom line, some investors began focusing instead on relative risk. "There were blue-chip companies that were the subjects of leveraged buyouts, and many of those leveraged loans and bond issues, while a bit pricey sometimes, weren't flawed," says Amero. "They certainly suffered [in the midst of the credit crunch], but they are still securities that we believe are fundamentally good." He points to the loans sold in connection with the $26 billion buyout of First Data Corp. by KKR as an example (although the company, as of early 2010, was recorded as incurring a loss for KKR itself).

Some investors couldn't react to the risks they identified. A bond fund mutual fund manager, for instance, has to invest in the kinds of fixed-income securities that are deemed permissible by the terms of the fund. But while such rules left many mutual fund managers in a bind, hedge fund managers had far more freedom of action. While raising capital, a hedge fund manager spells out the broad strategies that he intends to employ to generate returns in an offering document—a "long/short" or "event-driven" strategy, for instance— but he usually leaves himself with a lot of room to maneuver. So when John Paulson began to grow alarmed by what he believed was a credit bubble, all he had to do was decide how to profit from the reckless- ness of others.

Paulson, a former investment banker, decided that the subprime mortgage market was the part of the credit bubble that seemed the most overextended. He began using derivatives to short subprime mortgage securities in April 2005. It was the culmination of months of thought, analysis, and planning; the bigger any subsequent decline, the larger the profits Paulson's fund would capture. "We thought [this position] was a terrific risk-return tradeoff where you can risk 1 percent and make 100 percent," Paulson said in July 2007. "The exuberance in the credit markets and the massive liquidity was severely mispricing these securities."[5] That turned out to be the understatement of the decade. Paulson's Advantage Plus Fund returned 158 percent to investors in 2007 and another 37.6 percent in 2008, a year in which the Standard & Poor's 500 index *fell* 36.9 percent. The Credit Opportunities Fund fared even better, returning 600 percent to investors. Paulson himself pocketed an estimated $3.7 billion as his share of those returns; by paying heed to hidden sources of risk, suddenly he had become simultaneously a billionaire and a household name.[6]

If Paulson, working outside the mainstream investment banking community and relying on public information, could spot what was going on and take action, why couldn't Wall Street itself? Only a handful of mavericks such as Paulson spotted the opportunity to be a contrarian; few bankers seemed to have any sense of the risks associated with their own behavior and/or felt the need to act. Some of these were at Goldman Sachs, whose chief financial officer, David Viniar, convened a meeting in December 2006 to discuss subprime-related risks. The participants (who included risk managers) agreed they would kick off the new year by establishing a short position, a strategy that paid off richly for the investment bank and certainly contributed to its survival. Later, Lloyd Blankfein would attribute Viniar's initiative to what he described as Goldman's greatest "risk protection"—giving as much status, prestige, and compensation to the risk managers seeking to control the investment bank's finances as it did to the bankers and traders.[7]

For the most part, however, Wall Street seemed content to pursue its own peculiar brand of magical thinking. In the parallel universe as imagined by investment bankers, risk was minimal and readily managed, the supply of cheap credit was endless, and buyers were eager and plentiful. Wall Street's willingness to act as if reality was what they imagined it to be generated a toxic combination of blind faith in its own ability to manage risk and willful blindness to what should have served as warning signals. The result would be the effective demise of three of the five largest investment banks (Bear Stearns, Lehman Brothers, and Merrill Lynch, the last of which opted to be acquired by Bank of America) in little more than six months in 2008. It also brought about the near collapse of Wall Street itself.

Wall Street's Magical Thinking

Key to Wall Street's magical thinking was its reluctance to look risk straight in the eye. Of course, until the summer of 2007, there were few obvious signs that the bull market in credit would have such cataclysmic consequences. Those who persisted in voicing discomfort about the pace at which deals were being done, at the lofty valuations or at the degree of leverage, might be proven right in the long run, but for now would be laughed at and shunned, and perhaps even lose their jobs.

"Even to someone with a lot of expertise in risk management, it was hard for us to envisage while we were absolutely awash in liquidity that the biggest risk we faced was the sudden evaporation in market liquidity," says Leslie Rahl, founder of the risk consulting firm CMRA, whose "workouts" have included many of the derivatives debacles of the 1990s. What seems obvious now wasn't at the time, she adds. "It seemed illogical *not* to just keep doing what had worked." After all, until early 2007, there hadn't been a bank failure in nearly three years. Even when Pittsburgh's Metropolitan Savings Bank collapsed in February 2007, there was no reason for these magical thinkers to view it as anything other than an anomaly; only three institutions were shuttered by the FDIC that year, the same number as failed in 2003.[8] And 2003 had turned out to be a pretty good year for financial markets, they reasoned.

When Wall Street worried that they might be missing the warning signs of an extreme event that could threaten the financial system as a whole, the issue of a credit market bubble and subprime lending rarely served as the focus of those debates. Instead, risk managers at firms such as Lehman Brothers in 2006 worried about the impact of another terrorist attack like those of September 11, 2001, or of an epidemic of avian flu on global financial markets.[9] In contrast, the ultraliquid credit markets seemed unlikely to be the center of a financial markets disaster rivaling the 1929 stock crash in magnitude and significance. In the absence of any bank collapses and in the presence of record low bond default rates, the calculus made sense. Maybe there was a credit bubble out there, but bubbles can exist for a long time without bursting. An investor or banker who takes to the sidelines at the first hint of trouble can lose a lot of money and forfeit his credibility, the late 1990s had demonstrated only too clearly. Former Fed chairman Alan Greenspan wryly reflected on the relevance of that period, noting that "underpriced risk—the hallmark of bubbles—can persist for years."[10] (It took three years from the date Greenspan warned of "irrational exuberance" for the dot-com bubble to finally burst.)

Wall Street, by and large, wasn't listening to its risk managers. It wasn't doing its best to ferret out hidden warning signs. Instead, it seemed to be relying exclusively on a handful of quantitative risk-management models to save the financial system from disaster. The immense forward leaps in computing power that had made possible the creation of complex derivatives and other structured products had also made it possible for mathematical minds to devise ways to track and calculate different kinds of risk across a multitude of different business segments rapidly and efficiently. Computers also made it possible to simulate shocks to the system and watch how markets behaved.

This kind of calculation required computing power because the spread of derivatives made this a complicated task. If an investment bank had shares of Cisco and General Electric on its books, for instance, the impact of a market shock would be relatively straightforward to calculate; those stocks trade on an exchange and have a clear market value. But only a fraction of the world's financial instruments are that easily monitored. What would happen to a corporate bond? They don't trade as often, and dealers in those bonds make a market in them on an ad hoc basis when a potential buyer or seller requests price information. Who would be willing to be an intermediary in times of market stress? And at what price? Then there are the derivatives, which also aren't traded on an exchange (except for the plain-vanilla variants, such as options and futures contracts) and which often are highly customized products that don't have a logical buyer.

That's just the very tip of the iceberg. Today's investment banks are global: their risks can be related to the trading they do with a Kazakh oil and gas company, the loans they make to a Thai retailer, or a buyout they finance of a Mexican food processing company by a European conglomerate. Throw a stone in the waters of global markets today and the ripples will take a more unusual shape and stretch far wider than they would have a decade ago. Hence the allure of the quantitative risk management model in the eyes of investment bankers.

The Value at Risk Conundrum

The best-known of these models is the famous (or infamous) value at risk (VaR) model. "Essentially, that was the solution devised to the problem of a CEO who walked onto the trading floor and wanted a simple answer to the question of how much risk the investment bank was running today," explains Jaidev Iyer of GARP. "With VaR, you could give him a single number—how many dollars the bank could lose today if things went wrong." VaR vaulted into prominence when an international group of banking regulators, the Basel Committee on Banking Supervision, explicitly endorsed it as a way to gauge how much capital a financial institution is putting on the line, and thus to calculate how much capital it should set aside to shield itself should those risks backfire. The result was the Basel II accord, first published in 2004, which required financial institutions to incorporate risk into their balance sheet decisions.

After a lot of debate—it took five years to hammer out the basic principles, and implementation still isn't complete—the signatories (including central bankers and other regulators from twenty different countries) finally agreed that banks, investment banks, and other financial institutions could rely on VaR as a way to gauge risk. The lower the VaR, the less capital an institution needed to set aside to shield the firm from risk. But at the end of the day, no one was happy. "Nobody believed in it and nobody used it, except in the annual report and to tell regulators what was going on," says one former regulator. "Everyone in the regulatory community knew there were failings with this process. But at the same time, it had been so hard to agree on this, and so controversial, that no one who worked on Basel ever wanted to reopen the topic for discussion again."

The biggest problem with VaR—and with any other effort to model risk—is that while Wall Street may concern itself with numbers, human behavior is just as important a determinant of what happens there. And human behavior is notoriously difficult to quantify. But as VaR increasingly demonstrated throughout the Wall Street crisis, numbers didn't tell the whole story.

To start with, VaR couldn't give anyone an accurate picture of how well risk was being managed. For instance, the VaR associated with Goldman Sachs's sales and trading business was $101 million in 2007, meaning that on any given day, that was how much it might lose with a defined degree of probability. Goldman was second only to Citigroup in the amount of risk, and it also earned more in revenues than any other financial institution from those trading activities— $27.5 billion in 2007, up 21 percent from the previous year. On the surface, Lehman looks less risky in absolute terms. Its VaR was $92 million, and its revenues from sales and trading were about half of those at Goldman. But VaR doesn't tell the whole story. It was

Lehman, not Goldman, that experienced the biggest *increase* in VaR (it more than doubled, the highest rate of growth of any investment bank in 2007), while it increased only 37 percent at Goldman Sachs. Moreover, the size of Lehman's VaR relative to that of its trading revenue was higher than the same ratio at Goldman. Moreover, Goldman lost money on fewer trading days in 2007 than in 2006; the number of days on which Lehman's traders lost money jumped from five in 2006 to thirty-three in 2007. Goldman made more than $100 million on each of eighty-nine trading days; Lehman pulled off the same feat on only thirty-one days.[11] In other words, VaR alone gives a hopelessly inadequate view of the two organizations' ability to manage the level of risk that they were taking. "It didn't tell you anything at all about the caliber of assets on the balance sheet connected with those risks, or the skill of the bankers and traders," argues one veteran banker and risk manager.

The methodology is also problematic. VaR, like most other risk management models, is based on a series of assumptions, which in turn depend on probability and statistics. That means that VaR is shaped by what has happened in the past, and more specifically by what has happened most frequently. In some cases, there are a lot of data to draw on: the real estate market, for instance, has more than a century of reasonably reliable data, while the bond market has seventy or eighty years' worth. At the other end of the spectrum, risk managers can draw on only five years' worth of robust data available on credit default swaps, the newest breed of derivatives, which played a critical role in the market meltdown. VaR places more reliance on recent history than it does on the broad sweep of past events, but the biggest shocks have no historical precedent. As Greenspan sadly admitted to Congress, the models weren't designed around periods of maximum stress. Had they been, bank capital requirements would have been higher. Instead, Greenspan opined, "the whole intellectual edifice [of risk management] collapsed."[12]

VaR also relies on probability. The more frequently an event has occurred in the past, the greater weight it is given in VaR. By definition, therefore, VaR discounts the risk associated with an extreme event such as the 1987 stock market crash or Long-Term Capital Management's collapse. But while those are statistically unlikely to recur, such "unknown unknowns" are exactly the events that end up being the most destabilizing and thus the most critical to risk managers. Nassim Nicholas Taleb became just as famous as John Paulson (if not as wealthy) following the publication of his book *The Black Swan: The Impact of the Highly Improbable,* which points out just how frequently those events occur. Before the rest of the world "discovered" Australia, all swans were white; every empirical observation over the course of millennia supported that proposition. And yet, as the discovery of the first black swan in the antipodes proved, it was a false theory.

It was what Lehman's risk managers *couldn't* imagine, because it was outside of the realm of their knowledge, experience, or the all-important data, that would lead to the firm filing for bankruptcy two years later. In Taleb's view, these "Black Swans" are far more common than we'd like to think, and the biggest risk management flaw of all is the fact that we are so reluctant to admit that there is no such thing as a perfectly functioning crystal ball. Could someone in 1900, with the knowledge that was available as of that date, have predicted World War I and its consequences, including the Third Reich and the rise of the Soviet Union? he wonders. Of course not. The knowledge of the future available to a citizen at the dawn of the twentieth century was as limited as ours is today. That has ramifications for trying to manage risk on Wall Street. "In finance," Taleb concludes, "people use flimsy theories to manage their risk and put wild ideas under 'rational' scrutiny."[13] Black Swans are, by definition, impossible to quantify until they have occurred and thus become knowable, by which time it's too late.

Those who rise quickly to positions of power on Wall Street these days tend to be people with strong mathematical skills and a natural quantitative bent, because that's what it takes in order to come to grips with the complex financial instruments that dominate today's financial system. These individuals gravitate to quantitative tools for help in understanding risk. When they spot a possible Black Swan rising like a storm cloud on the horizon, their first instinct isn't to ask themselves the most basic question: "What might this be? Is it something I recognize, or is it something new that is going to force me to alter the way I think about the world?" Instead they plunge into their comfort zone—quantitative analytics—to see if they can make sense of this mysterious cloud. By the time they realize they can't, that it's something new and very ominous indeed, it's too late.

Even after the collapse of Bear Stearns and Lehman Brothers, in which liquidity risk had played a major role, bankers still continued to focus far more attention on credit risk and operational risk than on developing methods for predicting whether liquidity is about to evaporate. Ironically, the level of risk associated with flawed models (including risk management models) was even less of a priority, something that only 58 percent of respondents attempted to manage, according to a survey conducted by accounting giant Deloitte in late 2008.[14]

Quantitative risk measurement and management tools will remain problematic as long as financial institutions have a vested interest in interpreting the results the way they feel best helps them continue to pursue profits at all costs. A firm with a high VaR can reassure itself that its traders are better than their rivals at managing that risk, so the level or rate of increase is nothing to be concerned about. Moreover, as long as that high VaR is accompanied by a jump in revenues and profits from taking the risks, what is there to worry about? For Sir Deryck Maughan, plenty. At an industry conference in December 2009, the British banker, now a partner at KKR, warned his colleagues that many of the mathematical models that had led financial institutions to discount or overlook what proved to be toxic risks were still being used. The industry, he said, had not "faced up to the intellectual failure of risk management systems, which are still hardwired into many banks and many trading floors."

Above all, regulators still worry that the banks will try to compute VaR in such a way as to reduce their capital requirements. Since financial institutions can make money only on capital that can be used (and the leverage that they can apply while using that capital), the greater the capital they can use, the more likely the bank or investment bank is to generate an outsize ROE. An institution that has to set aside capital in reserve to guard against potential future losses is at a competitive disadvantage. That potential global competition to have the lowest possible capital, warned Sheila Bair, chairman of the Federal Deposit Insurance Corporation, in a June 2007 speech, "is a game with no winners." Bair worried that the Basel approach came too close to letting banks set their own capital adequacy standards, an approach she compared to letting each football player set his own rules in a championship match.

Bair's warnings, and her subsequent contributions to the debate over Wall Street's future, identify her as perhaps one of the most prescient Wall Street regulators of the last quarter century. At the time the Basel II signatories agreed to this approach, markets were unusually benign, volatility was at very low levels, and bank profits were strong and rising. That alone should make regulators think twice about what constitutes an acceptable level of capital, she cautioned. There is a "danger [in] thinking that banks will have enough lead-time to ramp up their capital as economic conditions deteriorate."[15] In light of the events of the next eighteen months, which included frantic and sometimes failed attempts to replace capital being eroded by write-downs, those remarks are striking. Bair, it seems, was able to do what Wall Street's best and brightest minds couldn't: envisage a day when the future might not be as rosy as the present. But then, regulators don't get bonuses for delivering profits to the banking industry.

The Lemmings, the Cliff, and the Laws of Physics

In 1831, well-trained English troops were marching in step across a suspension bridge near Manchester when it suddenly collapsed. Those assigned to investigate the tragedy discovered that the reasons for the collapse were tied to the laws of physics. British soldiers were drilled rigorously until they could march impeccably in step, or cadence, as it's known. But when it came to crossing the newly designed suspension bridges, this pattern proved to be disastrous. In some cases, the cadence of the marching can match the natural resonance frequency of a suspension bridge; in those cases, even though each step adds only a tiny amount of energy, cumulatively the impact of so many marching soldiers in cadence puts so much stress on the structure that the result is devastating. Once engineers realized what was happening, they set about devising new kinds of alloys that would reduce the natural resonance of a bridge to the bare minimum. Meanwhile, military officials recognized that marching in step, however desirable in nearly every other circumstance, was a foolish risk to take when crossing suspension bridges; they began instructing their troops to break cadence when crossing bridges.

This famous example of one of the laws of physics at work has an uncanny similarity to Wall Street. A Wall Street institution's employees are trained to pursue ROE at all costs, almost blindly, in the same way that soldiers are drilled to march in cadence, until it becomes second nature. Neither group questions the nature of that training until something goes wrong. In both cases, the result is a high level of systemic risk that no quantitative model can capture until it's too late. Just as each soldier concentrated only on making sure his steps exactly matched those of his fellow soldiers ahead of and on either side of him, on Wall Street few people seemed to pay attention to anything beyond the transaction at hand and its role in maximizing their group's profits and the firm's return on equity.

The groupthink worried Myron Scholes, coauthor of the Black-Scholes valuation formula, which made it possible for options and all kinds of other complex derivative products to find a home on Wall Street. Scholes (whose formula is the subject of much scorn from critics such as Taleb, who argue that it makes risk appear too understandable and too quantifiable) points out the inherent riskiness of ignoring systemic risk. "Any one bank can measure its [own] risk" using models based on Black-Scholes or other research, Scholes notes. "But it also has to know what the risk taken by other banks in the system happens to be at any particular moment."[16] In other words, just as no drill sergeant today would insist that his soldiers march in cadence at all times, regardless of the circumstances or the terrain, no financial institution can afford to ignore the possibility that what appears to be a riskless transaction in isolation can create risk to both the institution and the system if it's repeated endlessly across Wall Street. One bank doing subprime CDOs wasn't going to torpedo the financial system, but the banking system en masse cranking out so many subprime CDOs that subprime lending became the tail that wagged the dog came perilously close to doing just that.

That kind of copycat behavior also damaged regulators' efforts to rein in risk, recalls Sheila Bair. The banking regulator had a "peer intervention" analysis that was designed in the expectation that one banker had a better chance than a regulator of figuring out if another banker was taking on too much risk. The problem was that so many of the institutions were doing exactly the same thing, and the problems weren't flagged. Everyone was doing it; it was the new normal and everyone was making money doing it. No one caught on to the risk management flaw, Bair told the FCIC commissioners, "until the risky activities undertaken by all became unsustainable."

Wall Street needs to break out of its old ways of thinking about risk and leave behind the notion that it can always be identified, quantified, and controlled. What is needed more than a risk management system is a risk-aware culture, as Deloitte advocated in its survey. Those institutions the accounting firm spoke to in the latter months of 2008 were already aware that their risk management programs weren't doing a good job for them. Fewer than half of the respondents believed that those risk programs offered "significant value"; nearly a third told surveyors that risk management didn't generate *any* value when it came to either boosting the quality of their earnings or improving risk-adjusted returns. Only 38 percent believed their risk management systems helped limit losses when risks rose to the surface.[17] Indeed, almost the only area in which financial institutions felt that risk management programs were of significant value was keeping regulators happy.

Alan Greenspan may blame models for risk management failures, but it was human beings who devised those models, established their core assumptions, and then interpreted the results. As Sheila Bair had feared, there were ample incentives for misreading the level of risk in the financial system. Not surprisingly, most of them revolved around the two core drivers of everything else that happens on Wall Street—fear and greed. In this case, the fear was of being left behind in the battle for market share, profits, and return on equity, while greed was the allure of outsized bonus checks in exchange for taking risks and discounting the lurking presence of a Black Swan event that couldn't be quantified anyway. The only way to rein in risk taking, a growing number of risk managers argued, was equally behavioral. "Top managers and directors need to keep asking how the bank is making this money, whether the business is sustainable, what assumptions is the risk taking based on, can we get clear and accurate and objective information on the business and its risks," argues one banker turned risk consultant.

"Risk models always are a bit deceptive," says Leslie Rahl, the veteran risk manager at CMRA. Let's say there are two portfolios, one of which is full of complex structured products while the other contains only plain-vanilla securities such as stocks and bonds. Both are run through risk management models that show that they have an equal level of risk—something that can happen in periods of prolonged market calm. Rahl says the response should be not to heave a sigh of relief and move on but to become concerned and ask more questions about why two such disparate portfolios could appear to possess such a similar risk profile. "Until we come up with better methodologies, we have to find a way to adjust what the models say for the elements that the models can't capture," she points out.

Wall Street also needs to find a way to question its own assumptions, not just the conclusions drawn by models. The crisis we have just lived through wasn't as impossible to predict as some Black Swan theorists might argue. The risks associated with subprime lending were clear; as a study by Federal Reserve economists on the crisis showed, many Wall Street analysts correctly predicted that a slump in housing prices would batter subprime loans and the CDOs that contained them. But they ascribed a low probability to that ever happening.[18] "For fifty years, housing prices nationwide had always gone up, even if just a little bit," notes Michael Stockman, formerly a banker at UBS who now advises clients on portfolio construction as a managing partner of Corridor Quadrant. True, there were regional housing slumps, but one of the reasons that bankers felt comfortable giving mortgages to subprime borrowers was that even if they weren't good credit risks, the value of their collateral—the house they bought—would never deteriorate. Even movements in major real estate indexes were referred to as "appreciation," Stockman notes wryly. "No one could imagine depreciation." Indeed, when prices *did* fall, the move was dubbed "negative appreciation."

In medicine the adage that doctors first and foremost should do no harm causes physicians to second- and third-guess their original assumptions and send patients to other doctors for additional tests and second opinions. With no professional standard of that kind on Wall

Street, there was no motivation for anyone within AIG's head office to query the results that its London-based division, AIG Financial Products, was posting. Between 1999 and 2005, the division's revenues soared 342 percent, to $3.26 billion, as its financial engineers delved into the business of selling insurance to investors in CDOs in the form of credit default swaps. The business proved so successful that by 2005, AIG Financial Products was generating 17.5 percent of AIG's revenues, up from 4.2 percent in 1999; profit margins on the business had nearly doubled.

Across AIG, there seemed to be the will to believe that this business would be the insurance world's version of the Internet, an innovation that would utterly transform its business by enabling savvy firms such as AIG to sell insurance against credit risk in the same way they insured people against hurricane damage or death. Investors paid their premiums, just as someone buying fire or life insurance did. Because the CDOs AIG was insuring carried top-tier credit ratings, the firm didn't need to worry about setting aside capital to make good on the insurance claim. AIG figured that if CDO quality began to deteriorate, it would be able to respond. In fact, the calls for the firm to post collateral in connection with the slumping values of CDOs mounted faster than AIG could cope with; the firm had forgotten that it's the things that you fail to worry about or assume aren't risks at all that prove most toxic in the long run. AIG's de facto collapse and the more than $100 billion in bailout funds provided by the Treasury Department to keep it at least nominally afloat and prevent its collapse from fatally damaging every financial institution with which it had had dealings is one of the most clear-cut examples of what can happen when Wall Street stops thinking sensibly about risk on both an enterprise and the systemic level.

Enlightened self-interest may not be working to curb excessive risk taking. But Wall Street can't simply pass the buck, either, demanding that others perform this governance and risk management function on their behalf. For starters, it's by no means clear that regulators will do a better job; these days, some of them are likely to be the same former Wall Street risk management executives that stood by, oblivious, as the storm gathered and struck them.

Michael Alix, for instance, trumpeted the resilience of his risk management models and celebrated his risk management system's ability to ensure that Bear Stearns didn't hold too many risky securities at the same time in an interview with a *BusinessWeek* reporter back in 2006. Even when the markets were falling in response to a rise in interest rates, a computer screen full of flashing red lights (signaling securities whose prices were declining) didn't alarm him, he bragged. "The machine works!"[19] Less than two years after Alix was named head of risk management at the firm, Bear Stearns proved definitively that the machine *didn't* work: it hadn't anticipated all the problems that Bear would face or the extreme market conditions.

In one of the irony-rich moments of the Wall Street crisis, Michael Alix himself went on to be named vice president of the New York Federal Reserve's Bank Supervision Group in October 2008, at the heart of the crisis. The appointment raised eyebrows and prompted some scathing comments from across Wall Street, where Bear's former rivals were fighting to survive and figure out what to do next. But then, to many observers it was already clear that, far from helping Wall Street to rein in its worst instincts, regulators of all kinds—from the SEC down to the rating agencies—either were unable or unwilling to act or were even more oblivious to the risks than Wall Street itself. Wall Street may have been dancing as long as the music kept playing, in Chuck Prince's words. But to many it seemed as if the central bankers and securities regulators were calling the tunes and turning up the volume.

CHAPTER 7

Washington Versus Wall Street

The story of James Gilleran and his chain saw has become one of the most infamous in the growing annals of regulatory mismanagement of Wall Street. It dates back to the early summer of 2003, long before anyone on the Street realized that there was anything at all alarming going on in the real estate market, much less in the business of turning subprime mortgages into triple-A-rated packages of securities. Banking regulators were gathering to proclaim their support for the Bush administration's decision to reduce the regulatory burden that made it harder for the institutions they supervised to extend as many loans as they wanted. Gilleran, who had been named to head the Office of Thrift Supervision (OTS) in 2001, knew a great photo op when he saw it. At the press conference, he was one of four banking regulators to pose for dramatic effect behind a stack of paper representing regulations governing the lending business, all wrapped up in red tape. The other three regulators brought garden shears to demonstrate their willingness to attack the problem. In the photograph, Gilleran sported the biggest grin *and* the biggest weapon: a chain saw.

But then, James Gilleran had a lot of motivation to make his corner of the regulatory jungle happy by cutting red tape: the prospect of millions of dollars a year in fees from institutions that elected to operate a savings and loan institution, or thrift, as these entities are known. Just as the investment banks had every incentive in the world to maintain the lowest possible amounts of capital on their books, so many regulators—especially smaller, newer, and less well-known entities such as the OTS—had a built-in reason to lower their regulatory standards and overlook risky behavior on the part of their regulatees in an effort to woo and retain "clients." Anyone familiar with the basic rules of organizational behavior could have predicted this would happen. OTS's budget depended on the number of institutions it regulated. The more institutions it could attract under its regulatory umbrella, the better it would fare, organizationally speaking. On the other hand, if it adopted a regulatory stance that its "customers" viewed as unduly harsh, a number of thrifts might suddenly decide that they were really commercial banks at heart and thus subject themselves instead to the oversight of the Office of the Comptroller of Currency (OCC) and the Federal Reserve.

This was exactly the kind of development that the FDIC's Sheila Bair had feared—that lax regulation and a less-than-rigorous approach to risk management would cause the lowest common denominator to triumph. Gilleran kept slashing away at both regulations and his own ability to enforce whatever ones remained on the books, in hopes of wooing more "clients." Even as the mortgage lending business—a big part of the savings and loan industry—swung into high gear, Gilleran's chain saw whirred into life: the OTS honcho cut the size of his staff by 25 percent.

OTS-regulated institutions became the biggest providers of the mortgages that would end up contributing most to the subprime meltdown, such as option ARMs (adjustable-rate mortgages), but complaints about predatory lending didn't seem to register on Gilleran's radar. As is now well known, it was during Gilleran's tenure that the worst of the flawed mortgage products made their debut; complex loans that borrowers didn't understand committed them to larger mortgage payments than they would be able to make. Only reluctantly did OTS later sign an OCC-orchestrated pact to halt the practice.

John Reich, who took over the helm of OTS from Gilleran in 2005, showed nearly as much zeal as his predecessor had done in the quest to make the organization the regulator of choice for America's financial institutions. His publicly voiced concerns about the risk that overregulation would penalize both lenders and borrowers and keep Americans from the dream of owning their own home must have been music to the ears of Angelo Mozilo, CEO of Countrywide Financial.[1] By 2005, Mozilo was a bit fed up with having to account for all his actions to the OCC. The latter, as the *Washington Post* later reported, didn't want Countrywide's senior officers deciding which appraisers should be chosen to calculate the value of the properties against whose value Countrywide was lending money and structuring mortgages. Logically enough, the OCC feared that that presented a conflict of interest: appraisers might come back with the kind of inflated valuations that would allow Countrywide to write more loans and pocket more fees from selling them (and the risk they entailed) on to investment banks and commercial banks to be repackaged into CDOs. In 2006, Mozilo decided to leave the pesky OCC behind and to become a thrift, subject to the more benign regulation of the OTS. Its new regulator had, Countrywide executives later said, promised to take a more "helpful" view of the appraisal selection process.[2] It proved to be a classic example of what became known as regulatory arbitrage.

Indeed, it wasn't a coincidence that OTS ended up as the regulator of choice of many of the financial institutions that took on the greatest risks in subprime lending and would later pay the ultimate price for their risk management failures and the regulatory shortsightedness of Gilleran and Reich. For years, the OTS's single most important client was Washington Mutual (WaMu), the feisty thrift that had built up a nationwide banking network and was writing mortgage loans as fast as it could. The OTS certainly didn't want Washington Mutual to leave its regulatory embrace. Perhaps that was why its regulators allowed the institution to slash the amount of capital it allocated against possible future loan losses more and more with each year that passed, even when it became clear that the risks associated with the real estate business and mortgage lending were rising. By the summer of 2005, loan loss reserves at WaMu were a mere $48 for every $10,000 in mortgage and personal loans, about 25 percent below the already low average level for savings and loan institutions regulated by OTS.[3] Not surprisingly, in what would prove to be their final fiscal year as independent institutions, fees paid by Washington Mutual and Countrywide together accounted for nearly a fifth of the OTS budget.

One of the other institutions of which the OTS ended up as a major regulator was AIG, the giant insurance company that would become one of the biggest casualties of the Wall Street mayhem. As an insurance company, AIG was regulated by state agencies rather than federal banking or securities regulators. But it owned a savings and loan institution, and that meant the OTS received all the financial information about the company's operations. The OTS had warned AIG's board that its risk management procedures were full of holes. Nonetheless, when Federal Reserve officials put in a series of emergency phone calls on the critical weekend in September that led to the Lehman Brothers bankruptcy and the sale of Merrill Lynch, their OTS counterparts sounded downright bewildered to hear from them.

The OTS was oblivious to the fact that within the next two weeks AIG would face a demand for nearly $40 billion in cash from its counterparts to offset the declining value of the securities it had posted as collateral. The losses were in AIG's financial products division, which wasn't regulated by the OTS; still, given the magnitude of the obligation, they would certainly wreak havoc on the company's insurance and thrift operations. That would be even more true if, as seemed likely, AIG had to file for bankruptcy as a result of the losses. (Such a filing was averted only at the last moment by one of the largest direct infusions of government cash of the entire crisis.) The OTS couldn't even begin to help its fellow regulators unravel the mess; the Fed decided instead to summon AIG's CEO, Robert Willumstad, to help it understand the magnitude of the problem.[4]

The OTS approach to regulation ended up as the focus of an audit report by the Office of the Inspector General at the Treasury Department. The latter concluded that OTS-supervised thrifts were able to file misleading statements about their financial position, in particular the amount of capital they held on their books. While IndyMac—which collapsed in July 2008—was responsible for its own fate, the report says, the OTS had an opportunity to rein in the institution's hyperaggressive lending as early as 2005, when cash flow problems first surfaced.

The report is a review of several occasions on which the OTS permitted the institutions they regulated (including IndyMac) to backdate new capital infusions into the mortgage lending institutions, making their balance sheets look more stable than was really the case. In the case of IndyMac, that made the thrift look healthy only two months before the FDIC had to step in, close the doors of the suddenly insolvent institution, and reimburse its depositors. Even though at times IndyMac's thinly staffed regulator had up to forty people peering over the shoulders of the thrift's managers, the Treasury Department's forensic accountants concluded that they all either missed or didn't care about IndyMac's reckless behavior. (This included failing to verify that developers it was lending to had nailed down funding for all their projects and not overhauling its lax appraisal process for residential mortgages.) What *did* matter to OTS? "Growth and profitability [were] evidence that IndyMac management was capable" of managing their business and its risks, the report's authors concluded.[5]

Playing the Blame Game

When Wall Street's misaligned compensation policies set up incentives almost guaranteed to wreak havoc on the financial system, and when its internal risk management systems and models failed to work the way everyone believed they would, the theory was that the regulators and legislators—"Washington," for short—should have been able to prevent, control, or manage the crisis. After all, the raison d'être of the entire regulatory system is to serve as a last-ditch line of defense, one protecting the integrity of the financial system from Wall Street's worst instincts, referred to on the Street itself as "animal spirits." It was logical that investment banks were cheerleaders for their own interests. But the financial system needed its own team of cheerleaders—or guards—and that role is supposed to be played by the regulators. These groups, including the OTS, were established to protect the health of the system, because of the importance of the money grid to the economy and even to society as a whole. They weren't there to help individual businesses maximize their returns or to promote the philosophical concept of free enterprise.

Chuck Prince, the Citigroup of CEO until his ouster in the fall of 2007, might insist on continuing to dance to the music that he heard. But it was a regulator's job to ask whether the music that he claimed to hear was real or playing only in his head. And if exhausted musicians were collapsing one by one on the stage even as the Wall Street CEOs continued to polka, then the task of a regulator was to step in and declare that the party was over. A well-functioning regulatory system is one that is able to detect when the music is out of tune, when half the musicians can't keep up with the dancers, and when the dancers are cavorting to imaginary tunes.

On an unseasonably warm and balmy St. Patrick's Day in 2009, exactly a year after the collapse of Bear Stearns began the final chapter in the meltdown, some of Wall Street's survivors headed to the Upper East Side of Manhattan. They were bound for Rockefeller University's Caspary Auditorium, site of a sold-out Oxford-style debate about the causes of the financial crisis, sponsored by Intelligence Squared, a nonprofit organization backed by a hedge fund manager, Robert Rosenkranz. The resolution up for debate that evening: "Blame Washington more than Wall Street for the financial crisis." If it weren't for the occasional splash of green in the audience, no one would have known that the day was one that other New Yorkers were celebrating. In contrast to Intelligence Squared's other monthly debates, audience members hadn't come to this one to be entertained or even educated. They were cross, worried, and anxious; they wanted to vent. "I just know that *I* wasn't responsible for all this mess," said a twentysomething laid-off banker who gave his name only as Pete, his anger palpable. "We're the most hated guys out there. No one believes us. Even the president tells us we're shit. Come on! It *can't* be all about Wall Street!"

Indeed it can't, economic historian Niall Ferguson reassured Pete and others like him at the beginning of the debate. Ferguson admitted that he hadn't come to praise or defend bankers. "We blame them for much of what has gone wrong," he told the audience. "It's just that we blame the politicians *more.*" The Wall Street hometown audience erupted in laughter and cheers; declaring open season on Washington is universally popular. As for Citigroup's Prince, who claimed Wall Street had no option but to get up and dance, Ferguson pointed out slyly, "You have to ask yourselves, ladies and gentlemen, who was playing the music." Why, the historian wondered, do politicians love to point their fingers at financiers in times of trouble? "Could it just possibly be that they're trying to divert our attention away from Washington's own responsibility for the debacle?"

The possibility that the fatal flaw lies outside Wall Street itself is a comforting one to many financiers, especially as they confront the specter of heavy regulatory reforms. "Blaming Wall Street is like blaming the atmosphere for thunderstorms," exclaimed John Steele Gordon, part of Ferguson's debate team arguing in favor of the motion. Street "panics" happen periodically, he pointed out. "It's the nature of the beast." On the other hand, Washington regulators are "supposed to be the guys with the striped shirts and the whistles on the playing field. They make up the rules, and then they enforce them. And then they sometimes change the rules in order to accommodate some of their friends."[6]

It was an uneven contest: Ferguson and his two allies won the debate hands down, helped in equal parts by their debating skills, Ferguson's charm and Scottish accent, and the audience's determination to heap more of the blame on Washington, an attitude that reminded some observers of the age-old children's protest about being punished for a misdeed: "But, Mom/Dad, he *made* me do it!" Certainly, those New Yorkers seemed ready to believe that Washington made them do it: before the debate, 42 percent of attendees had voted in favor of the motion that Washington was more at fault than Wall Street, but two hours of debate later, 60 percent agreed with the proposition. Nearly ten months later, a somewhat cooler-headed Jamie Dimon insisted that, on the contrary, the buck stopped with Wall Street. "I do not blame the regulators," he testified before the FCIC hearings in January 2010. "The responsibility for a company's actions rests with the company's management." But there were still many to disagree with Dimon, to question whether Dimon believed his own argument, and to argue that Washington had actively urged Wall Street to pursue risky strategies, or at least served as an enabler of sorts.

Awarding the lion's share of the blame for the financial system's near meltdown to Washington rather than Wall Street is tempting, but it's also overly simplistic. True, Wall Street's regulators didn't try very hard to rein in the festivities at the height of the boom; some, such as Gilleran and the OTS, seem to have egged their constituents on to greater follies. But by the time the crisis was taking shape, the ability of regulators to fulfill their traditional role of protecting Wall Street's core functions—the smooth transfer of capital from those who had it to those entities that needed it—had been steadily eroded by several decades' worth of policy decisions. These culminated in a dysfunctional regulatory system that was rarely able to move beyond the nuts and bolts of each individual decision—separating research and investment banking divisions, moving to decimalization in trading systems, banning an "uptick" rule, promoting home ownership, fighting the prospect of an economic slump by keeping interest rates at rock-bottom levels for years, allowing parts of the financial system to shop for their own regulator—to focus on the big picture.

And when the big picture was mentioned, that picture wasn't one of the maintenance of a financial utility. No one discussed whether those initiatives contributed to the long-term health and stability of the financial system. Regulating other utilities is relatively straightforward, in both theory and practice, in part because there's a general acceptance among all interested parties that there is a broad public interest in having a reliable source of gas or electricity and an ample supply of clean water. (That's particularly true because most regulatory agencies are established to police the behavior of monopolies or oligopolies providing services that society deems to be essential.) Even the managers of power plants and water companies that might have an interest in keeping costs low and maximizing profits know that they will personally suffer alongside everyone else in the community if those financial goals result in the power grid collapsing or the water becoming contaminated.

When it comes to Wall Street, however, the picture is far blurrier, and not just because no single Wall Street institution can lay claim to monopoly or oligopoly status. Wall Street isn't a business like any other; it can't be compared to retailers such as Walmart or consumer goods manufacturers such as Colgate-Palmolive; even critics of excessive regulation will admit, especially after the events of the last few years, that all members of society have a vested interest in the survival of the financial system that can't be compared to even those giant corporate entities. (After all, we can always go shopping at Target.) Anyone who quibbles with that may want to discuss their views with the citizens of Iceland, who saw their own money grid almost completely disappear; now some Icelanders are returning to fishing to keep food on the table as the country's three McDonald's franchises closed their doors—good for the country's nutrition, doubtless, but a blow to its economy and psychology. It's deceptively easy for anyone to decide what makes for a good regulatory outcome in other utilities (clean water flows through the water pipes; electrical power is delivered when needed and in the quantity required to meet the demands of even the hottest summer days), and a failure is equally easy to spot (a blackout, for instance).

But on Wall Street, what makes for a good regulatory outcome is far more nebulous. Even the events of 2008 are subject to debate. Did they signify the failure of the regulatory function, because several major institutions collapsed, others required hundreds of billions of dollars of taxpayer capital to survive, and the entire money grid came within a fraction of an inch of the brink of disaster? Or was it a success, because legislators and regulators were able to pull together in a remarkable last-ditch effort in the worst days of the autumn of 2008 and rescue the most systemically important institutions, those deemed too big to fail? The definition of a good regulatory outcome is equally subjective. Ask an investment banking shareholder, and he will likely reply that a hands-off approach by regulators that allows the companies whose stock they own to capture a bigger market share and maximize their profits is the most desirable system. Corporations want a system that provides them with low-cost access to capital, even when the transactions that they seek to complete are ones that are uneconomic for Wall Street to undertake. Money managers and individual investors want a system that protects them from Ponzi schemes and other abuses.

The very disparate views of the goals of financial market regulation were part of the problem. Another major reason that the financial system would be left unguarded and unprotected (in the eyes of some, at least) at a crucial juncture was the fact that to many on Wall Street, the laudable goal of protecting the money grid required tolerating the intolerable: government intervention. By the dawn of the twenty-first century, the kind of deregulatory fervor that James Gilleran displayed in taking a chain saw to symbolic and actual red tape wasn't an anomaly but part and parcel of the political and regulatory ethos in the United States.

For government intervention in the shape of regulation to be acceptable, the proposed rules must be able to clearly demonstrate their value in advance, this camp argued, a burden of proof that was hard to meet. The FDIC's Sheila Bair admitted that when banking supervisors had to rely on judgment, the absence of clear reason for concern—such as losses from the risky activities—made it difficult to intervene. "Without hard evidence that the activities were creating unwarranted risk," trying to clamp down on risk taking would have been a provocative move, Bair suggests. (It would also have ignited a firestorm of controversy: Why were regulators seeking to meddle in a profitable business run by talented professionals?) "In retrospect, it is clear that supervisors were not sufficiently forward-looking in identifying and correcting imprudent risks," Bair testified at the FCIC hearings. "Current profitability alone is not a sufficient measure of safety and soundness." Indeed, profits—particularly the kind of record profits posted in the six straight years between 2001 and 2006—can be a red flag alerting a vigilant regulator to risky business. Only now, in the aftermath of the chaos made worse by the simultaneous failure of incentives, risk management, and regulation, is it philosophically acceptable to talk about preemptive regulation—protective regulation—once more.

Washington and Wall Street have coexisted uneasily for as long as there has been an independent national government and a national financial system. As long as financial markets have existed, what happens within them has consequences not only for the financiers but also for citizens who are far removed from Wall Street and who would be hard-pressed to distinguish a stock from a bond when asked to do so, much less define a derivative. The current crisis has wrecked the national economy of Iceland and caused havoc in German towns; everyone from marketing executives at consumer product firms to managers of geriatric nursing homes has had to frantically rewrite budgets to cope with the financing crisis that ensued. New college graduates, retirees, and entrepreneurs have seen their dreams shattered. Some economists calculate that the cost of the current crisis may reach as much as $4 trillion. That is a high price to pay for the de facto failure of governance, risk management, and regulation. American citizens, regardless of their level of wealth or personal opinions on the merits of regulation or government intervention, will end up paying for the government bailouts of Wall Street institutions and regulatory shortcomings in the form of higher taxes or lower government spending on other projects for years to come.

Deregulatory Fervor and Unintended Consequences

It shouldn't have been this bad. In the wake of the 1929 market crash and the nationwide depression that followed a wave of bank failures in the 1930s, politicians recognized the impossibility of controlling the fear-and-greed cycle that has governed financial dealings for centuries. People, left to their own devices, will fuel future bubbles, they knew, whether the focus of runaway speculation was tulip bulbs or railroad stocks. But, they reasoned, the federal government could put in place a set of institutions whose function was to take a pin to those bubbles (or even find a way to let the air gently out of them) before they could become so big that when they burst they would wreak havoc on the entire system.

In the 1930s, a battered and disgraced Wall Street had little ability to object to the array of reforms and regulatory measures introduced by Washington. When Congress passed the 1933 Glass-Steagall Act mandating the separation of commercial banks (entities taking deposits from individuals and businesses) from investment banks (those banks engaged in the riskier business of trading or raising capital via the debt and equity markets), even J. P. Morgan's heirs bowed to the inevitable. In September 1935, a clutch of J.P. Morgan office boys pushed eighteen heavy wooden rolltop desks out the doors of 23 Wall Street, the building at the corner of Wall and Broad that the financier had occupied from the day it was built until his death in 1913. They shoved them up a slight incline, past the New York Stock Exchange on their left, to the doors of a newer building at the corner of Wall Street and Broadway. A new investment bank, Morgan Stanley, had been born, in response to Washington's demand for risk reduction.

But Wall Street was never comfortable with the extent to which regulators restricted its collective ability to seek out new sources of business and profits. Every time a financier was blocked from doing something new and creative, he chafed at what felt like senseless and burdensome regulations. With the passage of decades and the disappearance of those who could all too vividly recall the horrors of the crash and the Depression, even rules like Glass-Steagall seemed increasingly unnecessary. With the transformation of Wall Street's business during the 1970s, and in particular as increasingly powerful competitors arose in Europe and Japan, Wall Street's leaders began viewing regulation as not only something that blocked their firms from earning as much as they could, but something that would lead, inevitably, to the loss of market share to overseas rivals and the erosion of Wall Street's unquestioned dominance of global markets. Banks such as Deutsche Bank and Credit Suisse didn't have to worry about Glass-Steagall, they fretted. They had giant balance sheets, the likes of which Morgan Stanley, Goldman Sachs, and Salomon Brothers could only dream about. Happily for Wall Street, this growing disgruntlement on its part coincided with the rise to power of a group of politicians with a distaste for regulation that, if anything, exceeded that of the financiers.

Ronald Reagan's vision of America harked back to a golden age of sorts, around the dawn of the twentieth century, when American lives were lived around the town square and the country store, where the Fourth of July was celebrated sedately and joyously with picnics of fried chicken and blueberry pie followed by fireworks after dusk. Free enterprise was part of being a free man or woman, in this worldview, and Reagan had an apparently endless series of witty and damning bons mots about the evils of government intervention. "The nine most terrifying words in the English language are, 'I'm from the government and I'm here to help,'" the former president quipped on one occasion. As for the government's view of the economy, that was easy to summarize: "If it moves, tax it. If it keeps moving, regulate it. And if it stops moving, subsidize it." Reagan's view of regulators themselves was equally jaundiced. "The best minds are not in government," he declared. "If any were, business would hire them away."[7] Regan's philosophy resonated deeply on Wall Street. Freedom, the new president proclaimed, was a core American value. Didn't that include the freedom from regulation for those on Wall Street?

Free market fundamentalists, as George Soros dubbed them, rose to power in the Reagan era but weren't confined to the Republican Party. When the Democrats took control of the White House and (briefly) Congress in 1992, policy toward Wall Street continued to revolve around deregulation, with few interruptions. (Robert Rubin, who later prodded Citigroup's bankers to take more and more risk at the height of the bubble, was a Goldman Sachs alumnus appointed by President Clinton to run the Treasury Department; not surprisingly, he advocated a hands-off approach to regulating Wall Street.) Increasingly, policy makers and legislators seemed to overlook the fact that an underregulated Wall Street could create havoc that wasn't confined to the financial system itself but stretched well into the broader economy and society. In other words, it wasn't just their own fate for which Wall Street firms were responsible. In the same way that a pharmaceutical company that didn't test its drugs properly (and didn't have an effective FDA overseeing those tests) would not only blow itself up but cause active harm to the general public, so the collapse of a Wall Street firm could have far broader consequences.

History spelled out the message quite clearly. The nineteenth century was punctuated by a regular series of panics on Wall Street: one in 1819, another in 1837, and still another in 1857. The Panic of 1873 (caused by a toxic combination of events that ranged from the railroad bubble to the effort by financier Jay Cooke to corner the gold market and his subsequent bankruptcy) led to a six-year-long national depression; the conflict between labor and management that followed it lasted well into the twentieth century and can be traced back to the decision of President Rutherford Hayes to use troops to break a strike by railroad workers. (Scores were killed.)

The 1873 crash caused bankruptcies across the United States and put an end to post–Civil War Reconstruction in the South; there was no money to continue political and economic reforms, meaning that African Americans in many former slave states had to wait another century to exercise their right to vote. The 1873 panic was followed by a boom revolving around more railroad speculation—which in turn produced yet another panic in 1893. That financial and economic crisis caused mayhem in eastern and midwestern manufacturing centers and sent displaced workers drifting westward to populate western cities from Portland to San Diego. One nineteenth-century panic caused the collapse of more than a dozen railroads; a later one was responsible for the demise of some six hundred banking institutions. In all cases, leverage was one of the culprits.[8]

Then came the Panic of 1907, an event that offers some uncanny parallels to the events of a century later: the complete disappearance of liquidity from financial markets, the collapse of one of Wall Street's largest financial institutions (the Knickerbocker Trust Company), the phenomenon of contagion as the crisis rippled through the system from one financial institution to the next, and the unwillingness of New York banks to extend even short-term credit.[9] Only the intervention of J. P. Morgan himself, playing the role of the then nonexistent Federal Reserve, saved the day. Summoning Wall Street's best and brightest to his Wall Street offices, he commanded them to cough up $25 million in the next ten minutes to keep the stock exchange open or watch the financial system itself collapse. Within half an hour of the arrival of the first banker at Morgan's offices, $23.6 million had reached the stock exchange; liquidity had been restored.

Morgan had saved the day, but his actions had created two separate sources of concern that led directly to the creation of a regulatory institution that could fill the role that Morgan had: the Federal Reserve. There were widespread fears that Morgan's power—so dramatically revealed—could be misused. Those who didn't worry about Morgan himself were concerned that after his death (which came in March 1913, months before the Fed's creation) there would be no other single individual with the same blend of skill, judgment, power, and force of character to perform the same function in the event of future panics. A regulatory agency was the solution that addressed both sets of concerns.

The chain of events that began in the summer of 2007 reminded even die-hard free market fundamentalists that in the midst of financial panics, regulation and regulators had their uses. Henry "Hank" Paulson, the former CEO of Goldman Sachs, had pleaded for years that Wall Street be allowed to regulate itself. Appointed Treasury secretary in 2006, he remained a staunch advocate of free financial markets. "An open, competitive and liberalized financial market can effectively allocate scarce resources in a manner that promotes stability and prosperity far better than governmental intervention," Paulson told an audience at the Shanghai Futures Exchange in the spring of 2007, a speech that was seen by global economists as part of an ongoing campaign by the United States and U.S.-based financial institutions to persuade China to follow their lead at a faster pace.[10] (China had already introduced new products such as foreign-exchange derivatives contracts and expanded its bond market, but it was slower in developing its asset-backed securities market and still imposed constraints on the local activities of U.S. financial institutions.)

Within eighteen months, Paulson was down on one knee in front of Nancy Pelosi in the Oval Office, begging for her help to get Congress to pass an unprecedented bailout package, one that would involve massive government intervention, to save the financial system from disaster. Meanwhile, the effort to preempt global competition had begun to look like an academic exercise. For now, at least, giant financial institutions had to worry more about surviving than about losing market share. And in China, local regulators were learning a lesson that their U.S. counterparts might have absorbed in 1873, 1893, 1907, or 1929. "Financial innovation is a double-edged sword," Fan Wenzhong, deputy head of research at the China Banking Regulatory Commission, said at a September 2008 conference in Beijing. "We can't just concentrate on product innovation and overlook the need to build the financial system."[11]

But by the time Paulson had learned that regulators and legislators (however flawed the individuals themselves might be) might have their virtues when it came to serving as a counterweight to the worst excesses of Wall Street's "animal spirits," it was late in the day. The regulatory framework had been established early in the twentieth century as a way to prevent another financial markets panic. But over the last twenty-five years, either the power of regulators to act had been curtailed or those individuals installed at the helm of regulatory agencies were unwilling to act.

Even if the new breed of regulators installed by the deregulatory zealots could bring themselves to admit that something more than just another normal market hiccup was taking shape, their hands-off philosophy left them powerless and paralyzed. Just as bankers used magical thinking to reassure themselves that the heavy winds and choppy seas they saw weren't a category 5 hurricane taking shape, regulators tried to convince themselves that the free market fundamentalists had it right and another panic wasn't on the way—it couldn't be, because an article of their faith was that market discipline would prevent any financial institution from taking silly or ill-considered risks. (Sheila Bair of the FDIC might note after the storm that a belief in self-regulating, self-correcting market was a fallacy; until that had become obvious, however, that view would have been deemed heretical by any in a position to act on it and beef up regulation.) By the time the storm made landfall, it was too late to act.

In just one example, the formal repeal of the Glass-Steagall Act in 1999 (after years of steady erosion) had helped create banking institutions that the Fed and the Treasury Department now realized were too big to be allowed to fail. Bailouts of AIG and the injection of billions of dollars of new capital to maintain institutions that might otherwise have collapsed, such as Citigroup, are part of the price that American taxpayers and businesses will have to pay for failing to protect the money grid. But the consequences of the near collapse of the money grid are liable to be far more dramatic and long-lasting than those of the actual collapse of the electricity grid in the northeastern United States and parts of Canada in the summer of 2003. The latter event, a daylong blackout, was unpleasant and caused chaos as well as millions of dollars of losses in spoiled food and lost business. But restoring the power grid to full effectiveness is a matter of willpower, capital, and equipment. Restoring the financial grid to health will take longer and cost trillions of dollars. And when it's done, Wall Street, and our relationship with it, will never be the same again.

Unintended Consequences

Perhaps someone should have warned these avid deregulators of the law of unintended consequences. But even in cases where a specific deregulatory measure didn't have unintended consequences (on which more later), the cumulative effect of the deregulatory ethos was such that over time, the idea that it might be appropriate or acceptable to regulate Wall Street became less and less politically acceptable. "If government appoints as regulators those who do not believe in regulation, one is not likely to get strong enforcement," economist Joseph Stiglitz pointed out in his testimony to Congress. Ultimately, those who did believe in regulation and who managed to survive within that kind of system found it difficult to actually regulate. Meanwhile, Congress—even before the financial crisis hit and the Madoff scandal dominated newspaper headlines—had concluded that regulators too often made a hash of their job even when they chose to do it.

It's hard to think of an excuse for the SEC's failure to figure out what Bernard Madoff was up to in his massive Ponzi scheme, especially since at least one concerned individual, financial analyst Harry Markopolos, presented an analysis of the whole scheme to them on a silver platter years before Madoff himself confessed. But perhaps there's an explanation for the agency's apparent inability to act, one that dates back to the events of 2005 that culminated in the SEC's decision to fire Gary Aguirre.

Aguirre, a staff lawyer, had spent months investigating a series of mysterious trades by hedge fund Pequot Capital Management, and believed that Pequot might have been tipped off to an upcoming merger by John Mack, then CEO of Credit Suisse and a friend of Pequot's founder, Art Samberg. (All the targets of Aguirre's investigation denied any wrongdoing and the SEC dropped the matter without bringing any charges, while a later congressional investigation into Aguirre's dismissal found no basis for his allegations. However, a second inquiry begun in 2008 prompted Samberg to close his firm the next spring.)

Aguirre wanted to subpoena Mack, then in the running for the CEO's job at Morgan Stanley, to question him about his relationship with Pequot and obtain records of any conversations related to the merger in question. His superiors at the SEC told him to back off, and within months Aguirre was fired. The 2007 congressional investigation that found Aguirre's specific allegations baseless nonetheless lambasted the SEC for its lack of backbone and specifically for paying "undue deference" to powerful potential witnesses such as Mack himself. (Mack testified, but the timing was unusual: his appearance was scheduled for a few days after the statute of limitations for any potential offenses had lapsed.) If trying to put John Mack into the hot seat got Aguirre into hot water, why would any regulator trying to keep his job pursue allegations about the equally powerful former chairman of the Nasdaq Stock Market, Bernard Madoff? It seemed tantamount to committing professional suicide.

That's the kind of message that the hands-off approach to regulation was sending, explicitly or implicitly, for much of the two decades leading up to the crisis. Regulators may have helped resolve the Long-Term Capital Management debacle, but they didn't help to prevent it.

Analysts and short sellers were the first to publicly discuss their concerns about Enron's opaque accounting; a detailed SEC investigation followed, but as short seller Jim Chanos of Kynikos Associates said at the time, "It just gave us all the gory details; it wasn't as if they were catching anything or discovering anything that anyone who had looked at their financial statements didn't already suspect was there. It wasn't regulating and preventing a thing; it was coloring in the picture we already knew."[12] Regulators, Chanos points out, were bolting the barn door long after the horse had fled. Speaking out again in 2009, Chanos argued at the Intelligence Squared debate that "there has not been one major financial fraud in the past 25 years uncovered by the government, outside auditors, or outside counsel. It's always been journalists, whistle-blowers, or short-sellers, or some combination thereof."[13]

Ultimately, the combination of regulation and deregulation created a particularly toxic brand of chaos. In the aftermath of the near collapse of AIG, Congress and other onlookers went hunting for the regulator that should have been scrutinizing the doings at AIG's financial products division. (That London-based unit was the part of the insurance company earning the big fees selling credit default swaps and failing to maintain any capital against potential losses, bringing AIG and the financial system itself so close to collapse that by mid-2009 the government had forked over some $170 billion to save AIG alone.) They found dozens of potential suspects; in every country where AIG did business—virtually every developed nation and many developing ones as well—there was a regulator responsible for overseeing part of their business. Then, on March 5, 2009, Scott Polakoff, the interim director of the Office of Thrift Supervision and heir to the chain-saw-wielding Gilleran, somewhat sheepishly asked to interrupt a Senate hearing into AIG's near demise to 'fess up. "It's time for OTS to raise their hand and say they have some responsibility and accountability here," Polakoff admitted. "We were deemed an acceptable regulator for both U.S. and domestic and international operations." Florida senator Mel Martinez seemed taken aback. "You [are] the regulator we've been looking for," he marveled. "I think we had assumed there wasn't one." "I'm the one," Polakoff responded. Anyone who had watched as one OTS-regulated institution after another collapsed as a result of poor risk controls might have been forgiven for whispering to himself, "I might have known."

Perverse Incentives

Without strong regulatory agencies in place—entities with the willingness to regulate prudently and the ability and resources to follow through on their regulations—there was little incentive for financial institutions such as Washington Mutual, Countrywide, or AIG to maintain prudent provisions against future losses. The proverbial carrot—the lure of higher earnings—pushed them in the opposite direction, and there seemed now to be no effective stick in the shape of curmudgeonly regulators determined to make them do the right thing.

A 2004 report by the Office of Federal Housing Enterprise Oversight (OFHEO) disclosed significant accounting irregularities at Fannie Mae and Freddie Mac that couldn't fail to raise questions about the judgment of the CEOs of both agencies. Nonetheless, Franklin Raines, CEO of Fannie Mae, responded to a question from a congressman about whether the agency's decision to set aside a mere 3 percent of its assets against possible future losses—a razor-thin cushion by most standards—by declaring that he felt it was actually too large a sum. The single- and multifamily home mortgages that Fannie Mae owned, Raines testified, were "so riskless that capital for holding them should be under 2 percent." While Raines didn't get any encouragement to slash those reserves further, his comments weren't met with howls of protest from anyone, from regulators to members of Congress. In fact, when Armando Falcon of the OFHEO testified about the accounting irregularities, Barney Frank of the House Financial Services Committee responded by saying, "I don't see anything in your report that raises safeness and soundness problems."[14]

Alan Greenspan, who had led the Federal Reserve for nearly two decades by this time, continued to believe that "enlightened self-interest" would cause Wall Street leaders such as Raines to act prudently. He cherished the illusion that their firms could regulate themselves, in the face of evidence showing him that enthusiastic risk taking was more integral to Wall Street than sober and attentive risk management. Sophisticated risk models and the even more elaborate derivative products from which Wall Street was earning more in profits (at higher profit margins) with every year that passed would do what they were designed to do, Greenspan was convinced. The only requirement was that the "enlightened self-interest of owners and managers of financial institutions [should lead] them to maintain a sufficient buffer against insolvency by actively monitoring their firms' capital and risk positions," he wrote a year after the collapse of Bear Stearns.[15]

Greenspan admits that he made a mistake. But rather than blame regulators for their failure to oversee what was going on, or the institutions for being imprudent, Greenspan directed his fire at the hypercomplex derivative products, which were "too much for even the most sophisticated market players to handle prudently." In other words, he said, there is nothing that any regulator or Wall Street rocket scientist could have done.

Greenspan may have been right, but the truth was that no one tried. Regulators didn't attempt to keep up with the pace of innovation on Wall Street, the growth in its use of and reliance on leverage, and its growth in size and reach. Even had they wanted to rein in what was going on, their efforts would have been doomed to failure.

There's a good reason why Greenspan is now widely viewed (particularly on Main Street) as one of the chief culprits responsible for the financial crisis. As is the case with most regulators, his errors were ones of omission rather than commission, but they were big ones. If anyone had the ability to realize clearly that Wall Street was motivated more by greed and the fear of losing a fraction of a percentage point of market share to a rival rather than by the fear of being seen to be less than responsible or honorable custodians and users of the financial grid, it was Greenspan. It was he who clung to the conviction that a prolonged period of ultralow interest rates wouldn't harm the financial system, who kept the punch flowing long after the partygoers were intoxicated and reeling around half senseless.

Greenspan, dubbed "the Maestro," was perhaps the single individual who had the gravitas and the power to stand up to Congress, the president, and Wall Street CEOs and warn them they were being reckless or shortsighted. Had he chosen to, he could have insisted that legislators transform the OTS into a powerful entity with the will and the ability to regulate the IndyMacs and AIGs. He could have sounded the alarm about inadequate reserves and risky derivatives, as a handful of respected financiers such as George Soros and Warren Buffett were already doing. (Buffett memorably and presciently described derivatives as "weapons of mass financial destruction.") Instead, Greenspan proclaimed in 2004, as the bubble was taking shape, "individual financial institutions [have] become less vulnerable to shocks," while the financial system as a whole was downright robust. And as for those derivatives, the ones that by 2009 he argued had been too much to handle? In 2003 he contended that they were an excellent device for transferring risk from those who couldn't handle it to those who could. He suggested to the Senate Banking Committee that regulating them would be a mistake.

The derivatives market is perhaps the single largest example of deregulatory zeal on Wall Street. When the regulatory framework that still governed Wall Street in 2007 was created in the 1930s, no one dreamed that these products would even exist. (Getting a 1940s-era policy maker to plan for derivatives was about as rational as suggesting to a Victorian policeman that he send off blood traces found at the scene of a crime to be tested for DNA.) Like all financial innovations, derivatives were a compelling addition to the tools at Wall Street's disposal. A corporate treasurer could use interest rate swaps to manage his company's exposure to interest rates; currency-related derivatives enabled companies that earned a lot of income outside the United States to manage the risk associated with unexpected moves in the value of the dollar. Used that way, derivatives reduced risk for Wall Street's clients.

But these high-octane instruments could also be used as outright bets on the direction or movement of markets, creating more risk for their users. It all came down to how they were being employed. And during the 1980s and 1990s, as derivatives became far more widely used (data from the International Swaps and Derivatives Association, ISDA, showed a jump from about $850 billion in 1985 to $8.5 trillion by 1993), concern that regulators didn't have a clue about how they were being used began to mount. ISDA's membership—which included most of the big Wall Street institutions along with other large and midsized banks—successfully fought off a first effort by the Commodity Futures Trading Commission to bring derivatives under its oversight. By the mid-1990s, when market events pushed regulation back up to the top of the agenda once more, ISDA had helped the industry prepare to fight back. "Market discipline is the best form of discipline there is," Mark Brickell, then head of ISDA, was guaranteed to proclaim, in one way or another, at every ISDA-sponsored event.

But some of these highly structured products now were causing losses on Main Street and attracting the attention of both legislators and regulators. Procter & Gamble and Gibson Greetings were hit with losses related to derivative-like instruments on their books that their treasurers insisted didn't perform as Wall Street had promised. (It remains up for debate whether the treasurers really didn't understand what they were being sold, or simply claimed not to when their bets later turned bad.) Meanwhile, Orange County had lost some $2 billion on leveraged bond derivatives called inverse floaters and in 1994 became the largest U.S. municipality to declare bankruptcy as a result. Its treasurer had bought the derivatives from Merrill Lynch after first trying to deal with J.P. Morgan. "Under no circumstances should we deal with this client!" concluded J.P. Morgan banker Bill Demchak, returning to New York after a meeting with the treasurer, Robert Citron, having realized just how clueless the bank's potential client was about what derivatives were, what they could and couldn't do, and the risks that were involved.[16]

Even before the losses, alarm bells were ringing. Richard Breeden, once known as an avid deregulator during his days at the helm of the SEC, warned corporate directors about the potential risks of derivatives in a *Wall Street Journal* editorial. In May 1994, the General Accounting Office (GAO) presented a 195-page report summarizing two years of study of the burgeoning derivatives market to Congress. The GAO—better known as a supporter of free markets than of regulation—concluded that there were "significant gaps and weaknesses" in the way that derivatives were regulated and urged Congress to appoint a federal agency to oversee "the safety and soundness of all major OTC derivatives dealers." A fierce fight followed in Congress and within the broader business community, with many regulators lining up alongside Wall Street, ISDA, and Greenspan. A handful of congressional leaders took up the regulatory battle. When in a hearing on proposed derivatives regulation ISDA's Brickell blasted Representative Jim Leach for treating derivatives differently from other securities, Leach retorted that they *were* different. They "are new, they are off balance sheet, they are a totally different dimension."[17]

Ultimately the free market fundamentalists prevailed, partly because some former critics saw the light. Gerald Corrigan, during his days at the helm of the New York branch of the Federal Reserve— the Fed post that gives its holder the closest view of what is going on on Wall Street—had once voiced concern about the newfangled and complex securities. Upon leaving the Fed, Corrigan went to work at Goldman Sachs; soon he was named cochairman of the fledgling Derivatives Policy Group, whose goal was to convince legislators that the bankers themselves were in the best position to both understand these complex instruments and manage their risks. Wendy Gramm, a former CFTC chair (and wife of former senator Phil Gramm, coauthor of the legislation reversing the Depression-era Glass-Steagall Act; she would become infamous as a member of Enron's audit committee), suggested that Washington should "resist the urge . . . to over-regulate what we just do not understand."[18] Greenspan's confidence in free markets remained unshaken; he continued to assure Congress and the public throughout the 1990s that the market could regulate derivatives usage just as ably as any agency.

As the usage of derivatives continued to grow and spread throughout the financial system, with more and more complex iterations being devised, the concern increasingly revolved around the lack of transparency in the market for these instruments. The existence of a stock exchange provides a degree of transparency that helps investors value a company's equity; the very liquid bond market, even in the absence of an exchange, made tracking bond prices relatively straightforward. An investor might quibble over whether the valuation the market was giving to the stocks or bonds was appropriate. But the transparency of the market meant that she could figure out what that valuation was with the click of a mouse.

In contrast, derivatives—which tended to be more customized instruments—didn't trade anywhere and didn't clear through any entity that was monitored by a regulator. Anyone requesting the most basic information on the industry—such as the notional value of credit default swaps written—could obtain only informed guesstimates. Brooksley Born, head of the Commodity Futures Trading Commission (CFTC) in the late 1990s, asked Wall Street and other interested parties to comment on ways that derivatives might be regulated in order to be sure that these increasingly ubiquitous and high-octane instruments didn't threaten the stability of the financial system before regulators were even aware of what was going on.

Within the blink of an eye, the deregulatory gang circled the wagons and began heaping scorn on Born. Even the crisis surrounding Long-Term Capital Management, whose losses were caused in part by the hedge fund's use of derivatives to magnify its bets on the bond market that later went sour, failed to save Born's initiative—or her career. Congress barred the CFTC from wielding any regulatory clout over derivatives for six months; Born resigned in 1999. (Born would be back. In 2009 she received the John F. Kennedy Library Foundation's Profile in Courage Award, presented to the public servants who have made courageous decisions of conscience without regard for the personal or professional consequences, for her efforts to bring the derivatives market under some kind of regulatory oversight. She was also named a commissioner of the FCIC, meaning that she is now in a position to shape the debate surrounding future regulation and closely question her former adversaries.) The same year, Greenspan and others (including then Treasury secretary Bob Rubin, who would later become vice chairman at Citigroup, a major player in global derivatives markets) proposed that Congress ban the CFTC from any future meddling in the derivatives universe.

Of course, like so many analyses—the Treasury's report on the shenanigans at the OTS, the UBS shareholders' report, and a chilling SEC survey of what went wrong at Bear Stearns—this chain of events looks more dramatic and alarming when viewed with the benefit of twenty-twenty hindsight. At the time, many Wall Street regulators believed the real threat was not lax regulation but overly oppressive regulation. Creating tough new derivatives rules wouldn't wipe out the demand for these products overnight, and it certainly wouldn't eliminate the eagerness of the global investment banks to earn fees from structuring and selling them. The impact of regulating derivatives would have been to drive the business offshore and undermine Wall Street's preeminence as a financial center. With every year that passed, this became a more likely scenario, it seemed. In the wake of economic liberalization in China, new businesses were being formed at a rapid clip; the demand for capital was at its height there, and an Asian financial institution could conceivably use success in China to establish itself as the next Citigroup or JPMorgan Chase. Then there was Europe, where the city of London was making determined efforts to compete head-to-head with Wall Street for the title of global financial capital.

As late as 2005 and 2006, those fears seemed even more intense. In the wake of the billions of dollars lost amid the accounting scandals revealed at the beginning of the decade, Congress passed the Sarbanes-Oxley Act. Sarbox, as it is familiarly (but not affectionately) known, tried to address a valid concern: the fact that corporate managers had been able to manipulate their earnings and distort the public portrayal of their financial position.

But Sarbox created a financial burden for the publicly traded companies that had to comply with the new law, particularly smaller companies. While the SEC had originally estimated the cost of meeting the new audit and governance rules at around $91,000 per firm, companies reported spending an average of $4.36 million each in 2004 alone, the first year that the rules took effect. Those figures were reported by the Committee on Capital Markets Regulation, which also noted that while half of all IPO proceeds raised in 2000 by companies (U.S. and foreign) selling stock occurred through a transaction on a U.S. exchange, by 2006 that had shrunk to only 5 percent. (It's unclear whether the reason was actually the competitiveness of American capital markets or other factors, such as the reality that a growing number of IPO candidates were non-U.S. companies that preferred to go public on an exchange based in their own country.) Meanwhile, the independent group noted that private equity funds were growing rapidly, a clear signal that regulation and the costs of complying with regulation were keeping both issuers and investors out of the public markets—at least in the United States.[19] In London, however, the London Stock Exchange's Alternative Investment Market (AIM) was increasingly appealing even to U.S. companies that might have been expected to go public on Nasdaq; it held regular marketing seminars in New York and San Francisco to which were invited investment bankers and promising young private companies.

The London exchange bragged about AIM's "pragmatic and flexible approach to regulation" (which involves the company picking one of a number of approved lawyers, accountants, or other corporate finance professionals to vouch for its bona fides, permitting both the company and the exchange to outsource regulatory issues to these nomads). Alarmed by this and other trends (companies were also going public in Amsterdam and Tokyo; U.S. investment banks viewed China and even Europe as higher-growth markets), groups such as the Committee on Capital Markets Regulation increasingly spoke out about the oppressive burden that regulations like Sarbox created for Wall Street. "Let's be frank—people liked London because it was less regulated than New York," says the head of one of the large hedge funds that began building up a presence in the city at the beginning of the new millennium. "If you were a company going public, that was what mattered, period. For hedge funds, there was the extra benefit of the time zone." (From London, hedge funds could trade in Asian markets in the morning, European markets throughout their working day, and U.S. markets in the afternoon and evening.)

The SEC, meanwhile, became the target of a very specific and intensive lobbying effort to reduce the burdens of regulation on the part of Wall Street in the spring of 2004. The big investment banks, led by Goldman Sachs, wanted to increase the amount of leverage they could take onto the balance sheets of their brokerage divisions. If the SEC agreed, the investment banks could stop holding so much capital in reserve against future losses by their brokerage divisions. Instead, that capital could flow up the corporate chain to the parent company, which could put it to work in ways best calculated to increase ROE and profits—ways that included investments in CDOs and mortgage-backed securities as well as credit derivatives and other complex structured products.

Since the net capital rule had been passed in 1975, investment banks had been required to limit the amount of leverage to $12 in debt for every $1 in equity on their books. They also had to tell regulators and shareholders if they approached that level too closely, and to stop trading if they exceeded it. In practice, that meant that leverage levels rarely topped 10 to 1. But in a low-interest-rate environment, taking more risk and building up leverage levels was more vital for investment banks trying everything they could to pump up their return on equity. And the SEC seemed to feel that Wall Street was now grown-up enough not to require any adult supervision, that the investment banks were interested enough in their reputations and self-preservation not to do anything stupid. So, after a brief meeting in April 2004, the SEC, under its chairman Christopher Cox, gave the go-ahead to switching to a new monitoring system, one that allowed the firms themselves to establish their own capital levels based on their own computer models. "I keep my fingers crossed for the future," quipped SEC commissioner Roel Campos, voting in favor of the measure.

Indeed, the decision proved to be the equivalent of firing a starter's pistol. The race itself was between the major investment banks, each of which seemed to be eager to claim the title of being the first to pile the largest amount of leverage on its balance sheet—or at least to deploy leverage to maximize return on equity and profits. At Bear Stearns, leverage peaked at around $33 of debt for every $1 of equity, while at one point Merrill Lynch had leverage ratios of 40 to 1. Not surprisingly, the golden years of finance followed the repeal of these net capital laws: by 2006, financial services companies made up nearly a quarter of the U.S. stock market's capitalization, compared to about 15 percent over the previous decades, and those companies earned 43 percent of all the earnings reported by companies in the Standard & Poor's 500 index.

Ironically, the SEC was able publicly to spin this de facto bit of deregulation as a way to *increase* its ability to keep an eye on what Wall Street was up to. That's because in exchange for the relaxation of the net capital rule, Wall Street firms agreed to let the SEC scrutinize their balance sheets, an agreement that conveniently dealt with another Wall Street headache—the threat by the European Union to regulate U.S. brokerage units doing business in England, France, and other parts of Europe. The EU authorities pledged not to do so if the SEC promised to regulate the parent entities. John Heine, the SEC spokesman, proclaimed that in fact the new 2004 rules "strengthened oversight of the securities markets, because prior to their adoption, there was no formal regulatory oversight" or liquidity standards for the parent holding company.[20]

That may have been true in theory, but in practice the SEC didn't seem terribly worried about what Wall Street was up to at either the brokerage firm level or the parent company level. Seven people were given the task of examining the finances of the parent companies. Performing that role, scrutinizing the balance sheets of the investment banking industry's largest players, should have given them enough insight into the levels of leverage and risk within the industry. However, they didn't act to rein in that risk taking, whether because

they didn't believe it posed a systemic threat to Wall Street or because they lacked the power to address any problems that they spotted. (The contents of the SEC's postmortem on Bear Stearns, which
not only clearly spelled out the firm's missteps but also suggested
that regulators were aware of those missteps as they occurred, suggests that the latter explanation for inaction was more probable.[21])
Nor between March 2007, when the first questions were beginning
to surface about the subprime crisis, and the autumn of 2008, after
the collapse of both Bear Stearns and Lehman Brothers and the sale
of Merrill Lynch to Bank of America, did that group have a director
to oversee their activities and lobby for action at higher levels within
the agency.[22]

If Greenspan was correct in his suggestion that it was the nature
of CDOs, derivatives, and other financial products that caused the
problem, together with the way financial institutions failed to manage the risks they created, regulators should have admitted their inability to control that risk. If the various regulatory bodies had simply
acknowledged that they couldn't monitor Wall Street anymore, much
less prevent investment banks from taking foolish risks, they would
have delivered a clear message to legislators and investors alike that
the latter would need to step up their own vigilance. Acknowledging
that the regulatory system wasn't up to the task of reining in the
increasingly complex world of Wall Street would have told other financial system participants to be still more prudent and protect themselves, since the regulators could no longer do it for them.

As it turned out, self-regulation remained the order of the day but
ended up making no one happy. It irked Wall Street, which disliked
having to pander (as bankers saw it) to regulators. In the eyes of Wall
Streeters, most of these officials weren't nearly as smart as the financiers they were overseeing; certainly, investment bankers argued,
they didn't understand what Wall Street's risk-taking culture was all
about. After all, if the regulators were really competent and capable

(or so the Reaganesque argument ran), they would have pursued a career on Wall Street itself, taking those risks and making big bucks, instead of becoming faceless bureaucrats. For their part, regulators were continually frustrated by their inability to get a clear picture of what was going on in the increasingly fragmented financial universe. Chaos seemed the most likely result of the potential information gap.

Most crucially, everyone seemed to want to defer to Wall Street. Politicians relied on Wall Street institutions for campaign donations; regulators such as the OTS relied on the same institutions to maintain their clout and budgetary power. (Even today, it is Wall Streeters who have been chosen to oversee the bailout and restructuring plans by government officials.) At first blush, it seemed as if the credit rating agencies had a unique chance to speak their minds. They had acquired the status of quasi-regulatory institutions thanks to Depression-era rules banning banks from owning non-investment-grade bonds; that made agencies providing the now urgently required ratings a de facto part of the Wall Street regulatory apparatus. Ratings agencies didn't report to Congress or rely on politicians for either their budgets or their ability to decide whether a corporate bond was a double-A or double-B. Ironically, as parts of the shadow banking system (such as securitization) became more important to Wall Street but also more likely to escape the oversight of other regulators, the ratings agencies became more crucial. At the same time, significantly, the nature of financial products became more complex. Only a triple-A rating could compensate for the complexity of the products emerging from the CDO-creation pipeline, enabling Wall Street to earn its fees and book the profits from its transactions.

Alas, the ratings agencies proved even more flawed in their ability to serve as some kind of guardian of the health of the financial system than the accountants who had blithely overlooked years of financial misstatements by the likes of Enron and WorldCom. Part of the problem lay in the deceptive simplicity of the ratings themselves.

The theory was that investors should be able to count on the credit quality of a triple-A asset to ensure that it would sail through the storm and emerge relatively unruffled, except perhaps in the event of a nuclear war or global pandemic. As bond managers liked to say, if a triple-A bond's quality deteriorated suddenly and significantly— enough, say, that it crossed into junk bond territory—then investors would have a hell of a lot more to worry about than what was happening to their portfolios. They'd be stocking up on canned goods and ammunition and heading for the hills. In contrast, a triple-B rating, while still investment-grade, signaled that an investor needed to monitor the transaction more closely. The ability to apply this very simple rating system to the extraordinarily complex world of structured finance was a coup for Wall Street, but it left investors with the perception that this new breed of security was just as easy for everyone to value and judge the risk of as a plain-vanilla bond.

The other problem was and remains the perennial one on Wall Street: the magnitude of the fees available for rating these CDOs and the identity of those footing the bill. Rating agencies may not have had to report to Congress, but they needed to report to their own shareholders. Turning down the opportunity to rate a CDO deal, a transaction that could generate $100,000 in fees for the agency, would have been just as hard to explain to their own investors as the decision by an investment bank not to structure the potentially lucrative CDO package in the first place. Not surprisingly, given the growing importance of structured finance products that required ratings, the ratings agencies became more deferential to Wall Street institutions, working with them on tweaking the design of the product in question. By 2005, about half of Moody's revenues came from the fees it earned for evaluating these and other structured products, and as much as 80 percent of its growth in revenue was coming from the same kinds of complex products. As the assets underlying the CDOs became more risky, the ratings agencies had become so dependent on fees they earned from them that turning down a deal became harder.

Marty Fridson, the veteran bond market analyst, says the real conflicts of interest didn't arise at the ratings agencies until recently, when they began to rate structured products such as CDOs. "For years, people objected in principle to the fact that the issuers selling the bonds paid the agencies for the rating, but in practice, it was rarely a problem," he argues. Information on the bond and the issuer's financial position was readily available to any analyst who wanted to check the accuracy of the agency's rating. And, Fridson points out, at the end of the day, a company that needs capital often has less clout than the rating agency. "The rating agency has an interest in maintaining the integrity of the rating; the issuer has to pay for that rating regardless of what it is, if they want to be able to sell the bonds."

In the world of structured finance, however, if the senior tranche of a CDO didn't get a triple-A rating, investors would be less likely to purchase it and the deal would be pulled. With no deal left to rate, agencies such as Moody's and S&P couldn't earn a fee. "The deal only worked if the top part could get a triple-A rating, and so it was in the agencies' interest to make sure they could do that," Fridson explains. The balance of power tipped definitely in favor of Wall Street. "No triple-A rating, no deal. No deal, no fee. Even if they'd had all the good intentions in the world, it would have been hard for them to manage that big a conflict of interest," suggests Fridson. "Both sides had a vested interest in getting it right—at least, getting it to the point where it could be sold." After that, it was caveat emptor.

No one in Washington or among the ranks of the quasi-regulators of the shadow banking system, it seemed, was both willing and able to oversee what was happening on Wall Street. To many, the debate over regulation felt increasingly academic, and little alarm was raised when an occasional regulator admitted that large parts of the financial system escaped not only the regulatory system's control but even its sight. In part, this was because of what Goldman Sachs strategist Abby Joseph Cohen once referred to (in the context of the dot-com years) as the "Cinderella economy"—nothing was ever carried to excess, and the level of market volatility remained low.

Initially, Ben Bernanke, Greenspan's successor as head of the Fed, was as phlegmatic as the Maestro himself. We were, Bernanke declared, living through "the Great Moderation," a period of market tranquility. As long as that lull continued, the gap between the regulators and their ability to monitor and oversee what was happening on Wall Street grew wider. Each Wall Street innovation ensured that the rules governing the Street became more outdated. Even the collapse of corporate giants Enron and WorldCom hadn't rattled confidence in the financial system for long. That financial markets could shake off such gigantic blows made even those worried about a looming subprime credit crisis confident that whatever happened, the financial system itself wouldn't suffer lasting damage; therefore, the fact that regulatory rules were outdated and agencies underfunded was less troubling.

When the government did respond to crises with new regulations, these tended to be too ad hoc to serve as well-considered responses to the root causes of whatever debacle they were intended to address. Many of them had just as many unintended consequences as deregulation had had. The settlement between regulators and investment banks in the wake of the conflict-of-interest scandals in investment research on Wall Street (finalized in 2002) required firms such as Citigroup and Merrill Lynch to rigorously separate research from investment banking activities. That laudable objective led to research itself being starved of resources; now that analysts couldn't use honest and objective opinions to help make money for the institution (even when those opinions were their own, developed without reference to their institution's financial interests), they were no longer a profit center. That meant that promising analysts ended up working in other areas of finance. The long-term consequences were damaging for both investors (who had access to less good-quality research on a wide range of stocks) and for smaller companies whose stock prices languished when investment banks cut back their research activities. There is certainly far less publicly available research on today's hot new market sector, green technology, than there was on the Internet in its early days. Then came Sarbanes-Oxley, which imposed costly new burdens on entrepreneurial companies, and which was passed in a matter of days to address the kind of governance problems detected at Enron only months previously.

In the view of some market participants, the need for well-considered and thoughtful regulation of Wall Street risk taking was growing as markets became faster-moving (with trades taking place in milliseconds rather than mere seconds), more global (with the advent of twenty-four-hour-a-day trading), and more interlinked. "Look, we're not known, as a group, for loving regulation for regulation's sake," says the CEO of one large hedge fund. "But someone, somewhere, should have had some kind of oversight of what was going on with Wall Street's balance sheets. And yes, I was saying so at the time. There should have been some risk-based guidelines on how big those balance sheets were allowed to grow."

On Main Street, there are lots of incentives for most of us to behave prudently. We try to keep some money set aside in cash for a rainy day—enough to cover our mortgage payment for a few months in case we lose our job or need to pay unexpected medical bills. In contrast, Wall Street seemed to be a kind of Wonderland, where normal rules of behavior were irrational. On Wall Street, all the incentives clearly urged financial institutions to believe that there would never be a rainy day and to behave accordingly. Washington succumbed to that way of thinking, whether it was due to Wall Street's lobbying (an appeal to legislators' self-interest) or to its preaching the virtues of self-regulation (an appeal to their idealism). By doing so, Washington seemed to suggest that this kind of magical thinking was just fine. As Niall Ferguson pointed out in the St. Patrick's Day debate, Washington-based institutions, from the SEC to the Fed, were great enablers of the hijinks on Wall Street. True, regulators didn't urge a financial institution to slash capital reserves to the bone—but they didn't protest when that happened. They even adjusted the rules, obligingly permitting the institution to do just that. Or, if the rules weren't changed, regulators such as the OTS quietly looked the other way.

Even after the collapse of Enron highlighted the risks associated with off-balance-sheet activities, Wall Street firms successfully lobbied for a rule that exempted them from consolidating their own offshore vehicles onto their publicly reported balance sheets. Suddenly, structured investment vehicles (SIVs) were being treated differently from off-balance-sheet vehicles at any other corporation. More and more, these SIVs became the place for financial institutions to park what they couldn't hold on their own balance sheets. While the SEC had relaxed rules pertaining to capital for the likes of Merrill Lynch, the Fed maintained tougher standards for the banks that it regulated. But neither the Fed nor any other regulator cared about SIVs, since they didn't show up on the balance sheet, and that balance sheet was what the regulators studied. So Citigroup shuffled lots of its hardest-to-manage securities into SIVs it had created offshore; when outside investors in the short-term securities used to finance the SIV began to protest, Citigroup pledged to buy back those securities at their full value if they ever ran into trouble—a promise that would come back to haunt the firm in 2007 and 2008.

But Washington's failure to monitor the health of the money grid went beyond its lack of oversight over complex securities and offshore off-balance-sheet transactions. As well as providing too little oversight, Washington was providing far too much credit, thereby permitting and even encouraging the institutions whose well-being was crucial to the health of the financial system to pile on more and more risk.

The lower interest rates fell and the longer they stayed there, the more demand Wall Street found among its investment clients for higher-yielding securities, even those that came with extra risk attached. "The Fed did not take away the punch bowl [of easy money]," says economist Nouriel Roubini, the new generation's "Dr. Doom." Instead, he suggests, the Fed responded by adding "vodka, whiskey, gin and [other] toxic stuff to it."[23] And even as individual members of Congress tried to rein in some of Wall Street's excesses, they failed to realize how their enthusiastic participation in other initiatives was actually fueling them.

Certainly, few members of Congress objected to the principles enshrined in the series of laws they passed designed to encourage home ownership among all strata of American society. "We want everybody in America to own their own home," declared President George W. Bush in 2002 before launching yet another round of initiatives aimed at that end. And yet, as Sheila Bair noted in her FCIC testimony, "There are both opportunity costs and downside risks associated with these policies."

In the name of the overarching virtues of home ownership, subprime loans made their debut. These loans were more and more affordable thanks not only to the creative financing by financial institutions but also to rock-bottom interest rates being maintained by Washington even as the rate at which house prices grew each year suddenly jumped from 7 percent to 17 percent. Even after Congress had become aware of the accounting problems at both Fannie Mae and Freddie Mac, they were slow to act to rein them in; by the time of their bailout, the two agencies had about $65 in debt for every $1 in assets. Those much-maligned subprime lenders could just claim that they were doing what their president commanded by turning more Americans into homeowners.

"Wall Street is one of the most competitive industries I have ever seen in my life," says Seth Merrin, founder of Liquidnet, who does business with nearly every major Wall Street institution. "If you put three or four of these guys in a room by themselves, within fifteen minutes they'll have some kind of bet going on, even if it's just how long it takes for a raindrop to hit the bottom of the window, and they'll all be yelling and screaming at their raindrop to move faster." These are the same people, Merrin wonders in disbelief, "that regulators expected to be rational and sensible and rein themselves in when the going got *really* exciting?" Merrin points out that the combination of government legislative policies that encouraged home ownership, fiscal policies that revolved around cheap money, and a deregulatory ethos was an environment designed to fuel ferocious competition between Wall Street institutions, each of which was intent on winning the biggest market share while maintaining the lowest possible capital reserves. "All the regulatory oversight catered to encouraging their self-interest, not to getting them to think about the fear part of fear and greed," he concludes.

The Fallout

Regulation is never perfect; every effort to shape the outcome of what Wall Street does leads to unintended consequences. Jeff Rubin, director of research at Birinyi Associates, a market analysis and investment firm, has studied the way markets work for decades and wonders, for instance, why regulators who oversee Wall Street have been so intent on pushing for ultra-high-speed transactions. "If an institution is investing for the long term, why does it make a difference that the trader can complete the trade in fifteen seconds instead of thirty seconds, and do it in pennies rather than eighths [of a dollar]?" Studies he has done show that speed doesn't necessarily produce a better price.

Rubin believes that many of the changes to the trading rules that have taken place over the last decade as markets have become more complex haven't benefited the entities for whose benefit Wall Street is supposed to exist—long-term investors and the companies who use Wall Street institutions to raise capital from that group of investors. "Those changes help Wall Street institutions like proprietary trading desks and hedge funds make money, not investors or issuers," Rubin declares bluntly. Regulators, he says, have been good at paying attention to the interests of the groups they are supposed to be overseeing but far less skilled at or interested in ensuring that the system their action and inaction produced was in the best interest of that core constituency.

Curiously, some of the beneficiaries of that lax regulation are now aligning themselves with Rubin (no relationship to Bob Rubin of Goldman Sachs, the Treasury Department, and Citigroup) and other critics. While no one has yet uttered the words "They made me do it!" some of the comments about regulators coming from senior figures on Wall Street don't fall far short of that. "Look, the people who were selling this stuff, they are being offered incentives to do it, in an environment where their bosses *and* the government knew, or could have known, what they were doing," says one top investment bank officer who worked closely with one of the former Wall Street CEOs dragged in to testify to Congress and the FCIC.

The executive is scornful of that process. "Oh, come on, it's for the TV cameras! It's like the car business; when the government is buying the car itself, why should I start worrying that this vehicle is unsafe at any speed? If Fannie and Freddie were buying these CDOs and subprime loans, if the regulators overseeing them and Congress weren't saying, 'Stop a second!' then even if at the back of your mind you say, 'Shit, I wouldn't buy this,' you justify it to yourself. It's your job to do this, you have bills to pay—and everyone, including the government, is telling you it's okay." At the back of Wall Street's mind, the former banker admits, was the thought that as long as Washington was putting its stamp of approval on the whole housing boom, those financial institutions that helped keep it moving wouldn't be held accountable for their actions; they would have a kind of get-out-of-jail-free card. That reasoning would prove valid for some, if not for those at Bear Stearns and Lehman Brothers.

To date, Congress has held several series of hearings to probe the various causes and consequences of the mess on Wall Street. If anything, however, they have showcased what seems like a lack of knowledge among representatives and senators about how Wall Street works, its purpose, and the reasons it came so close to the brink of disaster. Those hearings and the myriad public debates on the causes of the crisis have also shown how ready each group—Washington and Wall Street—is to toss the burden of responsibility to the other. It may be that the FCIC hearings prove to be more meaningful, although the first round of the discussions shed little new light on the topics under discussion. Still, at least this time around, those asking the questions are knowledgeable insiders rather than politicians who are trying to shed their past Wall Street affiliations and reflect their constituents' outrage at the Wall Street shenanigans. That alone may mean that the report—due by the end of 2010—will be informative and thoughtful, even though it may come too late to influence the shape of the first round of reform legislation in Congress.

Ultimately, both groups are culpable. After all, Washington didn't hold a gun to the head of Chuck Prince or any other investment bank CEO in order to force Wall Street to keep dancing. But regulators and legislators alike, instead of pulling the plug on the jukebox in order to preserve the health of the money grid, looked the other way and allowed the music to keep playing and Wall Street to keep dancing. In some cases, they took actions that resulted in the volume moving higher and tempting more participants onto the dance floor. The regulators and their overseers in Congress and the White House knew—or should have known—that the nature of those on Wall Street would be to boogie enthusiastically until the last note sounded. They could have insisted that the band play a mournful pavane in order to change the atmosphere. They could have taken away the toxic punch bowl that Roubini describes in order to restore sobriety to the proceedings. At the very least, they could have confiscated the car keys of all the revelers, to ensure that the damage they caused was limited to a few smashed glasses.

When regulators did wake up from their long nap and act, it was too late. They opened the Fed's lending window, in time to rescue Goldman Sachs and Morgan Stanley but too late to save Bear Stearns. By forcing a last-ditch rescue of Bear in the shape of the JPMorgan Chase takeover and bailing out Fannie Mae and Freddie Mac, regulators sent the signal to Richard Fuld at Lehman Brothers and other Wall Street CEOs that bailouts might be available for them, too. Not until the last minute, until a series of marathon meetings over the course of a now famous and stressful weekend in mid-September 2008 at the fortress-like headquarters of the New York Fed, did it become clear just how dire the situation was.

Timothy Geithner, then head of the New York Fed, urged the assembled bankers to try to find a way to finance Lehman's toxic assets, a measure that would have averted a bankruptcy filing and facilitated the company's sale to Barclays or another acquirer as a going concern. The Wall Street senior bankers, summoned at the eleventh hour and fifty-ninth minute, balked. How costly would this bailout be? Certainly far more so than Long-Term Capital Management had been, at a time when their own balance sheets were under pressure. And why should they help a competitor acquire Lehman? The bankers focused instead on finding a solution to prevent other investment banks from following Lehman down the drain; Geithner tried to refocus the discussion on the immediate problem of Lehman. "You guys have got to try harder," he demanded.[24] Ultimately, however, there was no alternative to Lehman's collapse; the effort was too little, too late.

Should Washington's legislators and regulators have treated Wall Street the same way that parents of irresponsible teenagers treat their children—setting curfews and restricting access to the family car? Your answer to that question probably depends on the philosophical perspective from which you approach it. But in the wake of the financial crisis and the credit crunch that rippled throughout the broader economy, leaving mayhem in its wake, it has become nearly as difficult to suggest that Wall Street be left to regulate itself as it has always been for parents to let their teenagers follow their instincts, however destructive, in the name of laissez-faire parenting philosophy. As George Soros—who himself has profited richly from free markets—suggests, "The stability of financial markets is not assured; it has to be actively maintained by authorities."[25]

What happens next will follow the script written in the 1930s, in the wake of the last great systemic crisis. Washington is about to rewrite the rule book according to which Wall Street must live, and build or rebuild a set of institutions that can enforce those rules. Only when it's evident what form those new rules will assume—a process that may take another five years or more to become clear— will it be possible for Wall Street to move beyond the current range of interim responses and figure out how it will perform its core function for the rest of the twenty-first century.

In order to develop more than simply a Band-Aid solution, Washington and Wall Street will need to join forces and create a kind of accountable capitalism. Like it or not, Wall Street is not the type of business that can be allowed to simply collapse if its members behave foolishly and its investors don't rein them in. That means that somehow legislators and regulators will need to inculcate an awareness of that overarching duty among Wall Streeters, from the Lloyd Blankfeins right down to the greenest junior banker. Without a sense of fiduciary duty, on the part of both Wall Street and its overseers, to the financial system itself—and not just to those who earn short-term profits by participating in that system—there is little reason to be optimistic about Wall Street's ability to avoid a future catastrophe.

Without free enterprise, there's no reason for Wall Street to exist, just as there's no reason to have cars if you don't have roadways on which to drive. But those roads have to be maintained, and cars have to be driven at safe speeds. Now it's up to a new generation of regulators and financiers to devise a new set of rules of the road for Wall Street, one that will emphasize its role as a utility.

PART III

THE NEW FACE OF WALL STREET

In the gloomy days of mid-January 2010, Wall Street's biggest players, led by Goldman Sachs and JPMorgan Chase, popped champagne corks in celebration of a rapid return to extraordinarily profitable operations. Goldman Sachs reported $13.39 billion in profits for 2009—thanks in large part to a special and unofficial Wall Street "stimulus" plan in the shape of ultralow borrowing rates. (The results dwarfed the forecast of even the most bullish analysts; the firm's earnings totaled $8.20 a share, compared to a consensus estimate of $5.19.) And then there was the bonus pool, which for 2009 would add up to $16.19 billion. Meanwhile, JPMorgan Chase announced that its profits had more than doubled since 2008, hitting $11.7 billion in 2009; its employees would share a $26.9 billion compensation and bonus pool. But while Wall Streeters—those who had survived the last two years—celebrated in a mixture of relief and joy, Main Street erupted in outrage. And even on Wall Street, the party didn't last long.

Even as we were all still digesting the fine print of those and other Wall Street earnings announcements, President Barack Obama presented his own vision of what Wall Street could and should look like in the future. Unlike most of those who have publicly discussed their ideal Wall Street in public since the crisis began, the president's plan was specific: he wants to see an end to institutions that are "too big to fail," or at least to firms whose size and level of risk taking together make them likely to threaten the entire financial system in the event of a collapse. Henceforward, Obama announced, banks that accept deposits from customers won't be allowed to conduct any proprietary trading; they would also be barred from advising or investing in hedge funds. On top of that, the president proposed that no bank have more than 10 percent of the nation's assets—not just its FDIC-insured assets.

While all of those proposals will require some form of new regulation, public outrage from Main Street at Wall Street's profits and pay packages meant that the president couldn't have timed his bombshell better. And if it is translated into the form of new rules, Wall Street firms will be forced to make a choice: remain a banking institution or cease treating other Wall Street institutions as their best clients. While he didn't use the word *utility* in his announcement, he might as well have done so. Investment analysts who only days earlier had voiced excitement about the potential future earnings power of firms like JPMorgan Chase and Goldman Sachs suddenly switched their focus to calculating the hit to the bottom line of these and other firms should the Obama proposals become the law of the land. Within a day of the announcement, a team of analysts at JPMorgan Chase itself calculated that the curb on proprietary trading—if carried through—would cost Goldman, Morgan Stanley, Credit Suisse, UBS, and Deutsche Bank about $13 billion in lost revenue in 2011. Goldman Sachs would feel the biggest hit, seeing a $4.67 billion loss of earnings in 2011.[1]

The catalyst for his plan, the president made clear, was his dislike for the rival plan adopted and pursued by Wall Street itself: a rapid return to the status quo ante. "My resolve to reform the system is only strengthened when I see a return to old practices," Obama said in announcing the proposals. Particularly enervating, he said, were the claims by financial institutions that they couldn't lend more to Main Street, even as they raked in big profits. Certainly, the trend on Wall Street in the months that led up to Obama's bombshell was a cautious kind of willful amnesia. Now that even some of the most troubled behemoths, like Citigroup, no longer seemed in danger of collapsing and taking the financial system down with them, perhaps the survivors could simply pick up and carry on, as if nothing had really happened? After all, as Jamie Dimon had told his daughter in response to her question, a financial crisis is just one of those things that happens every five to seven years.[2]

During the week that the investment banks reported their block-buster profits and Obama announced his intentions, Democrats were still reeling from the loss of their prized sixtieth Senate seat in a special election held to fill the seat once owned by the late Edward Kennedy. Bashing the banks, the pundits proclaimed, was one way to curry favor on Main Street ahead of the upcoming midterm elections in November 2010. But that overlooks the fact that the "too big to fail" conundrum was one that Wall Street, its regulators, and the administration had all been grappling with since the bailout of AIG in the summer of 2008. Size isn't always evil, insisted Josef Acker-mann, CEO of Deutsche Bank, in one of several PR pushes made by big bankers to take the edge off populist fury in the closing weeks of 2009. No, but size combined with a propensity to take risk, and the duty to earn profits even if that happens at the expense of the financial system, *is* a problem.

So, too, is the fact that banking analyst Richard Bove could recommend purchasing shares of Citigroup in the summer of 2009 not because it had brought in new, stronger management (it hadn't) or because the quality of its loan portfolio was improving (it wasn't), but simply because the institution had an ace up its sleeve: the fact that the government couldn't afford to let it fail, and that de facto government guarantee would provide a cushion for shareholders. Even John Reed, who served as co-chairman of Citigroup until retiring in 2000, seemed sheepish at the fact that the institution he helped create had swollen in size from $740 billion in 1998 to $1.9 trillion by 2009. "I'm sorry," he said, with more sincerity than was mustered by those other Wall Street figures who have consumed, publicly, their own doses of humble pie since the markets stabilized and talk of financial system reform began. If Reed were to do it over again, "I would compartmentalize the industry for the same reason you compartmentalize ships—so leaks don't spread and sink the whole ship."[3]

Just because it becomes possible to build a giant conglomerate like Citigroup, and to run it in such a way that it is taking onboard far too much risk because government policies seem to permit or encourage that, doesn't mean that bankers like Reed and his heirs *should* do so. And that's the problem at the heart of any discussion of Wall Street's future as well as the push by the industry to return quickly to business as usual. If the Obama administration's proposals to reshape the banking world aren't implemented—or are watered down—what other initiatives can or should be taken to address the problems? In a pinch, we can muddle along with the dysfunctional health care system that existed prior to 2010; we can't exist without a financial system. So what kinds of corporate structures, regulation, and policy frameworks will encourage Wall Street institutions to behave in the interests of *all* their stakeholders and in a way that doesn't jeopardize the health of the financial system itself?

The solution is to start thinking of and treating Wall Street as the utility that it really is. That doesn't necessarily mean that its institutions must be government-controlled monopolies or that the industry must accept a regulated rate of return set by the Fed or some other agency. Rather, it requires that everyone from within those regulatory bodies to the most junior bankers and traders understand in their bones that Wall Street is there not to enrich them but to serve its users. We must redefine the meaning of "success" on Wall Street to mean more than just profits for Wall Street firms themselves. The mantra caveat emptor is no way to run a utility.

In the final chapter of this book, I'll explore some of the reasons why action—whether by policy makers or regulators—is necessary to prevent Wall Street from following the same toxic path all over again once the panic and the level of scrutiny have abated. So far the incentives haven't really changed, despite all the talk about "clawbacks," increased regulatory oversight, and a decline in leverage. If new regulations aren't put in place to prevent Wall Street from following the path of least resistance (now the president's clear preference) and returning to the risky behavior of yore, then regulatory measures making it prohibitively expensive to do so are required. Because, as Morgan Stanley's chairman, John Mack, admitted to a standing-room-only crowd of financial journalists and others in late 2009, Wall Street simply can't rein itself in; self-control is not part of its DNA. Without changes, the Street's participants will always be chasing their most successful rival, whether that is Goldman Sachs or some other firm.

But before dealing with those major strategic issues, I'll show you the ways in which the trauma of the financial crisis has already begun to reshape the world of Wall Street. Some firms have vanished from the landscape altogether, but new players are emerging. And entirely new *types* of Wall Street players may end up delivering intermediary-type services in the way that investment banks like Goldman Sachs once did; those players may not even be investment banks as we would define them today. A quarter of a century ago, if the five most powerful Wall Street figures had been summoned to Congress to testify on any particular issue, odds are that their ranks would have looked very similar to the five men we could see in front of the FCIC commissioners in January 2010: the heads of the biggest banks and investment banks. A quarter century from now, that lineup may look very different, not just because the names of the firms have changed, but because the nature of the most powerful firms fulfilling Wall Street's core function as the money grid may change dramatically.

A new idea of what Wall Street is, or should be, is in the earliest stages of emerging, and it's up to all parties to ensure that the system that results is one that serves the interests of all, from Goldman Sachs down to the smallest client of the money grid. The ethos of "chasing Goldman Sachs"—pursuing the maximum level of profits and return on equity, without heed to systemic risk or the interests of all the stakeholders in the money grid—is a model that has to be left behind as part of the wreckage of the "old" Wall Street. The definition of being a winner on Wall Street needs to evolve beyond that of the firm that manipulates the grid to earn the highest level of profits, because that is what its shareholders demand of it. Perhaps, one day, Wall Street will rediscover Jack Morgan's pledge of doing "first-class business in a first-class way."

CHAPTER 8

Too Big to Fail, Too Small to Thrive?

Were the events of 2008 the end of one era and the beginning of another? Or would the cataclysm that caused the collapse of two of Wall Street's premier investment banks, the emergency sale of a third, and the transformation of the remaining two large institutions into plain-vanilla banks end up causing nothing more than cosmetic changes to the landscape and its myriad participants?

It will take a decade, perhaps, to fully understand the postcrisis lay of the land on Wall Street. That is how long it will take for the full range of regulatory reforms to be announced and implemented and for financial institutions, investors, and consumers to react to them. By early 2010, it was finally becoming clear that the Obama administration wouldn't be content to stop with a first level of reforms, giving more powers of oversight to the Federal Reserve with the goal of protecting the financial system as a whole and creating a new regulatory body to monitor financial products, like mortgages, that Wall Street might in future pitch to the average consumer. Some Wall Streeters kicked up a fuss and made a few grumpy public comments about the heavy hand of government, but by and large these were policy initiatives that many of them could accept were necessary, or at least inevitable.

Then came the bombshell. The same week that many Wall Street firms triumphantly sealed their return to profitability and (they hoped) the status quo ante, the president lived up to all their worst fears. Wall Street institutions, Obama said in announcing his plans to overhaul the entire financial system, had taken "huge, reckless risks in pursuit of quick profits and massive bonuses." And that state of affairs couldn't be allowed to continue. So the president decided to tackle, squarely, the biggest issue of them all: the structure of the banks. If his proposal makes it into legislation and is approved by Congress, Wall Street's major banking institutions would no longer be able to make proprietary trades with their own capital, nor could they invest their own money in hedge funds or private equity divisions. In other words, they would have to return to serving Main Street and would no longer be able to rely on reaping rich rewards by serving themselves and their inside circle first and foremost.

The plan would help address some of the growing fury on Main Street at the extent to which Wall Street has bounced back to life while they continue to struggle, while also starting to address the perplexing issue of moral hazard. If financial institutions like Goldman Sachs can't undertake ultrarisky activities in the first place, then the chances that it will need to be bailed out diminish at least slightly. That, in turn, means that the government isn't in the odd position of saving nominally private institutions from the consequences of their misjudgments, simply because those institutions have been deemed "too big to fail." "Just because things seem populist doesn't mean they're not the right thing to do," Treasury secretary Timothy Geithner commented in the wake of the announcement of the Obama plan.

The Obama plan will undoubtedly play a major role in helping to redefine what Wall Street is and how it works, in ways that we may not come to understand for years. And yet, even before the president stood up in the White House to launch what may be the biggest fight between Washington and Wall Street since the Great Depression, the Wall Street landscape had already begun to change, slowly and almost imperceptibly. While policy initiatives and lavish bonus packages grabbed the headlines throughout 2009, other forces were at work. Even before the president weighed in with his views, Wall Street insiders were already asking themselves and each other some of the big questions. What does Wall Street do, and what should it do? How does it function, and how should it function? The magnitude of the crisis and the dislocation it produced are so great that almost anything now seems possible, at least in theory. Wall Street players, for the first time in some seventy-five years, have received a glimpse of entirely new vistas and possibilities. It's almost as if they have just arrived in the Wild West, been shown a·map on which all the territory is up for grabs, and been told to go out and stake a claim. Everyone, from the newest member of the tiniest regional brokerage to the most eminent Wall Street veteran, is free to take part in the game of reinventing Wall Street.

Among those now free to at least try to reconceive Wall Street according to his or her own vision are the president and one of the chief advisors on his reform plan, former Fed chairman Paul Volcker. To be sure, some of the rules of the road will be laid down by reinvigorated regulators and angry and aggressive legislators from both parties. But within those constraints, many Wall Street veterans still see more opportunity than risk. In some cases, those opportunities may influence how we redefine Wall Street. Winners can come from anywhere. They can be found among the ranks of the giant financial institutions (such as Goldman Sachs, with its outsized profits and employee bonuses); the boutique institutions launched by star bankers that try to emulate what Goldman Sachs was two to three decades ago and replicate its success; and the midmarket players that end up grabbing a dominant market share of a particular kind of banking, from serving health care companies to working with a new crop of green technology businesses. At least one giant hedge fund sees its own future including the construction of a classic intermediary Wall Street business, bringing together investors with those in need of capital in the tradition of the money grid.

While these businesses dream of becoming the next Goldman Sachs, the actual Goldman Sachs and its peers are trying to stop too much transformation from taking place, either in the day-to-day business of keeping the financial system working or in the regulatory and legislative arenas, where a host of new policies are being developed. "They will fight—ferociously—to recapture any ground that was lost during the storm," says Jimmy Dunne of Sandler O'Neill. "We have a window of opportunity, yes, but it will close, and we'll have to fight just as hard to hang on to whatever we gain."

In place of the magical thinking that dominated Wall Street in the years leading up to the near collapse of the financial market had arisen a kind of willful amnesia. Surely, the large legacy institutions (those that were caught up in the storm but had so far survived more or less intact) reasoned, the events of 2007 and 2008 were nothing more than a giant nightmare from which they were now awakening? Announcing Citigroup's first-quarter results in early 2009, Vikram Pandit, its CEO, suggested that write-downs on troubled assets "may be largely behind us." Glenn Hutchins, cofounder of Silver Lake Partners, a private equity firm, argued in an interview that the buyout industry could be on the brink of entering a new golden age, now that companies could once again raise capital from the stock and bond markets. "Investors are being paid to take risk again," Hutchins said.[1] And nowhere, it seemed, was it easier to find someone to take those risks again than on Wall Street itself.

Up until early 2010, at least, events seemed to conspire to support that perspective. Goldman Sachs and JPMorgan Chase, the two clear winners among the legacy institutions, went from strength to strength. JPMorgan Chase, which had spent the dismal months of the winter of 2008–2009 snapping up market share in every conceivable area of commercial and investment banking to the point where its dominance was becoming unquestioned, announced a second-quarter profit of $2.7 billion. Over at Goldman Sachs, whose employees seemed capable of spinning straw into gold, the second quarter of 2009 reassured the world that the bank was back big-time. Only days after repaying the $10 billion of government bailout money it had received the previous fall, Goldman reported the largest quarterly profit in its 140-year history: $3.4 billion. By the third quarter, the two giant institutions were neck and neck, each having earned in excess of $8 billion of profits for 2009 and both reported lofty profits at year-end. "The nightmare is over," exulted one Goldman Sachs employee as 2009 drew to a close. "We can start dreaming of better days, of getting back to normal."

But while some on Wall Street celebrated, the nightmare was still under way on Main Street. Around the same time that Goldman announced its third-quarter results, unemployment broke above 10 percent in the United States for the first time since 1983. Not surprisingly, Goldman's huge profits and its plans to pay out record bonuses to its employees triggered more envy, anger, and outright resentment than at any other time in its 140-year history. Even the announcement that it would set aside another $200 million of its profits to add to its charitable foundation didn't dampen the outrage; that figure was a drop in the bucket compared to the bonuses—perhaps more than $20 *billion*—that Goldman would begin paying out to its top producers in early 2010.

Goldman didn't give up. In the run-up to its January 2010 announcement of its 2009 earnings, the firm pondered making it mandatory for top employees to donate at least a certain amount of their own winnings to charity. That still didn't quell the popular fury. The outrage was reflected in the tone and content of Matt Taibbi's scathing profile of the firm published in the July 2009 edition of *Rolling Stone*. Rehashing every conspiracy theory surrounding Goldman, Taibbi concludes (in some of the most memorable prose ever crafted in a work of business journalism) that Goldman is "a great vampire squid, wrapped around the face of humanity, relentlessly jamming its blood funnel into anything that smells like money."[2]

Lloyd Blankfein was well aware that his deep desire to return to the good old days as soon as possible could be derailed by legislators and regulators in light of just this kind of adverse publicity, by just the sort of plan that Obama would indeed announce in January 2010. He warned his business heads and the rank and file alike to rein in their enthusiasm and avoid any public demonstrations of affluence. Blankfein even embarked on a PR campaign of sorts, granting a lengthy interview to the *Times* of London. Alas, that backfired as badly as did the charitable donation. Blankfein tried to emphasize Goldman's role in the financial grid, arguing that "we help companies to grow by helping them to raise capital. Companies that grow create wealth. This, in turn, allows people to have jobs that create more growth and more wealth. It's a virtuous cycle." But then, he went on to declare that Goldman Sachs is "very important" and that it serves a "social purpose." Blankfein even told the interviewer that he believes he is "doing God's work."[3] His performance during the January FCIC hearings was equally erratic.

More important than Goldman's hubris, or even whether its bankers flaunt their wealth too much, is the fact that they are earning it by once again embracing risk. While that is what lies behind the firm's lavish profits, it's also what put Goldman in the president's cross-hairs. Throughout the year, the firm's average daily VaR level rose steadily, following a 20 percent jump in the first quarter. Much of that came from its trading, particularly in the risky bond and currency markets. For most of 2009, the gap between bid and ask spreads remained extraordinarily wide, offering savvy traders a way to buy at very low prices, then hang on and wait for a recovery or tighter spreads. Or, if the trader was executing a transaction for a client, those spreads justified much higher fees. In the second quarter alone, in the midst of the spring market rally, Goldman earned more than $100 million in revenues on at least forty-six separate days of trading—a record— according to an SEC filing. Its value at risk during the same period hit an average of $245 million daily, up from $184 million in the year-earlier period. In other words, on any given day, Goldman could lose as much as $245 million (within a certain range of probability). Still, Goldman's profits drew irritable comments even from the Wall Street–friendly, such as Larry Fink, founder and CEO of BlackRock and himself a former investment banker. "They are making very luxurious returns," he commented, and went on to imply that this came very close to profiteering at the expense of the money grid's users, including investment firms such as BlackRock.[4]

Many of Wall Street's legacy institutions, particularly still-troubled firms such as Bank of America and Citigroup, will face a major battle to reclaim their past power and prestige and resume behaving as if the last three years had never happened. By the same token, however, regulators and critics of Wall Street's excesses, who have their own set of dreams about what the new Streetscape should look like, will find it difficult to force those behemoth institutions to change the way they think about their business; their hope is to alter their behavior by restricting what activities are permissible. Meanwhile, smaller firms will be busy trying to seize on the disarray within the ranks of Wall Street's giants as a way to carve out a new and much larger role for themselves as part of the morphing money grid.

There is every incentive for the rest of Wall Street to continue chasing Goldman Sachs. Indeed, with Goldman itself poised to become the biggest loser of all the Wall Street "winners" and survivors as a result of the Obama plan—its private equity, hedge fund, and proprietary trading activities, responsible for a large part of the firm's earnings, will suffer disproportionately, analysts were concluding within hours of the White House proposal being made—there is more opportunity than ever before for some other institution to displace Goldman at the top of the Wall Street hierarchy. Chasing Goldman Sachs could take on an entirely new meaning.

"Too Big to Fail"

If there was one phrase that everyone on Wall Street was already sick of hearing by 2009, it was "too big to fail." The idea that the collapse of a Wall Street institution couldn't be permitted because it would trigger a series of shock waves that would ultimately shatter the entire financial system wasn't a new one. Indeed, back in 1998, that rationale was behind the government-proposed, Wall Street–financed bailout of Long-Term Capital Management; the hedge fund had so many ties to so many Wall Street firms and other players that they would be impossible to unravel. In the years that had followed, the fate and fortunes of Wall Street's investment banks, commercial banks, hedge funds, private equity funds, and other players had become even more interwoven, creating a kind of labyrinth that daunted even those who labored within the belly of the beast, such as Goldman Sachs banker turned Treasury secretary Hank Paulson. Even normally calm veterans of Wall Street were rattled by what they believed could happen following the collapse of one of these systemically important firms because of this web of counterparty relationships. (A counterparty is an institution or individual that takes the opposite side of a trade or a derivatives contract; as Blankfein was quick to point out to the FCIC commissioners, financial institutions expect that a counterparty is able to look out for itself. Certainly, he said, a bank like Goldman Sachs has no obligation to be a protective parent figure, shielding a counterparty from any potential harm.)

Mohamed El-Arian, CEO of Pacific Investment Management

Co., the largest manager of bond funds in the world, is normally a phlegmatic observer of "noise" in the markets. But in the days leading up to the crucial weekend meeting of Wall Street's leaders with Fed officials in New York in September 2009, El-Arian called his wife and told her to take out as much cash as she could from an ATM machine. When she asked why, El-Arian responded, "I don't know whether the banks are going to open tomorrow." The financial system, he says, was freezing shut before his very eyes.[5]

When the Fed and the Treasury Department brokered the purchase of Bear Stearns by JPMorgan Chase, it was in hopes of preventing a firm-wide tragedy from becoming an economic catastrophe. But others on Wall Street didn't learn the lesson. Back in 1998, when investment banks were asked to chip in $250 million to save LTCM, Bear Stearns's Jimmy Cayne flat-out refused. Merrill Lynch's then-CEO, David Komansky, demanded to know what Cayne thought he was doing. "When did we become partners?" a furious Cayne shot back.[6]

That attitude was still one of Wall Street's biggest problems a decade later. They might have a common interest in fending off regulation or other outside interference, but Wall Street's firms have always seen a rival's woes as their opportunity—and vice versa. During the boom years, every firm had thought of nothing more than grabbing the biggest possible share of whatever fee-generating business was available, without considering the risk created to the system when they and their peers were all doing the same thing at the same time. Each firm on Wall Street put its own interests ahead of those of the system and paid attention to what its rivals were doing only insofar as those activities affected its own ability to grab market share and profits. (They certainly weren't thinking of what so many firms following the same business strategy might do to the sustainability of that strategy, their business model, or the system itself.)

They could take comfort in the fact that the precedents set by LTCM and Bear Stearns signaled that the larger they became as a result of all that risk taking, the more inclined the government would be to help them out of their troubles. They were right, up to a point. No one could allow the system to fail; it was too crucial. So it wasn't until the eleventh hour and fifty-ninth minute in the negotiations to salvage Lehman Brothers that it became clear that this time Paulson and Bernanke would let the firm collapse rather than bail it out. Finally, John Thain, Merrill Lynch's CEO, realized what he had to do. Within twenty-four hours, he had hammered out an emergency deal for his own firm, recognizing that if Lehman did collapse, Merrill likely would be the next to place its head on the chopping block, and no one would be there to rescue it, either.

That moment of resolution didn't last long. Within days, AIG was on the ropes, and its web of ties with other institutions dwarfed those of Lehman in both size and complexity. Bernanke and Paulson agreed that AIG posed an unacceptable systemic threat. And "too big to fail" was back. As the nature of the bailout plan unfolded over the autumn of 2008, it became clear that the biggest beneficiaries would be Wall Street's biggest players. Goldman received $10 billion of direct help (since repaid); it also received about $13 billion from the bailout of AIG as one of the insurance giant's counterparties. The government's infusions of vast amounts of cash into the economy and the banking system (some $12 trillion as of late 2009, by some estimates) also fueled Goldman's trading and underwriting businesses; the rock-bottom interest rates meant the firm's cost of doing business was cheaper than at nearly any time in its history. It's to be hoped that Blankfein sent Paulson, his successor (Timothy Geithner), and Bernanke boxes of gourmet chocolates for the holidays as a token of his gratitude.

The policies to preserve the financial system by designating (de facto, if not officially) some institutions as being "too big to fail" is likely to continue to affect the new Wall Street landscape. Some institutions, including Goldman and JPMorgan Chase, have been able to leverage that status into a rapid return to making hefty profits. True, the Obama plan tries to address this; it would demand that no single financial institution control more than 10 percent of the system's total assets, not just 10 percent of the FDIC-insured assets of the banking network. That would certainly reduce the growth in concentration, and, on the margins, trim back the market share of some firms. But it doesn't tackle the core problem, the one that rightly concerns the public: the fact that their tax dollars could once again be used to shield financial institutions from the consequences of their actions, simply because of their size and systemic importance.

And what would happen if Goldman decided to relinquish its status as a bank rather than forfeit its most profitable businesses? That wouldn't make the firm any less important to the system, only remove it from the new Obama-Volcker rules. Addressing risk taking, as the Obama plan does, is a step in the right direction, to be sure. Still, without the threat of market discipline in the shape of bankruptcy, it's hard to envisage a Wall Street environment in which Citigroup, Bank of America, and other still-troubled firms take a sober and realistic look at their position and undertake the dramatic kind of changes that may be necessary for them to stand on their own two feet. Those institutions that can use their access to cheap, government-guaranteed financing to do business more profitably now seem to have an edge in the battle for market share on Wall Street. An oligopoly seems to be emerging.

Wall Street's Barbell

The panic that swept across Wall Street in 2008 had receded by the spring of 2009, when credit markets began gradually to unfreeze and the stock market rallied. However, that panic left behind in its wake a heated debate over the right model for Wall Street, one that began to intensify in early 2010 with the launch of Obama's plan.

Should the "new" Wall Street be a completely fresh set of institutions, carved out of the strongest parts of the legacy firms and supplemented by the array of midmarket firms and a host of boutiques and new players? Or should it be back to business as usual, only with a smaller number of ultralarge players dominating Wall Street?

As early as the autumn of 2008, it was clear that in the first stage of the evolution of a new Wall Street, the financial system that would emerge from the wreckage would take the shape of a barbell, with large groups of institutions clustered at each end and not much in the middle. At one end would be the oligopolistic behemoths, smaller in number but just as powerful as before and, in the case of players such as Goldman, JPMorgan Chase, Barclays, and perhaps Wells Fargo, even more formidable competitors. At the other end would be a host of boutiques and specialized investment banks, some already in existence and others newly formed by star bankers who had fled the giant firms. While the former were battling to return to business as usual as rapidly as possible, the latter were arguing that business as usual was no longer either possible or desirable.

Some of those now scrutinizing the tabula rasa they believe that the Wall Street crisis has left in its wake, imagining how different things might be in the future, are what might be called the usual suspects. They are the bankers and traders who, after spending the first decade or two of their professional lives working within Goldman Sachs, Morgan Stanley, or Merrill Lynch, found themselves suddenly unemployed or underemployed, or who came to believe for the first time in their lives that the best way to deploy their skills isn't within one of those blue-chip firms. Nor are they taking what has until now been the traditional alternative path to fame and fortune by launching a hedge fund or joining a buyout fund. (For the most part, those options look far less attractive or even possible than they did as recently as mid-2008.) Some of their peers have simply abandoned the Darwinian struggle to find and hang on to the few available new posts at the big Wall Street firms; they have joined Main Street businesses or launched their own companies. (One former Lehman banker now provides Manhattan kids with cupcake-baking experiences; another Wall Street refugee teaches yoga to her stressed-out former colleagues.)

The lion's share of the business—the outsize profits from underwriting stock and bond deals, advising companies on mergers, and providing trading services to clients—may still rest in the hands of the giants. But the buzz is all about the boutiques, which have more chance than ever before of unseating some of the powerhouse firms. All of them are building their business plans on one incontestable fact: the distaste for and widespread distrust of "big Wall Street," represented by firms such as Goldman Sachs and Citigroup. Their potential clients may not believe in the kind of conspiracy theories involving Goldman Sachs fueled by Taibbi in *Rolling Stone*. But they do have lingering misgivings about the giant institutions that peddled subprime CDOs to their clients while selling the same securities, or even shorting them in hopes prices will fall further. That anger runs deep: clients watch the government funnel a steady supply of capital to a group of institutions that might otherwise have collapsed, even as those on Main Street struggle to keep the doors of their own businesses open as the recession bites deep, or try to renegotiate their home mortgage without any assistance. Everyone is aware of the taint associated with old-model Wall Street. Brokers and investment advisors who once loved to boast that they belonged to Merrill Lynch's famed "thundering herd" are now deserting; many have set up independent advisory firms. The same phenomenon is being seen among investment bankers and traders.

"Some of the changes that we've seen happen in the wake of the crisis aren't likely to be unraveled any time soon, and they are changes that favor the creation of new business models on Wall Street," argues John Costas. He's putting his money where his mouth is. For more than a quarter of a century, Costas worked for some of Wall Street's biggest firms, rising to become head of investment banking at UBS. Now he has launched the PrinceRidge Group with former colleague Michael Hutchins. The new broker-dealer will trade mortgage-backed securities and an array of corporate debt, but that's just the beginning of Costas's ambitions. He plans to turn to his own advantage both the anger at the perception that Wall Street's big institutions are being given an unfair edge and the reality that the size of those giant institutions has left a void in the market that he believes PrinceRidge can fill.

"On a normal day in 2008 and into 2009, about half the market share has been up for grabs and little firms were making ten times more money than they had ever made before," Costas says, almost visibly delighting in the prospect of beating the big institutions at their own game. When the behemoths are worried about their own balance sheets or too preoccupied with straightening out problems with their subprime mortgage or credit card portfolios, PrinceRidge can move in and grab the trading business, helping to meet demand for those interested in buying debt and to execute sales for those looking to reduce their exposure. Only weeks after opening, PrinceRidge was "in a very healthy position indeed," says Costas. "It's a very unique time, where you can open a business and right away have trading clients doing business with you." He believes PrinceRidge's edge will prove lasting. "Back in 2006, the twenty biggest institutions handled about 80 percent to 85 percent of the trades in this space; over the next three to five years, 50 percent or so will be up for grabs by firms like ours."

Potential clients such as hedge fund manager Nick Harris* are already seeing the impact of that transformation. Like all hedge fund managers, Harris relies on Wall Street traders to help him move in and out of trading positions at a second's notice. Over the course of

2008 and into 2009, he had begun to realize that some of the trading desks at big Wall Street institutions were no longer as able or willing to help him put together trades in the way they once had, even though Harris oversees a few billion dollars in assets. J.P. Morgan was scaling back their trading with hedge funds, he discovered, perhaps in an effort to contain risk. "I've met with the new guys at Barclays [which acquired most of Lehman's investment banking assets after the latter filed for bankruptcy], and they just have very little interest in helping us," he commented in the summer of 2009. So as Harris set out to raise new capital he simultaneously embarked on a quest to develop a whole new set of trading relationships.

"There's a great opportunity for anyone who is interested to come and grab market share in the trading universe—the Canadian banks, European institutions like BNP Paribas, or the midmarket firms like Jefferies," Harris says. "Anyone with any kind of appetite for risk and the ability to manage it could grab the business away" from the legacy banks. "There are guys like Key Bank and Jefferies that I had never really dealt with before but who are now starting to be more important to us because they are the guys providing the liquidity," in place of Wall Street's biggest players, including JPMorgan Chase and Citigroup. Harris now has a long list of those firms and individuals, and he's forging a new set of trading partnerships. Wall Street's winners may be thousands of miles away from Wall Street itself; it was a relatively small Texas-based firm that helped Harris execute some crucial trades in the stock of a tobacco company. That firm will now be added to the speed dial on his traders' phones, occupying the space once reserved for Citigroup's trading desk, Harris says.

Jeffrey McDermott has his own dreams of grabbing market share from the big institutions. Unlike some other refugees from the big Wall Street institutions, McDermott (like Costas, a UBS alumnus) initially thought about launching a private equity firm when he left the world of the big banks in 2007. But fund-raising in that environment was difficult, and McDermott quickly switched his focus to something he found both more compelling and a model that was more differentiated and, he believes, more likely to thrive in the midst of the tabula rasa that is postcrisis Wall Street: a boutique investment bank dedicated to raising capital for clean technology and other green businesses.

"From the point of view of the economy and society as a whole, it was pretty clear to me that climate change and global sustainability were going to continue to be a big area of interest and investment for a while," McDermott explains. Just as happened in the earliest days of the technology revolution and the evolution of the Internet, McDermott figured that smaller companies would be in the vanguard. But with Wall Street's power players caught up in the battle both to return to their old ways and to fight off Washington's increasingly major reform proposals, firms like Goldman Sachs just weren't interested in any but the top 0.01 percent of those businesses. McDermott calculates his new firm, Greentech Capital Advisors, can fill the void, making up for this lack of undivided attention on the part of the giants to the three hundred or so companies in this sector he believes are today "underbanked." The technology industry may have had Frank Quattrone; in McDermott's vision, fledgling green energy businesses will have him on their side, helping them negotiate multimillion-dollar deals—even billion-dollar deals!—when giants like Siemens, General Electric, and United Technologies come calling. A bonus is the fact that in his days working for the big boys on Wall Street, McDermott got to know the big clients, such as GE and United Technologies. He almost chuckles with glee when discussing the nature and scope of the opportunity. "This whole industry has only grown up in the last two years or so, so there's no embedded firm with specialized knowledge and a competitive advantage. It's all new intellectual capital, and I'm in on the ground floor."

Try to Forge a New Reality from Opportunity

Nearly every part of Wall Street's traditional business is under siege. But while dislocation is creating opportunities for players like Costas and McDermott, it remains to be seen whether a lucky break can be transformed into a real and sustainable business advantage. The firms most likely to do that are those that had an early start and a competitive edge, such as the advisory boutiques founded by the likes of Morgan Stanley alumnus Bob Greenhill (whose departure from that firm was described in chapter 1) and former star UBS banker Ken Moelis. These firms, which once worked quietly but very profitably on the margins of Wall Street, have moderate fixed costs because they didn't run giant trading desks or underwriting and distribution operations. They had no giant debt load, and they hadn't been pursuing return on equity for its own sake to keep shareholders happy. In the dark days of November 2008, a boutique was what everyone wanted to be, and where every Wall Street banker worth his bonus suddenly discovered he had always yearned to work.

Greenhill, for instance, had never tried to—or needed to—chase Goldman Sachs. In 2006, when Goldman reported a return on equity of 33 percent and was the envy of all its peers among the diversified investment banks (most of which had to scramble to post a 20 percent ROE), Greenhill had an ROE of 56.3 percent. It did even better the next year, providing its shareholders with an 82 percent ROE. It seemed to be good evidence in support of the proposition that chasing Goldman Sachs wasn't the only possible business model on Wall Street. Greenhill, like other advisory boutiques, never aspired to offer as all-encompassing a suite of products and services to its clients as Goldman did. At the height of the market meltdown, in November 2008, it managed to attract an extra $80 million from investors who were eager to support its business model and figured that Greenhill would thrive even as the bigger firms seemed likely to collapse or simply deflate. (It took only hours to raise the money; Bob Greenhill later bragged to Fred Joseph that he could have raised twice as much.)

The capital would come in handy, since Greenhill, like Wall Street's other boutique advisory firms, was expanding rapidly. Why, the boutiques calculated, would companies looking for advice and guidance on a corporate restructuring, merger, or acquisition turn for help to the big banks, which seemed to have mismanaged their own businesses so dramatically? And since the boutiques didn't sell debt or engage in proprietary trading, they could point out to potential clients that they had no hidden agenda. They would be there to provide the best advice possible, not to insist that the firm be retained in a host of other areas as well in a quid pro quo for its advice.

The boutiques were hoping to pick up clients; they were already luring top bankers—future rainmakers—away from their bulge-bracket rivals such as Citigroup and Morgan Stanley. Greenhill alone added fourteen managing directors to its roster in 2008, bringing the total to forty-nine. Three of them were Lehman Brothers refugees in Chicago, giving the boutique a footprint in that city for the first time. It also opened a Los Angeles office staffed with big-bank refugees, and expanded its range of activities in London.

Sure enough, the deals began flowing in: Greenhill advised Roche on its $46.8 billion battle for control of biotechnology giant Genentech. While the Wall Street crisis and the credit crunch put a crimp in mergers, the boutiques were suffering less than their larger counterparts. They were also getting seats at some of the best tables in town, advising on deals such as InBev's $52 billion purchase of Anheuser-Busch, the $68 billion acquisition of Wyeth by Pfizer, and the $58 billion mega-merger of mining giants BHP Billiton and Rio Tinto. And overall, the boutiques' share of the merger advisory business was climbing, hitting 15 percent by mid-2009 while the share belonging to the giants dipped a few percentage points. Boutique investment banks were gaining traction faster than ever before, even amid a downturn that might have been expected to favor their bigger rivals, firms such as Citigroup and JPMorgan Chase that could offer easy access to financing along with advice. But in a tricky economic and market environment, it seemed that clients valued the independent nature of the boutiques' advice as much as they did the money they would need to complete a deal.

Ken Moelis, for one, seems intent on parlaying the short-term strategic edge created by the havoc on Wall Street into a long-term advantage. A veteran of such feisty second-tier institutions as Drexel Burnham Lambert and Donaldson, Lufkin & Jenrette, Moelis went on to become a power player at what became during his tenure one of the biggest Wall Street banking firms, the U.S. division of Swiss giant UBS. He displayed impeccable market timing, walking away from UBS to launch his own boutique within weeks of the bank's realization of the magnitude of its subprime lending problems. (Moelis wasn't directly involved in the business of churning out CDOs.) After making UBS a viable competitor to Goldman and Morgan Stanley in the investment banking businesses—underwriting stock and bond sales and providing advisory services—he decided to repeat the feat, this time for his own benefit. Now it would be Moelis & Co. that went head-to-head with Goldman Sachs.

At the dinner in Los Angeles celebrating Moelis & Co.'s official opening in July 2007, attended by the small team of veteran bankers that he had convinced to join him, Moelis gave a brief motivational speech. To anyone paying attention, it was clear that he saw his new firm's future as involving something more exciting than simply becoming yet another member of the cluster of high-end boutique investment banks. "I hope this is the beginning of something that, a hundred years from now, people will look back on and say, 'That's when it started,'" Moelis later recalled saying. In fact, he added, it was the kind of moment that deserved to be preserved in a photograph—the kind of photograph that hung on the walls of the big firms that Moelis had once worked for and now set out to beat; the photograph featuring Messrs. Goldman and Sachs, for example.[7]

Within twenty-four hours of opening his doors, Moelis issued a challenge to those venerable players, as well as his former firm and other boutiques. He parlayed his long-standing professional relationship with Stephen Bollenbach, the CEO of Hilton Hotels, into a $13 million fee in exchange for advising Hilton, which was about to be acquired by buyout firm Blackstone. Since then he's worked on the InBev purchase of Anheuser-Busch and helped Yahoo fend off the unwelcome corporate embrace of Microsoft. To be sure he's ready for anything, he also poached a forty-person team of restructuring bankers from midmarket firm Jefferies & Co. to handle what he expects will be a wave of bankruptcy-related workouts; by 2009, about half of the boutique's work would be advising on restructuring. (For its part, Jefferies snagged a team of star health care bankers from Moelis's former firm, UBS; only in the midst of the uncertainty that now reigned would such rainmakers have considered leaving a top-tier investment bank for one that had traditionally been viewed as a haven for those not good enough to cut it in the big leagues.) Over the course of 2008, as larger rivals were melting down, Moelis tripled the size of his staff and opened offices in Chicago and London.

Even firms that previously had abandoned the investment banking and market-making parts of the financial services business seemed to revive and take a new interest in their potential in the midst of the shake-up. Sanford C. Bernstein & Co., a noted investment research firm, announced in December 2009 that it had recruited Thomas Morrison, a former Bank of America securities banker, to launch a new business underwriting securities issues for clients. Bernstein, now a division of asset management company Alliance Bernstein Holding L.P., had previously walked away from this capital markets side of the business, amid controversy surrounding potential conflicts of interest between its noted research and its banking activities. In the face of the size of the opportunity, that concern now appears to have taken a backseat.

The arrival of new rivals like Bernstein is an additional threat to the survivors, even those who emerged from the storm stronger in relative terms. "The risk is on the side of JPMorgan Chase and the other big players," says Dick Bove, an investment banking analyst who himself now works for a smaller firm, Rochdale Securities. "They are the ones that could end up losing some business here." At the very least, Bove says, the boutiques will put themselves in the position to be acquired—at a healthy premium—by the big banks in a few years' time. That would be repeating the pattern of the early to mid-1990s, when established large banks snapped up feisty and fast-growing investment banks like First Boston and Donaldson Lufkin & Jenrette and folded them into their larger firms with varying degrees of success.

Some of the boutiques aren't waiting to get the merger ball rolling. Eric Gleacher, a veteran M&A banker (he founded the M&A department at Lehman Brothers and later advised KKR on its legendary buyout of RJR Nabisco), took a step in that direction, deciding to sell his firm, Gleacher Partners, to Broadpoint Securities Group in a deal valued at about $68 million. Instead of clinging to the boutique model, Gleacher has taken a step toward creating something altogether different. "There's a space at the top of the investment banking world, where firms like Lehman, Bear, and Merrill Lynch once were—and yes, Goldman too, before it and Morgan Stanley became banks," Bove points out. "That's the space that is up for grabs, and it remains to be seen whether a new hybrid model—a firm more diversified than a traditional boutique, but that isn't driven by the need to post big returns on equity—will emerge and grab that, or whether it will be divided up between big guys and the small, specialized boutiques."

The big banking institutions are unusually vulnerable, and sometimes publicly display that, as when UBS filed a lawsuit against Jefferies in June 2009, claiming that the latter had been "surreptitiously planning" a raid on UBS's talent. After all, Benjamin Lorello and his group had earned more than $1 billion in fees for UBS over the previous last four years; given that the ties between a star banker and his clients tend to be stronger than those between the clients and the institution (with the exception, of course, of Goldman Sachs), the suit showed just how aware UBS is that its brand name now counts for much less than it once did. In this environment, even a once-marginal firm can emerge overnight as a potentially formidable competitor. But can the boutiques or a new hybrid firm parlay their short-term strategic edge into a long-term advantage, and remake Wall Street in the process?

Big Banking's Revival?

Wall Street's giant firms aren't going to simply slink away into the night. Most on Wall Street argue that the big firms had an unbeatable advantage. At times when capital was scarce, they had it. "To stay in the game, you need capital," points out one Goldman Sachs banker. "Do you think that we just take an order to sell so many shares of General Electric and don't execute it until we find someone else who's willing to buy it at that price?" Nonsense, he says. Being an intermediary these days—serving a client efficiently—means knowing what price to pay for a big block of stock the client wants to sell, being willing to keep that stock on the firm's own balance sheet until it can find a buyer at the right price (or, preferably, at a profit), and managing the risk associated with it. That takes a big balance sheet; it's a necessary service that the boutiques can't fill. "They're just too small," he adds dismissively. "The phrase I hear is 'too small to thrive.' I don't know about that, but they'll be thriving in their own little corner of the world, not expanding into ours." (The difficulty drawing a clear line between when a trade is proprietary in the true sense of the word and when a firm is using its own capital to facilitate client transactions, is going to be one major hurdle to the Obama plan to reduce risk taking by banks: most financial institutions that retain large prop trading desks insist that a fraction of the trades taking place there are truly proprietary, i.e., having no connection to any client trade, past or present. Defining what is and what isn't "proprietary" will be a major challenge to the Obama proposals.)

Whether or not that dismissive view is valid—after all, building a new investment bank isn't cheap, Bove points out—what is clear is that none of the rivals has a monopoly on the winning Wall Street model. If the boutiques launched by Costas, Greenhill, and Moelis are winners or potential winners, so, too, are Goldman Sachs and JPMorgan Chase as well as some of the still-struggling firms, once they are stable and recapitalized.

After years spent stuck beneath Citigroup, Goldman, and Morgan Stanley in Wall Street's pecking order, J.P. Morgan had become the deal maker that everyone else on Wall Street had to envy by the summer of 2009. Of every $100 of fees that companies paid to Wall Street banks for underwriting stock sales, J.P. Morgan collected $15, while Goldman Sachs pocketed only $10. J.P. Morgan had vaulted from sixth to first place in the much-watched underwriting league tables since 2005, when it had picked up only $5 of every $100 in fees. At JPMorgan Chase's annual meeting, CEO Jamie Dimon was thanked at least twice for his leadership by shareholders and was able to wrap up with a comment that the institution might be able to boost its dividend in 2010, if not earlier.

Another potential winner is Barclays Capital, the investment banking division of the British bank that picked up the bulk of Lehman's investment banking franchise for a bargain-basement price after the latter's bankruptcy filing and now may succeed in doing something that American bank CEOs have been warning anxiously about for nearly two decades: become the foreign bank to unseat JPMorgan Chase and Goldman Sachs in much the same way Toyota and Nissan did General Motors and Chrysler. At the head of Barclays Capital stands an American, Bob Diamond, who has long operated in a world in which his firm wasn't the biggest kid on the block; now it looks like one of Wall Street's strongest market players. When Diamond transformed Barclays de Zoete Wedd into Barclays Capital in 1997, he recognized that competing head-to-head against Goldman Sachs would be nearly suicidal; today that has become possible.

But it's unclear that he will seek to chase Goldman Sachs in the same way that Lehman, Merrill, and Citicorp once did, trying to capture an ever-larger market share and return on equity, regardless of the risks. Diamond's attitude toward Wall Street has always stood in stark contrast to that of many of his peers. While they pursued proprietary dealings in CDOs, he was less aggressive, emphasizing his bank's role as intermediary. "We take risks, but prefer to keep them client-focused," he said in early 2006, just as Citigroup, Merrill, and their peers were rushing to emulate Goldman Sachs and become principals in the deals they did. "A large prop [proprietary] shop shifts the amount of risk it will take to its own book and by necessity away from its clients." Diamond noted the growing disaffection among Wall Street's corporate clientele, which felt that as their bankers relied more and more on proprietary deals for profit and on deals for Wall Street entities for fees, they were less on the same side of the table as the CEOs they ostensibly represented.[8] He was also amazed at the risks they were running. "They lend as if they had balance sheets," he said of stand-alone investment banks such as Bear Stearns and Lehman Brothers in 2009.[9] (The two investment banks didn't have balance sheets in the sense that Diamond meant; instead of shareholder deposits, they relied on short-term financing from the capital markets, giving them little in the way of long-term assets.)

. For those winners, in the months leading up to the announcement of the Obama plan, it sometimes seemed as if time had stood still and it was still 2006. True, Lehman's dark green and gold logo had disappeared from the firm's midtown office building and the trading booths of the floor of the New York Stock Exchange, to be replaced with the pale blue signage of Barclays. But the big banks were bigger than ever, and, public pronouncements notwithstanding, were trying to turn back the clock as quickly as possible. JPMorgan Chase, thanks to the deals that permitted it to acquire not only the investment banking business of Bear Stearns but also the deposits of Washington Mutual at bargain-basement prices, had emerged as one of three large banks that collectively issued an astonishing two-thirds of all credit cards and half of all mortgages by 2009.

To give the bigger banks a helping hand, regulators and administration officials had actually encouraged "big" banks, waiving antitrust rules that once barred any single institution from owning more than 10 percent of the country's deposit base. Barclays even managed to reverse the trend of banker flight to the boutiques, snapping up a health care banker from Moelis & Co. who had fled Citigroup to the boutique world only a year earlier. By late 2009, that showed up in compensation as well. JPMorgan Chase ended the freeze on salaries of employees earning more than $60,000 a year in late 2009, just in time for the annual bonus season. Reflecting the jump in risk taking, traders were expecting to be the biggest winners of all in that bonus pool, raking in a 60 percent increase in total compensation, compared to only about 20 percent for investment bankers.

Even the losers among the big banks were behaving as if they were winners and returning to taking risks that could create fresh havoc within the financial system if left unchecked. Citigroup, for instance, had been mulling plans to revamp and relaunch its alternative investments division before the Obama plan raised questions about its ability to do so. A rebranding would have been advisable, certainly, since several of its hedge funds had to be liquidated in the wake of the crisis. (One of those funds, which had banned investor withdrawals for nearly a year, returned only 3 cents out of every investor dollar entrusted to it.) Now Vikram Pandit, Citi's CEO and a former hedge fund manager, wants to get back to the exciting world of running alternative asset funds, which can return higher-than-average management fees as well as performance fees. (That assumes, of course, that Citi's managers are better able to identify both opportunities and risks than recent evidence would suggest.) Happily for the financial system, perhaps, investors seem reluctant to reenlist. While Citi hoped to raise another $2.5 billion sometime in 2010, by late 2009 investors had contributed a mere $150 million.[10] Perhaps if Citigroup's new shareholder, the U.S. government, can't demand that Citi take a hard, strategic look at its own businesses, investors will impose the same kind of discipline. Or at least they will as long as they remain fearful; it is when greed returns and regulators are even less watchful than they are today that the system will be most at risk.

Even before it became clear that the government would intervene more dramatically in trying to shape the future of Wall Street's biggest players, it was already clear that winners and losers alike would need to respond to regulators and shareholders in new ways. By the autumn of 2009, Citigroup found itself with the federal government as its single largest shareholder, in possession of a 34 percent stake in the giant bank. It's hard to say which side was more uncomfortable with the arrangement. On one hand, Congress has put limits on the government's ability to try to change Citigroup's risk-taking culture, making regulators unhappy about their relative lack of influence. Still, the latter were able to press Citigroup to replace its chief financial officer amid widespread discontent about what was seen as a lack of commercial banking expertise in Citi's executive offices. His replacement, the bank agreed, would have "relevant financial, accounting or other experience acceptable to the [regulatory] agencies."[11]

Sheila Bair, in her role as head of the FDIC, had been working the phone lines on a related issue, urging Citigroup directors to clear the decks not only of some people but also of problematic assets and business units. To the bank—and to Wall Street as a whole—this kind of attempt to influence Citigroup was greeted with horror. True, the bank probably would have imploded without a series of capital infusions and wasn't a textbook example of a healthy financial institution. But telling the bank how to run its daily affairs? That was a sign of creeping socialism and tantamount to nationalization.

Those big banks that have repaid the assistance they received from the federal government's Troubled Asset Relief Program (TARP) will find other parts of the new regulatory ecosystem unwelcoming or downright hostile, even if they don't have to deal with phone calls from Bair or her counterparts. Even Goldman Sachs will have to live with regulators peering over its shoulder—especially given the level of public hostility to the firm. During the FCIC hearings, in response to a question about whether he favored a higher level of regulation on Wall Street, Blankfein made a point of mentioning the large number of regulators who now swarm over Goldman's downtown Manhattan headquarters on a daily basis, even when financial markets are calm. Still, he carefully avoided answering the question of whether that heightened scrutiny made for better or more effective regulation, and certainly history isn't reassuring. (After all, as noted previously, IndyMac had a flock of OTS regulators tripping over each other at its office, none of whom were able to prevent the institutions from collapsing.)

"The regulators are hell-bent on not having this happen again," says Leon Cooperman, the former Goldman Sachs banker who currently heads a large hedge fund group. "When I was a partner at Goldman Sachs, we would sit around the partners' dining room and talk about how we never, ever wanted to become a bank; that the banks were too regulated, that the returns were much less in that

business, and what have you." In September 2008, Goldman Sachs
did become a bank, subjecting itself to regulation by the Federal Reserve and potentially forcing it to reshape its business, something
that could lead to lower rates of return. "You can rest assured that
Goldman Sachs and Morgan Stanley became banks not because they
wanted to, but because the government made it clear to them that
that was what was going to happen," Cooperman opines.

But will Goldman Sachs remain a bank for long? Under the
Obama plan—which is largely the brainchild of former Fed chairman Paul Volcker, and which the president himself quickly dubbed
"the Volcker Rule"—banks with federally insured deposits wouldn't
be allowed to trade for their own account, to own hedge funds, or to
run their own private equity divisions. "When banks benefit from
the safety net that taxpayers provide, which includes lower-cost capital, it is not appropriate for them to turn around and use that cheap
money to trade for profit," President Obama declared, in what many
interpreted as a very thinly disguised shot at Goldman Sachs. His
subsequent remarks, apparently addressed at Goldman's decision to
short the risky subprime CDOs for its own account, even as the firm
continued selling them to clients, made the real target of the Volcker
Rule even more clear. "That is especially true," the president continued, "when this kind of trading often puts banks in direct conflict
with their customers' interests."

And yet these business lines are very lucrative ones for Goldman
Sachs in particular. (Morgan Stanley seems to have been more willing to adopt the banking ethos, expanding its asset management operations and scaling back its proprietary trading.) Even when the
ultimate point of a trading position is to accommodate one or more
clients' positions, Goldman's trading desks deploy a lot of their own
capital, positions that the government could decide to define as being
"proprietary" even as Goldman executives claim they aren't. For
Goldman, the choice may come down to either remaining a bank or

hanging on to some of its most profitable business divisions—not much of a choice at all, really. That's one of several weaknesses of the Volcker Rule. If it becomes law, and Goldman does opt out by returning to being an investment bank rather than a bank holding company, that won't change the firm's systemic importance or its risk appetite. If Goldman's Midas touch deserts it a decade from now, it's hard to imagine that the government wouldn't step in to save it, and with it, the financial system.

Even before the Volcker Rule made its debut in early 2010, it was clear that regulators and policy makers wouldn't put up with Wall Street firms taking quite as much risk as they once had. As bank holding companies, Goldman and Morgan Stanley had already come under the new and more intensive scrutiny of the Fed and more restrictive rules on the amount of leverage they could use to generate profits. The Obama plan simply delivers an even larger challenge to Wall Street's ability to return to being a profit-generating machine for its shareholders and employees. If they can't pursue some of their most profitable business lines and can't use leverage, then what?

"By and large, you can't make large sums of money without taking risks," and risk taking is out of fashion as well as hard to pull off in the current political climate, commented Franklin Allen, finance professor at the Wharton School of Business, as firms like Goldman resumed reporting blockbuster earnings in the summer of 2009. "The more money you make, the indication is that you probably took a lot of risk to do it. . . . And I think that's part of the problem."[12] Those high value at risk numbers may yet return to haunt Goldman Sachs. In contrast, Morgan Stanley—which posted nine straight months of losses, continuing long after Goldman's financial recovery—is not as eager to embrace risk once more. The firm that once ousted its CEO, Phil Purcell, in part for his reluctance to take risk is now a more conservative place to work; John Mack, Purcell's successor, stepped down as CEO in 2009 only after hiring one hundred new risk managers. Still, by mid-2009, rumblings of discontent over this relative caution were spreading within Morgan Stanley as some executives claimed that the firm would be standing "shoulder to shoulder" with Goldman again before the end of 2010.[13]

For the time being, at least, the incentives to take risks remain in place. For Goldman Sachs, using its skilled traders to earn profits simply makes sense—that is the firm's edge, and volatile markets demand those skills. Elsewhere, bankers are trying to find a source of revenues and profits to replace CDO issuance and junk bond underwriting for buyout firms, just as they had sought to replace the trading fees they had earned before Mayday in 1975. Wall Street may still cherish a hearty appetite for risk taking, but the same can't be said for its clients at either end of the money grid, and that's why the Volcker Rule may find a lot of support across Main Street.

As long as investors remain reluctant to take big risks, as long as they refuse to chase higher yields at any cost, it will be easier for Wall Street firms to stick to more stable plain-vanilla businesses. The faster hedge funds and buyout funds return to normal and the cycle begins again, the more cautious regulators will need to be. For now, says buyout fund manager Jake Martin, highly leveraged and ultra-risky deals are as dead as the dodo. "We can't do deals that rely on financial engineering, but only on those that we're willing to work on to transform," he says. "Those deals are likely to be smaller, they're likely to be fewer in number, and it will take longer between the time we do them to the point where we're ready to exit" and generate another fee for Wall Street in the form of IPO fees. Any transactions will be smaller, meaning that banking fees will be smaller.

Plain-vanilla deal making sounds attractive, and Wall Street tried hard to pretend that it was throughout much of 2009. In his written testimony to the FCIC, Mack drew attention to the firm's renewed commitment to Wall Street's core function: Morgan Stanley had helped clients raise nearly a trillion dollars of new debt and equity capital between the fourth quarter of 2008 and the opening days of 2010. By the end of the summer, financial institutions had raised nearly $4 billion through the sale of bonds for corporations. Some of those were incredibly good deals for the businesses themselves: Procter & Gamble needed to offer only 1.35 percent in annual interest payments to sell its bonds, the lowest rate ever paid by a corporate issuer in the dollar-denominated bond market. At the other end of the money grid, investors eagerly snapped up those newly issued bonds, which offered higher returns than it was possible to earn from Treasury securities without forcing them to take on risk, to which they had just discovered they suffered a life-threatening allergy.

But Wall Street is going to have to work harder and put up with more to earn fees from those kinds of transactions, fees that in any case don't measure up to what they once earned from their CDO machines and fast-paced deal making for buyout funds. Many of those buyout targets will be going public once more in the coming years, and firms such as KKR and Blackstone will be just as hard-nosed in negotiating the smallest fee possible for those deals as they were when it came to demanding the cheapest available financing on the buyouts. The only way an underwriter can make a lot of money on those IPOs is by increasing the number of deals they do. And that, of course, raises the risk that banks will relax their underwriting standards and allow poorer quality companies to slip through the net and go public, just as happened at the height of the dot-com boom, in 1998 and 1999.

It's not only buyout firms that will play hardball with Wall Street. In 2009 Robert Benmosche, CEO of AIG, began to award underwriting and advisory mandates to banks who helped the firm break itself into smaller and more manageable pieces. Those financial intermediaries stood to earn as much as $1 billion in fees, four times the sum that investment banks earned from working on the breakup of AT&T in the late 1990s. One piece of the action was the IPO of

AIG's Asian insurance business, a deal that the New York Fed (overseeing the process) said could raise $5 billion to $8 billion when it was completed in the first half of 2010. The IPO would take place on the Hong Kong Stock Exchange, where large companies going public have traditionally paid their underwriters 2 percent to 2.5 percent of the proceeds in fees. The New York Fed disclosed just how much joint underwriters Morgan Stanley and Deutsche Bank stood to earn, and Benmosche promptly dug in his heels. It was too much, he told employees at a staff meeting in August 2009. "I said, 'How about 1 percent?' So then everybody's face turned red, and I said, 'So change it,'" Benmosche claimed. "So we're talking about 1 percent, not 2 percent to 2.5 percent."[14] (In fact, the IPO never happened; instead British insurer Prudential acquired the business weeks ahead of the IPO for $35.5 billion. Bankers would have to be satisfied with the fees they would earn helping "the Pru" to finance the deal.)

It's in that context that the Volcker Rule looks particularly ominous. If Wall Street's institutions are forced to rely *solely* on these plain-vanilla transactions for profits, those profits are going to be thinner on the ground and shareholders more dissatisfied. That translates into a lower stock price—and less wealth creation for the bankers themselves. They may yet—gasp—end up looking like a real utility.

Tug-of-War

The incentives for Wall Street to return to its past practices are all in place, and there are signs that it is beginning to happen. The only question is what factors will rein in that behavior. While regulators place their faith in their ability to craft new rules, others argue that a cultural transformation is needed, as I'll discuss in the next chapter. Ultimately, however, it may be the arrival of entirely new kinds of competitors on the new Wall Street landscape that will serve as a reminder to keep risk taking in check. What if those firms that had been Wall Street's biggest clients over the last decade—hedge funds and buyout firms—now became its rivals? What if they began to try to serve as their own intermediaries and dispense with at least some of the services of Wall Street's traditional money grid operators? Could a firm such as Blackstone replace Goldman Sachs and beat it at its own game?

It may sound outlandish, but buyout fund manager Jake Martin, who has been helping to structure financial transactions for a specialist buyout firm for nearly two decades, believes he and his peers have all the skills that are required. "I think it's quite possible that some of these large and very diversified buyout firms could bypass institutions like Citigroup altogether and sell bond deals for their portfolio companies directly to the buy side," Martin remarks. A firm such as KKR knows who the logical investors are for the debt it wants to issue to finance the purchase of, say, a medical devices company. "They have the same knowledge and skills as Citigroup—their ranks are full of bankers." Battered legacy institutions aren't attractive banks to work with, Martin adds. "At some point, it will be KKR and not Citigroup knocking on the door of other investors. They'll say, 'Hi, we're here to get you to buy a piece of this bond or loan deal, which we've taken a big piece of ourselves.' They'll be part investor and part banker, and the change will occur relatively seamlessly."

KKR is one buyout firm that is already taking baby steps in that direction. Back in 2007, it recruited Citigroup banker Craig Farr to build an in-house investment banking division, KKR Capital Markets, to serve the firm's own portfolio companies and give the buyout group more control over the whole investment banking process. In 2009, KKR Capital Markets signed an unusual pact with Fidelity, giving the investment giant exclusive access to KKR's share of any of its portfolio companies in the wake of an IPO or other public issue. This gives KKR an exit strategy for its holdings, and Fidelity the option to pick up some stock in any businesses that its money managers find intriguing without having to compete for them on the open market. But some of Farr's recent transactions have raised speculation that KKR has more in mind than just catering to its existing portfolio companies. While buyout funds may band together to execute a buyout, they have traditionally been less comfortable as minority owners of already public companies. (Indeed, transactions of that kind executed in 2000 and 2001 produced some memorably large losses.)

Nonetheless, Farr and KKR provided the struggling Eastman Kodak with a cash infusion in 2009, a transaction that gives it the option to acquire a 17 percent stake in the firm down the road as well as two board seats. "Who knows where they could take this?" says one investment banker. "It's not inconceivable that they could begin providing at least advisory services for a fee to Kodak now, and maybe develop more businesses for which they traditionally had to go to Wall Street. This is not a time to rule out anything."

Martin's own firm, which he didn't want to name publicly, is already investigating ways to make this work for its portfolio companies. One option is to raise a new fund that would invest in bonds issued not only by its own portfolio companies (it already does that) but for other businesses as well. Instead of turning to Citigroup, the CEOs of those companies could cut out the middleman and come straight to Martin's firm for capital. "Why do we need to have Citigroup as an intermediary?" Martin wonders, allowing his eyes to drift toward the Park Avenue skyscrapers outside his office window, a small smile playing around his mouth. The smile broadens. "We can be our own intermediary; we have the know-how, the contacts. The technology exists to help us. And we have the kind of capital that we can put into these deals in a way that Citigroup obviously wasn't able to manage to do sustainably."

In an era in which Jefferies can overnight shake off the curse of a nonexistent brand name by recruiting a star health care banker and his team, and the combination of lavish bonuses and the vampire squid label mean even Goldman's brand isn't quite what it was, why shouldn't a KKR or a Blackstone step into the breach, not just by investing its own capital but by acting as a de facto underwriter by persuading others to join it? "If we do our own due diligence and say we're putting our own money in alongside those of others, wouldn't that be a selling point?" Martin demands. "I've got to believe it. After all, while Citi would only be interested in selling it on to the next guy, we'd be there for the long haul. There's an intermediary, and then there's an intermediary with skin in the game beyond how to make a quick buck."

If buyout funds are still only pondering this kind of dramatic transformation, at least one hedge fund has taken a definite first step toward branching out beyond being a principal to take on an intermediary role as well. By late October of 2008, Ken Griffin, the founder of Citadel Investment Group, one of the world's largest and most influential hedge fund empires, was drawing up plans to take advantage of the carnage and chaos he was witnessing all around him. For now, that mayhem was wreaking havoc in Citadel's hedge fund portfolios and fueling rumors (unproven) that Citadel itself was in jeopardy. But in Griffin's eyes, those losses were short-term hiccups; he was looking ahead to the day he believed Citadel would emerge as a new kind of player on Wall Street.

True, the Chicago-based firm was already enough of a heavyweight to irritate the investment banking community. When JPMorgan Chase decided to punish the Chicago upstart for stealing too many of its top traders by refusing to handle any trades for Citadel's funds, the bank couldn't afford to keep the boycott in place for longer than a day. After all, Citadel commanded up to 4 percent of all trading volumes worldwide on any given day. Now Griffin figured the chaos gave him the chance to transform Citadel into something more than just another big hedge fund. He could put his firm on the same level as JPMorgan Chase or Goldman Sachs, and himself on the same level as Lloyd Blankfein or Jamie Dimon. Why couldn't a hedge fund such as Citadel become an intermediary, an investment bank in its own right? Why did it have to rely on these other institutions? And why couldn't Wall Street clients have access to another competitor to the behemoths that dominated the landscape?

Griffin confided his plans to Rohit D'Souza and Todd Kaplan, two Merrill Lynch alumni. Citadel had long possessed a market-making division, a business that both offers to buy stocks, bonds, and other securities at a bid price and maintains an inventory of them to sell at the posted ask price. It's a technology-intensive, client-centered business that requires top-notch risk management; only the best can pocket enough from the spread between the bid and ask prices to make it worth their while. Citadel was good at the business and had become one of the world's biggest market-makers. "It was clear to all of us early on in these discussions that the market-making business could serve as a hub for a new kind of investment bank," Kaplan recalls. "We started out by discussing what might be possible, and it quickly evolved into us working on a full-fledged business plan, on the way to add client-facing bankers to that existing model." Before the end of the year, Griffin, Kaplan, and D'Souza were all convinced: Citadel had a chance at becoming one of the great investment banks on Wall Street, they agreed. So what if it was technically still a hedge fund?

All three believed that the only way to try to launch a viable competitor to the existing investment banks, with their still-impressive (if tarnished) brand names, was to return to Wall Street's roots. In many ways, the business plan harked back to the model that investment banks such as Lehman Brothers had begun to discard in the 1980s. Kaplan's vision was of an investment bank that would serve as an intermediary, not a principal. Above all, Kaplan wanted Citadel's new investment bank to focus on earning fees rather than on generating a return on the equity portion of a giant balance sheet, as Wall

Street firms had been doing for the last decade or two. No more chasing Goldman Sachs, he decided. "I watched the big firms lose their way when it came to client service, and I don't want that to happen again."

While the classic investment banks had been sustained by the stream of revenues coming from high-margin trading operations up until Mayday in 1975, this twenty-first-century reincarnation of that model would be financed by the high-volume market-making business. (It didn't hurt that Citadel itself was making some $1 billion a year from the newfangled high-frequency trading platform it had built, a way to make even more money from rapid-fire computerized trading.) It was just a new twist on an old theme, some Wall Street veterans suggested as the details began to leak out in the summer of 2009. But the one thing that stunned everyone was that the initiative was coming not from someone such as Costas or Moelis but from a hedge fund. From a hedge fund in *Chicago* to boot.

"I just don't see it," says Roy Smith, a finance professor at New York University and a former partner at Goldman Sachs. "How do they imagine they can achieve overnight what it took firms like Goldman more than a century to build?" Of course Griffin has built up a hedge fund empire with $15 billion in assets under management since 1990 and, his supporters say, is one of the most opportunistic investors around. "If he sees an opportunity, it's there," says one former senior colleague. Even though D'Souza announced his resignation from the business in late 2009, by then the fledgling investment bank had recruited eighty bankers, sales reps, and traders. Kaplan resigned in early 2010 to spend more time with his Chicago-based family; by this point, the New York–based business had one hundred employees and was still growing. They were already working on trades for other hedge funds—something naysayers said could never happen, since rival funds would fear that Citadel's traders would try to use the insight into their rivals' business to their own advantage—and have won mandates to advise corporate clients, including a bankrupt casino operator. Griffin sees himself not as chasing Goldman Sachs but rather as *becoming* Goldman Sachs. "I do believe in the next five years we will have created one of the great sales and trading operations" on Wall Street, he said in an interview.[15] And they will be able to do so, Kaplan argues, because returning to business as usual is neither possible nor wise for Wall Street as a whole. "This is a whole new ballgame."

Whether they acknowledge it or not, across Wall Street and into the far reaches of the financial system, bankers, traders, investors, customers, and regulators are all rethinking what Wall Street means. While it's clear that no single model will triumph, the fear haunting the minds of many is that those who emerge as winners won't do so because of their devotion to their customers or the health of the financial system, or even because they undertook some kind of strategic review of their businesses as a result of the crisis.

Regardless of whether Citadel succeeds with its plan to graft an investment bank atop a hedge fund, Kaplan has come to believe that simply trying to emulate the Street's biggest and most successful firms was at the root of the problem. Wall Street's institutions should have pondered whether or not they had a real competitive advantage in the businesses they were entering as well as a real understanding of the risks as well as the potential for those businesses to boost their ROE. "The need to make a return on the balance sheet was all-important, but then the balance sheet became the tail wagging the dog," Kaplan acknowledges.

He believes the new Citadel model—serving as a classic intermediary for clients—will help shape the Wall Street of the future. But he found it hard to recruit bankers who share that vision. As wave after wave of layoffs occurred on Wall Street, Kaplan's inbox rapidly filled up with résumés from displaced bankers with blue-chip pedigrees. But he remained picky. "Not everyone gets it," he explains.

"When guys I talked to about a job asked me what our ROE target is, I had to explain we're not going to be managing the business that way." Instead, he pointed out that financial metrics such as ROE are "outcomes, not objectives. Our objective is to win, and winning means being the best client service provider."

Perhaps the biggest question about Wall Street today isn't the shape of the winning institutions of the future, but whether or not its denizens will ever manage to internalize that ethos. Certainly, government policies and new regulations won't succeed in swaying Wall Street's hearts and minds.

CHAPTER 9

Chasing Goldman Sachs?

As fate would have it, two of the most illuminating and thought-provoking comments on the future of Wall Street weren't made in one of the innumerable and carefully scripted congressional hearings in which regulators, legislators, and members of the financial industry debated the causes of the financial crisis and haggled over what should happen next. Both were throwaway remarks, one made with little thought to a radio talk show audience and the other in response to a question during a panel debate by financial journalists.

The first of these comments came from Richard Parsons, the lawyer (and former CEO of AOL Time Warner) who had been named chairman of Citigroup early in 2009. In May of that year, the still-struggling bank had passed its government-mandated stress test. Perhaps in order to celebrate that event, Parsons was a guest on a morning talk show on WNYC, the New York affiliate of National Public Radio, and chatted with the host, Brian Lehrer, about the results of the stress test and the future of New York as a global financial center. Parsons's soft, warm voice carried a tone calculated to reassure and even soothe any Main Street residents still fuming about the billions of dollars of bailout money Citigroup had received and the fact that taxpayers would end up owning more than a third of the bank. That voice stayed calm as Parsons made one of the most significant statements about how Wall Street's giant legacy institutions—those behemoths that, with the help of taxpayer dollars, survived the crisis and still dominate the financial markets—view the future. Citigroup, Parsons declared, is committed to weathering the storm. After that, he said, the bank feels obliged to "do right by our two major constituencies."

That's where Parsons unwittingly showed just how little those on Wall Street had changed their perception of the world and their place in it in light of the events of the previous two years. Citigroup may have come close to following Lehman Brothers into bankruptcy; its stock price may have slumped below $1 a share earlier that year. But the fact that only significant help from the federal government had prevented far worse disasters, or that Citigroup had played a role in destabilizing the entire financial system, didn't seem to have registered with Parsons. Certainly he didn't cite the financial system as a whole, or even the taxpayers who indirectly financed the bailout, as one of those two constituencies. Indeed, not even the bank's clients—its depositors, its borrowers, its credit card holders, the companies for which Citigroup had helped raise capital—got a nod from Parsons. "Our two main constituencies," the Citigroup chairman explained, "are our shareholders and our employees."[1]

In other words, the same kind of slavish catering to bonus-hungry employees and profit-hungry investors came first and foremost. Why this would produce better outcomes for the financial system and for shareholders than it had during the past decade, why Citigroup would be better able to manage the kinds of risks that single-minded approach created than it had been in all-too-recent memory, remained unclear. (Via a spokesman for the bank, Parsons declined to elaborate.)

John Mack, on the other hand, seems to have emerged from the mayhem with a very different view of what went wrong, one he revealed in what seemed to be an unscripted comment during a panel discussion convened by Bloomberg News and *Vanity Fair* about how the financial press had covered the financial crisis. Mack, weeks away from stepping down as CEO of Morgan Stanley, was sitting in the audience when he was pressed to answer a few questions by the panel. The critical moment came when the discussion shifted to how regulation of Wall Street should change in the years to come. "We cannot control ourselves," Mack told his audience. Regulators, he said, will have to do the job that those on Wall Street can't do for themselves: they "have to step in and control the Street." So what if at least ten or fifteen federal regulators now roam the halls at Morgan Stanley, which became a federally regulated banking institution to save its corporate life at the heart of the crisis? "I love it," Mack said. That kind of scrutiny "forces firms to invest in risk management."[2]

Two senior bankers, two events, two throwaway remarks, and two very different pictures of Wall Street, past and present. Taken together, however, they point to the conundrum at the heart of the crisis. When left to their own devices, financial services firms such as Citigroup and Morgan Stanley will focus almost monomaniacally on what is in their own best interest, seeking out ways to earn higher returns and recruit the top talent by paying the most lavish bonuses and offering the most enticing perks. Mack is absolutely correct: they cannot help themselves. As Parsons's remarks show, the crisis has not reshaped the fundamental attitudes toward the financial system on the part of those participants most responsible for making the money grid work efficiently and safely in the interests of *all* of its beneficiaries, not just themselves or those able to reward them most richly. But with a few high-profile exceptions—those running the troubled financial institutions, their closest allies, and those directly responsible for overseeing the most troubled areas, such as subprime lending and CDO origination—most of the players on Wall Street are the same as they were three years ago.

Until leaders such as Citigroup's Parsons come to believe that they are acting in the interests not only of their shareholders and employees but of their clients and the broader financial system—and until they act in a way that is consistent with that conviction—any transformation in the way Wall Street works will be cosmetic at best. True, there will be no more excessive subprime lending; there will be less leverage. The products triggering the next bubble won't be CDOs, junk bonds, or dot-com stocks. But as long as hedge funds and private equity funds generate the bulk of the fees and wish to undertake transactions in other parts of the financial markets—perhaps involving products that have yet to be invented—there will be no reason to say no, and every reason to go along with them. Financial institutions will seek out the riskiest businesses, and emphasize them, because that's where the biggest profits are made.

Former Treasury secretary and onetime Goldman Sachs CEO Hank Paulson tried to drive home to Wall Street's leadership the message that they had a common interest that transcended their individual corporate self-interests during the fateful weekend in September 2008. According to the accounts of the meetings that took place at the Federal Reserve's headquarters in lower Manhattan, the assembled bankers pressed Paulson to structure a bailout for Lehman. For his part, Paulson tried to get them to shoulder some of the responsibility for what all were finally prepared to acknowledge was a systemic failure, and thus play a role in preventing a collapse that could have systemic ramifications. "You have a responsibility to the marketplace," Paulson told them.[3]

Because they didn't acknowledge that collective responsibility—whether they couldn't agree that they had a common responsibility in the first place, as had happened when Cayne refused to become "partners" with rivals such as Merrill in the Long-Term Capital

Management bailout a decade earlier, or whether they couldn't act on it because of their own internal woes—nothing happened. Lehman filed for bankruptcy protection, and the intermediary function at the heart of the money grid came within hours of not just freezing but collapsing altogether. "It's impossible to understate the sense of fear people in that room felt—they were going into the unknown," says one former top banker familiar with the weekend's events. He went on to compare it to the fear among scientists at Los Alamos just before the atomic bomb was tested for the first time in the spring of 1945. "For all those guys knew, they were going to set fire to the earth's atmosphere when they set off the first nuke, and some of us wondered if we'd blast our financial system back to the days of the horse and buggy and the quill pen," the former banker says. "As it turns out, after Lehman, the government stepped in and did everything it could to make sure we never had to find out."

The Utility and Fiduciary Duties

To whom or what do the institutions at the heart of the money grid owe their primary loyalty? Should they have acted as partners to save the system, even at the last moment? Or, by 2008, was that kind of action so unfeasible as to be impracticable? Without understanding how Wall Streeters might respond to that, it's impossible to address the corollary question that haunts most Americans on Main Street: Will Wall Street return to behaving recklessly once the crisis is past, even with more restrictive rules governing its behavior? What happens once the government is no longer peering over the shoulders of financial institutions that are now larger and more systemically important than ever?

Unfortunately, in the absence of major changes to the DNA of these giant legacy institutions and their inhabitants, the question isn't whether but when, as John Mack admitted in his cri de coeur. The giant legacy institutions have strong incentives to return to business as usual, and little motivating them to develop a new path that will put less stress on the system as a whole in the absence of the Volcker Rule or even more sweeping restrictions. Moreover, these restrictions may backfire by curtailing the "good" kind of risk taking that the money grid requires in order to fulfill its role in the economy. After all, while classic utilities such as gas and electric companies are economically and socially useful, they aren't very profitable. One reason why many on Wall Street recoil at the idea of describing their business as fulfilling a utility-like function is the fact that utilities' profits are typically overseen and its fees approved by regulators fearful that businesses running effective monopolies will take advantage of their customers.

Wall Street's intermediaries don't need to worry about being allowed to earn only a regulated rate of return, as are their counterparts in other utility-like businesses. To date, policy makers of all kinds tend to acknowledge that while members of the money grid fulfill the same kind of utility function that a power or water utility does and exist to meet a social good of some kind, they aren't a typical utility. They have opted to allow the industry to regulate itself, constrained only by rules passed and overseen by organizations such as the Securities and Exchange Commission and the Office of Thrift Supervision. The problem is that as the financial system has become more concentrated and oligopolistic—the ten largest banks ended up holding 40 percent of all commercial banks' insured deposits in 2000, more than double the level of two decades previously—those organizations have been lackadaisical in their enforcement of what rules existed. And the banks and investment banks regulated by the SEC, the OTS, the Fed, and other agencies—those institutions at the hub of the money grid, on which the health of the grid's intermediary functioning relies—were paying attention to an altogether different set of incentives.

Unless you work for or invest in a power company, you probably can go through your entire life without becoming familiar with the phrase "regulated rate of return." Similarly, unless you happen to be a corporate governance activist, a securities lawyer, or a corporate director, odds are that you've heard the phrase "fiduciary duty" only in passing and dismissed it as one of those bits of jargon that is just academic. That's only half true. While it *is* jargon, understanding the concept of fiduciary duty is essential to understanding what happened on Wall Street and why it might happen again. The concept of fiduciary duty is straightforward enough—the idea that an individual or a group has an overwhelming duty to another group that overrides every other possible interest, including self-interest. It's the same kind of relationship that a lawyer owes to his client, the kind that pops up on television crime shows when a lawyer is put in an impossible bind when he can't publicly disclose information that would solve a murder because that information was entrusted to him by a client.

That's the level of duty that every director of every corporation has to its shareholders. Every decision the director makes must— legally—be in the best interests of the company's shareholders; that extends to the selection of a CEO and employees who are bound by the same duty. The smaller the number of shareholders, and the greater the extent to which they overlap with the directors and employees—as in a private partnership, for instance—the more likely it is that they will be vigilant about the kind and nature of the risks the company is taking, as investment banker John Costas noted earlier: "The partners' capital was on the line; we thought about the long-term implications of all the business we pursued; we knew that our long-term profits depended on being responsible stewards of our capital in the short term." If a potential source of new profits seemed too risky over the long haul, Costas says, the partner had an incentive to speak up and the ability to make his voice count, as one of those shareholders in whose interests the company was legally required to function.

But what if those investors weren't the firm's partners, those charged with running it? Even at those financial institutions where employees were major owners—Lehman Brothers among them—the culture had changed over time. Few investors saw themselves as long-term holders of any company; with the freedom to sell their stock whenever they chose came an intensified focus on short-term profits. Increasingly, higher profits *now* were being demanded by the investors, all of whom had the clout to win an audience with an investment bank's chief financial officer or CEO and to influence their decisions in a way that employees couldn't.

The very nature of Wall Street institutions as publicly traded companies has emerged as part of the problem, one that is perhaps a bigger issue in determining the health of the Street than the risky activities Obama and Volcker seek to curtail, because the fact that these firms are public may push them further in the direction of high-risk businesses. The trade-off for a stable and large capital base was a fiduciary duty to shareholders that began to feel to many like an ever-greater burden, especially given the way many of those shareholders came to define that duty.

Before Brad Hintz moved to Alliance Bernstein and began to track the business of Wall Street's investment banks as a research analyst, his job was to communicate to investors that Morgan Stanley, where he worked in the firm's investor relations division, was doing everything it could to maximize profits and the all-important return on equity. As profits and outsized ROE levels became harder to earn, that message was simply that Morgan Stanley would deliver "superior" returns. Increasingly, those outside shareholders almost exclusively defined the bank's fiduciary duty to them as a matter of earning and distributing the largest profits possible in the shortest possible time frame.

The pattern was repeated all across Wall Street. Each quarter, bankers at publicly traded companies scrambled to beat the results of the previous three months to keep investors happy. And those big investors themselves—pension fund managers, hedge fund managers, mutual fund managers—weren't shy about making known their demands for higher rates of profit growth and return on equity. One former Citigroup executive says, "That just didn't happen within a private firm. The pressures were there, sure, but there was more of a likelihood that someone worried about the long-term impact of a short-term move to grab market share could get a hearing and be heeded."

In other corporate scandals that have rocked the United States in recent years, shareholders have been betrayed by managers who violated their trust in the pursuit of personal profit or power, sometimes by selling faulty products, in other cases through fraudulent accounting schemes. Ironically, as Leo Strine, vice chancellor of the Delaware Court of Chancery (one of the places where a lot of shareholder lawsuits end up being filed and adjudicated), points out in one of the most damning postmortems on the Wall Street crisis yet published, a failure to abide by shareholders' interest isn't what can be blamed for the catastrophe. Indeed, Strine argued, directors and managers were perhaps too responsive to demands from their investors to do whatever it took to boost profits and stock prices. "The more pressure business leaders are under to deliver high returns, the greater the danger that they will violate the law and shift costs to society," Strine concludes.[4] (In this case, those costs included the direct cost of the plunge in asset values when the bubble burst, as well as the financial burden of the bailout.) As of this writing, no one has been convicted of any offense in connection with the crisis—the only criminal charges yet filed, against two Bear Stearns employees (the collapse of whose hedge fund in 2007 now seems to be the first in a series of dominoes), ended in an acquittal. It may be, as Strine cautions, that on today's Wall Street, firms "are free to engage in behavior that is socially costly without violating" the law.

Indeed, even if firms such as Lehman and Merrill Lynch had consciously taken on excess risk and leverage, a savvy lawyer could still argue—legitimately—that they were acting in the fiduciary interest of investors by trying to maximize profits. As long as investors continue to believe that a firm's board and management are pursuing their best interests by maximizing short-term profits, that is what those Wall Streeters will do regardless of whether they realize the damage they could cause (as John Mack seems to) or not (as Parsons's comments appear to indicate he does not). Altogether missing from this equation is the kind of ethos that Dennis Weatherstone, former chairman and CEO of the firm then known as J.P. Morgan & Co., once tried to instill in the aggressive bankers underneath him.

Weatherstone worried about the potential of the burgeoning derivatives trading business to wreak havoc even on those firms, such as Morgan, that managed its own risks prudently. If this aspect of Wall Street was left to grow without any restrictions, Weatherstone was fearful of what would follow. In his view, the fates of all players in the financial system were intertwined and the entire system was only as strong as its weakest member. "If you are driving along the motorway in a smart Maserati and see an old car belching fumes, it's no good just driving on," Weatherstone told J.P. Morgan's aggressive young bankers, according to Gillian Tett's chronicle of the bank's adventures in the world of derivatives. The fumes might signal a problem with the car that could become a problem for everyone else on the highway. "If that old car crashes, it could wipe out the Maserati, too."[5]

Weatherstone's warning was delivered in the early 1990s. But wisdom from such elder statesmen was received with less and less respect as the years passed and it became harder to make money by sticking to low-risk business and plain-vanilla transactions on behalf of customers. What the clients wanted was more complex, too. Clients who had a complicated basket of investments or a large block of stock to sell wanted to do it as quickly and easily as possible. Ideally, they wanted to call a few top trading desks, have each one of those desks calculate a price it would be willing to pay for that portfolio, and pick the best one. It's like Amazon's customers placing an order for a new flat-screen TV. When you click on "buy now" online, you expect to be able to buy now, not be asked to wait to place your order and be informed of the price while Amazon goes off to locate the TV and haggle over the price with the manufacturer. You want Amazon to take the business and financial risk of holding those televisions on its own balance sheet.

Similarly, Wall Street's big institutional clients didn't want to sit around and wait to sell big blocks of stock until the trading desk could assemble a group of willing buyers on the other side of the transaction. The firm that was willing to offer the best price immediately won the business—and the client's loyalty. A bank or trading desk that dithered around, unwilling to take the risk of keeping the securities on its own balance sheet for a few hours or a few weeks before passing them on, would lose out.

These days, no Wall Street firm can function only as a pure intermediary, scoffs a senior banker at one large financial services firm. "What, do you think the client will sit around waiting while you put together a group of twenty-seven bidders who together will pay an average price of X for what he's selling? You've got to be kidding! They count on us to be not the intermediary, but the guy on the other side of the deal." From there, the trading desk will hedge the positions (limiting the risk of owning the stock by establishing trades that will increase in value should the value of the just-purchased securities decline) and, over time, unload them—ideally at a profit. "That is the game that we are in today."

Some firms, such as Goldman Sachs, played that game extremely well. Others, faced with the harsh reality that making money easily the old way was no longer possible, concluded that they would have to follow Goldman's lead, even if they couldn't do as well at it. And they would need to seek out other sources of large profits—even if those profits came accompanied by large risks—in order to stand a chance of offering their own investors a return on equity that measured up to that of Goldman Sachs.

Viewed through that prism, Merrill and Citigroup simply were doing what they were legally required to do, by virtue of their status as publicly traded companies with an obligation to their shareholders. When they set up their CDO-creation machines in 2003 and 2004, they were taking risks in order to maximize shareholder value. Only rules banning such activities outright would have outweighed that fiduciary duty, and right up until the end of the bubble, Wall Street ferociously fought off any effort to limit their freedom of action. (The Volcker Rule is likely to trigger even more feverish lobbying by the Street.)

Leaving the business to their rivals would have been foolish on a personal level—especially once Phil Purcell's ouster from the helm of Morgan Stanley in a shareholder-led coup reminded them of the career risk of not pursuing the maximum possible profit. But it would also have violated their fiduciary duty to investors. What manager or board member, confronted with the choice of earning profits for investors by taking on some risk in anticipation of a greater reward down the road and leaving the business to a rival when there is no indication that the level of risk is unacceptable, could make the latter decision and feel she was on legally sound footing? "There was evidence that these businesses were profitable; there was no evidence that they were built on quicksand," argues one lawyer who represents one of the large legacy institutions. "When there is no evidence of any *E. coli* or other tainted food, should a restaurant stop serving its customers steak or hamburgers?"

Certainly John Mack didn't see the risks when he succeeded Purcell at the helm of Morgan Stanley. Some of Mack's earliest meetings were with the hedge funds that were of ever-growing importance to Morgan Stanley and other Wall Street firms; Mack wanted to reassure their managers that while Purcell had favored sticking to the old, classic role of Wall Street firm as intermediary, Mack had no problem with Morgan Stanley taking on more risk as a proprietary actor, especially with the objective of helping its hedge fund clients. As Charles Gasparino chronicled in *The Sellout*, his narrative of the meltdown and the events leading up to it, one of those Mack met with was Stanley Druckenmiller, manager of Duquesne Capital and a former colleague of legendary hedge fund manager George Soros. Morgan Stanley had what it took to replicate Goldman's trading prowess, Mack told Druckenmiller. "The old agency model is gone, and it's never coming back," he added. "The proprietary model is here to stay."[6] And with it came a willful blindness to the degree and nature of the risks that his firm and others would take to maximize their own profits and serve clients such as Druckenmiller, who themselves were ramping up their risk taking and leverage with the help of Wall Street.

Today, evidence is all around us that the risk taking Wall Street institutions either facilitated or undertook on their own behalf could and did damage the financial system; Mack himself seems prepared to admit that the result was inevitable. Yet the concept of fiduciary duty to the institution's shareholders being paramount remains intact. As long as banks such as Citigroup are legally required to pursue the maximum return for their shareholders, and as long as senior executives such as Parsons don't comprehend the problems inherent in that, will it even be possible to talk about reforming the world these giant institutions inhabit? The former Citigroup financial executive laughs at the paradox that creates. "Well, that's the 64-trillion-dollar-question. You'd like to think that the banks' directors and top managers would see that their fiduciary duty would stretch to include the well-being of the financial system as a whole, since without a Wall Street, who cares who's on top of the heap? But then, where is the evidence that that is happening?" Henry Kaufman, the onetime Salomon Brothers economist who won the nickname "Dr. Doom" for his predictions of rising interest rates during the 1970s and early 1980s, fears that there is only one logical outcome even today. "Incentives to leverage [and risk taking] always will overshadow prudent judgments."[7]

The late Fred Joseph agreed with that assessment. "It's a bit inevitable, because that's human nature at work," he argued. "At least, it's the risk we all run, and hopefully we learn over time not to let our animal spirits run away with us. But it happens." Joseph was particularly concerned by the fact—always true at any point in time—that Wall Street is a young person's world. That means a prolonged period—even ten or fifteen years—without a major market shock that wreaks havoc on everyone can leave Wall Street without a large enough body of people who have "seen it all happen before." Only with the experience of going through a gut-wrenching meltdown— when someone isn't sure where the market's bottom is, or whether he'll still have a job the next morning—comes the kind of judgment needed to offset those animal spirits, Joseph said. "Memories fade fast here," he said. "Look, we're already seeing people just try to move on from the events [of 2007 and 2008]."

Another Wall Street veteran, Peter Solomon, suggested to the FCIC that they at least revisit the merits of old-style Wall Street structures like the separation between risk-taking businesses and consumer-oriented ones, or the private partnerships, as a way to limit the degrees to which risk taking becomes destructive. "Our firm is a throwback to the era of the early 1960s when investment banks functioned as agents *and fiduciaries* advising their corporate clients," he said. (The italics are mine.) "We do not act as principals or take proprietary positions. We do not trade and we do not lend." That model, he suggested during the questioning that followed his presentation, had its advantages.

Even if the incentives to take risk don't come from investors egging on the bank's board and top managers to earn more and more with every fiscal quarter that passes, other factors are likely to tempt those large banks to seek out deals that offer the certainty of higher risk in exchange for the possibility of higher returns. As Kaufman points out, these factors are likely to be part of Wall Street's DNA. Once a Wall Street intermediary accepts a certain set of growth and profitability targets as reasonable, once it becomes accustomed to being able to use a large balance sheet to help earn those profits, once it relies on "financial ingenuity" to generate income and a "financial framework that prescribes no effective limit," then it becomes as hard for it to change its modus operandi as it is for a supertanker to change course on a dime.[8]

Policing the System

As of late 2009, there were clear signs that risk taking was returning to Wall Street, and it was in that context that Obama proposed the Volcker Rule as policy. True, some legacy institutions, such as Citigroup and Bank of America Merrill Lynch, are still struggling with the fallout from the crisis and coping with intense global scrutiny of their businesses and hence are in no position to take on much new risk. Nonetheless, the amount of capital that Goldman Sachs was willing to lose on any given trading day was rising at a double-digit pace throughout 2009. Investors seemed to become more comfortable with risk as well, bidding up the prices of junk bonds—the riskiest corporate bonds on the market—in search of higher yields.

At the same time, Wall Street was able, for the first time in many years, to make money on the kind of plain-vanilla intermediary transactions that it had once despised as uneconomic. By 2008, however, it had become tricky for a company to sell debt or raise new equity capital, and so clients were willing to pay more for the service. Meanwhile, investment banks could also make more from the difference between bid and ask prices in both the stock and bond markets; that spread had always been how a trading desk had earned a large chunk of its profits, and with the volatile and risky markets of 2008 had come much wider spreads. At least in the short term, Wall Street could make money by taking more conventional kinds of risks within limits that were acceptable to the vigilant Federal Reserve. Some of the transactions that boosted their collective revenues and fattened their profits were deeply ironic in nature: Wall Street was now profiting from the repairs it was making to its own balance sheets. Every time that Bank of America, Wells Fargo, or another financial institution raised capital to repay money borrowed from Washington via the Troubled Asset Relief Program, or TARP, they did it by selling stock into the public market; each of those transactions generated some kind of fee for underwriters. By some estimates, fees for the equity issues by financial firms in the United States alone during 2007 and 2008 hit well north of $5 billion—or more than had been issued in the previous two decades rolled together. The three big offerings in December 2009 alone raised nearly $1.2 billion in fees for the underwriters. And yes, those were the same firms who were the recipients of the capital. In one particularly ironic twist, Citigroup paid itself enough of a fee for underwriting *its own* stock issue to jump to the rank of fourth-largest equity underwriter of 2009. In other words, Citigroup used its own misfortunes and desperate need for capital to win league table bragging rights.

But how long will the taste for plain-vanilla products and transactions linger on Wall Street when its inhabitants are all well aware that only more exotic flavors—the riskier deals—are the ones that generate more profits? Bankers point out that the link between compensation and risk taking is still intact: the more aggressively a firm uses its balance sheet, the higher its return on equity and profits and the larger the bonus pool. "No one is being paid to be prudent with shareholder capital," says one veteran banker. As the months and years slip past and the financial crisis becomes as much a part of history as, say, the 1987 stock market crash or the LTCM collapse in 1998, risk taking will reemerge as something necessary to do in order to earn profits. "Déjà vu is just around the corner," argues Leo Tilman, a risk management specialist. "Soon enough, calming markets and competitive pressures of fully commoditized financial businesses will compress margins and fees" once again.[9] And the vicious circle will begin again, he predicts, with Wall Street's intermediaries taking risks they don't always understand and rarely are capable of managing.

After decades of working on Wall Street, Ralph Schlosstein, the CEO of boutique investment bank Evercore, has formulated a theory for what happens on Wall Street. In a normal year, the economy grows at a nominal pace—one that includes the rate of inflation—of about 5 to 6 percent. At the same time, Schlosstein points out, investment banks have consistently managed to earn between 17 percent and 20 percent on their equity—in other words, their ROE has been anywhere from 11 to 15 percentage points higher than the rate of growth in the underlying economy. "If you're in a business generating that much more in returns than is being provided by the economy, you either have to find a way to give the excess capital you are making back to your shareholders [through dividends or stock buybacks] or you figure out some way to [use and ultimately to] lose that extra capital by involving yourself in some new business." Wall Street, Schlosstein believes, has proven itself adept at the latter option. "We lost money in the energy markets, in the emerging markets, in junk bonds, and now by securitizing subprime assets."

This toxic state of affairs was the product of two separate trends on Wall Street. The first was the kind of laissez-faire behavior outlined in chapter 7. The other is the culture that has just been discussed above, the one that not only enabled but required managers to deliver, with slavish attention to detail, exactly what their short-term-oriented investors were seeking: the maximum possible short-term profit. Had Wall Street itself been more attuned to the risks it was running—if it had a compensation system that paid gargantuan bonuses to those employees who earned the greatest *risk-adjusted* returns for the firm and its investors—the results might have been less destabilizing. But it takes time, perhaps years, for the results of a given new business to become clear, for the real risk level to become apparent, and for the actual (as opposed to modeled) risk-adjusted return to be computed.

Had it been possible for the CEO of a Wall Street firm—such as a Phil Purcell—to decide to forgo a source of potential profits that he believed to be too risky without jeopardizing his career, would that have limited the scale of the damage? Had Wall Street's culture been less of a beat-thy-neighbor-at-his-own-game affair and instead one where those like Mike Gelband (the Lehman executive who tried to get his bosses to listen to and act on his concerns about the risks lurking beneath the surface in the real estate market) are heeded instead of escorted to the company's front doorstep, it might be a less exciting place, but one that is more stable and less risky. And just as we don't need a power utility that tries to cut costs so much that it can't invest in new transmission networks or generating capacity and thus risks blackouts on hot summer days, so we don't need a money grid whose participants, in the pursuit of profits for themselves and their investors, put the entire system in jeopardy.

To stop Wall Street from repeating its mistakes, we have two options. One seems impossibly complex; the other is deceptively straightforward. The latter is the one that is now being suggested by nearly everyone, including John Mack, Barack Obama, and Paul Volcker. Protect Wall Street from its own worst instincts, Mack declared. "Regulators have to be much more involved" in keeping an eye on what his (now former) firm and its rivals are getting up to. That's quite a statement coming from Mack, who, like his fellow CEOs, has more traditionally been an advocate for *less* regulation or, indeed, *self*-regulation.

Nonetheless, it's a school of thought that, in one form or another, had been gaining ground even on Wall Street before Obama's Volcker Rule bombshell, if only because it manages to shift the burden of responsibility from Wall Street altogether. "When you are sitting within one of these institutions, it's hard to even grapple with the concept of systemic risk," says Evercore's Schlosstein. "You are so focused on your own institution and how it is doing relative to its peers that it's hard to take enough of a step back to see the whole big picture."

He grapples for the right analogy, one that will illustrate the kind of risk that is involved and the need for *someone* beyond Wall Street to shoulder the responsibility. "Imagine," he says, "that there's a wall, and on one side of it is someone with a giant canister of gasoline. On the other side of it is a guy with a giant match. Neither of them can see the other or know that the other is doing something that places them both at risk." The regulator, Schlosstein explains, is the person placed in such a way that he can not only see both of those people but perceive whether the gasoline is being stowed safely, where no fire will cause it to explode, or whether the person on the other side of the wall is playing with his matches in a way likely to cause a conflagration.

"In banking, we train people to react to a problem by finding a way to make money out of it," Schlosstein points out. That's what hedge fund manager John Paulson did when he became an overnight celebrity and wealthy beyond his wildest dreams after identifying the ways in which the subprime lending problem was about to wreak havoc on Wall Street. His instinct wasn't to warn Lehman or Bear Stearns; it was to short their stocks. And in early 2009, Paulson became an active buyer of stock in all of Wall Street's legacy institutions, betting that the survivors will be able to return to posting big profits that will succeed in propelling stock prices sharply higher. Paulson, like any other short-term investor, is risk-agnostic—as long as the risks pay off, and for as long as the risks pay off, he's happy to be at the party.

Mack and Schlosstein are correct to argue that more active and better-considered regulation of the money grid is needed. The form that regulation takes—whether the Volcker Rule becomes law, what agencies supervise the Street—is less important than the impact it has on the way Wall Street functions. If the new rules work properly, someone such as Paulson, who is betting on a return to normal, will walk away from his investment disappointed by the lack of windfall profits. As I explored in chapter 2, the two periods over the last fifteen or twenty years in which Wall Street transactions become extremely profitable for the investment banks and other institutions undertaking them also turned out to be the peak of a cycle; within a year of those fee levels hitting their highest points, a bubble had burst, causing mayhem not only in the financial markets but also in the real economy.

An effective regulatory system is a dynamic one. It must be able to spot trends as they materialize; it must analyze those trends to understand whether or not they pose a real danger to the health of the financial system (or just to the health of a single institution); it must be able to react in an appropriate fashion. An effective regulatory institution is one that functions as a counterweight of sorts to Wall Street's infamous "animal spirits." When a bubble builds up—whether that shows up in the level or nature of risk taking, in the valuation of certain kinds of assets or certain markets, in the level of compensation paid to Wall Streeters, or in any kind of shift in the nature of the business being done on the money grid, especially a new business that doesn't seem to be linked to any fundamental business associated with the grid—then regulators must be prepared to act.

True, Alan Greenspan spoke out when he spotted "irrational exuberance" taking shape in the stock market in the early stages of the dot-com bubble. But that was late 1996; it took more than three years for the bubble to grow to extreme levels and burst. By that time, it had probably grown to claim millions more victims worldwide, including those who lost their retirement savings as well as those who lost their jobs amid the fallout. Imagine what could have happened if Greenspan had gone beyond jawboning and instead had summoned the CEOs of the major financial institutions involved in the emerging bubble to a meeting during which he laid down the law and told them that he didn't want them to underwrite excessively speculative companies, or that they would be held accountable for investor losses in some manner, or, if they insisted on forging ahead with this business, that they should be prepared to contribute a share of their fees to an investor protection fund.

In all probability, such dramatic steps wouldn't have been possible, but neither would they have been necessary. A gentle hint by the powerful Fed or the SEC that the regulators were thinking about such measures and were watching might have been enough to take some of the steam out of the market at a critical point. It might also have lent credibility to the concerns of in-house naysayers such as Lou Gelman, who watched his role at Morgan Stanley morph from that of gatekeeper to the capital markets to one he compared to being a croupier at a Vegas casino.

Good regulators think countercyclically. When they see the boom taking shape, they worry about the bust that could follow. Just as a good electrical utility regulator makes sure that a Consolidated Edison power plant has enough generating capacity to serve the citizens of Manhattan on the hottest summer days—that it can cope with a week or two of peak demand without a blackout—so a good financial regulator will make sure that the institutions it regulates have their own version of excess capacity in the form of large capital reserves. Those capital reserves—the amount of money that is set aside to be touched only in an emergency, when unforeseen losses wreak havoc on a bank's balance sheet—can't be static; they can't be the function only of how a bank is defined (size, types of business, etc.) or even by virtue of how much risk now-discredited models tell the regulator that the institution is running with its capital. It needs to change along with the institution, so that a bank that suddenly starts paying out large bonuses to employees in a new business segment that could potentially put at risk a lot of the institution's capital is required to set aside more of that capital, even if nothing else has changed. If that new business line suddenly begins to generate a third of the company's revenues or profits, that might trigger other regulatory scrutiny and possibly other capital requirements.

The idea, says Sheila Bair, is to make the kinds of business strategies that proved so destructive in the first decade of the new millennium so unappealing and unrewarding that Wall Street firms will shun them on their own, without being required to do so, or manage them more carefully in the future. "One way to address large interconnected institutions [those deemed too big to fail] is to make it expensive to be one," Bair suggested to the FCIC in the commission's first round of hearings, during which she proposed the creation of an FDIC-style fund to finance the breakup of any failing Wall Street giant. That kind of proactive approach would be better for taxpayers and other members of the financial system than an after-the-fact capital raising or bailout, she suggested, and is the only way to make sure that a firm that could fail is given a financial incentive not to do so.

The more risky the business model—the more it relies on proprietary trading or structured finance, like CDOs or derivatives—the higher its "insurance" payment would be, Bair proposed. She went further still, suggesting that the kind of large and interconnected firms that post the greatest systemic threat to Wall Street should be asked to create a plan for their own liquidation in the event of insolvency—a kind of corporate living will that would serve as a blueprint for them to be broken up and sold if needed.

The real enemy of effective regulation is stasis. Static rules tend to be those created solely in response to the last crisis, such as Glass-Steagall in 1933. Developed to address the problems that made the

1929 Wall Street crash a crisis for the entire banking system, Glass-Steagall separated the two businesses, ordaining that a commercial bank that took client deposits could not engage in the more speculative business of investment banking. Glass-Steagall was under siege for part of its sixty-six-year existence precisely because it didn't provide a way for financial institutions to consolidate in an efficient manner.

Ultimately, it was honored more in the breach than the observance. While there is a lot of debate over the possibility of reviving a Glass-Steagall-style barrier between the risky parts of Wall Street and its utility function, doing so now may prove tricky; Bair's proposals may be a creative alternative, and one that the financial industry is more likely to support, given that they can still choose to pursue businesses they believe will be profitable, as long as they are willing to undergo extra scrutiny and/or pay more into an FDIC-style fund.

Good regulations are those that cause those institutions being regulated to stop and think about the nature of the business that they are pursuing, and to second-guess themselves, to ask themselves the tough questions: "If I am wrong about this, what is the worst that can happen, and am I prepared for that and whatever consequences follow?" The hallmark of a poorly conceived regulation is one that has all and sundry devising ways to outwit it before it is even passed into law, as was the case with a recent attempt to regulate the derivatives business. The goal? To try to shed some light on the extent of the risks being taken by participants in these specialized contracts, which can range from the very straightforward (a swap in which two parties agree to exchange fixed for floating interest rate debt, or a future stream of income in Swiss francs for one in U.S. dollars) to the extremely exotic (pretty much anything you can imagine—such as the risk that the currency of Swaziland, the lilangeni, will move in a certain direction relative to the value of the Brazilian real and the price of coffee).

The bill seeks to get these instruments traded on an exchange or cleared through some kind of intermediary organization so that the markets and regulators have a better handle on where potential risks exist. That's a laudable objective. But lawmakers wanted to exempt some players from this kind of oversight, such as farmers, mining companies, and others who typically use relatively straightforward kinds of commodities to hedge their day-to-day business risks rather than to speculate. A farmer, for instance, may lock in a price for the soybean crop long before it is harvested by selling soybean futures; that eliminates his risk that he will see his income plunge should the price fall before the harvest, as well as the potential for a higher return on the crop if it rises.

As long as those who are exempt from that law really aren't speculating, and as long as they have an economic purpose behind their actions, that might not be so bad. But quite apart from the prospect that these players, once given their exemption, would then have carte blanche to do whatever they want without the same kind of oversight applied to others, or the fact that their business dealings may be large enough to create some kind of systemic risk and thus merit monitoring, there is a sizeable additional risk. What is to prevent a big hedge fund, such as Steve Cohen's SAC Capital, from opening a division dedicated to oil and gas exploration and production? Once established, with the exemption given, would the rules prevent the hedge fund from routing all kinds of derivatives transactions through its new division?

The legislative process is a lot like making sausages: even those who happen to like the product don't much enjoy watching the process. In the case of developing new financial rules of the road, it's unlikely that the kinds of trade-offs and compromises necessary to pass the new laws will result in a set of new regulations and regulatory bodies capable of meeting the demands placed on them. Already, for instance, the proposed consumer financial protection agency wouldn't shield consumers from loans made by car dealer-ships. True, as car dealers pointed out in their lobbying efforts, they weren't the architects of the Wall Street crisis. But their loans are a financial product, one that—like a mortgage or credit card, the other kinds of products covered by the new agency—can be complex and misunderstood by consumers and misrepresented by lenders.

If regulators are to be able to protect the financial system from Wall Street, as John Mack suggests is necessary, their ability to do so may be constrained by the kinds of agencies they work in and the terms of their mission as laid out in the legislation creating those agencies. But even in the best possible scenario—one in which Con-gress manages to pass a collection of coherent and well-thought-out new regulations that effectively address the issue of systemic risk and create new institutions able to tackle that on a dynamic basis, stifling the wrong kind of innovation while encouraging the right kind (and being able to distinguish between the two)—the success of those institutions will hinge on their ability to attract and retain the best talent. In other words, whatever agency replaces the SEC and takes on its role and function needs to begin chasing Goldman Sachs.

In order to be effective, regulators need to be as aggressive and as knowledgeable as the brightest banker on Wall Street. Too often, the brightest and the best regulators are quickly lured away from the SEC and the CFTC to the financial institutions they once regulated, where they can earn multiples of their civil service salaries in their first year on the job. When those regulatory jobs are just a way for future bankers to maximize their future utility to Goldman Sachs or JPMorgan Chase (former heads of enforcement at the SEC have moved on to firms such as those, as well as Deutsche Bank, Credit Suisse, and Morgan Stanley, among others), that limits the effective-ness of the regulator today. What regulator wants to take a hard-line stance against one of the handful of remaining large financial institutions, knowing subconsciously that in order to repay her student loans and put her own children through private school within a few years she may approach those same organizations for a better-paying job? For the money grid to function in the interests of all of those who have a stake in it and not just those who run it, the regulators who ensure that the rules are being applied fairly deserve to be rewarded lavishly for containing risk, just as bankers and traders are for running it in-house or helping their clients pass it on.

Chasing Goldman Sachs?

At the end of the day, the question boils down to one of culture. Is Wall Street's culture of reckless risk taking one that can be constrained only by force, in the same way that a serial killer is doomed to repeat his behavior unless confined to a maximum-security prison for the rest of his life or sentenced to death? That seems to be what John Mack was suggesting when he declared that "we can't control ourselves," and what the Volcker Rule implies. One of Mack's former Wall Street peers, Charles Prince, had put forth much the same case, if slightly more poetically, when he argued that as long as the music kept playing, he had to keep dancing along with everyone else.

But isn't it possible for someone on Wall Street to break step and decide to sit out the dance? And if not, why not? And what can we, collectively, do to make that possible? While we can use the regulatory system to protect Wall Street from its worst instincts (and to protect us, as users of the money grid, as well), surely we are all better off in the long run if Wall Street itself can develop its own modus operandi, whether as Bair has proposed or in some other way.

It's impossible—and undesirable—to remove greed as a factor in the way Wall Street thinks and operates. "We cannot and should not take risk out of the system—that's what drives the engine of our capitalist economy," John Mack told the FCIC commissioners. But perhaps it is possible to think about ways in which greed can be displaced as the deciding factor. Instead of playing yesterday's game, chasing Goldman Sachs and trying to earn the highest possible return without heed to anything else, could the financial institutions at the heart of Wall Street's money grid shift their focus to *emulating* the best characteristics of Goldman Sachs?

Why and how did Goldman Sachs become the firm that everyone else on Wall Street envied? The mystique predates the tenure of ex-Goldmanites such as Robert Rubin and Hank Paulson at the helm of the Treasury Department. Long before it had the easy access to cheap government capital that turbocharged its earnings power in 2009, it was earning a higher rate of return on its capital than many of its competitors and often paying out heftier bonuses at the end of every year. And it was doing so year after year, with relatively few missteps.

When, in the late 1990s, other firms decided that catering to the man in the street or retail investor was the wave of the future, Morgan Stanley merged with Dean Witter, and others set off to either build a retail brokerage network or acquire one. Goldman insiders say that when the topic surfaced for discussion there, it was rapidly dismissed. Goldman wasn't Merrill Lynch; that wasn't its core business. It was a firm that worked with institutional clients—big pension funds, mutual funds, or companies in search of capital—and a handful of ultrawealthy individuals and families, but not Joe Sixpack. That wasn't a business it knew, and it came with a set of risks the Goldmanites didn't feel sure that they could manage. Sure enough, within a few years, the Internet craze was over and several of the firms that had made massive investments in developing a broad retail presence were forced to retrench or refocus. In the wake of the dot-com bubble's bursting, individual investors weren't as active traders or as lucrative clients as they had been only a short while before. But Goldman had never jumped on that bandwagon, and it let the next one pass it by as well. Less than a decade later, firms such as Merrill Lynch were snapping up mortgage origination companies in order to secure as much proprietary deal flow as possible for their CDO-creation machines. Goldman Sachs again pondered the merits of jumping on the bandwagon—and was criticized by some shareholders for failing to do so when it again decided to stick to its knitting.

Goldman went further. Over the course of a two-and-a-half-hour meeting on December 14, 2006, that has now become part of Wall Street's folklore, chief financial officer David Viniar talked through the housing bubble with key members of Goldman's mortgage underwriting team, its risk managers, its traders, and others. They emerged with a resolution that this was indeed a bubble, and one that needed to be shorted. (As Schlosstein suggested tends to happen on Wall Street, their instinct was to find a way to profit from a market aberration, not try to remove the problem.) Not only did Goldman not buy a mortgage originator, but it reduced or removed the amount of credit it was willing to extend to mortgage originators. It established short positions in the credit and derivatives markets that would boost its profits if the real estate market began to crumble, and it began to sell off its own holdings of mortgage-backed securities, both subprime and investment-grade.[10]

Goldman Sachs and its employees are no saints, as the *Financial Times* noted in naming Blankfein its Man of the Year in 2009. The firms that bought the CDOs they had structured and sold were clients—Goldman was their counterparty and didn't owe them any fiduciary duty. As Blankfein told the FCIC commissioners, they were mainly professional investors who could look out for themselves. That argument didn't impress Angelides, who pointed out that many of these institutions managed money on behalf of ordinary middle-class or blue-collar American workers, but it's not an argument that he will win: Goldman may have been in morally muddy waters but not illegal ones, doing just what it was required to do, but no more.

Did anyone really expect a Wall Street firm to suffer from a sudden attack of altruism? They didn't advise the rest of the world of the decision Viniar and the trading team had come to by issuing a press release, any more than John Paulson issued a press release when he established his own positions. It was up to Goldman's clients to look at the same set of facts—they were there for anyone alert and astute enough to spot them—draw the same conclusions and take the same measures. Most didn't, as history would quickly demonstrate.

What is worth chasing about Goldman Sachs isn't its rate of return; what is worth replicating isn't its outsized bonus pool. Rather, what the rest of Wall Street can learn from Goldman Sachs is that strategic thinking and planning pays off—and can pay off disproportionately well when done by some of the smartest people on Wall Street. "Trying to simply mimic Goldman Sachs is likely to lead to disaster," says Evercore's Schlosstein. Rather, he and others suggest mimicking elements of their strategy.

That, says another former senior Wall Street figure, is harder than it sounds. "When I talked to people who worked for me, I would ask them to come and tell me what their strategy was going to be for next year; how they were going to change the business and adapt to the changes that they found," he recalls of his first years overseeing a business division. "Don't tell me you're going to run faster than everyone else, shoot straighter, and win. Because that is not ever what works on Wall Street, not *ever.*" The harsh reality of life on the Street, he adds, is that few people look ahead very far and think strategically; even fewer try to combine that analysis with a hardheaded evaluation of their own competitive strengths and weaknesses. "There may be a lot of very smart people on the Street, but they are always playing yesterday's game or today's game, not thinking about tomorrow," he says. "They are not thinking about how the markets are changing, how they might change in the future, how they can organize today to prepare for that."

The result is that when change happens, Wall Street scrambles to cope, just as it did when new technology wreaked havoc on its business model and just as it did when Mayday removed—overnight— the stable source of trading fees that made that business model sustainable. "Because they are clever and smart, these Wall Street guys from the better firms, they develop a solution and survive," the banker-turned-consultant says. "But it's not done in such a way that they plan ahead and try to control the outcome and position themselves to win. It's not that Wall Street discourages strategic planning; it just doesn't reward it. It's all about what is this year's performance, or how did your group do last quarter? It's about maximizing this year's bonus, and worrying about next year when it happens." To the banker, a chess player, it's like the difference between a game of poker and a game of chess. At poker, he says, what happens in one hand doesn't affect the outcome of future hands—that's a function of the cards he is dealt. Chess, in contrast, is a game of strategy, where each move limits future options or creates fresh opportunities. "It doesn't surprise me that the guys on the Street tend to play poker more often than chess," he comments drily.

One firm that has chosen to emulate Goldman Sachs rather than to chase it is the boutique founded by former Morgan Stanley star deal maker Robert Greenhill. In the autumn of 2009, in a move that received almost no attention from the financial press amid the hubbub surrounding new regulatory initiatives and the speculation surrounding who would succeed Ken Lewis at the helm of Bank of America Merrill Lynch, Greenhill & Co. calmly announced that it would spin off its proprietary private equity investment division, Greenhill Capital Partners. At least one firm, it seemed, had decided that trying to replicate Goldman Sachs by becoming bigger and more diversified and doing more proprietary deals wasn't the only path to success on Wall Street. Indeed, Greenhill himself believed that the biggest opportunity for his firm, with its particular set of skills and team of bankers, lay in helping companies negotiate mergers and acquisitions or in advising clients on other strategic matters. "The scale of the opportunity," Greenhill declared, "merits our undivided attention."

There is no question that Greenhill and his bankers are good at deal making. But the firm's decision wasn't made out of an altruistic desire to serve their clients more adeptly, but from a realization that the move played to their strengths in a way that trying to become a player in merchant banking didn't. Thus it was where they could capture higher profits. The Rolodexes of Greenhill's bankers are the envy of those who toil at many larger banks and who are all too aware that the sole reason they are invited to participate in some merger deals is because they bring access to capital along with them.

But capital can become a commodity, as it did in recent years; skill is the one thing on offer on Wall Street that can't be commoditized and is likely to continue commanding a premium fee. It is skill that helps Goldman Sachs earn a substantial return on its shareholders' equity (and that return is even bigger when given a boost by access to cheaper, government-supplied capital). Skill, like strategic thinking, can be acquired and honed, but not imitated or chased. Nor can strategic planning. Clayton Rose, a former investment banker and now a senior lecturer at the Harvard Business School, says that Greenhill's move was not only a reflection of the boutique institution's clear understanding of its skills but also a recognition of its weaknesses. These insights can only come from strategic thought. "Smaller players [like Greenhill], in this environment, don't enjoy a competitive advantage in terms of access to credit or deal flow for their private equity or merchant banking businesses," says Rose. "So they don't have the ability to outperform their larger investment banking peers in this area" on an ongoing basis.

If you can't beat them, why chase them at all? That's a question that too few Wall Street firms have been asked or, it seems, tried to ask themselves. The firms that now dominate the money grid—JPMorgan Chase and Goldman Sachs—do so because they have a culture that puts a priority on risk management, and part of that risk management process involves asking tough questions of oneself. Some of the firms that chased Goldman Sachs without a real understanding of what made its model work—as opposed to what kinds of businesses helped it generate big profits—are now gone, or absorbed into other institutions.

So far, too few Wall Street firms have tried to answer the question of why they're chasing Goldman Sachs, much less the broader question of what Goldman Sachs represents. Some of those who have done so have come up with the wrong answer, judging by Dick Parsons's throwaway comment about Citigroup's priorities; others don't see any reason to undertake that exercise at all. When these firms are once again on a stable footing, will they resume chasing Goldman Sachs—or JPMorgan Chase, if that firm succeeds in unseating Goldman and emerges as the model to emulate on Wall Street? Will smaller rivals try to replicate what Goldman Sachs has done, rather than carve out their own path to success based on their own strategic analysis of the opportunities and challenges and their own strengths and weaknesses?

"There is significantly more capital on the books of Wall Street's banks than is needed for them to fulfill their core role of providing liquidity to investors," says Evercore's Schlosstein, alluding to one of the basic utility functions at the heart of the money grid. As long as that is the case, he adds, there will remain an incentive for parts of those firms to take outsized risks and to behave as if they are running a casino rather than a utility. "Something needs to provide Wall Street with a wake-up call and remind it that shocks like those of 1998 and 2008 will not be aberrant events as long as the risk-taking culture remains so central," Schlosstein argues. "Memories fade faster on Wall Street than on Main Street."

But Main Street's need for Wall Street is the reason that Wall Street still exists. The one certainty is that, regardless of which particular institutions or investment banking models endure and triumph over the next decade, its functions must remain intact. Unless we want to return to the days when we had to save for decades to buy a house, couldn't buy furniture for that new home until we had saved the cash, and had to keep our savings in a bank account paying us less in interest than the rate of inflation (or, worse still, buried in the backyard or in our mattresses), we all have a healthy interest in ensuring that Wall Street functions smoothly, just as we have an interest in being sure that when we flick a switch the light comes on, or that clean water flows through our taps.

That means we have a vested interest in ensuring that Wall Street begins to adopt some kind of long-term strategic planning, that it collectively stops trying to chase Goldman Sachs and instead starts trying to emulate the best features of the Goldman Sachs model. At the same time, all the financial institutions that collectively make up the money grid—including Goldman Sachs itself—must accept that as long as they collect the profits from running the grid, they must be prepared to pay the price when things go awry. A system in which the intermediaries profit while those at either end suffer outsize losses is not one that is sustainable.

Going forward, all of those who have an interest in the survival of the money grid that is Wall Street must decide collectively what kinds of actions and compromises are necessary to ensure that the grid and its functions remain healthy and vibrant over the long haul. Otherwise, we risk a systemic meltdown that could make us look back on the events of 2008 almost wistfully. Ultimately, we will get the Wall Street that we deserve.

NOTES

Introduction

1. The chronicle of the final six months of the "old" Wall Street is told in great detail in Andrew Ross Sorkin's survey of the events leading up to the Wall Street bailout in *Too Big to Fail* (New York: Viking, 2009).

2. Author's reporting with New England Power Pool (NEPOOL) and North America Electrical Reliability Council (NERC) in September 2003.

3. James Saft, "Goldman, Where Are the Shareholders' and Taxpayers' Yacht" [sic], Reuters, July 16, 2009, retrieved from http://www.reuters .com/article/idUSTRE56F3SR20090716?pageNumber=2&virtual BrandChannel=0&sp=true

Part I: Dancing to the Music

1. Michiyo Nakamoto and David Wighton, "Bullish Citigroup Is 'Still Dancing' to the Beat of the Buy-out Boom," *Financial Times,* July 10, 2007, retrieved from http://www.ft.com/cms/s/0/5cefc794-2e7d-11dc -821c-0000779fd2ac.html?nclick_check=1

Chapter 1: From Utility to Casino

1. Elizabeth Hester and Peter Cook, "Former Bear Stearns CEO Green- berg Says Investment Banks 'Gone,'" Bloomberg News, December 8, 2008.

2. "RightScale Raises Another $13 Million," *New York Times,* December 8, 2008.

3. Data provided by National Venture Capital Association.

4. Eric Dash, "Return of High-Yield Debt Raises Concerns," *New York Times,* September 17, 2009.

5. Krishna Guha, "Man in the News: Hank Paulson," *Financial Times,* September 26, 2008.

6. Author's research in the Amsterdam Stock Exchange archives, 1998.

7. An excellent history of the evolution of America's capital markets and Wall Street is Charles Geisst, *Wall Street: A History from Its Beginnings to the Fall of Enron* (Oxford: Oxford University Press, 2004).

8. Author's research; discussion with Exchange archivists in Amsterdam and Paris, 1998.

9. Axel Madsen, *The Deal Maker: How William C. Durant Made General Motors* (New York: John Wiley & Sons, 1999), 72.

10. Steven Watts, *The People's Tycoon: Henry Ford and the American Century* (New York: Knopf, 2005), 59.

11. Madsen, *The Deal Maker,* 115.

12. Details of Google's early financing rounds and of the IPO underwriters' pitches came from those involved in both processes and from Google insiders.

13. Randall Smith and Suzanne McGee, "Major Institutions, Led by Fidelity, Get Most of Hot IPOs," *Wall Street Journal,* January 27, 2000, C1.

14. Data from National Venture Capital Association.

15. Henny Sender and Francesco Guerrera, "BlackRock Chief Attacks Wall Street Banks," *Financial Times,* July 22, 2009.

16. Data from Dealogic LLC.

17. Ibid.

18. Patricia Beard, *Blue Blood and Mutiny: The Fight for the Soul of Morgan Stanley* (New York: William Morrow, 2007), 57–62.

Chapter 2: Building Better—and More Profitable—Mousetraps

1. Return on equity data cited throughout the book was calculated and provided to the author by Jeff Harte, banking analyst at Sandler O'Neill. It is calculated using the Dupont ROE methodology.

2. Fee data was calculated using the estimates for fee revenues provided by Dealogic LLC. Fees include those earned on debt and equity underwriting transactions, as well as merger and acquisition advisory fees.

3. Bonus data from the Office of the State Deputy Controller of New York, retrieved from http://www.osc.state.ny.us/press/releases/jan08/bonus.pdf.

4. Paul Muolo and Mathew Padilla, *Chain of Blame: How Wall Street Caused the Mortgage and Credit Crisis* (New York: Wiley, 2008), 181.

5. William Cohan, *House of Cards* (New York: Doubleday, 2009), 177.

6. Eric Weiner, *What Goes Up: An Uncensored History of Wall Street* (New York: Back Bay Books, 2007), 166.

7. Ibid., 116.

8. Ibid., 123.

9. Charles Ellis, *The Partnership* (New York: Penguin Press, 2008), 92.

10. Alan D. Morrison and William J. Wilhelm Jr., "The Demise of Investment Banking Partnerships: Theory and Evidence," Center for Economic Policy Research, February 2005, retrieved from http://gates.comm.virginia.edu/wjw9a/Papers/IBDemiseFinal%20Aug%2030%2006.pdf, 15.

11. Beard, *Blue Blood and Mutiny,* 14.

12. Ken Auletta, *Greed and Glory on Wall Street: The Fall of the House of Lehman* (New York: Random House, 1986), 11.

13. Connie Bruck, *The Predators' Ball: The Inside Story of Drexel Burnham and the Rise of the Junk Bond Raiders* (New York: Penguin, 1989), 31.

14. Marty Fridson has traced the origins of today's "junk" bonds or high-yield securities back to the nineteenth century, when there were debates about whether these offered better investment returns. He says the term "high-yield bond"—the phrase that the junk bond bankers, issuers, and analysts prefer—was used as early as 1919 by John Moody.

15. Bruck, *Predators' Ball,* 246–47.

16. Lewis Rainieri, interview by Mara Der Hovanesian, "A Smart Idea Spoiled," *BusinessWeek,* June 30, 2008, retrieved from http://www.businessweek.com/magazine/content/08_27/b4091040380049.htm.

17. Ellis, *The Partnership,* 378.

18. Ibid., 379.

19. Patrick Hosking and Suzy Jagger, "'Wake Up, Gentlemen,' World's Top Bankers Warned by Former Fed Chairman Volcker," December 9, 2009, retrieved from http://business.timesonline.co.uk/tol/business/industry_sectors/banking_and_finance/article6949387.ece.

Chapter 3: What's Good for Wall Street Is Good for . . . Wall Street

1. All data are from Dealogic LLC.

2. Special dividends have been paid by many private equity–acquired companies to their new owners as a way of quickly returning the capital

those funds invested in the original buyout; the company uses its own cash or must raise new debt to pay that dividend.

3. Darla Mercado, "Hedges Claim 30% of Bond Trading," *Investment News,* August 30, 2007, retrieved from http://www.investmentnews.com/apps/pbcs.dll/article?AID=/20070830/REG/70830016.

4. Jennifer Popavec, "How to Get in on High-Yield Real Estate Debt," *Registered Rep.,* April 1, 2007.

5. Author's interviews with current and former Goldman Sachs executives.

6. Data contained in KKR's S-1 filing with the SEC; retrieved electronically: http://www.sec.gov/Archives/edgar/data/1404912/000104746 908010826/a2187975zs-1a.htm.

7. Anecdotal information from Adelsbach, hedge fund managers, and an executive banker working within prime brokerage divisions of Lehman Brothers.

8. Ellis, *The Partnership,* 248.

9. Ibid., 249.

10. Hedge fund return data from Hennessee Group index, retrieved from http://www.hennesseegroup.com/indices/returns/year/2002.html.

11. Data from Dealogic LLC.

12. Tom Braithwaite and Francesco Guerrera, "Wall Street Titans Face the Flak," *Financial Times,* January 13, 2010.

13. Auletta, *Greed and Glory,* 6.

14. Ibid., 17.

15. Ellis, *The Partnership,* 391.

16. Nikhil Deogun, "The Future of Finance: Is Wall Street Over?" *Wall Street Journal,* March 30, 2009.

Chapter 4: To the Edge of the Abyss—and Beyond

1. Lawrence G. McDonald, *A Colossal Failure of Common Sense: The Inside Story of the Collapse of Lehman Brothers* (New York: Crown Business, 2009), 132.

2. Ibid., 133.

3. Ibid., 138.

4. Steve Fishman, "Burning Down His House," *New York,* November 30, 2008.

5. Michael Flaherty, "Blackstone CEO Says Public Markets 'Over-rated,'" Reuters, February 27, 2007.

6. James Stewart, "The Birthday Party," *The New Yorker,* February 11, 2008.

7. Data contained in Blackstone's S-1 filing with the Securities and Exchange Commission.

8. Robert Litan, "Reuniting Investment and Commercial Banking," *Cato Journal* 7, no. 3 (Winter 1988): 807.
9. All ROE data provided by Jeff Harte of Sandler O'Neill.
10. Christine Harper, "Goldman's Bonus Pool Jumps 23% to Record $12 Billion," Bloomberg News, December 18, 2007.
11. All data on fees from Dealogic LLC.
12. Data provided by Jeff Harte, Sandler O'Neill.
13. Data from Dealogic LLC.
14. CDO data from SIFMA, retrieved electronically: http://www.sifma .org/research/pdf/CDO_Data2008-Q4.pdf.
15. Ranieri's own bank would be among the victims of the 2008 meltdown.
16. Muolo and Padilla, *Chain of Blame,* 198.
17. Fishman, "Burning Down His House."

Part II: Greed, Recklessness, and Negligence

1. James Stewart, "Eight Days," *The New Yorker,* September 21, 2009.
2. Morrison and Wilhelm, "The Demise of Investment Banking Partnerships."

Chapter 5: "You Eat What You Kill"

1. Christine Harper, "Whitehead, Ex-Goldman Chief, Blasts Wall Street Pay," Bloomberg News, May 16, 2007.
2. Merrill Lynch's 2007 proxy statement, retrieved electronically from the SEC's EDGAR system.
3. Thomas Philippon and Ariell Resheff, "Wages and Human Capital in the U.S. Financial Industry 1909–2006," retrieved from http://pages .stern.nyu.edu/~tphilipp/papers/pr_rev15.pdf.
4. Data from Merrill Lynch's financial reports, as filed with the SEC, and available electronically as 10-K and 10-Q reports on the SEC's EDGAR system.
5. Kyle Bass, written testimony to the Financial Crisis Inquiry Commission, retrieved from http://www.fcic.gov/hearings/pdfs/2010-0113-Bass.pdf.
6. The DeSantis letter and the responses were published in the online edition of the *New York Times,* March 25, 2009.
7. Deposition by John Thain obtained from the office of Andrew Cuomo, New York state attorney general. Thain went on to say, "I think I've done exactly what my board asked me to do."
8. Data on number of derivatives trades that Lehman Brothers had outstanding provided by Jeffrey McCracken in the *Wall Street Journal,* December 30, 2008.

9. Patricia Beard discusses the way Morgan Stanley executives viewed compensation as part of the firm's culture in the decades before the 1980s in *Blue Blood and Mutiny,* 19–50.

10. Ibid., 47.

11. Recalled by Gelman and two other former Morgan Stanley executives.

12. Philippon and Resheff, "Wages and Human Capital," 29.

13. Calculated based on Office of the (New York) State Deputy Controller's budget data, and information from the investment banks themselves on their individual budget "pools."

14. Press reports and author interviews with art consultants and hedge fund managers familiar with Cohen's collection.

15. Harper, "Whitehead Blasts Pay."

16. Gretchen Morgenson, "Bullish Analyst of Tech Stocks Quits Salomon," *New York Times,* August 16, 2002.

17. Ellis, *The Partnership,* 292.

18. David Weidner, "Fortress Has Another Weakness," MarketWatch, August 11, 2008.

19. Deogun, "The Future of Finance."

20. Claire Hill and Richard Painter, "Berle's Vision Beyond Shareholder Interests: Why Investment Bankers Should Have (Some) Personal Liability," presented to symposium "In Berle's Footsteps," University of Seattle Law School, November 2009. Retrieved from http://papers.ssrn.com/sol3/papers.cfm?abstract_id=1510443.

21. Ibid.

22. "Archbishop of Canterbury: Repent, Bankers," Associated Press, September 16, 2009.

Chapter 6: The Most Terrifying Four-Letter Word Imaginable

1. The UBS report to its shareholders was published only weeks before the Swiss bank's annual meeting in April 2008, 11.

2. Ibid., 42.

3. Leo Tilman, *Financial Darwinism* (New York: Wiley, 2009) and author interviews with Tilman.

4. UBS report.

5. Christine Williamson, "Excellent Timing: Face to Face with John Paulson," *Pensions & Investments,* July 9, 2007.

6. Survey of top-paid managers of 2007, "Alpha's Top Moneymakers," *Alpha* magazine, April 2008.

7. "Lloyd Blankfein and Ken Moelis on Wall Street Risks, Rewards and Opportunities," Knowledge@Wharton, November 14, 2007,

Wharton School of the University of Pennsylvania. Retrieved from http://knowledge.wharton.upenn.edu/articlepdf/1844.pdf?CFID=69374443&CFTOKEN=77959103&jsessionid=a8307ad1e1d5027db5e53426ca7e55614075.

8. Data from FDIC, retrieved from http://www.fdic.gov/bank/individual/failed/banklist.html.

9. Emily Thornton, David Henry, and Adrienne Carter, "Inside Wall Street's Culture of Risk," *BusinessWeek,* June 12, 2006.

10. Alan Greenspan, "We Need a Better Cushion Against Risk," *Financial Times,* March 26, 2009.

11. Shanny Basar, "Wall Street Treads a Wary Path Over Risk," *Financial News,* March 17, 2008.

12. Greenspan was testifying before the House Committee on Oversight and Government Reform in October 2008. His testimony revealed many flaws in his thoughts and assumptions, including his belief that Wall Street's self-interest would protect the system. "I made a mistake in presuming that the self-interests of organizations . . . were such as that they were best capable of shielding their organizations and shareholders from harm," he confessed.

13. Nassim Nicholas Taleb, *The Black Swan: The Impact of the Highly Improbable* (New York: Random House, 2007), 296.

14. Global risk management survey, "Risk Management in the Spotlight," 6th edition, Deloitte Touche Tomatsu, June 11, 2009.

15. Retrieved from http://www.fdic.gov/news/news/speeches/archives/2007/chairman/spjun2507.html.

16. Deborah Solomon, "Crash Course," *New York Times,* Q&A with Myron Scholes, May 17, 2009.

17. Deloitte risk management survey.

18. Kristopher Gerardi, Andreas Lehnert, Shane Sherlund, and Paul Willand, "Making Sense of the Subprime Crisis" (Brookings Institution, Brookings Papers on Economic Activity), September 11, 2008. Retrieved from http://www.brookings.edu/economics/bpea/~/media/Files/Programs/ES/BPEA/2008_fall_bpea_papers/2008_fall_bpea_gerardi_sherlund_lehnert_willen.pdf.

19. Thornton, Henry, and Carter, "Inside Wall Street's Culture of Risk."

Chapter 7: Washington Versus Wall Street

1. Binyamin Applebaum and Ellen Nakashima, "Banking Regulator Played Advocate over Enforcer," *Washington Post,* November 23, 2008.

2. Ibid.

3. Ibid.

4. Stewart, "Eight Days."

5. Retrieved from http://www.treas.gov/inspector-general/audit-reports/2009/oig09037.pdf.

6. Intelligence Squared Debate, March 17, 2009, transcript, pp. 5–9, and later p. 17. Transcript provided courtesy of Dana Wolfe at Intelligence Squared.

7. Retrieved from http://www.quotationspage.com/quotes/Ronald_Reagan.

8. Henry Kaufman, *The Road to Financial Reformation* (New York: Wiley, 2009), 5.

9. In the context of the 2008 market crisis, the following definitive survey of the 1907 Panic has taken on a new relevance and attracted many new readers: Robert F. Bruner and Sean D. Karr, *The Panic of 1907: Lessons Learned from the Market's Perfect Storm* (New York: Wiley, 2007).

10. The text of the speech is located on the Treasury Department's website and that of the Shanghai Futures Exchange. Retrieved from http://www.treas.gov/press/releases/hp301.htm.

11. Zhao Yidi and Kevin Hamlin, "China Shuns Paulson's Free-Market Push as Meltdown Burns U.S.," Bloomberg Markets, September 23, 2008.

12. Interview with author, October 2001.

13. Intelligence Squared Debate, transcript, 24.

14. Caroline Baum, "Imagine Pandit Querying Barney Frank," Bloomberg News, February 12, 2009.

15. Greenspan, "We Need a Better Cushion Against Risk."

16. Gillian Tett, *Fool's Gold: How the Bold Dream of a Small Tribe at J.P. Morgan Was Corrupted by Wall Street Greed and Unleashed a Catastrophe* (New York: Free Press, 2009), 38.

17. Frank Partnoy, *Infectious Greed: How Deceit and Risk Corrupted the Financial Markets* (New York: Holt Paperbacks, 2004). Partnoy's book summarizes this debate and ISDA's growing influence in Washington.

18. Wendy Lee Gramm, "In Defense of Derivatives," *Wall Street Journal*, September 8, 1993.

19. The committee publishes quarterly reports on U.S. market competitiveness, which have shown a steady decline in the competitive position of the capital markets. They can be retrieved from http://www.capmktsreg.org/press.html.

20. Stephen Labaton, "Agency's '04 Role Let Banks Pile Up New Debt," *New York Times,* October 8, 2008.

21. Mark Pittman, Elliott Blair Smith, and Jesse Westbrook, "Cox's SEC Censors Report on Bear Stearns Collapse," Bloomberg News, October 7,

2008. The unredacted version, while distributed to many members of the press, has never been made public.

22. Author interviews with former regulators; contents of the still-private SEC reports.

23. Intelligence Squared Debate, transcript, 28.

24. Stewart, "Eight Days."

25. George Soros, *The New Paradigm for Financial Markets: The Credit Crisis of 2008 and What It Means* (New York: Public Affairs, 2008), 117.

Part III: The New Face of Wall Street

1. Gavin Finch, "Obama Plan May Cost Banks $13 Billion, JPMorgan Says," Bloomberg News, January 22, 2010.

2. Jamie Dimon's testimony to the FCIC, January 11, 2010, retrieved from www.fcic.gov.

3. Bob Ivry, "Reed Says 'I'm Sorry' for Role in Creating Citigroup," Bloomberg News, November 6, 2009.

Chapter 8: Too Big to Fail, Too Small to Thrive?

1. Daniel Bases, "Private Equity May Be on Cusp of 'Golden Age,'" Reuters, September 22, 2009.

2. Matt Taibbi, "Inside the Great American Bubble Machine," *Rolling Stone,* July 2009.

3. John Arlidge, "I'm Doing God's Work; Meet Mr. Goldman Sachs," *Sunday Times,* November 8, 2009, retrieved online at http://www .timesonline.co.uk/tol/news/world/us_and_americas/article6907681 .ece.

4. Sender and Guerrera, "BlackRock Chief Attacks Wall Street."

5. Stewart, "Eight Days."

6. Roger Lowenstein, *When Genius Failed: The Rise and Fall of Long-Term Capital Management* (New York: Random House, 2000), 205.

7. Scott Eden, "The Networker," *Dealmaker,* April/May 2008.

8. Jeff French, "On the Road Again," *Investment Dealers Digest,* January 29, 2006, retrieved from http://www.iddmagazine.com/issues/20060129/ 11932-1.html.

9. "Barclays in $1.75 Billion Deal for Lehman's Core," *New York Times,* September 17, 2008.

10. Henny Sender and Francesco Guerrera, "Citi to Relaunch Troubled Hedge Fund Unit," *Financial Times,* November 6, 2009.

11. Francesco Guerrera and Joanna Chung, "Regulators Urged Citi to Replace CFO," *Financial Times,* August 18, 2009.

12. "Wall Street Report: Big Profits Among the Ruins," Knowledge@ Wharton, http://knowledge.wharton.upenn.edu/article.cfm?articleid =2291.

13. Graham Bowley, "Red Ink Stains Bank and Banker," *New York Times,* July 22, 2009.

14. Hugh Son and Zachary R. Mider, "AIG's Benmosche Wants to Halve Wall Street's IPO Fees," Bloomberg News, September 2, 2009.

15. Katherine Burton and Saijel Kishan, "Griffin Rebounding from 55 Percent Loss Builds Bank," Bloomberg News, October 29, 2009.

Chapter 9: Chasing Goldman Sachs?

1. *The Brian Lehrer Show,* WNYC, May 13, 2009, via podcast.

2. Katya Wachtel, "Morgan Stanley CEO Calls for More Regulation of Wall Street at *Vanity Fair*–Bloomberg Event," *Huffington Post,* November 18, 2009, http://www.huffingtonpost.com/katya-wachtel/morgan -stanley-ceo-calls_b_363233.html?dlbk.

3. John Helyar, Alison Fitzgerald, Mark Pittman, and Serena Saitto, "Ten Days Changed Wall Street as Bernanke Saw 'Massive Failures,'" Bloomberg News, September 22, 2008.

4. Leo Strine, "Why Excessive Risk-Taking Is Not Unexpected," *New York Times,* DealBook, October 5, 2009.

5. Tett, *Fool's Gold,* 29.

6. Charles Gasparino, *The Sellout* (New York: HarperBusiness, 2009), 183.

7. Kaufman, *Road to Financial Reformation,* 34.

8. Ibid., 45.

9. Leo Tilman, "Needed: Strategic Vision, Not More Regulation," *Harvard Business Review* online, September 18, 2009.

10. Gretchen Morgenson and Louise Story, "Banks Bundled Bad Debt, Bet Against It and Won," *New York Times,* December 24, 2009.

ACKNOWLEDGMENTS

Writing a book is never a solo venture, even though it may feel like it some days. My greatest thanks have to go to my editor, John Mahaney, for spotting the potential in an unconventional kind of book, one that looked at the concept of Wall Street. When the dramatic events of the summer and autumn of 2008 forced me to rethink the project from soup to nuts, John was unfailingly and amazingly patient and supportive—just as later he was there to prod me to deliver something better whenever I needed it. This book would never have seen the light of day without the efforts of my intrepid agent, Giles Anderson. I was astonished to learn that some agents consider their job done when the contract is signed; Giles was always there for me to lean on or bounce ideas off of through the whole process.

I wish it were possible for me to thank by name all those who have toiled on Wall Street—some for decades—who made this book possible by sharing with me their experiences and reflections. Unfortunately, most of them would be furious if I did, and perhaps that is one of the saddest comments about Wall Street as it functions today: the inability to be self-critical in public.

Paul Bennett was an admirable research assistant, scrambling around in search of esoteric facts and figures. The folks at Dealogic LLC never batted an eyelash at the most extraordinary data requests; a special thank-you is owed to Dimitri Kiriazov, who has since left the firm. The idea for this book—and the awareness of the magnitude of the gap that exists between Wall Street and "Main Street"—grew out of the series of classes I taught for Media Bistro: my thanks to Carmen Scheidel and her group for giving me that opportunity. Rachel Elson, the queen of the headlines, spent an entire dinner (and consumed an entire paper tablecloth) trying to come up with just the right headline for the book. An eclectic group of individuals helped me find an even more diverse group of Wall Streeters, past and present, to talk to: my thanks, in particular, to Tony Guernsey, Heather Fontaine, Jonathan Cunningham, Bill Thompson, Aline Sullivan, Steve Martiros, Mary Sedarat, and Laura Congleton. Thanks to the folks at Intelligence Squared for access to the St. Patrick's Day 2009 debate on Wall Street—and the transcript. Bob Kurucza tried to keep me from wandering too far afield in my speculations about who's to blame and what happens next; I owe him thanks for serving as a sounding board. Without the technical assistance from Chris Manigan, I don't think I would ever have completed the manuscript.

An incredible number of friends, family members, and editors have had to put up with my distraction and absences for nearly two years, from the time I began working on the project until I finally bade farewell to the galleys. Jo Rodgers at Crown kept reminding me that there is a light at the end of the tunnel; Michelle Moran, having been through all of this, convinced me that it wasn't an oncoming train. Alice Finn helped me on my way during some of the darkest days, and Elizabeth Wine's amazing cake-baking skills were always appreciated. My brother, David, came up with some smart ideas for the book's structure, while the drawings from my niece and nephews, Julie, Connor, and Jamie, were pinned up by my desk to make me smile. Special thanks to Joy Russell, Freya Kristjanson, Glenys Babcock, Bev Mazzarella, Glenn Becker, Gerit Quealy, Judith Dobrzynski, Solange de Santis, Marion Asnes, and Ron Bunn for cheering me on while never asking me the dreaded question "When will it be done?"

This book could never have been written without the help in decades past of some great editors. I'd like to thank, in particular, Mike Malloy, Barbara Donnelly Granito, Justin Schack, Dan Colarusso, Phil Roosevelt, and Anita Peltonen for demanding the best work I could deliver. Much of any credit for this book belongs to them and the other editors I've worked with; any flaws and shortcomings are, of course, my own responsibility.

INDEX